Social, Ethical and Policy Implications of Information Technology

Linda L. Brennan
Mercer University, USA

Victoria E. Johnson
Mercer University, USA

 Information Science Publishing

Hershey • London • Melbourne • Singapore

1/2007

B+T 365

Acquisition Editor:	Mehdi Khosrow-Pour
Senior Managing Editor:	Jan Travers
Managing Editor:	Amanda Appicello
Development Editor:	Michele Rossi
Copy Editor:	Alana Bubnis
Typesetter:	Jennifer Wetzel
Cover Design:	Michelle Waters
Printed at:	Integrated Book Technology

Published in the United States of America by
Information Science Publishing (an imprint of Idea Group Inc.)
701 E. Chocolate Avenue, Suite 200
Hershey PA 17033
Tel: 717-533-8845
Fax: 717-533-8661
E-mail: cust@idea-group.com
Web site: http://www.idea-group.com

and in the United Kingdom by
Information Science Publishing (an imprint of Idea Group Inc.)
3 Henrietta Street
Covent Garden
London WC2E 8LU
Tel: 44 20 7240 0856
Fax: 44 20 7379 3313
Web site: http://www.eurospan.co.uk

Library of Congress Cataloging-in-Publication Data

Social, ethical and policy implications of information technology /
Linda L. Brennan, editor, Victoria Johnson, editor.
   p. cm.
Includes bibliographical references.
  ISBN 1-59140-168-2 (hardcover : alk. paper) -- ISBN 1-59140-169-0
(ebook)
 1. Information society. 2. Information technology--Social aspects.
3. Information science--Moral and ethical aspects. 4. Communication of
technical information. 5. Computer scientists. 6. Copyright--United
States. 7. Information technology--Government policy--United States.
I. Brennan, Linda L. II. Johnson, Victoria (Victoria Elizabeth)
  HM851.S635 2004
  303.48'33--dc22

                    2003014952

Paperback ISBN 1-59140-288-3

British Cataloguing in Publication Data
A Cataloguing in Publication record for this book is available from the British Library.

Social, Ethical and Policy Implications of Information Technology

Table of Contents

Preface

Information systems have effects far beyond their operational or functional uses. As information systems become more pervasive in human organizations, these effects pose increasingly significant ethical dilemmas and create unintended social costs and consequences. Management practice and public policy lag behind the advances in technology and their impact on social systems.

Today's leaders must be able to anticipate and address these challenges, although they are often unprepared to do so. Technical professionals, who have been taught to think in terms of logic, structures and flows, also experience difficulties in addressing such situations. By creating awareness and offering analytical frameworks for a variety of issues stemming from information systems' implementations, this book can contribute to the development of these professionals' ability to cope—and perhaps avert—these problems.

We have developed this book with the following audiences in mind: professionals entering information systems management; undergraduates in computer information systems programs; graduates in management information systems programs; students of public policy and public administration; and professionals entering public sector management.

The book is divided into three sections. The first section highlights several social implications of information systems. We start broadly with "Global Perspectives on the Information Society" and then delve into specific challenges. "Digital Divides: Their Social and Ethical Implications" examines the impact of technology access on societies, while "The Perils of Access and

Immediacy: Unintended Consequences of Information Technology" explores the impact on organizations and individuals. "What, Me, Worry? The Empowerment of Employees" and "Managing Workplace Privacy Responsibly" provide different perspectives on the relationships among organizations, individuals and the technologies they use. We close the section about social system effects with a provocative examination of technology-mediated interpersonal interaction with "Virtual Harms and Real Responsibility."

The second section is devoted to several chapters addressing many of the ethical challenges posed by information systems. "Ethical Challenges for Information Systems Professionals" provides an introduction to ethical viewpoints and an overview of the difficulties professionals face in the implementation of information systems. The next chapter, "Living Within Glass Houses: Coping with Organizational Transparency," describes the increasing pressures corporations face for ethical behavior and corporate social responsibility. This is followed with the specific illustrations of "Ethical Challenges of Information Systems: The Carnage of Outsourcing and Other Technology-Enabled Organizational Imperatives." The last chapter in this section, "A Contrarian's View: New Wine in Old Bottles, New Economy and Old Ethics—Can it Work?," questions whether ethical questions and implications have really changed with the advent of information systems.

The last section provides an overview of policy considerations, highlighting several of the legal ramifications of information systems. We begin with consideration of questions of responsibility and accountability for systems, with "Liability for Systems and Data Quality" and "Software Engineering as a Profession: A Moral Case for Licensure." The next two chapters address the protection ("Copyright Law in the Digital Age") and preservation ("'Digital Orphans': Technology's Wayward Children") of technology-based intellectual property. "Compliance with Data Management Laws" then highlights interesting legal issues of data management.

We end this book with a chapter that suggests how future efforts might address these difficult issues and implications. "The Central Problem in Cyber Ethics and How Stories Can Be Used to Address It" offers a different way to learn, discuss, and think about the social, ethical and policy challenges posed by information systems.

Acknowledgments

These chapters represent a wide diversity of viewpoints, carefully crafted to stimulate thinking and challenge perspectives. Our thanks go to the chapter authors, all of whom were valuable and collegial contributors to this project. We sincerely appreciate the sponsorship and assistance of everyone at the IGP Press. We are also indebted to G. Russell Barber, Frank Ghannadian, Samuel Juett, James Hunt, Spero Peppas, Mary Saunders, and Steven Simon, our colleagues from Mercer University who truly supported this project.

Finally, we thank Bob, Jonathan, and Larry for their encouragement—and our canine children for their companionship—as we worked our way through the process of editing hundreds of pages of manuscripts.

We hope you will find the result worthwhile.

Linda L. Brennan
Victoria E. Johnson
Mercer University
May 2003

Section I

Social Implications

Chapter I

Global Perspectives on the Information Society

William J. McIver, Jr.
University at Albany, USA

ABSTRACT

This chapter surveys issues and priorities being raised internationally by governments, civil society and the private sector in conceptualizing a global information society. Examinations of social, ethical and policy implications of information and communication technologies are often limited in scope, by region, constituency, issue, or other social dimensions. It is critically important, given growing global interdependencies in terms of labor, trade, communications resources and other factors, that social informatics and community informatics research begin to include more international perspectives and analyses. Efforts initiated within the United Nations sphere and other international bodies in recent years are offering unique opportunities to develop such perspectives. This chapter examines the body of issues being raised through these processes. This chapter seeks to show the diversity of perspectives that exist globally on these issues. Global perspectives on social, ethical and policy implications of information systems introduce the consideration of both the common and the diverse needs of the world's many cultures, regions and nations. Information and communication technologies are seen in this context as both enabling solutions to the world's many social problems and as potential sources of threats to labor, environment, culture, and other facets of society.

INTRODUCTION

This chapter surveys current issues and priorities being raised internationally by governments, civil society and the private sector in the context of developing an information society. Examinations of social, ethical and policy implications of information and communication technologies (ICTs) are often limited in scope, by region, constituency, issue, or other social dimensions under study. It has become critically important, given growing global interdependencies in terms of labor, trade, communications resources and other factors, that social and community informatics research begin to include more international perspectives and analyses.

Social informatics has been defined by Kling (1999) as "the interdisciplinary study of the design, uses and consequences of information technologies that takes into account their interaction with institutional and cultural contexts." Social informatics research has three principal areas of focus:
1. The development of models and theories that explain the social and organization uses and impacts of ICTs;
2. The development of methodologies that improve the design, implementation, maintenance and use of ICTs; and,
3. The study of philosophical and ethical issues that arise due to the use of ICTs in social and organizational contexts.

Community Informatics is an emerging field of computer and information science—and arguably a part of social informatics—concerned with developing a coherent theory, methodology and praxis to support the development, deployment and management of ICT-based solutions to community problems. Community informatics has been described as a discipline with a scope and purpose analogous to the well-established field of management information systems (MIS) (Gurstein, 2002). The characteristics and needs of communities can be significantly different from those of the types of organizations for which ICTs have traditionally been developed: well-funded businesses and governmental organizations. The major differences are as follows:

Socio-Technical Geographies

Communities are geographically situated and, thus, there are often significant geographic components to their problems. For example, rural communities worldwide have historically faced major geographic barriers in gaining access to infrastructure necessary to use ICTs, including electrification and telephony.

Technology Life-Cycle Constraints

Communities also often face tighter financial constraints than business or governmental organizations in attempting to address their problems in terms of the costs of implementation and long-term maintenance. The seeking of IT-based solutions must, therefore, include consideration of low cost, public domain or open source solutions (Dinkelacker, 2002; Johnson-Eilola, 2002; PicoPeta Simputers, n.d.; Yajnik, 2002). The development process must also devote greater attention to issues such as the training needs and capabilities of communities to provide technical support and respond to changes in system requirements.

Accessibility and Universal Design

Community informatics must also have a commitment, as both a matter of principle—and law in many countries—to the development of ICTs for communities such that the widest range of citizens can enjoy their benefits, particularly those with disabilities (Glinert & York, 1992). The concept of universal design has evolved out of the objective of designing systems that are accessible to people with disabilities. It has been recognized, however, that universal design benefits all people, not just those who have disabilities. General principles for universal design have been developed by a number of organizations (Bergman & Johnson, 1995; Connell, 1997; NYNEX, n.d.; Pacific Bell Advisory Group for People with Disabilities, 1996). Universal design principles have also been developed for the specific software engineering domain of Web applications (World Wide Web Consortium, 2001).

Prioritizing Social Requirements

Community informatics also differs from MIS in that it must, in the interest of social and cultural goals, be open to creative solutions for communities that may be outside the orthodoxy of traditional MIS solutions or cost-benefit analyses.

The development of technology for communities without due consideration of these unique requirements has often had unfortunate consequences (see Margonelli, 2002; Benjamin, 1999; Rudolf, 2002).

International research on social, ethical and policy implications of ICTs has been performed since at least the founding of international bodies, such as the International Postal Union and the International Telegraphy Union, in the late 1800s (McIver & Birdsall, 2002). In the past two decades, social informatics research of an international nature began to emerge in both traditional academic research and non-governmental organizations (NGOs). Much of this work, like social informatics research (Kling, 2001), has been distributed across many diverse sites. NGOs focusing on ICT issues have emerged, and NGOs whose initial primary foci were on issues not related to ICTs have expanded their agendas to include social, ethical and policy implications of information systems. International social informatics research has emerged out of a number of areas, including examination of the concept of communication for development (Figueroa et al., 2002), communication rights (Fisher & Harms, 1983; Hamelink, 1994; Birdsall & Rasmussen, 2000), and telecommunications policy and governance (Heeks, 1999; Mueller, 1999).

Unified perspectives on international social informatics issues have been difficult to come by, perhaps due to the distributed and diverse sites of knowledge production. However, efforts initiated within the United Nations sphere of organizations and several other international bodies in recent years are offering unique opportunities to develop such perspectives. This has been due both to a shift in focus to "information society" issues at the international level and to modalities of participation that have yielded input from not only member states and the business sector, but also from broad cross sections of civil society, across many regions of the world.[1] Arguably, the most important site and catalyst for this unification is currently the process behind the United Nations-sponsored World Summit on the Information Society (WSIS) that has been unfolding since the middle 1990s, culminating in 2005.

This chapter is not about the World Summit on the Information Society itself, but it examines the body of information being generated by the preparatory processes of the Summit and other international processes to develop a survey and analysis of international social informatics issues being raised in the development of a global vision of an information society. This chapter seeks, in particular, to show the diversity of perspectives that exist globally on what should constitute an information society and what social, ethical and policy relationships should exist between such a society, its citizens, member states, and the private sector.[2]

The spectrum of viewpoints on these issues range from the notion of an information society as merely a collection of technologies and communications channels to viewpoints that integrate the technical with the social. In the latter case, some conceptions of an information society are explicit in their inclusion of such notions as citizenship; community participation in decisions about ICTs; economic, political, and social justice; and the use of ICTs for development.

Within these viewpoints, there exist issues that are often overlooked or taken for granted in developed countries. For example, many constituencies from developing nations have been highly critical of the models of an information society that now dominate in developed countries because they tend to overlook non-digital communications modalities, such as radio and television, which remain far more accessible and practical in developing regions. The merging of these two viewpoints raises unique issues.

BACKGROUND: A HISTORICAL PERSPECTIVE ON SOCIAL, ETHICAL AND POLICY IMPLICATIONS OF AN INFORMATION SOCIETY

Innis (1964) showed that media of communication and transitions to new types of media have made profound impacts on civilizations. He demonstrated, in particular, how the characteristics unique to different types of media have determined the natures and biases of the impacts they were able to make in terms of space and time. This has been shown to be true for information systems in general. Global perspectives on the social, ethical and policy implications of information systems have most certainly been considered since the introduction of technologies of communication such as writing and ancient postal services (see Scheele, 1970, pp. 7-10; Postman, 1992, pp. 3-39). These perspectives have been shown to have co-evolved in a complex interaction between the capabilities afforded society by each generation of technology and the evolution of civil, political and economic rights in those societies (see McIver & Birdsall, 2002).

Administrative and Technical Implications

The earliest global perspectives on information systems were concerned primarily with administrative and technical issues. These included the creation of universal administrative zones of operation through interconnection, political protections for free transit of information through third countries via networks (e.g., postal and telegraph), and technical interconnection standards. International perspectives on telecommunications began to develop since at least the ninth century C.E., after the fall of the Roman Empire and its postal service, the *cursus publicus*, when inter-city-state and private courier services began to fill the void (Scheele, 1970, pp. 7-10). Formal international structures for dealing with ICTs did not emerge, however, until 1865 when the International Telegraph Union (2002) was founded (Hamelink, 1994). The desire to achieve both cross-border administrative and technical interoperability between the then proliferating telegraphy networks motivated its formation. This was to be followed by the formation of the Universal Postal Union in 1874 (Codding, 1964, p. 1). Telephony was first addressed in the International Telegraph Union (ITU) starting in 1885, and was fully integrated by 1925 (International Telecommunication Union, 2002; Codding, 1995). Radio's first application was radio-telegraphy in 1896. Its international regulation was first taken up in the period from 1903 to 1906, resulting in the formation of the International Radio-Telegraph Union. Governments initiated the merger of all of these policy activities to form the International Telecommunication Union in 1934 (2002).

Cultural and Social Implications

In 1948, the United Nations was founded, bringing about a new generation of human rights—adding economic, cultural and social rights to civil and political rights—and a different set of perspectives on what is now considered in the conception of an information society. Understanding of administrative and technical implications of information systems at an international level was, by this time, fairly mature (though these understandings are also always evolving). Regulatory models for broadcast media, for example, had been created in most developed countries by this time, with government control being the norm (see McChesney, 1995). The new generation of human rights added cultural and economic issues to the consideration of the social, ethical and policy implications of information systems.

The Universal Declaration of Human Rights, the founding document of the United Nations, was perhaps the first document of its kind to articulate rights that could be directly linked to social implications raised by information systems and to technological advancement in general. Article 19 (United Nations, 1993) states:

Everyone has the right to freedom of opinion and expression; this right includes freedom to hold opinions without interference and to seek, receive and impart information and ideas through any media and regardless of frontiers.

Article 27 section 1 states:

Everyone has the right freely to participate in the cultural life of the community, to enjoy the arts and to share in scientific advancement and its benefits.

By the 1950s, developing nations were raising concerns about the impacts of broadcast media. They objected to the one-way flow of information made possible by the broadcast technologies of radio and television. These flows originated at the time almost exclusively in the developed world, often by colonizing nations, and were sent into developing and colonized countries (UNESCO, 1980a; Hamelink, 1994). The broadcasting of culturally and politically- biased information with no means of reply was seen as an undemocratic form of communication. This concept has recently come to be called "content dumping." These issues were raised at an international level in 1955 at the Bandung Conference, a forum initiated by 29 African and Asian nations that came to be known as the Non-Aligned Movement.

The advent of satellite-based communications in 1957 with the launching of Sputnik raised fundamentally new social, ethical and policy implications for ICTs. Satellites made global information systems possible for the first time, providing a means of broadcasting over much wider areas, as well as a new means for the transmission and networking of point-to-point communication modalities such as telephony. The cultural implications were phenomenal. Comor observed that "...the 'intimate' quality of the human voice and image entering one's home, DBS provides an effective means through which both a literate and non-literate population can be reached," and, as a result of this level of intimacy, "an effective and immediate expression (and manipulation) of human emotion is a well-recognized political and commercial advantage relative to other forms of mass media" (1994, pp. 87-88). Once again, the international community addressed a transition to a new technology. In 1961, the United Nations General Assembly adopted resolution 1721D(XVI), which supports the right of access to satellite communications by all countries on a non-discriminatory basis. It states: "Communication by means of satellite should be available to the nations of the world as soon as practicable on a global and non-discriminatory basis" (Hamelink, 1994, p. 67). Later that decade, Jean d'Arcy, Director of Radio and Visual Services in the UN Office of Public Information, published an article on the implications of direct broadcast satellites in which he called for a new right: the right to communicate (d'Arcy, 1969).

Collective Implications

Over the five decades following the Universal Declaration of Human Rights, the conception of human rights has evolved to include the notion of collective rights. Collective rights seek to address guarantees and protections that should be enjoyed by entire communities. These might include development rights, rights of self-determination for indigenous groups, and rights related to gender, ethnicity, cultural and linguistic preservation, and environmental protections for whole communities or regions (see United Nations, 1997). These have all come to be taken into account in the context of information systems.

Sites where the domain of collective rights first began to intersect with social, ethical and policy implications of information systems include the Bandung Conference and the ITU Plenipotentiary Conference at Montreux in 1965. The earlier conference began to address the social and cultural impacts of broadcast

ICTs in developing countries. The Montreux Conference began to deal with the economic, social and political impacts of ICTs (Markle Foundation, 1972, pp. 3-6). In particular, developing nations began to link communication with development. Recommendations were made to the Plenipoteniary that the ITU support technical assistance, establish a regional presence, and that member states establish a fund for use by developing countries for this assistance (Codding, 1995). This initiated a movement that has continued to the present, with mixed results in achieving these recommendations. By 1982, the ITU's mission had been changed to include the "[maintenance] and [extension] of international cooperation...for the improvement and rational use of telecommunications" (Codding, 1995. p. 506). A number of civil society organizations involved in communication rights have extended this conception of development to include not only technical assistance for member states, but also for communities therein. Among many other issues, they maintain that assistance must extend from the technical level to that which would allow communities to both make use of information transmitted over ICTs and to participate in its formation (see Rockefeller Foundation, 1999; World Summit on the Information Society - Coordinating Group on Civil Society, 2002).

Technological and Social Convergence Toward a Global Information Society

The period from 1965 to the early 1970s saw the development of a number of technologies that would help lead to a crystallization of the concept of a global information society. Packet switching was crucial in the development of data networks, leading to the inception of the ARPANET in the U.S. in 1969 (Press, 1997). Packet switching had the broader impact of enabling broadband communications and the convergence of many media of communication, including data networks, broadcast radio and television, satellite, and cable television. While the ARPANET was not developed for use by average citizens, it was crucial to the evolution of modern conceptions of an information society. It, along with the present day Internet, fostered the development of a number of technologies that have subsequently become the basis for much of a global information society, including SMTP (i.e., for e-mail), FTP, TCP/IP, and HTTP. Between 1969 and 1990, use of the ARPANET and its technological and organizational offshoots such as CSNET and NSFNET remained largely outside of the realm of average citizens. Mostly academic, government and industrial scientists had access to these networks (Zakon, 2001).

During the 1980s, the emergence of the personal computer and the establishment of community networks and proprietary dial-up information services allowed the broader public to become familiar with technologies such as e-mail, electronic bulletin boards, chat rooms, and other online services. In 1986, the first FREENET was started in Cleveland, Ohio in the U.S. to provide free access to a virtual community in which people could share information and discuss issues. The Cleveland FREENET was soon followed by the creation of many community networks in North America and around the world. The private sector also began to contribute in a more direct way to the public's increasing exposure to notions of information society during the 1980s. New and existing online information services such as CompuServe and AOL began offering dial-up services geared toward personal computer users.[3] These would also soon expand to have global reach.

During this period, NGOs and other entities in the broader civil society became more involved in moves toward an information society. From 1985 to 1986, PeaceNet, GreenNet and EcoNet were formed to provide networking for peace and environmental activists around the world. In 1987, the Institute for Global Communications (IGC) was formed. It provided services to an increasing number of organizations and other networks over the next decade (Institute for Global Communications, 2002). In 1990, Association for Progressive Communications (APC) was founded by a coalition of civil society-oriented activist networks around the world (Association for Progressive Communications, 2000, pp. 11-15). These networks and their users were perhaps the first to see ICTs as tools for responding to what they perceived as injustices around the world and, ultimately, as tools to form a human-centered information society.

The last major episode leading to explicit calls for the formation of an information society involved a confluence of events: the start of commercial access to the Internet for the public; the advent of the World Wide Web in 1992; and the impacts of divestiture, privatization and mergers in the telecommunications industry. Changes in U.S. government policy allowed commercial dial-up access to the Internet starting in 1990 (Zakon, 2001). In 1992, the World Wide Web was released for public use by CERN (European Organization for Nuclear Research) and, by 1993, the first general purpose Web browser—Mosaic—was made available to the public (World Wide Web Consortium, 2000). The World Wide Web initiated a rapid increase in Internet usage by government, business and civil society (Mueller, 1999, p. 5). The backdrop of all of these events was the move toward greater private control of telecommunication networks since the divestiture of AT&T in 1984.

All of these developments helped to accelerate the convergences of policy interests and technological development toward the construction of an information society. Widespread public access to the Internet and wide dissemination of the protocols for World Wide Web technologies enabled, for the first time, a platform-independent environment in which users could share and disseminate more types of information with far greater ease than ever before. The new business environment created both competition and mergers that helped to push the enabling technologies of a future information society into the public.

Calls for an Information Society

These developments culminated in 1993 in the U.S. with a call for a National Information Infrastructure (NII) initiative. The agenda of the NII was to create a "seamless web of interconnected, interoperable information networks, computers, databases, and consumer electronics that will eventually link homes, workplaces, and public institutions together" (National Research Council, 1994, p. 1). It was also in this time period that calls for a global version of such an infrastructure were made (Gore, 1994). On a technical level, a global information infrastructure had long been in existence and use by government, business and civil society for a variety of purposes, from research to commerce to citizen participation in society (National Research Council, 1994, pp. 269-281).

Major developments began on an international level around the technical and administrative aspects of Internet governance; legal issues related to Internet technologies, such as copyright, trademark and taxation; and the development by government, business and civil society of positions on a broad spectrum of social, ethical and policies issues, including digital divide issues, development and culture-specific impacts of information technologies. Mueller chronicled the complex struggle over Internet governance between 1994 and 1998, which originated in a U.S. political context, but was subject to interventions on an international level (1999). The U.S. government pursued a model of self-regulation for Internet governance that revolved initially around U.S.-based entities. Other governments demanded internationalization of the model and greater governmental involvement. Governments were also concerned about the impact of U.S. trademark law and, in general, the dominance of the U.S. over Internet governance (Mueller, 1999, pp. 9-10). The resulting formation of the Internet Corporation for Assigned Names and Numbers (ICANN) was a formal framework ostensibly designed to be international, representative and accountable to governments, business and civil society (p. 13). [4]

Many influential scholars from Norbert Weiner (1948) to Marshall McLuhan (Levinson, 1999) foresaw and contemplated social and ethical issues related to what has become known as the "Information Society" long before the World Wide Web. Likewise, civil society organizations such as Computer Professionals for Social Responsibility had long developed social, ethical and policy positions related to enabling technologies of an information society. [5] A number of notable government studies involving this concept had also been conducted as early as the 1970s. The Canadian Department of Communications' task force called the Telecommission (1971) issued the report *Instant World* in 1971, which examined the societal implications of the combined use of computing and telecommunications, and studied the concept of a right to communicate. In 1978, Simon Nora and Alain Minc published a critically important report in the history of computing—*L'Informatisation de la société* (The Computerization of Society)—that had been commissioned by Valéry Giscard d'Estaing, the then president of

France (1980). Their report defined a new industrial policy necessary to restructure civil and political society in France via the synthesis of telecommunications and computing technologies, a concept they called *télématique*.

It was arguably not until the advent of the World Wide Web, however, and the subsequent rush to the Internet by citizens, business and government agencies that comprehensive positions on social, ethical and policy issues relating to an information society began to form. Business formed influential organizations in which such positions were developed, including CommerceNet in 1994.[6] Similarly, civil society organizations arose, including the Platform for Communication Rights 1996.[7] Most important and potentially far reaching has been the development of integrative and summative processes within the UN sphere that have brought together inputs from stakeholders from governments, business and civil society. The United Nations' Millennium Declaration is a milestone in this context (United Nations, 2000). Drafted in 1999, it established a process by which member states are to meet a set of ambitious goals to improve the global community. ICTs are expected to play a major role in pursuing these goals (p. 6). The ITU, under the sponsorship of the UN, subsequently started the process for the World Summit on the Information Society (United Nations, 2001). The G8 nations also started a similar process at their 2000 summit to work on digital divide issues called the Digital Opportunity Task Force—commonly known as "DOT Force" (Coordinating Committee of Business Interlocutors, 2000, p. 11). These efforts have been yielding important information about the diverse perspectives on the notion of an information society, across member states, regions, the private sector, and civil society. They are also providing information about social and community informatics issues that are unique to different regional and issue-based constituencies. These preparatory processes have included regional summits and consultations held with and between non-governmental organizations (NGOs), member states and the private sector. A survey of social, ethical and policy implications that have been identified in these processes is given in the next section.

A THEMATIC PERSPECTIVE ON SOCIAL, ETHICAL, AND POLICY IMPLICATIONS OF AN INFORMATION SOCIETY

As discussed in the previous section, a focus on discrete information systems in social contexts was broadened to the notion of an information society during the 1990s. This section attempts to synthesize themes that have come to be seen as constitutive of a hypothetical information society. These themes have been articulated by government, business and civil society through their input into processes in the UN sphere and other selected bodies such as ICANN. These include declarations to which UN member states were signatories; input into the WSIS by the Coordinating Committee of Business Interlocutors (CCBI), which includes the World Economic Forum; and regional and international statements of civil society formations involved in the WSIS process. The themes that will be examined here are: the foundations of an information society; digital divides in an information society; the development of a framework for an information society; a knowledge society perspective; defining rights and governance; infrastructure development; development and employment; tools, services and applications; citizens and communities; and gender perspectives.

The Foundations of an Information Society

The concept of an information society is the current context in which the social, ethical and policy implications of information systems are being dealt with by many actors at the international level. This first theme is necessarily epistemological. It is one that attempts to establish the philosophical and legal foundations upon which other information society themes should be elaborated. Information systems have long been seen as entities that not only embed society, but also as agents that help to define it. From a global perspective, the major task here has been to develop a shared understanding of the concept of an information society. Such a vision might be best articulated in terms of the fundamental basis of an information society and the roles of societal actors—governments, business and civil society—within it.

Two general perspectives on the fundamental basis of information society seemed to have emerged: information society as a consumer-oriented environment containing tools, applications and services; or information society as a global commons enabled by ICTs in which human needs are central. Evidence for the first perspective can be seen in recent proposals into the WSIS process by member states and the business sector. Here, the theme "user needs" is given the same status as other broad thematic areas such as "building infrastructure" and "services and applications" with minimal explicit reference to human rights (World Summit on the Information Society - Executive Secretariat, 2002a, pp. 1-8). This general perspective is one that is held by business (see Coordinating Committee of Business Interlocutors, 2002). Many civil society entities have, on the other hand, articulated positions that would place human rights at the center of a conception of an information society. In this viewpoint, an information society's purposes, development, operation, and governance would take place within established human rights frameworks and would be evaluated on its ability to meet human needs (see World Summit on the Information Society - Coordinating Group on Civil Society, 2002).

Governments have articulated a spectrum of positions on their roles in an information society. These articulations have been made individually and collectively. The Millennium Declaration of the United Nations states that governments should "...ensure that the benefits of new technologies, especially information and communication technologies..." are enjoyed by all people (United Nations, 2000, p. 6). One implication of this declaration is that ICTs are to be seen as major tools for meeting the series of highly ambitious goals it set forth, including the provision of elementary education to all children by 2015. The G8 nations articulated a similar, but less-specific message (G8, 2000). One role of government in an information society that is implicit in these efforts is as a catalyst and organizer for business and civil society processes concerning an information society. For example, the G8 initiated the Digital Opportunity Task Force (DOT Force) to address the digital divide and other societal matters. Positions of member states with respect to these declarations vary. The European Union sees, in part, its role as bringing "the Information Society closer to all citizens of Europe, develop the economic wealth, address growing social needs, and focus on cultural identity and diversity" (European Union, 2002, p. 7). The U.S. commentary on the first preparatory conference, PrepCom-1, of the WSIS, for example, argued against linking the Millennium Declaration to the goals of the WSIS (United States of America, 2002, p. 2).

Business, as represented by the Coordinating Committee of Business Interlocutors (2002), has articulated its roles in an information society as providing services and applications, facilitating trade in goods and services, facilitating the delivery of government services, performing self-regulation of its actions within information society, and ensuring "sustainable economic growth" (pp. 1-9).

A significant number of IT-related NGOs and other NGOs that have added IT issues to their agendas have adopted positions on the role of civil society that might be characterized as running counter to positions articulated by some governments and business or, at the very least, as acting as a balance. Many see civil society as providing oversight for governmental and business activities within an information society that has become global and increasingly privatized. To this end, many entities within civil society have called for greater transparency and citizen involvement in the operation of an information society (World Summit on the Information Society - Civil Society Plenary, 2002a).

The views between stakeholders from government, business and civil society have not been entirely antagonistic. Business has been acknowledged by many stakeholders as providing key innovations and other contributions creating the possibility for an information society. At the same time, it is recognized that the contributions of business may not have been possible without the support of governments for the development and operation of technologies that are forming the basis for an information society, most especially the Internet. Civil society is also seen as contributing in major ways to the evolution toward an information society, primarily in its continuing support for open source development and knowledge sharing.

Digital Divides in an Information Society

One of the most critical sets of social, ethical and policy issues that must be dealt with in realizing an information society is the phenomenon known as the digital divide. In domestic contexts, this is often defined as a gap between individual citizens having access to Internet technologies and those who lack such access. In a global context, the concept of a digital divide has been expanded to include communities, nations and whole regions. Citizens in many parts of the world still do not have basic access to ICTs. This includes not just Internet, but basic telephony. Democratic access to and use of ICTs, such as digital government services, cannot be truly realized in a society as long as there remain citizens who lack access to both appropriate technologies and technical skills to make use of these services.

It is now being explicitly recognized that a complex of different types of barriers exist, not just the proverbial, monolithic "digital divide" (European Union, 2002; G8, 2000; World Summit on the Information Society - Civil Society Plenary, 2002b; World Summit on the Information Society - Executive Secretariat, 2002a). A major focus is on addressing barriers faced by those nations defined by the United Nations Development Program (2002) as the least developed countries (LDCs). Given this broader understanding of the digital divide, the other issues that many see as needing to be addressed include: social, economic, and educational barriers; political and social barriers; requirements for achieving universal and equitable access; information as a public good, with due consideration for intellectual property; freedom of expression and of the media; supporting cultural and linguistic diversity in circumventing barriers; and the distinct roles of governments, civil society and the private sector in bridging barriers to an information society.

Access to information (e.g., digital government services) is not only characterized by access to technologies, however. Access to information has been studied on several levels, including the properties and characteristics of access, as well as the means and availability of access. Means and availability of access are not dependent only on the economic status of individuals or their communities, but also on information usage skills and geography. Access to the equipment, software and telecommunication services necessary for Internet access must obviously be accompanied by skills to make use of them.

Telecommunication-based information technologies have come to be seen as spatial systems that change space and time relations to create new "virtual" geographies (Gillespie & Robins, 1989; Kitchin, 1998). These include geographies defined by communication, economics and social formations. Access to the benefits of an information society then clearly requires access to a geography in which access points (e.g., telephones, computers or kiosks) or other appropriate telecommunications infrastructures exist. Such geographies include work environments, libraries and schools where access points likely exist.

Less obvious are the relationships between the deployment of these technologies and urban planning by both public and private sectors. Urban geographies must have an evolving telecommunication infrastructure for citizens to make use of the latest digital services. It is becoming less practical, for example, to download government documents using 56K modems as their sizes and quantities increase, but newer technologies may not be practical either. Certain advanced data communications standards such as ISDN, DSL and cable television-based Internet access, which provide solutions to bandwidth problems, may be unavailable in certain areas due to a lack of infrastructure.

A digital divide can also be characterized by the information itself: its costs, representations, communication processes used to convey it, and ways it is collected from one's surrounding environment. These issues have been examined extensively at both conceptual (McReadie & Rice, 1999a, 1999b) and implementation levels (December, 1996). Of particular concern here are potential cost barriers for information and representations of government information. Certain sources of public information are not free. Large collections of legal briefs and other documentation about legal cases in the U.S. are available through subscription services such as Westlaw. Such arrangements have raised serious questions about the ability of citizens to access public information they need.

Communication researchers have demonstrated that the valuation of information in general presents a unique problem for those who are economically disadvantaged (McCreadie & Rice, 1999a, p. 68). Beyond the basic consideration of whether one can afford to pay for information, the value of information is more uncertain than most other types of goods. Its usefulness cannot be conclusively determined until it is used. Thus, those who are less able to afford information are also less likely to take chances buying it because its usefulness may be highly uncertain to them.

Finally, the cost of technology may present a barrier to information. Policy making to address the digital divide must mandate the leveraging of ICTs to provide access points via more widely available technologies. These include telephony-based applications and low cost Internet appliances such as handheld computing devices or Internet appliances. Policies must also encourage innovations that allow electronic government documents to be used in the context of human agent environments, wherein citizens can still communicate directly with government officials.

Developing a Framework for an Information Society

This theme attempts to develop a holistic legal and policy perspective on the concept of an information society. A framework for an information society would define the functional, regulatory and developmental aspects of the society, as well as its relationship to existing human rights and international law frameworks. Functional issues would include education, addressing the needs of workers, facilitation of technical literacy, and support for commerce. Regulatory issues are seen as including data protection, privacy and network security, intellectual property rights, public domain and fair use, and the establishment of appropriate policy and market structures. Developmental aspects of an information society would address sustainable and environmentally responsible development of ICTs, appropriate use of new and traditional ICTs, capacity building in governments, civil society and the private sector, financing and deployment, and examination of social and regulatory impacts of this framework. In this context, participatory design is recognized by many as an indispensable tool for ICT development. An integral part of the developmental processes of an information society would also include a continuing process of implementation and review of the framework itself.

A Knowledge Society Perspective

This theme considers the special relationship between information and knowledge, where knowledge is derived from processes of organizing data and information to convey domain-specific understanding, experience, expertise, and learning. An information society has often been characterized as a knowledge society (United Nations, 2000). From this perspective, an information society is seen as enabling the creation and management of knowledge as the primary benefit to humankind. Social, ethical and policy considerations in this context relate to: the establishment of general educational goals sought through the use of an information society; enabling distance learning; facilitating both formal and lifelong learning; the development of information literacy, including critical appreciation of information and content development skills; access to knowledge; support for cultural and linguistic diversity; and support for the needs of young people (World Summit on the Information Society -Youth Caucus, 2002). This perspective also recognizes that capacity building in academia is necessary to support a knowledge society.

Defining Rights and Governance

A major area of contention in the development of an information society has been in defining and enforcing the rights of all stakeholders, as well as the particulars of its governance. An exemplar here is the ICANN and public criticisms of it (Mueller, 1999). Critical issues in addressing rights and governance are: democratic management of international bodies dealing with ICTs; information and communication rights of governments, business and citizens; privacy and security policies and rights; censorship and regulation of content; the role of the media; defining, identifying and responding to criminal activities within an information society; the application of ICTs for government and decentralization (see McIver & Elmagarmid, 2002); and media ownership and concentration. A major emphasis here for civil society and some governments has been to establish support for the empowerment of citizens. In addition, many see an information society as enabling the reform and strengthening of democracy.

Business, as represented by the CCBI, would like to see a limited role for governments and civil society in the rights and governance of an information society. In its Global Action Plan, it called for governments to "rely on business self-regulation and the voluntary use of empowering technologies as the main drivers behind the creation of trust across the whole spectrum of users and providers of e-commerce goods and services" (p. 6). In the fundamental principles it articulated for the WSIS, the CCBI called for government intervention to the extent necessary to support a "stable, international legal environment, allow a fair allocation of scarce resources and protect public interests" (p. 8).

Infrastructure Development

Infrastructure is a nexus for many of the major technical, social and policy issues in the realization of an information society. The goal here is the evolution from the present technical state to one in which all of the benefits envisioned from an information society can be realized. Key issues here are: the extension of Internet connectivity to areas that are under-served or not served at all; the application of wireless technologies, particularly to realize the economic benefits that technological "leap frogging" affords developing nations (see Norman, 1998); the development of new advanced ICTs to meet outstanding human needs in all societies; the building of bridges between different types of media, including radio, television, print, and the Internet; addressing the needs of rural communities; and the availability of ICTs needed to address emergency situations around the world, as articulated in the Tampere Convention (International Telecommunication Union, 1998). Perhaps the most contentious set of social, ethical and policy issues in this category has been in defining the balance of roles between private sector investment, government subsidy and civil society efforts in creating information society infrastructure (see Coordinating Committee of Business Interlocutors, 2002; World Summit on the Information Society - Coordinating Group on Civil Society, 2002; World Summit on the Information Society - Executive Secretariat, 2002c).

Development and Employment

An information society is seen as having the potential to greatly affect development and create employment. This can be seen, as discussed above, beginning with the communication for development movement among members of the ITU. The key issues here are: the creation of economic opportunities; the role of ICTs in health, agriculture, labor, culture, and other life-critical sectors (see World Summit on the Information Society - Executive Secretariat, 2002b for a detailed compilation); the role of ICT-based communication for development;

the training of workers for an information society; a consideration of the realities and dangers of labor exploitation in ICT-based sectors; an examination of the roles and impacts of investment and speculation in ICT-based development; and the role and limits of e-commerce in development and employment.

Tools, Services, and Applications

Being enabled mainly by scientific and technological achievements, the dominant focus of conceptions of an information society through the early 1990s was techno-centric, viewing an information society merely in terms of the technical feasibility of classes of tools, services and applications. The increasing influence of social and community informatics perspectives has, however, changed the focus to one of considering which tools, services and applications should be used or developed with regard to their social impacts and human needs that must be addressed (e.g., as articulated in United Nations, 2000). The broad technical issues in this category are: the development of technologies that facilitate active citizenship and improved government; technological support for universal access to knowledge and global communication and cooperation; and the improvement of the standard of living adequate to the health and well-being of all citizens. Specific issues include: the building of bridges between the communication modalities of radio, television, press, and Internet; the development of ICTs for e-government, including citizen input into political processes (Macintosh et al., 2002); support for disaster mitigation and relief operations (International Telecommunication Union, 1998); support for long-term data retention and archiving for cultural preservation (InterPARES, 2002); and tools to facilitate cross-sector co-operation (Coordinating Committee of Business Interlocutors, 2002).

Citizens and Communities

A number of issues have been contributed mainly by civil society to the conception of an information society that falls outside of commercial and governmental perspectives. The major issues here are: the creation and preservation of an electronic commons, free public spaces and technical resources that can be used to meet human needs (see Lessig, 2001); community control of ICT infrastructures; continuing support for open source technologies; capacity building for communities to participate in an information society; and addressing the multiplicity of dimensions of diversity, including linguistic and cultural diversity. Specific issues here are: the empowerment of communities through ICTs; preservation of culture and language; support for oral information and cultures; support for independent, community controlled media; meeting the needs of people with disabilities; meeting the needs of the elderly; providing support for cross-cultural communications; stemming the technological "brain drain" from developing countries; content dumping, which is the subsidization of information production and its delivery far below cost to culturally vulnerable populations (World Summit on the Information Society -Youth Caucus, 2002); and geographic-specific issues, such as problems of rural access to ICTs.

Gender Perspectives

It is well understood, as Jansen (1989, p. 196) states, "technological designs are also social designs" (see also Muller et al., 1997). The social designs in information technologies and processes used to achieve them reflect society's gender biases—among others. Design processes that do not take gender issues into account run the risk of producing information technologies and services that do not adequately address the needs of women. The Millennium Declaration of the United Nations stressed the need to address gender as a basis for overcoming major problems in societies (United Nations, 2000, p. 5):

We also resolve:
To promote gender equality and the empowerment of women as effective ways to combat poverty, hunger and disease and to stimulate development that is truly sustainable.

The promotion of gender equality has been recognized by growing numbers of stakeholders as an issue that is not only important to women, but a necessary condition for improving all societies given the central roles and responsibilities that women have. The broad issues that have been raised in this context are reducing gender discrimination and improving participation of women in an information society, capacity building and training for women, and the use of ICTs to improve the lives and livelihoods of women worldwide. Specific issues include: supporting wide participation by women and gender ICT specialists in policy and decision making at all levels in the ICT sector; supporting women's greater access and control over resources necessary for their empowerment; improving the participation and representation of women and gender equality advocates in all levels of policy making; reform of decision-making processes in the ICT sector; the development of ICT applications for supporting women's reproductive and productive roles, and in education and literacy programs; the development of ICT applications for reducing violence against women; and addressing issues of pornography and other forms of exploitation that are enabled by ICTs (Hafkin, 2002; Ramilo, 2002; Sylla, 2002). Two other themes that have been identified by the Women's Caucus of the WSIS are ensuring that ICTs contribute to the goals of peace, equality and development, and the use of ICT applications for conflict resolution and peace building (Walker, 2002).

FUTURE TRENDS: THE FIGHT FOR HUMAN RIGHTS AND DECIDING ON THE ROLE OF BUSINESS

The one future trend evident at this date is the continuing coalescence of government, business and civil society toward a well-defined declaration of an information society. The trajectory of this trend is being directed through the two phases of the World Summit on the Information Society: Geneva in 2003 and Tunis in 2005. There seems to be two overriding areas in which social, ethical and policy implications of an information society are being considered as these summits approach. One area concerns the debate over whether an information society should be defined relative to human rights frameworks. Recent proposals for the summit agenda contain few explicit references to human rights (World Summit on the Information Society - Secretariat, 2002a). Given its sponsorship by the UN, many civil society stakeholders have seen this as a serious contradiction (World Summit on the Information Society - Coordinating Group on Civil Society, 2002). The summit is a response to the UN Millennium Declaration, which commits member states to "the rule of law, while respecting internationally recognised human rights and fundamental freedoms" (2000, p. 6). Influential stakeholders, such as the U.S., have called explicitly for the de-linking of the Millennium Declaration from the summit agenda, stating that it "provides just one of many possible goal-setting options" (2002, p. 2).

A second area concerns the changing role of business within UN-sphere processes in the context of the WSIS, from one in which business was represented through non-profit, industry-wide organizations to one in which individual businesses (or "business sector entities") are allowed to represent themselves directly in the proceedings. This is an unprecedented idea that has been raised recently in debate over the rules of procedure for the summit (World Summit on the Information Society - Secretariat, 2002c). This possibility raises a number of issues around balanced representation across all categories of stakeholders and what is seen by many in civil society as raising the possibility of undue influence by the business community in the formation of an information society (see World Summit on the Information Society - Civil Society Plenary, 2002a). Recent scandals in the IT business sector—such as the WorldCom debacle—and their potential impacts on society are cited as key reasons for maintaining a proper balance of representation among all stakeholders in the formation of an information society.

CONCLUSION

Global perspectives on social, ethical and policy implications of information systems introduce consideration of both the common and the diverse needs of the world's many cultures, regions and nations. ICTs are seen as both enabling solutions to the world's many social problems and as potential sources of threats to labor, environment, culture, and other facets of society. These realities are now being considered at the international level in the development of comprehensive frameworks for an information society. This is taking place, in part, in the preparatory processes for the World Summit on the Information Society, the G8's DOT Force, and ICANN. These efforts have come about as the result of a long history of international policy making around individual telecommunication technologies, the evolution of human rights through UN processes, and the increased use of advanced ICTs, such as the Internet, by the public, business and governments. International efforts, such as those sponsored by the UN, have often engendered major controversies based on differences in cultural and political perspectives, but they have arguably contributed to the major progress that has been seen in human development over the past century (see United Nations Development Programme, 2001). The promise of efforts such as the WSIS and the DOT Force is that such benefits will accrue to humankind through the application of advanced ICTs to the formation of a just information society. The success of these efforts will depend on the diligent and democratic consideration of the social, ethical and policy implications of information systems.

ACKNOWLEDGMENT

This work was partially supported by a Rockefeller Foundation Bellagio Fellowship. The author expresses appreciation to all of his colleagues in CPSR and the WSIS process for their contributions to the body of knowledge presented here. Finally, the author thanks the anonymous reviewers for their insightful feedback.

REFERENCES

Association for Progressive Communications. (2000). *APC Annual Report 2000*. Retrieved November 2002 from the World Wide Web: http://www.apc.org.

Benjamin, P. (1999). Community development and decratisation through information technology: Building the new South Africa. In R. Heeks (Ed.), *Reinventing Government in the Information Age: International Practice in IT-Enabled Public Sector Reform*, London: Routledge, pp. 194-210.

Bergman, E. & Johnson, E. (1995). Towards accessible human-computer interaction: Sun Microsystems Accessibility Program. In J. Nielsen (Ed.),

Human-Computer Interaction (Volume 5). Retrieved November 2002 from the World Wide Web: http://research.sun.com.

Birdsall, W. F. & Rasmussen, M. (2000, February). Citizens at the crossroads: The right to communicate. *Government Information in Canada/Information Gouvernementale au Canada, 20.*

Codding, Jr., G. A. (1964). *The Universal Post-Union.* New York: New York University Press.

Codding, Jr., G. A. (1995). The International Telecommunications Union: 130 years of telecommunications regulation. *Denver Journal of International Law and Policy, 23*(3), 501-511.

Comor, E. A. (1994). Communication technology and international capitalism: The case of DBS and U.S. foreign policy. In E. A. Comor (Ed.), *The Global Political Economy of Communication: Hegemony, Telecommunication and the Information Economy* (pp. 83-102). London & New York: MacMillan Press & St Martin's Press.

Connell, B.R., Jones, M., Mace, R., Mueller, J., Mullick, A., Ostroff, E., Sanford, J., Steinfield, E., Story, M., & Vanderheiden, G. (1997, April 1). *The Principles of Universal Design, Version 2.0.* North Carolina State University, The Center for Universal Design.

Coordinating Committee of Interlocutors. (2002, July 1-5). *Coordinating Committee of Business Interlocutors Input, WSIS PrepCom 1.*

d'Arcy, J. (1969). Direct broadcast satellites and the right to communicate. *EBU Review, 118*, 14-18.

December, J. (1996, Winter). Units of analysis for Internet communication. *Journal of Communication, 46*(1), 14-38.

Dinkelacker, J., Garg, P.K., Miller, R., & Nelson, D. (2002, May). Progressive open source. In *Proceedings of the 24th International Conference on Software Engineering* (pp. 177-184). New York: ACM Press.

European Union. (2002). *The U.N. World Summit on Information Society: The Preparatory Process—Reflections of the European Union* (Document WSIS/PC-1/CONTR/3-E). Retrieved August 2002 from the World Wide Web: http://www.itu.int/wsis.

Figueroa, M.E., Kincaid, L. D., Rani, M., & Lewis, G. (2002). *Communication for social change: An integrated model for measuring the process and its outcomes.* The Rockefeller Foundation. Retrieved June 2002 from the World Wide Web: http://www.rockfound.org.

Fisher, D. & Harms, L. S. (eds.) (1983). *The Right to Communicate: A New Human Right.* Dublin: Boole Press.

G8. (2000, July 23). *G8 Comminique Okinawa 2000.* Retrieved November 2002 from the World Wide Web: http:// www.g7.utoronto.ca/g7/summit/2000okinawa/finalcom.htm.

Gillespie, A. & Robins, K. (1989, Summer). Geographical inequalities: The spatial bias of the new communications technologies. *Journal of Communication, 39*(3).

Glinert, E. P. & York, B.W. (1992, May). Computers and people with disabilities. *Communications of the ACM, 35*(5), 32-35.

Gore, A. (1994, March 21). Vice President Remarks — International Telecommunication Union. Retrieved October 2002 from the World Wide Web: http://clinton1.nara.gov/White_House/EOP/OVP/html/telunion.html.

Gurstein, M. (2002, Winter/Spring). Community Informatics: Current status and future prospects. *Community Technology Review*. Retrieved May 2002 from the World Wide Web: http://www.comtechreview.org.

Hafkin, N. (2002, November 11-14). Gender issues in ICT Policy in developing countries: An overview. *United Nations Division for the Advancement of Women (DAW) Expert Group Meeting on "Information and communication technologies and their impact on and use as an instrument for the advancement and empowerment of women."* Seoul, Republic of Korea.

Hamelink, C. J. (1994). *The Politics of World Communication: A Human Rights Perspective*. London: SAGE Publications.

Heeks, R. (ed.) (1999). *Reinventing Government in the Information Age*. London: Routledge.

Innis, H. (1964). *The Bias of Communication*. Canada: University of Toronto Press.

Institute for Global Communications. (2002). *About ICG*. Retrieved November 2002 from the World Wide Web. http://www.igc.org.

International Telecommunication Union. (1998). *Tampere Convention on the Provision of Telecommunication Resources for Disaster Mitigation and Relief Operations*. Geneva.

International Telecommunication Union. (2002*). ITU Overview: History*. Retrieved September 20, 2002 from the World Wide Web: http://www.itu.int.

InterPARES (International Research on Permanent Authentic Records in Electronic Systems). (2002). *The long-term preservation of authentic electronic records: Findings of the InterPARES Project*. Retrieved November 2002 from the World Wide Web: http:// www.interpares.org.

Jansen, S. C. (1989, Summer). Gender and the Information Society: A socially structured silence. *Journal of Communication, 39*(3), 196-215.

Johnson-Eilola, J. (2002, October). Open source basics: Definitions, models, and questions. *Proceedings of the 20th annual international conference on computer documentation*. ACM Press.

Kitchin, R. M. (1998). Towards geographies of cyberspace. *Progress in Human Geography, 22*(3), 385-406.

Kling, R. (1999, January). What is social informatics and why does it matter? *D-Lib Magazine*, 5(1). Retrieved May 2002 from the World Wide Web: http://www.dlib.org.

Kling, R. (2001). Social Informatics. *Encyclopedia of LIS*. Kluwer Publishing.

Lessig, L. (2001). *The Future of Ideas: The Fate of the Commons in a Connected World*. Random House.

Levinson, P. (1999). *Digital McLuhan: A Guide to the Information Medium*. London: Routledge.

Macintosh, A., Malina, A., & Farrell, S. (2002). Digital democracy through electronic petitioning: E-petitioner. In W. J. McIver, Jr. & A. K. Elmagarmid (Eds.), *Advances in Digital Government: Technology, Human Factors, and Policy*. Boston, MA: Kluwer.

Margonelli, L. (2002, April). The Rainmaker: How a low-cost, lightweight pump is changing the economy of a nation. *Wired*, 10.04. Retrieved August 2002 from the World Wide Web: http://www.wired.com.

Markle Foundation. (1972). *Global communications in the Space Age: Toward a new ITU*. Report of an International Conference Sponsored by the John and Mary R. Markle Foundation and the Twentieth Century Fund.

McChesney, R. W. (1995). *Telecommunications, Mass Media, and Democracy: The Battle for the Control of U.S. Broadcasting, 1928-1935*. New York: Oxford University Press.

McCreadie, M. & Rice, R.E. (1999a). Trends in analyzing access to information. Part I: Cross disciplinary conceptualizations of access. *Information Processing and Management, 35*, 45-76.

McCreadie, M. & Rice, R.E. (1999b). Trends in analyzing access to information. Part II: Unique and integrating conceptualizations. *Information Processing and Management, 35*, 77-99.

McIver, Jr., W. J. & Birdsall, W.F. (2002). Technological evolution and the right to communicate: The implications for electronic democracy. *Proceedings of the European Institute for Communication and Culture (Euricom) Project: Electronic Networks and Democratic Life. Electronic Networks & Democratic Engagement Colloquium*. Njimegen, The Netherlands, October 9-12, 2002.

McIver, Jr., W. J. & Elmagarmid, A.K. (eds.) (2002). *Advances in Digital Government: Technology, Human Factors, and Policy*. Kluwer.

Mueller, M. (1999, December). ICANN and Internet governance: Sorting through the debris of 'self-regulation.' *Info., 1*(6), 497-520. Retrieved November 2002 from the World Wide Web: http://www.icannwatch.org.

Muller, M., Wharton, C., McIver, Jr., W. J., & Laux, L. (1997). Toward a future of HCI research and practice agenda based on human needs and social responsibility. *CHI 97 Conference Proceedings*, Atlanta, Georgia, March 22-27.

National Research Council. (1994). *Realizing the Information Future: The Internet and Beyond. Computer Science and Telecommunications Board*. Washington, D.C.: National Research Council.

Nora, S. & Minc, A. (1980). *The Computerization of Society: A Report to the President of France*. Cambridge, MA: MIT Press. (Originally published 1978, L'Informatisation de la société. Paris: La Documentation Française).

Norman, D. (1998). *The Invisible Computer*. MIT.

NYNEX. (n.d.). *NYNEX Accessibility and Universal Design Principles*. Trace Research & Development Center. Retrieved November 2001 from the World Wide Web: http://trace.wisc.edu.

Pacific Bell Advisory Group for People with Disabilities. (1996). *Universal Design Policy: The Advisory Group's Recommendations and Pacific Bell's Response*. Trace Research & Development Center. Retrieved November 2001 from the World Wide Web: http://trace.wisc.edu.

PicoPeta Simputers (n.d.). *About PicoPeta Simputers*. Retrieved December 2002 from the World Wide Web: http://www.picopeta.com.

Postman, N. (1992). *Technopoly: The Surrender of Culture to Technology*. New York: Knopf.

Press, L. (1997, January/February). Seeding networks: The federal role. Retrieved November 2001 from the World Wide Web: http://www.isoc.org.

Ramilo, C. (2002). *National ICT Policies and Gender Equality Regional Perspectives: Asia*. United Nations Division for the Advancement of Women (DAW) Expert Group Meeting on "Information and communication technologies and their impact on and use as an instrument for the advancement and empowerment of women." Seoul, Republic of Korea. November 11-14.

Rockefeller Foundation. (1999, January). *Communication for social change: A position paper and conference report*. Retrieved September 2002 from the World Wide Web: http://www.rockfound.org.

Rudolph, S. (2002). Digital Ecologies. *Jiva Institute*, November 5. Retrieved in December 2002 from the World Wide Web: http://www.jiva.org/report_details.asp?report_id=49.

Scheele, C. H. (1970). *A Short History of the Mail Service*. Washington, D.C.: Smithsonian Institution Press.

Sylla, F. S. (2002). *ICT as an Instrument for Participation: The Regional Perspective from Africa, Examples of the Internet use at the Grassroots Level*. United Nations Division for the Advancement of Women (DAW) Expert Group Meeting on "Information and communication technologies and their impact on and use as an instrument for the advancement and empowerment of women." Seoul, Republic of Korea. November 11-14, 2002.

Telecommission. (1971). *Instant World*. Ottawa: Information Canada.

UNESCO. (1980a). *Many Voices, One World: Towards a New More Just and Efficient World Information and Communication Order*. Paris: UNESCO.

UNESCO. (1980b). *The New World Information and Communication Order*. (Resolution 4/19). Adopted by the Twenty-First Session of the Unesco General Conference, Belgrade, October 27, 1980.

United Nations. (1993). *Human Rights: The International Bill of Human Rights: Universal Declaration of Human Rights; International Covenant on Economic, Social and Cultural Rights; and International Covenant on Civil and Political Rights and Optional Protocols*. New York: United Nations.

United Nations. (1997). *Human Rights: A Compilation of International Instruments (Volume II: Regional Instruments)*. New York: United Nations.

United Nations. (2000). United Nations Millennium Declaration. Draft Resolution referred by the General Assembly at its fifty-fourth session, Item 61(b) of the provisional agenda. Retrieved January 2001 from the World Wide Web: http://www.un.org.

United Nations. (2001). *Resolution A/RES/56/183 of the General Assembly of the United Nations* (adopted in December 12, 2001). Retrieved November 2002 from the World Wide Web: http://www.un.org.

United Nations Development Programme. (2001). *United Nations Development Programme Report. Making new technologies work for human development*. Retrieved November 2002 from the World Wide Web: http://www.undp.org.

United States of America. (2002). DOCUMENT WSIS/PC-1/CONTR/9-E. Retrieved November 2002 from the World Wide Web: http:// www.itu.int/wsis.

Walker, A.S. (2002). *Statement re: Participation of women in the WSIS preparatory process*. World Summit on the Information Society PrepCom 1. July 2, 2002, Geneva. Retrieved November 2002 from the World Wide Web: http://www.wsis.info.

Wiener, N. (1948). *Cybernetics, or Control and Communication in the Animal and Machine*. New York: MIT Press.

World Summit on the Information Society: Civil Society Plenary. (2002a, July 5). *Civil Society Plenary Statement on Rules of Procedure, Accreditation and Modalities for NGO participation* (Final Statement). Geneva.

World Summit on the Information Society: Civil Society Plenary. (2002b). *Putting People First in the Information Society: A statement on WSIS content and themes, endorsed by 22 NGOs and civil society entities*. Retrieved August 2002 from the World Wide Web: http://www.itu.int/wsis.

World Summit on the Information Society: Coordinating Group on Civil Society. (2002, September 12). *Civil Society Coordination Group Statement to the Informal Meeting on Content & Themes: Geneva, 16-18 September 2002* (Document WSIS/CSCG/3). Retrieved September 2002 from the World Wide Web: http://www.itu.int/ wsis.

World Summit on the Information Society: Executive Secretariat. (2002a). *Proposed themes for the Summit and possible outcomes* (Document WSIS/PC-1/DOC/4-E). Retrieved September 2002 from the World Wide: http:// www.itu.int/wsis.

World Summit on the Information Society: Executive Secretariat. (2002b, June 14). *Compilation of Contributions Submitted by Members of the High Level Summit Organization Committee (HLSOC) and Others on the Themes and Activities of the World Summit on the Information Society. Note by the WSIS Executive Secretariat* (Document WSIS/PC-1/CONTR/ 1-E). Retrieved September 2002 from the World Wide: http:// www.itu.int/ wsis.

World Summit on the Information Society: Executive Secretariat. (2002c). *Draft Rules of Procedure for the Preparatory Committee* (Document WSIS/ PC-1/DOC/5). Retrieved September 2002 from the World Wide: http:// www.itu.int/wsis.

World Summit on the Information Society: Youth Caucus. (2002, July). WSIS PREPCOM I YOUTH CAUCUS DECLARATION OF PRINCIPLES AND PRIORITIES. Retrieved September 2002 from the World Wide Web: http://www.geneva2003.org.

World Wide Web Consortium. (2001, August 24). *Web Content Accessibility Guidelines 2.0* (W3C Working Draft). Retrieved November 2001 from the World Wide Web: http://www.w3.org.

Yajnik, N. M. (2002, December 1-2). Challenges in the Design and Implementation of Sustainable Innovations in Developing Nations. "Development by design:" 2nd International Conference on Open Collaborative Design of Sustainable Innovation. Bangalore, India. Retrieved January 2003 from the World Wide Web: http://thinkcycle.media.mit.edu.

Zakon, R. H. (2001). *Hobbes'' Internet Timeline v5.4*. Retrieved November 2001 from the World Wide: http://www.zakon.org.

ENDNOTES

[1]   Civil society is taken in some contexts to mean Non-Governmental Organizations (NGOs). In this chapter, the term refers more generally to citizens, non-profits organizations and other entities not representing government or business.

2   Disclaimer: the author is also a representative for an NGO participating in
     the WSIS.
3   Compuserve's consumer-oriented services evolved out of an earlier packet-
     switching service for corporate customers.
4   Since its inception, controversies have continued to arise around ICANN
     issues of accountability and representation (see Mueller, 1999).
5   http://www.cpsr.org
6   http://www.commercenet.org
7   http://www.comunica.org/platform/index.htm

Chapter II

Digital Divides: Their Social and Ethical Implications

Emma Rooksby
Charles Sturt University, Australia

John Weckert
Charles Sturt University, Australia

ABSTRACT

This chapter considers the social and ethical significance of digital divides, where a digital divide is taken to be an intra- or international inequality in levels of access to information and communication technologies. The authors argue that digital divides are not necessarily morally objectionable in themselves. Digital divides are instead morally objectionable to the extent that they create, perpetuate or exacerbate morally objectionable conditions of other sorts, such as material deprivation, or abridgement of liberty. The authors also propose a method for assessing the moral significance of digital divides. They hope that the chapter will help analysts of inequalities in access to information and communication technologies to provide more specific accounts of the moral harms caused by instances of such inequalities.

INTRODUCTION

This chapter addresses three important questions about the nature and moral significance of digital divides. The three questions to be addressed are the following: First, what is a digital divide? Second, what empirical features determine the moral status of a digital divide? And third, why are social inequalities morally undesirable anyway? Digital divides, while fairly easy to characterize in terms of the distribution of technologies within a society, are far more difficult to assess in terms of their moral significance. Not all digital divides are morally significant. Further, the moral significance of a digital divide will depend on empirical features of the divide beyond the distribution of technologies, as well as on social context. These facts have implications for policy approaches to digital divides: policy approaches to the digital divide should be established, for particular regions, prior to substantial empirical investigation of whether and to what extent inequalities in access to ICTs are creating morally objectionable social impacts.

The approach used in this chapter is that of analytic moral philosophy. The chapter also draws on empirical research, including qualitative research conducted by the authors on attitudes towards the Internet among members of socially disadvantaged groups.

A word about the origin and uses of the term "digital divide" is in order before we present any argument. The term "digital divide" originated as a catchphrase to describe inequalities in access to information and communication technologies (ICTs), usually among members of some specified nation or community. It has been most commonly used to describe societies in which some portion of the population has access to Internet-related technologies and the remainder does not. The term normally carries normative "overtones," for instance an assumption that it is morally or socially undesirable for a society to be characterized by a digital divide.

The term "digital divide" is also used to describe inequalities in access to information and communication technologies (ICTs) between different communities or nations; it is often altered to "global digital divide" in such contexts. Again, the term carries some normative overtones.[1] However, the "global digital divide" is a comparatively unexplored topic, with much of the literature in this area drawing on literature from national or sub-national contexts, within particular developed countries.

BACKGROUND AND LITERATURE REVIEW

There is a burgeoning literature on the digital divide. Most contributions attempt to characterize digital divides, and to provide policy guidelines on how they might be reduced or removed from a society. However, there is some debate in the literature as to the precise characterization of a digital divide, resulting in a range of proposed solutions.

Some contributors argue that there is in fact no "digital divide" problem to solve. The most common argument is not that there are no inequalities in access to ICTs between different groups within a given society, but rather that these inequalities do not matter from either a moral or a public policy perspective. For example, Brady (2000) argues that "computers and Web appliances are now relatively cheap, and free Internet access is available in many areas. Even lower income families could find a way to get wired if they viewed it as a high enough priority." But even if lower income families could not so easily gain access to ICTs such as the Internet, Brady does not see this as a great problem, arguing that the differences merely reflect differences that already exist between rich and poor. Lack of access does not matter much anyway, Brady concludes; many other social circumstances and inequalities matter more from the public policy perspective. Compaine (2001), too, argues that the term "digital divide" does not refer to any new phenomenon, and that the term is just a new label for the old concept of information "haves" and "have-nots."

Other writers take a similar but more reserved view, holding that, whether or not disparities in access to new ICTs exist at present, and regardless of their moral desirability, they will so soon cease to exist that no policy or other action is required. Such arguments are usually framed relative to a single technology, the Internet, while disparities in access to different types of qualities of Internet service, or to other ICTs, are put to one side. Arrison (2002), for example, argues that evidence shows that there has been a dramatic increase in Internet use in most developed countries in recent years. He concludes that, "if things continue at this rate, it won't be long before virtually everyone who wants to connect can" (Arrison, 2002, n.d.).

There is indeed evidence that levels of access to the Internet are growing in developed countries such as the USA, most EU countries and Australia. However, the figures fall short of proving that there are no inequalities in access to ICTs, or that inequalities will be removed completely in the future, let alone that the inequalities have no moral significance. For one thing, it may be the case that, while the *numbers* of people lacking access to new ICTs may be decreasing in these countries, the *benefits* that those lacking access miss out on are increasing in range and significance. Many new ICTs, particularly the nexus of personal computer, Internet and associated technologies, are *all-purpose* information and communication technologies, capable of supporting interactions and transactions germane to all areas of life. If this technology nexus is taken up, like writing was in an earlier age, as the primary medium for a significant proportion of interactions and transactions, then lack of access will translate into lack of benefits. Additionally, arguments that the "digital divide," treated solely as disparities in levels of Internet access, will soon disappear, fail to take into account the constant development of new ICTs, and the constant upgrading of Internet-related technologies. A society in which most of the population uses high-speed latest-generation Internet technologies, and the remainder has Internet access so slow and old that they cannot access information and services with their equipment is not well characterized as a society with no inequalities in access to ICTs. Again, though, the question of whether these inequalities have any moral significance remains unaddressed.

Among those who hold that the digital divide *does have some moral significance*, a range of views is present. At the simplest level, the digital divide is interpreted as merely a difference in access to a computer connected to the Internet. Brady (2000) compares it with inequalities in the amount of jewelry or sports cars that the rich and poor are likely to own respectively. By treating ICTs as luxury goods (like sports cars), performing no practical function or a practical function available by other cheaper means, such accounts treat inequalities in access to ICTs as lacking any distinctive or interesting features. In other words, approaches such as that of Brady (2000) assume that there is no *particular* moral significance to inequalities in access to ICTs, over and above the moral significance of distributive inequality as such. Of course, the moral significance of distributive inequalities is a matter of much debate, within moral philosophy and in public policy discussions as well.

Many accounts of the digital divide, typically those presented in policy documents rather than academic works, assume it to have intrinsic moral significance, but do not explain exactly what its intrinsic moral significance might be.[2] A great deal of effort is devoted to developing policy solutions to digital divides without providing any detailed normative account of what, exactly, is wrong with inequalities in access to ICTs. Numerous reports to governments around the world take this format. Some examples include UK Government Policy Action Team 15's "Closing the digital divide: information and communication technologies in deprived areas" (2000), and the U.S. Department of Commerce's early "Falling through the net: a survey of the 'have nots' in rural and urban America" (1995).

Other accounts of the digital divide that hold it to have intrinsic moral significance (that is, significance over and above that of distributive inequality as such) are more sophisticated. The majority agrees that a digital divide, broadly, consists in the existence of inequalities in the levels of access to new ICTs within a society; their degree of sophistication lies in the explanations they give for the existence of such inequalities. Many, for example, attempt to develop a comprehensive account of the various factors that influence differences in access to ICTs, and thus to explain why it is that particular individuals fall on the "wrong side" of the digital divide. Shade (2001) explains the development of the notion of the digital divide as follows:

Initially, use of the term digital divide took on a simplistic definition, with access defined solely as technical access (computers and telecommunication services). Later, definitions of the digital divide began to encompass more complex measures of access—not just access to the technical infrastructure—but access to the social infrastructure. A variety of socio-demographic characteristics were recognized as increasing (or inhibiting) access, including income, education, gender, race, ethnicity, age, linguistic background, and location (rural vs. urban).

More sophisticated approaches include those presented by Lisa Servon in *Bridging the digital divide: technology, community and public policy* (Servon 2002), and Pippa Norris's *Digital divide? Civic engagement, information poverty and the Internet worldwide* (Norris 2001), which considers digital divides in an international rather than intranational context.

Other sophisticated views of digital divides are elaborated in a recent issue of *Computers and Society*. For example, Adams (2001) argues that merely giving the numbers of those who do and those who not have technical access to the Internet cannot answer "serious qualitative questions regarding the *lived expectations* of the divide." Culture, context and personal experiences are just as important as "the affordances of the computer or the content of the Internet." More specifically, "education, geography, age, income, ethnic origin and so on, are all important." In other words, while figures on the levels of access may illustrate inequalities of access to ICTs within a society, they do not explain why such inequalities exist, or give any guidance on how they might be reduced.

According to Kretchmer and Carveth (2001), in the same volume, only 50% of the digital divide relative to the Internet, a key new ICT, can be explained by differences in income and education. The other 50% is explained by factors such as what the Internet 'means' to people and how experiences of using it are made meaningful. People who do not use the Internet might be avoiding it because for them it has negative value: someone might associate the Internet with commercial culture, or with the depersonalization of social interaction, or with an unstoppable and undesirable wave of technological change affecting contemporary societies. Kretchmer and Carveth (2001) conclude with some suggestions of how their explanation of the demographic features of inequalities in access to the Internet can be used as the basis of policies designed to reduce such inequalities:

[O]ur research suggests that successful programs to combat the digital divide must start with access, but cannot stop there. Useful solutions require content relevant to people's lives to motivate underserved groups...Concern for content, motivation, and culture needs to be brought into the mix... (Kretchmer & Carveth, 2001, p. 13)

A similar argument is developed by Monahan (2001), to the effect that technological and educational inequalities will persist within a society even if universal access to new ICTs were achieved in that society. Monahan argues that technologies should be seen as operating within larger contexts of inequality, rather than as solely responsible for *new* inequalities. Discussion of the digital divide artificially focuses attention on a single experienced reality, technological artifacts, whereas in fact the wider social context of distributive inequality itself supports inequalities in access to new ICTs. The debate about the digital divide must be placed within specific contexts of meaning, that is, within the meaningful lives of the disadvantaged.

Bolt and Crawford (2001) discuss the digital divide in relation to children, in the Australian context. And they too argue that figures on access to ICTs are just the starting point. The principal components in the divide, they claim, are education, gender, employment, and race. The education problems are that computers in schools are not equally accessible, and that computers are not handled well by all educators. There is a problem of teacher training, and properly trained teachers make the most difference in bridging the divide. The employment issue is that there is not enough understanding in schools of the role of IT in employment. Problems arise with gender because there is preferential treatment of boys in classroom, and girls approach technology differently and this is often not recognised by teachers. Finally, race is a factor, and the racial digital divide is not just income-related. There is often a lack of identification with IT among members of nonwhite groups, and there is a lack of relevant content online. These four factors lead to a complex situation with respect to the digital divide amongst children in Australia.

While all these accounts are more sophisticated than "level of access" accounts such as Brady's, they all make fundamental and unsupported assumptions. Most significantly, all of the above accounts assume that, however it is to be characterized, the digital divide is morally undesirable, not only for societies as a whole, but for all of the members of that society who lack access to ICTs, for whatever reason. Such writers talk of "combating" or "finding solutions to" the digital divide, and their more sophisticated explanations of patterns of access to ICTs are presented as providing a firmer grounding than "level of access" accounts for policies and strategies to reduce inequalities in access to ICTs. Even where such writers acknowledge that inequalities of other kinds exist independently of inequalities of access to ICTs, they still see inequalities of access to ICTs as a distinctive social ill to be rectified.

To summarize, then, there is a large literature around the concept of the digital divide. Much of the literature is interdisciplinary in nature, and much of it focuses on particular ICTs, predominantly the Internet and personal computers (PCs). Many contributions to the literature are policy-focused rather than theory-focused. Perhaps because of the policy orientation of the literature, the majority of contributions do not provide any analysis of the moral status of digital divides. Most contributors tend to assume, without much argument, either that a given digital divide is morally insignificant or that it is morally undesirable and ought to be removed.[3]

Why is this the case? It is the case because the majority of accounts of digital divides take it for granted that access to new ICTs brings substantial benefits to all individuals who use them, so that all those who do *not* use them are assumed to be "missing out" on those substantial benefits. The majority of accounts assume on this basis that inequalities of access to ICTs are morally undesirable in their own right.

But this conclusion by no means follows; nor is the premise uncontestable. For one thing, access to new ICTs does not always or automatically bring benefits to people, for two reasons. First, unless properly used, new ICTs may have few benefits to their users. Second, some people are simply not in a position (due to social disadvantage or physical or mental incapacity) to make beneficial use of some new ICTs. For example, someone who is too disabled to use e-commerce cannot benefit from the time and money savings currently available via the Internet in many countries; and a socially disadvantaged person who cannot afford to purchase airtickets is not benefited by having access to slightly cheaper airtickets via the Internet. Given the contestability of the premise, the conclusion is not well supported.

WHAT IS A DIGITAL DIVIDE?

As we have seen, the majority of accounts of digital divides do not distinguish between the distribution of ICTs within a society and the degree of moral significance to be attributed to that digital divide. The acknowledgment of this distinction is important for analysis of digital divides, since its existence means that the normative significance of such a divide cannot be read off neatly from empirical facts, such as that the poorest 20% of a society lack home Internet access. This distinction should be clearly marked. The empirical qualities will of course vary widely depending on the ICT in question and the uses to which it is put in the society in question. The moral significance of a digital divide will depend, in part, on the empirical properties of a digital divide itself, but will also depend on other features of the society in question. For example, whether or not that society maintains alternative modes of access to the goods accessible via new ICTs will determine the extent to which a digital divide in that society is morally pernicious. Other features of the society in question that help determine the moral status of a digital divide include what social inequalities already prevail.

The empirical aspect of a digital divide is most accurately characterized with respect to individual ICTs (or commonly used complexes of ICTs, such as computer and Internet), rather than encompassing all ICTs at once. There is a case to be made for assessing digital divides in relation to all ICTs. This is because interaction among divides may create very different effects than would each divide taken in isolation. For example, on its own, a digital divide relative to computer and Internet access may create one sort of effect, and a digital divide relative to mobile phone use may create another, but a further, quite different set of effects might be created by the interaction between these two digital divides. But such an assessment can always be made as well, based on analyses of digital divides with respect to the various individual ICTs in use within the society in question, by devoting additional efforts to assessing the interaction of the different divides.

We propose the following condition for the existence of a digital divide in relation to distribution of an ICT, best characterized merely as "an inequality in access to an ICT." *An inequality in access to an ICT exists within a society when some members of that society have access to that ICT and other members of that society lack access to that ICT.*

Some clarification of the term "access" is appropriate at this point. "Access" cannot be taken to mean mere physical access to an ICT, since physical access alone will be of little or no benefit to many people. It will not benefit someone who is physically incapable of using that ICT (for example, through disability), or to someone who has not learned to use that ICT, or to someone for whom the activities and interactions available via that ICT are not seen as being of any benefit. Nor is ownership the only way for individuals to gain access to ICTs, which may also be shared or public resources.

Access to an ICT consists, then, of the following components:

1. Regular and reliable physical access to the ICT (whether through personal ownership or though shared or public resources);
2. Regular access to any assistive devices necessary for a person to make use of the ICT; and
3. Sufficient knowledge, training and confidence to make use of the ICT.

A person who has all three of these components will have full access to an ICT, even if that person prefers not to use the ICT, or would not find use of it beneficial.

The definition given above addresses the existence conditions for an inequality in access to an ICT in terms of the distribution of an ICT within a society. It says nothing at all about the moral status of a digital divide. Even if we know the levels of access to an ICT within a society, we still don't know much that will help us discover the moral significance of those levels. Further information about the nature and social context of the digital divide is also necessary. What is the ICT characteristically used for? What benefits does it provide to users? How morally or practically important are the benefits provided by the ICT to its users? Are the benefits provided by the ICT available to nonusers via other means?

This article is no place for large-scale empirical analyses of this sort. However, a method can be developed for analyzing the moral status of digital divides, by specifying the *types* of empirical circumstances that are likely to make a digital divide morally undesirable. We now turn to this task.

WHAT EMPIRICAL FEATURES DETERMINE THE MORAL STATUS OF A DIGITAL DIVIDE?

This section makes a start on developing a method for analyzing the moral status of digital divides. The issue is, of course, very large, but some progress can be made by developing a general framework for analysis. The moral significance of any particular digital divide depends on the empirical qualities of that divide, together with the social and political context in which that divide exists. More specifically, a digital divide is morally undesirable if it creates, perpetuates or exacerbates fundamental social inequalities. We here develop an account of empirical circumstances and context, other than the distribution of a technology, which are likely to make a digital divide morally undesirable. The final section of this chapter moves on to address the issue of why social inequalities more generally are morally undesirable, even in societies where nobody is seriously deprived.

An interesting analysis of the digital divide in Steyaert (2002) is our starting point. Steyaert's main argument is that while a range of problems is associated with the development and use of new ICTs, it is misplaced to give primary concern to particular information and communication technologies such as the Internet. The primary focus for moral and political concern should be on the more fundamental issues of "accessibility of information, relevance of information and information literacy" (Steyaert, 2002, n.p.), via whatever media are available or predominant. Principally, Steyaert's position is that focusing on access to particular ICTs overlooks the fact that it is how the ICTs are *used*, rather than the mere existence of the ICTs that creates, perpetuates or exacerbates social inequalities. His point is fairly narrow, with his list of more fundamental issues limited to issues concerning information. But the point has more general relevance: the uses of ICTs within a society can create, perpetuate or exacerbate inequalities in other areas besides those related to information, such as political participation, or economic activity and transactions.

By this sort of account, inequalities in access to ICTs are morally undesirable *if* they have morally undesirable social impacts. In other words, in so far as they have moral significance, inequalities in access to ICTs will have *derivative* rather than *primary* moral significance. If, for example, inequalities in access to an ICT create or perpetrate severe poverty or morally undesirable levels of political or economic inequality within a society, then the poverty, or political and economic inequality are primarily morally undesirable, while the inequalities in access to ICTs that contribute to them are *derivatively* morally undesirable.

The social impacts of inequalities in access to ICTs depend in part on the social context into which new ICTs are introduced. We see four main dimensions along which empirical qualities of a digital divide (relative to a given ICT) may have morally significant social impacts on a particular society. These dimensions are as follows:

1. *Nonpositional benefits of access:* What the benefits of access to the ICT are, in nonpositional terms ("in nonpositional terms" means: without reference to the advantage that access gives one person *over another person or people*);

2. *Positional benefits of access:* What the benefits of access are, in positional terms ("in positional terms" means: with reference to the advantage that access gives a person *over another person or people*);

3. *Availability of alternative means:* To what extent the ICT becomes the sole means of access to further morally significant benefits or activities (such as government services, political activities or commercial activities); and

4. *Disbenefits of access:* Access to an ICT may involve certain disbenefits to those who use it, perhaps by reducing opportunities for exercise and face-to-face interaction. If an ICT brings disbenefits to users, then this to some extent may offset the degree of morally objectionable social inequalities associated with a digital divide.

Some discussion of these normatively significant empirical features of digital divides and the social context in which they exist is in order.

1. *Nonpositional benefits of access:* Inequalities in access to an ICT may give those with access a benefit that does not make those without access any worse off than they would have been if nobody had access. Examples of such nonpositional benefits available via currently existing ICTs would include, primarily, new opportunities for leisure and relaxation. Another important nonpositional benefit of access to currently existing ICTs would be opportunities for communication and social interaction. Nonpositional benefits of access to an ICT certainly have the potential to contribute to social inequalities, because while some are better off with these new benefits, others' circumstances remain the same. But the benefits can be said to be nonpositional because there is no competition for the benefits in which access to an ICT gives its possessors a competitive advantage.

2.   *Positional benefits of access:* Inequalities in access to an ICT (within a given community) may give rise to inequitable distribution of benefits (or opportunities for benefits) the *equitable* distribution of which is morally desirable. For example, a digital divide may produce inequalities in timely access to advertisements of job positions, in such a way as to disadvantage those who lack the ICTs necessary to access those advertisements. Other positional advantages provided by access to an ICT might include cheaper prices on various goods and services relative to prices paid by those without access (e.g., banking services); access to greater or more accurate information than is available without access to an ICT (e.g., government planning information); or opportunities to make certain purchases ahead of those without access (e.g., in the real estate market or in large-scale trade and commerce).

Generally, if an ICT provides its users with substantial positional advantages, it will tend to increase distributive inequality to the extent that inequalities of access to that ICT mirror existing patterns of distributive inequality. If inequalities of access to an ICT mirror existing patterns of distributive inequality, then those who are already better off will be the ones who gain further positional advantages. On the other hand, if inequalities of access to an ICT do *not* mirror existing patterns of distributive inequality, then the introduction of that ICT may tend to encourage *redistribution.*

3.   *Availability of alternative means:* Whenever and wherever access is the only means to access services and gain benefits, then that proportion of the population lacking access will be disadvantaged relative to those benefits, the moral importance of access to the benefits determines the moral significance to be attributed to lack of access to the ICT that is a means to the benefits. Where only a small proportion of the population lacks access to an important ICT, it is particularly easy for service providers to overlook their lack. Commercial service providers in particular may overlook those who lack an ICT if that section of the population is too poor to be a potential "market."

For example, in developed countries such as Australia, or the U.S., where high levels of access obtain, increasing numbers of commercial companies provide services only via Internet technologies (airline companies), or provide a discount to customers using their services via Internet technologies. This currently seems not to constitute a disaster, morally speaking, since lack of access to the benefits available this way hardly seem to be an absolute deprivation: not all airline companies operate online, having no access to airlines seems not to be too huge a deprivation either.

The following are commonly cited examples of goods and services only available by means of some new ICTs (primarily Internet technology). First, some jobs are only advertised via the Internet, or can only be applied for online. Second, some companies offer their commercial services (e.g., airline tickets, banking and financial services) only via the Internet, or available at a significant discount online. Third, some government services, primarily information, are available only via the Internet. (Some governments make information available free via the Internet, but charge for hard copies, an example of a positional advantage given by access to the Internet.) And finally, some educational services are only available via the Internet. (This is particularly prevalent in some developing countries, in which no homegrown tertiary education institutions exist, and the countries depend on Internet-based institutions for tertiary education services.)

4.   *Disbenefits of access:* An important and sometimes overlooked empirical feature of societies characterized by inequalities in access to an ICT is whether or not those who lack access to that ICT do so out of choice or out of necessity. This point might be clarified by illustrating some of the disadvantages that are produced for some people who currently lack access by the acquisition and maintenance of access. The following disbenefits were listed by seniors in qualitative research work we conducted into the attitudes of people lacking access to the Internet towards the Internet and related technologies (Rooksby, Weckert, & Lucas, 2002): Reduced opportunities for (face-to-face) social interaction; reduced opportunities for exercise, since tasks that would have required travel no longer do so; and immense expenditure of time on the acquisition of ICT-related skills.

This feature also addresses the fact that many people who currently lack access to certain ICTs do not *perceive* themselves as thereby disadvantaged. This finding is supported by qualitative research, such as focus groups conducted with people who lack access to Internet technologies (see, for example, Rooksby, Weckert, & Lucas, 2002). An explanation is not far to seek: some people who lack access would indeed be worse-off overall if they had access to Internet technologies. It may well be the case that those people who do not feel that they are disadvantaged by lacking access to ICTs such as the Internet will indeed have better lives without regular access to ICTs, despite the fact that they thereby suffer some positional disbenefit, relative to those who do have regular access. Although these people would miss out on a range of benefits provided by ICTs, this is not in itself sufficient evidence that, all things considered, these people are not made worse off overall by not regularly using ICTs, given the current costs of using them. Further, people who are already poor may simply not be able to afford to take advantage of either positional or nonpositional advantages of the Internet. (People most likely not to benefit from access to

Internet technologies would be those with mental disabilities that make computer use difficult even with training, the very poor, for whom the expense of ICT access currently outweighs the benefits in most countries, and seniors who find adaptation to using ICTs extremely difficult and time-consuming.)

While these features are all ones that are likely to make a digital divide normatively significant, the list is only a start; we make no claim that it is complete. Other empirical features of digital divides and their social contexts, such as the cost of ICTs, and the prevalence of other, fundamental inequalities in the society in question, are also likely to determine, to some extent, whether those divides are morally significant. The key point is that a digital divide is not automatically a moral problem for a society, since the empirical features of that divide may not contribute to the moral significance of that divide. If, for example, a society characterized by inequality in access to the Internet is one in which the Internet is used only predominantly for recreational purposes, and in which e-commerce is not prevalent, then the "digital divide" in question is unlikely to be morally significant, and almost certainly not significant enough to warrant policy intervention by government. We do not wish to cast doubt on the claim that many digital divides *are* morally significant, but merely to illustrate that their significance does not result *merely* from the existence of an inequality in distribution of an ICT, but in fact depends on empirical features of those divides and their social contexts.

So, to summarize, we have here provided a list of some empirical features of a digital divide, and the societies in which they emerge, that help to determine whether that digital divide is morally significant. We suggest that an assessment of the moral significance of any particular digital divide should take account of these empirical features relative to that divide. Assessments ought, in addition, to appraise the potential of new ICTs to create, perpetuate or exacerbate morally undesirable social impacts in the future, as well as to assess the present situation. This task is notoriously difficult, due to the rapid development of new ICTs and the wide range of ways in which they may be taken up and used. Finally, we have tried, in this section, to emphasize that the moral status of a digital divide does not depend solely on the presence of inequalities in access to new ICTs. It depends to a large extent on how ICTs are used, what they are used for, and what type of society they are used in; in a word, the moral status of a digital divide depends on the social impact of that divide on the society in question.

WHY ARE SOCIAL INEQUALITIES MORALLY UNDESIRABLE ANYWAY?

We have argued above that a digital divide, relative to an ICT, is morally undesirable if it creates morally undesirable social impacts that outweigh its morally desirable social impacts. And we have begun the task of developing a list of empirical features that contribute to a digital divide's being morally significant. But we have not yet said much to support the claim that social inequalities within a society, such as inequalities in access to ICTs, are themselves morally undesirable. Since many philosophers and other theorists today are of the view that it is only absolute deprivation that matters morally, and that social inequalities do not matter as such, this issue is worth addressing in some detail. Social inequalities encompass a range of inequalities, such as inequality of political influence, economic inequality (inequality in wealth, income or both), and inequality of standing among the members of a society.

Social equalities *are* arguably valuable in their own right. Some philosophers have argued that societies characterized by economic equality or equality measured in terms of well-being are good simply by virtue of that equality (see for instance Sen, 1992). However, as we have noted, there is a great deal of controversy about the value of equality in its own right. Many philosophers, political theorists and economists (not to mention many politicians and social analysts) argue that social inequalities are morally acceptable, and that it is only absolute material deprivation that is a legitimate cause for moral concern or policy intervention. But we can leave aside the debate about whether social inequalities are morally acceptable in their own right. This is because there are plausible arguments that social equalities are also valuable for reasons other than having value in their own right. These other reasons are called derivative reasons. Social inequalities may be morally objectionable for other reasons than simply being inequalities. As Charles Beitz has put the point, we "treat a social inequality as a bad thing because of its consequences for values which are distinct from equality itself. Derivative reasons hold that these (nonegalitarian) values would be better served if steps were taken whose result would be to reduce the social inequality" (Beitz, 2001, p. 97). This is the line of reasoning that we shall be following here, taking Beitz (2001) as the basis of our position.

Inequality and Material Deprivation

The first derivative reason to object to inequality is that inequality is a marker for material deprivation of some sort. This objection holds that a social inequality is objectionable if some people are living in "terrible conditions" and it would be possible to alleviate their suffering by means of a transfer from the better off "without creating hardships of comparable severity" (Scanlon, 1997, p. 2). The point here is that the inequality itself is not the problem; rather the inequality signals that people are suffering through material deprivation, and that those who are better off are in a position to help the sufferers.

As Beitz notes, it may well be the case that the force of concern with (material) deprivation signalled by inequality fades away as people's level of (material) conditions reaches some level of sufficiency. That is, so long as those who are deprived are only *relatively* deprived, and in absolute terms pass over some threshold level of material possession, then there is nothing morally objectionable about the inequality in that case. However, even if the weight we attach to such an objection does diminish as a person's material condition improves, it may still have force at a surprisingly high level of material possession. "There is no clear or sharply defined threshold of 'serious deficiency' above which a concern to improve a person's material conditions simply ceases to operate" (Beitz, 2001, p. 101).

For example, even in an affluent society, someone without access to some fairly expensive commodities (such as ICTs) might be not just relatively, but absolutely deprived, *if access to ICTs were to become essential* for activities such as finding paid employment, accessing government services or purchasing commercial goods and services. It is fairly clear that ICTs are not currently generating such absolute deprivation in any country as things stand, either within any country or between countries. However, in line with our fourth condition, monopoly, this *might* well happen in the future.

Inequality and Abridgement of Liberty

A second indirect objection to social inequalities is that they are associated with (or even help to create) societies in which those who are advantaged have an unreasonably large say about the organization of those societies. If those who are advantaged have an unreasonably large say about social organization, then those who are disadvantaged are, by the same token, deprived of a reasonable say in social organization. This is morally undesirable since those who lack a reasonable say in how their society is organized are likely to benefit less, or even to become deprived, under social organizations resulting from processes in which they have not had a reasonable say.

The existence of social inequalities means that those who are advantaged have an unreasonably large amount of power over the disadvantaged, in such a way that the liberty of the disadvantaged is unjustifiably limited. Beitz argues that those who have greater material resources and political influence "can often determine what gets produced, what kinds of employment are offered, what the environment of a town or state is like, and what kind of life one can live there" (Beitz, 2001, p. 106).

Social inequalities do indeed sometimes lead to this unacceptable degree of control, although the circumstances in which it occurs are usually complex. Examples would include the unreasonable degree of control some local government counselors have over the way land is used and developed; the influence that some wealthy individuals and organizations have over governments; and the influence that wealthy employers have over the working lives of their employees under highly deregulated labor laws, such as exist in Australia today. Institutional mechanisms may support control of this type, for instance through labor laws, by denying legal standing to individuals in certain types of case, or through political donations systems.

A digital divide might create or exacerbate this type of social inequality under some circumstances. If, to use a hypothetical argument, access to the Internet were made necessary for political participation in Australia, then inequality of access to the Internet in Australia would prevent those lacking access from exercising the fundamental capability to participate in the social and political life of their community. Those who lacked access would have a smaller say than those with access in political opinion-forming, deliberation, and decision-making, just because they lack the expensive and complex equipment that has become or been made necessary for such participation. It is therefore perfectly possible for members of quite developed societies to be deprived, by virtue of the social structures in which their lives are lived, of fundamental human capabilities.

Of course, social inequalities will not always result in the disempowerment of the poorer members of society. The institutions within which a social inequality occurs can take steps to protect against or compensate for the capacity of economic power to constrain the liberty of the poor. And when they do so successfully, the effects of the social inequality will not be so disastrous in moral terms. An example of a state in which institutions have these protective and compensative powers is the modern welfare state, which protects labor organisations, provides a social safety net and so on. Many developed countries currently fund digital divide-related initiatives of various sorts, designed primarily to provide access to various ICTs, but also to provide training and in some instances to encourage higher usage of ICTs.

Inequality and Procedural Unfairness

A third objection to social inequalities is that inequality "undermines or disrupts the conditions on which the fairness of many other processes (like most competitions) depends" (Beitz, 2001, p. 107). We recognize procedural unfairness in several forms. It may appear "as unwarranted exclusion from a decision-making process in whose outcomes an individual has an interest; as an asymmetry in the terms of participation in a process not justified by its aims; as reliance on irrelevant or partial information, or as exclusion of relevant information; or as 'background conditions such as inequalities in training and resources' (Scanlon, 1997, p. 4) that cause an agent's interests to be given either more or less weight than would be reasonable in light of their nature and urgency" (Beitz, 2001, p. 107).

Procedural unfairness is perhaps the most significant of the morally objectionable (but nonegalitarian) consequences of inequalities in access to ICTs. Of those listed by Beitz, the most prominent for our purposes is that of background conditions such as inequalities in training and resources. A digital divide relative to an ICT that provides its users with positional advantages (our third empirical condition) is, in effect, an example of an inequality of resources, where those who lack access cannot compete on equal terms for goods open to competition, such as employment or scarce resources. And it is *unfair*, not merely undesirable, for some members of society to lack access to a resource, if access to that resource gives its users positional advantage over nonusers in morally significant areas of life. (The qualification "morally significant" is necessary here, since, clearly, not all the positional advantages of access to an ICT *are* going to be in morally significant areas of life. To take just one example, the positional advantage of having "better" or "more desirable" games to play is an unlikely candidate for an advantage in a morally significant area of life.)

To summarize, these arguments illustrate that social inequalities may have morally repugnant consequences, in addition to any intrinsic moral ill associated with inequality itself. Thus, in cases where digital divides do indeed create, perpetuate or exacerbate social inequalities, such as economic inequality or inequalities of social or political standing, an argument is available to the effect that such divides are themselves morally repugnant.

CONCLUSION

In this chapter, we have taken issue with the common assumption that "digital divides" are intrinsically undesirable features of a society. We argued that digital divides, considered simply as inequalities in the distribution of ICTs, do not have any intrinsic moral significance. Rather, substantial investigation is required to establish the moral significance of a given digital divide. A digital divide is only morally repugnant if it takes certain forms, and only within certain social contexts. We have illustrated some empirical features of digital divides and social contexts, which, if fulfilled, will increase the chances that a digital divide is likely to create, perpetuate or exacerbate social inequalities within a society. Digital divides that do not create, perpetuate or exacerbate social inequalities will not require government (or other) intervention. We concluded by providing some more detailed grounds for the claim that social inequalities are morally undesirable.

REFERENCES

Adams, A.R. (2001). Introduction: Beyond numbers and demographics: "Experience-near" explorations of the digital divide. *Computers and Society*, *31*(3), 5-8.

Arrison, S. (2002, March 13). What digital divide? *Tech news* - CNET News.Com. Retrieved January 21, 2002 from the World Wide Web: http://news.com.com/2010-1078-858537.html.

Beitz, C. (2001). Does global inequality matter? *Metaphilosophy, 32*(1/2), 95-115.

Bolt, D.B. & Crawford, R.A.K. (2000). *Digital Divide: Computers and Our Children's Future.* New York: TV Books.

Brady, M. (2000, August 4). The digital divide myth. *E-commerce Times.* Retrieved January 21, 2002 from the World Wide Web: http://www.ecommercetimes.com/perl/story/3953.html.

Compaine, B.M. (2001). *The Digital Divide: Facing a Crisis or Creating a Myth?* Boston, MA: MIT Press.

Kretchmer, S.B. & Carveth, R. (2001). The color of the Net: African Americans, race and cyberspace. *Computers and Society, 31*(3), 9-14.

Monahan, T. (2001). The analogue divide: Technology practices in public education. *Computers and Society, 31*(3), 22-31.

Norris, P. (2001). *Digital Divide?: Civic Engagement, Information Poverty, and the Internet Worldwide.* New York: Cambridge University Press.

Rooksby, E., Weckert, J., & Lucas, R. (2002). *Bridging the digital divide: A study into connectivity issues for disadvantaged people.* Unpublished.

Scanlon, T.M. (1997). *The Diversity of Objections to Inequality* (The Lindley Lecture). Lawrence, KS: Department of Philosophy, University of Kansas.

Sen, A.K. (1992). *Inequality Reexamined.* Cambridge, MA: Harvard University Press.

Servon, L. (2002). *Bridging the Digital Divide: Technology, Community, and Public Policy.* Malden, MA: Blackwell.

Shade, L. (2001). *Review of "The digital divide: Facing a crisis or creating a myth."* B. M. Compaine, Cambridge, MA: MIT Press, 2001. *Computers and Society, 31*(3), 42-43.

Sidorenko, A. & Findlay, C. (2001). The digital divide in East Asia. *Asian-Pacific Economic Literature, 15*(2), 18-30.

Steyaert, J. (2002). *Much ado about unicorns and digital divides.* Retrieved January 21, 2002 from the World Wide Web: http://www.steyaert.org/Jan/

UK Government Policy Action Team 15. (2000). *Closing the digital divide: information and communication technologies in deprived areas.* Retrieved May 15, 2002 from the World Wide Web: http://www.pat15.gov.uk.

US Department of Commerce. (2000). *Falling through the net: A survey of the 'have nots' in rural and urban America.* Retrieved May 1, 2001 from the World Wide Web: http://www.ntia.doc.gov/ntiahome/fallingthru.html.

ENDNOTES

[1]   For example, work in economics has indicated the potential of new technologies to enable less developed countries to participate more fully and successfully in global trade, with consequent benefits for those countries' economies (Sidorenko & Findlay, 2001).

2   That such reports do not make arguments for the moral significance of the digital divide is probably because they assume such justification to have been made by others, and not because the authors do not believe such justification is unnecessary.

3   Some contributors argue for policy intervention without specifying the grounds for their intervention. In such cases, the grounds might be economic (providing universal access will benefit the national economy) or political (providing universal access will be popular with voters). We do not address arguments of this sort, as the vast majority of accounts of the digital divide pay at least lip service to the claim that digital divides are morally objectionable.

Chapter III

The Perils of Access and Immediacy: Unintended Consequences of Information Technology

Linda L. Brennan
Mercer University, USA

ABSTRACT

What are the potential issues created by the increased access and immediacy offered by information technology? The following chapter suggests how to anticipate these "perils" by applying a conceptual framework, as well as by understanding specific examples and by anticipating future trends. Implications for developers and users of information technology are discussed with suggestions for leveraging access and immediacy while mitigating their perils.

INTRODUCTION

"It's not my fault—I didn't mean to do it!" Whether it is for a fly ball through a window or an information system gone awry, we are held accountable for the consequences—intended or otherwise—of our actions. The key to dealing with unintended consequences is to anticipate them—beyond realizing that you're "playing ball" too close to the building. By anticipating potential issues, you can address them before they turn into big problems.

What are the potential issues created by the increased access and immediacy offered by information technology? The following chapter suggests how to anticipate these "perils" by applying a conceptual framework, as well as by understanding specific examples and by anticipating future trends. Implications for developers and users of information technology are discussed.

CONCEPTUAL FRAMEWORK

To develop a general idea of the challenges that can arise from information technology applications, it is helpful to use a conceptual framework for analyzing the impact of technology. Sproull and Kiesler (1991, p. 1) offer that framework:

"Predicting the potential consequences of any new technology is an extremely complex problem. Simply forecasting the direct costs of a new technology can be hard, and that is the easiest step. Understanding how the technology will interact with ongoing routine practices and policies is even more difficult. Imagining how that technology will lead to long-term changes in how people work, treat one another, and structure their organizations is harder still. A two-level perspective on technology change can help in anticipating potential consequences."

This two-level framework identifies different types of effects: first, in terms of the efficiency of an organization and second, in terms of its social system. Consider a rock thrown into a pond: the first level effect is how far and how deep the rock goes; the second level effect is how extensively the water ripples. Such is the impact of information technology.

Specifically, **first level efficiency effects** of information systems are the ones that are most easily anticipated, e.g., increases in productivity, changes in costs, improvements in value-added. These effects are typically factored into whatever cost justification is required for a new information system.

Productivity improvements result in increases in the ratio of outputs to inputs. This may occur because the organization can achieve the same level of output with less input, or because the organization can achiever greater output with the same level of input (or both). These improvements typically stem from the greater ease afforded by information systems, such as the:

- Ease of access to information and people,
- Ease of revision of work product,
- Ease of distribution of information,

- Ease of leverage with greater use,
- Ease of programming for information access and creation.

Consider the scenario of arranging a meeting for a project approval. Without information technology, the project manager asks a secretary to contact each of the attendees (or their secretaries) in an attempt to find a mutually convenient time. This is quite time-consuming to arrange. In the meeting the project manager presents a chart, manually drafted, of the proposed project schedule. The project is approved, with the proviso that the schedule be adjusted to include some additional constraints. The project manager then gives the handwritten notes for the meeting minutes to the secretary to type, and the project plan to a technician to redraft. Once completed, these deliverables are then routed to each of the participants, confirming the decision days, or even weeks, after the meeting occurred. Fast forward to today: the project manager uses an online calendaring system to schedule the meeting at the first available time for all of the participants. The meeting notice is automatically distributed via e-mail, with a meeting agenda. The project manager brings a laptop computer to the meeting and is able to project the project plan for everyone to see. As additional constraints are noted, the project manager can capture those in the plan right in the meeting. After the meeting is over, the project manager sends a copy of the plan, and a cover note, containing the meeting minutes to everyone who participated *that same day*. With this illustration, we can see how the supporting technologies (commonly available office automation tools) have created greater first-level effects of access and immediacy.

Cost changes often arise because of reductions in the cost of inputs, i.e., the ability to "do more with less." Technology implementations also incur costs, such as those associated with development and deployment of the technology. It is important to consider the total cost of ownership when evaluating technology options; i.e., what are the ongoing support and maintenance costs? There are often "hidden costs" to consider. For example, a cost justification of a sales force automation project might include the expense associated with hiring trainers for the new users, but is the opportunity cost of the salespersons' time considered? What if a decision is made to NOT train the new users (i.e., the system is so "easy-to-use" they don't need training…)? Will they take the time to learn the new system on their own? What are the cost implications for support? Consider also the impact of the learning curve; typically the productivity of new users decreases before any productivity improvements from a new system are realized. While the long-term benefits of such a system may be profound, such hidden costs can also be significant.

Value-added improvements may arise from the cost displacement, i.e., additional work that people may be able to do with the spare time created by productivity improvements. The value-added may be in terms of quality improvements, enhanced information content, higher product or service consistency, or increased measurement and feedback for continuous improvement of products and processes. Additionally, these improvements may be manifested as timeliness gains, such as faster time to market or a shorter sales cycle.

Sometimes subtle and usually profound, **second level effects** are harder to anticipate and measure than are first level effects:

"Second-level effects from...technology [lead] people to pay attention to different things, have contact with different people, and depend on one another differently. Change in attention means change in how people spend their time and in what they think is important. Change in social contact patterns means change in whom people know and how they feel about them Change in interdependence means change in what people do with and for each other and how these coupled functions are organized in norms, roles, procedures, jobs, and departments" (Sproull & Kiesler, 1991, pp. 4-5).

Social system changes are evident in the transformation of work content and skills requirements for employees. Consider the role of a secretary now (with desktop computing expertise) as opposed to 20 years ago (with stenographic skills). Professionals are more self-sufficient because of office automation. Managers have a broader "span of control" with more subordinates having direct reporting relationships due to the empowerment of distributed information. Researchers, marketers, and engineers collaborate earlier in the product development cycle with "design for manufacturing" capabilities afforded by computer-aided design. The access provided by communication technologies enable line workers to send an electronic mail message to a chief executive officer—with a reasonable expectation of a personal reply.

These systemic changes are evident at the workgroup and organizational levels, with widespread efforts to reengineer business processes, leveraging immediacy and access to better rationalize information and product flows. The extensive internetworking and untethered (i.e., wireless) communications that are becoming commonplace mean that, at least conceptually, anyone can reach any information anywhere—and any information can reach anyone anywhere. Time and space are transcended. Sales force automation, enterprise resource planning, supply chain management, electronic commerce and selective outsourcing are examples of such integration made possible by information systems.

This integration can become a competitive advantage, making it difficult for suppliers and customers to disengage from one another. This is just one way in which, at an industry level, there are technology-driven changes in the basis of competition. Barriers to entry are lowered. For example, a "local" retail outlet can create a "global" presence by implementing a website with product ordering capability. Information asymmetries between sellers and buyers are reduced with the extensive search capabilities available on the Internet.

The access and immediacy of information has generally increased corporations' accountability to all of their stakeholders—not just customers, suppliers, employees and shareholders, but to the community at large. Technological sophistication has extended the context and the content of the business/society relationship (Johnson & Brennan, 2002, p. 114). Environmental practices, fiscal integrity, international activities, and philanthropic work are easily scrutinized and questioned.

The impact of technology is not all positive, however. A study of 350 executives from major corporations revealed several common frustrations (Velga & Dechant, 1997, p. 75) with more than half expressing concern that:

- Information technology (IT) has not made their lives better, just busier,
- IT wastes as much time as it saves,
- IT has caused work relationships to deteriorate,
- IT means serious information redundancy and overload,
- IT means my office is always with me 24 hours a day, leaving me with little time for friends, family, or myself.

Personal experience and other research studies provide evidence of these "wired world woes" (not the least of which is a family's "virtual vacation" with one of its members tied to his wireless communications capability, exchanging frequent and invasive messages on his Personal Digital Assistant). In the following section, some other specific examples of unintended consequences are presented.

SPECIFIC UNINTENDED CONSEQUENCES

These examples are offered as illustrations of the two level framework as our conceptual model. Efficiency gains may arise from immediacy and access, but at the cost of flexibility. Social system changes triggered by access or immediacy may be dehumanizing. Our dependence on computing may be crippling.

Immediacy is hard to undo. Whether it is an inflammatory electronic mail message, an incorrect company Web page, or an electronic banking transaction – the harm may be done before you can correct the problem (if you *can* correct it):

- Receiving a forwarded message that angered him, a sales professional sent an inflammatory reply. The reply was intended for the person who forwarded the message, not the originator of the upsetting comments. The wrong person received the message. The ease by which it was distributed led to an embarrassing situation.

- A pharmaceutical company posted a form on its website, enabling people to request information about an antianxiety medication. This form generated a data file that the pharmaceutical company neglected to secure, unintentionally creating ease of access. After hundreds of names were in the data file, the company realized and corrected its error. It is unknown if that information was accessed and used improperly.
- A newspaper report tells of a man who, when banking online, "missed a decimal point and paid $27,566 to his gas company...instead of $275.56...It took several calls...and...over two weeks before he was reimbursed" (Higgins, 2003, p. D1). The efficiency afforded by technology can be at the cost of flexibility.

Immediacy takes time from courtesy. The terse informality of electronic communications (when was the last time you received a thoughtful, handwritten note?) encourages people to bypass the formalities and courtesies. The volume of communications has exacerbated this problem. For example, Geller (2003, 1C) reports that "employers, deluged with resumes and increasingly leaving it to computers to sort through them all, are abandoning the courtesy letter and the polite callback as quaint, but outdated customs."

Such informality has had a profound effect on the written English language. A recent article published by Congressional Quarterly (2000) notes an increase in the use of contractions as well as a decline of emphasis on grammar and spelling. This is attributed, at least in part, to the use of electronic mail.

Access limits the privacy of individuals. The more information that is available about you, the less privacy you have. Consider an example where that is not necessarily a bad thing: the Aware Home. In a prototype built by the Georgia Institute of Technology, the sensors and computers in this home are helping researchers find ways in which technology can help the elderly live more independent lives. Or think about a parent embedding a microchip under a child's skin, using global positioning technology, to be able to recover him or her from abduction. Or even the government integrating information about individuals to profile suspected terrorists. Privacy has costs. Access has benefits. And vice versa.

Access magnifies the impact of software errors. The capabilities afforded by information technology have been applied to extremely critical and very complex systems. The ability to assure the quality of these systems is limited:

"Writing code...is like writing poetry: every word, each placement counts. Except that software is harder, because digital poems can have millions of lines which are all somehow interconnected.   Try fixing programming

errors, known as bugs, and you often introduce new ones...So far, nobody has found a silver bullet to kill the beast of complexity" (Feldman, 2001).

The increasing reliance of individuals and organizations on such complex systems makes them more vulnerable to system failures. On a personal level, O'Malley (2001, p. 6.) describes his frustration with this vulnerability:

"Intellectually, I know we're living life in the fast lane. But viscerally, it feels a lot like we're spinning our wheels. I've got a great new computer system that freezes about once a week and occasionally refuses to let me use the...[disk] drive. My cell phone is pretty sleek, but it often sounds like I'm dialing up another country when I call home, and it routinely drops my calls to colleagues in other states...But nothing symbolizes the disconnect between high technology and low problems better than this: I don't know what time it is...my telephone display says it's 4:02 p.m., my watch says it's 4:05...my...sophisticated...PC declares it to be 3:37—a full half-hour behind the desk it sits upon—and it's busily stamping all of my e-mail and documents accordingly."

Beyond these specific examples, trends can be examined to apply the conceptual framework and leverage prior experience. We can see how efficiency effects lead to greater access and immediacy, which in turn lead to social system effects, including the unintended consequences. In the following section, future trends are noted with the intent to aid in the anticipation of unintended consequences.

FUTURE TRENDS

The pace of change in technology has accelerated, is accelerating, and must continue to accelerate (Leavitt, 2002, p. 82). Information technology developments are continuing to make computing faster and cheaper. Laudon and Laudon (2003, p. 144) suggest that these capabilities in turn raise—or exacerbate—ethical issues. For example, with networking advances, copying data and information goods (e.g., digital audio) is much easier, making it harder to protect intellectual property. With database advances, companies can easily maintain and analyze vast quantities of personal data, making it harder to protect individuals' privacy.

The next wave of personal computers is labeled "pervasive" computing, defined as "an abundance of networked mobile and embedded computing devices that individuals and groups use across a variety of tasks and places" (Dryer & Eisbach, 1999, p. 652) or as "ubiquitous and mobile systems and technologies that interact seamlessly in everyday life (Soares, 2002, p. 26).

Collins (1999, p. 15) described this as a "trend toward convergence—that old Dick Tracy audio/video wristwatch thing." Add "smaller" and "wireless" to "faster" and "cheaper" as technology trends. More access. More immediacy.

For quite some time, futurists such as Alvin Toffler (1991) and John Naisbitt (1982) described a variety of dehumanizing effects resulting from information technologies. Clearly, the impact is not all positive. The nature and content of our work, our relationships, our identities are changing. The technology is becoming pervasive and possibly invasive. Yet the potential for positive change is compelling as our technological capabilities grow.

Kelly (1998) identifies 10 "rules" that project success in the light of accelerating immediacy and access in his view of the future. He asserts that the "only true scarcity" is human attention; gaining that attention is a competitive advantage. Relationships in the vast network of human organization will be of critical importance. Kelly also foresees that the more successful companies will be the ones who can leverage decentralized points of control and unleash innovation.

Perhaps the real key to success is finding an appropriate balance. The balance is between aggressively leveraging the immediacy and access and proactively insulating against them. The same capability that causes a "virtual vacation" enables a professional to work at home to be near a sick child. Electronic "cookies" that capture information about website preferences can lead to unsolicited advertisements as well as online sessions customized to the individual.

In order to balance between leverage and insulation, the unintended consequences of immediacy and access must be anticipated. As Leavitt (2002, p. 84) suggests, "Let's learn to look—with a very wide angle lens—further ahead and faster, at the possible effects of new technologies, before those down-the-road effects clobber us." The "down-the-road" effects are the second level effects in our framework, the social system effects. Some are desirable; others are not. If the effects can be anticipated, then appropriate plans for leverage and insulation can be implemented. A structured approach to such planning is presented in the following section.

IMPLICATIONS

Suppose that you are implementing a new information system, either as a user or as a developer. What do you expect to result from this effort? Clearly, there will be some expected benefit to warrant this investment of time and money. But what else is likely to occur? It may be helpful to structure your thinking as is presented in Table 1, posing access and immediacy against leverage and insulation. This approach can help to create an action plan for addressing the now-anticipated—and newly intended—consequences.

Table 1. Illustration for Analyzing Unintended Consequences

	Changes in Access From First Level Effects	**Changes in Immediacy From First Level Effects**
Opportunities for Leverage of Second Level Effects	Strategies to leverage access, e.g., to: • apply flexibility • promote innovation	Strategies to leverage immediacy, e.g., to: • emphasize responsiveness • accelerate cycles
Needs for Insulation from Second Level Effects	Strategies to insulate from access, e.g., to: • prevent overuse • address overload	Strategies to insulate from immediacy, e.g., to: • assure quality control • protect users

Now that the full potential impact of the information system has been identified, it is also important to address the process of introducing the system so as to achieve the changes as intended. Consider Figure 1 as an illustration of an organization embarking on such an implementation. "X" marks the current state of the organization, "?" represents the state of the organization without the change, and the star represents the intended state resulting from the change.

This assumes that the difficult steps of first assessing the current state and then determining the intended state have been accomplished. It should be a straightforward matter, then, of charting a course to take the organization from "X" to the star state. Right? Not really.

Figure 1. Model of Planned Change (Adapted from Brennan & Hoffman, 2001)

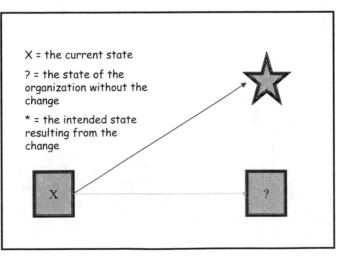

Figure 2. Illustration of Individuals' Perceptions of Change (Adapted from Brennan & Hoffman, 2001)

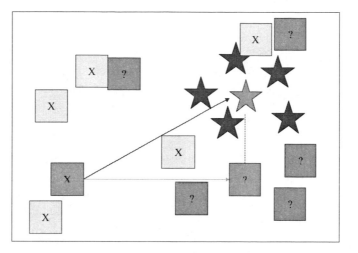

The reality is that individuals affected by the organizational change will have different perceptions of all three of these states, making it hard to convince all of them to move in the same direction. This is illustrated by Figure 2.

The stars are clustered around the actual vision showing that it is very hard to achieve a common understanding of what is to be accomplished. The myriad of boxes marked "X" represent the various perspectives held by the individuals faced with the change. Similarly the different "?" boxes show that these individuals will likely view the future prospects without the system very differently. As a result, the individuals will perceive the need for change differently, if at all.

The challenge, therefore, is to not only to anticipate and extend the intended consequences of the information system, but also to communicate them. People involved in and affected by the change (i.e., "stakeholders") must have similar perspectives in order to have similar motivations. This entails anchoring their assessments: those of the current state of the organization, the consequences of not changing, and the vision of the future state. Creating this common understanding among the stakeholders makes following the charted course achievable and the perils of access and immediacy less threatening.

REFERENCES

Abel, R. (1997). The Internet: Some unintended consequences. *Publishing Research Quarterly, 13*(1), 73-77.

Brennan, L. & Hoffman, G. (2001). CIO as change and innovation officer. Working paper.

Collins, C. (1999). Heads up, multitaskers. *Christian Science Monitor, 91*(235), 15.

Congressional Quarterly. (2000). New informality? *CQ Researcher, 10*(40), 946-947.

Dryer, D. C. & Eisbach, C. (1999). At what cost pervasive? A social computing view of mobile computing systems. *IBM Systems Journal, 38*(4), 652-676.

Feldman, S. (2001, May 7).   In R. Dalton (Ed.), *A Look into Future Technohazards. Byte* Retrieved October 17, 2002 from EBSCOHost on the World Wide Web: http://www.gallileo2.usg.edu.

Geller, A. (2002, October 20). Technology, tide of job applications spell end of courtesy letter. *The Telegraph*, 1C(2).

Higgins, M. (2002, October 17). The dark side of online billing. Wall Street Journal, D1(2).

Johnson, V. & Brennan, L. (2002). Examining the impact of technology on social responsibility practices. *Re-Imagining Business Ethics: Meaningful Solutions for a Global Economy, 4*, 107-123.

Kelly, K. (1998). *New Rules for the New Economy: 10 Radical Strategies for a Connected World.* New York: Viking.

Laudon, K. C. & Laudon, J. P. (2003). *Essentials of Management Information Systems* (5th ed.).   Upper Saddle River, NJ: Prentice-Hall.

Leavitt, H. J. (2002). Technology and Organization: Where's the off button? (Reprinted). *IEEE Engineering Management Review, 3Q2002*, 82-90.

Naisbitt, J. (1982). *Megatrends.* McNally & Loftin Publishers.

O'Malley, C. (2001). Low-tech blues. *Popular Science, 258*(6), 6-7.

Soares, S. (2002). Forecast for a multimodal future. *Communications News, 39*(9), 26.

Sproull, L. & Kiesler, S. (1991). *Connections: New Ways of Working in the Networked Organization.* Cambridge, MA: MIT Press.

Toffler, A. (1991). *Future Shock.* Bantam Books.

Viega, J. F. & Dechant, K. (1997). Wired world woes: www.help. *Academy of Management Executive, 11*(3), 73-80.

Vrana, G. (2002). Pervasive computing: A computer in every pot. *EDN, 47*(3), 75-78.

Chapter IV

What, Me, Worry? The Empowerment of Employees

Marsha Cook Woodbury
University of Illinois, Urbana-Champaign, USA

ABSTRACT

This chapter deals with the training and education of business personnel about the ethics, manners and responsibilities of e-mail, voicemail, cell phones, and instant messaging, including international etiquette. The author argues for empowering employees by helping them learn to handle these electronic tools in a manner that causes the least harm to others and promotes the best records management and communication. The author outlines suggested topics and practices, and argues that companies should direct their energy into training and setting solid, understandable policy rather than relying on invasive oversight. Illegal activities, such as destroying company records, are also covered.

THE EMPOWERMENT OF EMPLOYEES

Socialization: The process whereby an individual acquires the modifications of behavior and the values necessary for the stability of the social group of which he is or becomes a member. Oxford English Dictionary

The varied uses of the Internet and all its features, the explosion in e-commerce, and the revolution in interpersonal and group communication are challenging modern business culture. Gambling, gaming and shopping have moved outside of casinos, arcades and malls and into the office place. Workers can download the latest music, zap instant messages across the country, look at lewd pictures, and play Solitaire during working hours.

Like a note passed during a meeting, e-mail is colorful, short, unedited, and usually spontaneous. When sending e-mail, most employees are not thinking about seeing their messages in a courtroom, blown up on poster board and used as evidence, nor do they want the local newspaper to quote their e-mail on the front page. The same observation can be made about voicemail. Certainly, a revealing tape can be embarrassing, as when Hewlett-Packard CEO Carly Fiorina said in a voicemail to another top executive that the company might "have to do something extraordinary" to sway two large stakeholders to approve their merger with Compaq (Fried, 2002).

With these factors in mind, this chapter about the introduction of new technologies develops in three stages. First, the focus is on the main theme, educating workers to use the artifacts in a constructive manner, because acculturation and training are the preferred way to create honest, loyal employees. Then the chapter shifts to "acceptable use" policies, and how they might help. Third, the focus turns to legal and illegal activities that might occur.

This chapter contains suggestions for empowering workers, helping people to be well-trained and responsible users of the new tools. The technology demands adaptation and consideration on all sides, and business is currently in a transition phase. If a company cannot train its employees, or prefers a top-down, Big Brother approach, will that make workers perform better? How will employees handle the lack of privacy that comes with computer infiltration of all parts of their working lives?

THE SOCIALIZATION PROCESS

Historically, developing "acceptable" or "understood" ethical practice lags well behind new introduction of new tools. Owners of automobiles, for example, still receive only rare punishment for unsafe or antisocial behavior. Some areas do a better job than others of instilling responsible car use; driving habits around Boston would bring approbation in rural California. The two words, "cellular phone," underline that point—training and understood practice are vital to blending that technology into everyday life. The cell phone is still in its infancy, interrupting concerts and plays, weddings and funerals, classes and worship, and society is only beginning to cope.

Businesses seldom educate new hires or re-educate established employees about netiquette, the etiquette of communication in business and cyberspace. Perhaps they assume that people today do not need this knowledge, that employees have learned "the ropes" in college. This failure can have an adverse effect on business and cyberspace communication, yet the necessary training may not be difficult. Here is how Jeff Johnson (1998), president of UI Wizards, recalls being acculturated:

Though e-mail was new to me in 1984, it was not new to Xerox: researchers in Xerox Palo Alto Research Center (PARC) had used it since the mid-1970s. They had successfully spread e-mail, and the culture that went with it, throughout the rest of the company. Part of that culture was a set of guidelines and "best-practices" for using e-mail and networks: called the Electronic Mail Briefing Blurb. By 1984, it was required reading for new employees. It contained such suggestions as the following: reply only to a message's sender rather than to everyone who received the message, wait a day or two before replying to an e-mail message that makes you mad, don't send anything via e-mail—especially to a list—that you wouldn't want public; and so on. Although the guidelines in the Briefing Blurb were neither extensive nor comprehensive, they made a big impression on me, and have stuck with me over the 14 years that I've used the Net. I believe that they have served me well. I have worked at several companies since, all of which used e-mail and provided access to the Internet, but none of them provided such guidance to newcomers.

Suggestions for Employee Training

If a manager is speaking sarcastically or out of anger, the listener can discriminate the emotion through observing the stress in the voice, the posture, and the preceding conditions, such as the departure of a government inspector. Nonverbal cues such as shrugging, hand waving and smiling are a remarkably rich source of information. Physical presence is akin to a well-lit room, for when communication moves into the technological realm, the light dims and reality is harder to discern. The richness of information—the vibrancy of color—is lessened.

In most instances, text-based messages neutralize the communication more than voicemail does. This absence of inflection and tone can lead to radical misinterpretations, while it can also be a great equalizer, allowing the more timid souls to express themselves on par with the louder, more fluent, or more domineering people. Given these attributes, companies do well to review the common courtesy of electronic communication, the rules of netiquette.

Instant Messaging

Among employee activities, "instant messaging" attracts attention for devouring time from the workday. Employees download products such as AOL IM (Instant Messenger) or MSN Messenger and use them for "live" chatting (typing messages to one another in real time). IM traffic may be a business record for some firms, as federal regulators require that all securities communications with clients be kept for auditing.

Businesses have the ability to track and save IM sessions, recording the length of time and the content, and perhaps they should do so for their own protection in case of a lawsuit later. On the other hand, such monitoring seems to be an unwarranted invasion of an employee's privacy.

Instant Messaging Netiquette

Instant messaging (IM) in the business world requires a certain amount of restraint. The issue for most busy people lies in keeping focused on each conversation. E-mail can be answered later, while IM demands immediate attention, so use each tool when appropriate.

- *Keep it brief.* Use e-mail if you need to write more text.
- *Be professional.* You are at work, and whatever you write is a reflection on you and your company.
- *Limit the number of things you are trying to do at once.* Multitasking can go too far. Pay attention to each virtual conversation, and try not to have many of them going on at once.
- *Show courtesy.* If you are unavailable, make sure the IM software conveys that information to someone trying to contact you.

E-Mail

E-mail and voicemail have many characteristics in common largely because they are both stored on computers and are dealt with not in real-time but *asynchronously.* That is, the communication is not concurrent, taking place only when the sender and receiver choose to write or read, talk or listen. Voicemail and e-mail are both one-sided.

E-Mail Netiquette

People at work can find their e-mail accounts fill up like a parking lot on big game day. In order to maintain a semblance of control on this surge of traffic, they need help from their friends and co-workers. The basic rules of e-mail communication are rather extensive and are on the Internet. However, some are important enough for inclusion here, used (and elaborated on) with permission from an Internet RFC, Request for Comment, #1855 (Netiquette Guidelines, 1995).

Do not "copy" people unnecessarily. People are swamped by e-mail. No one appreciates getting unnecessary messages, so restrict the people on the cc: list.

A good subject line helps enormously. Again, people work through piles of e-mail every day. If the subject line is carefully chosen, people can delete messages without having to read them.

Think before sending. People are often amazed at how many errors they catch when they reread a message completely before hitting the send button. Take the time to be clear. In e-mail, people are what they write. Be slow to send and generous in receiving. Do not send flames (heated messages) even if provoked; talk to people in person when angry. If flamed, it most often serves no good purpose to respond.

Think about seeing the message in court. An e-mail message appears more authentic than other forms of evidence, with its date and time stamp and electronic path clearly marked. Juries respond to it because of its colorful language and brevity.

For example, in the U.S. government's Microsoft case, one of the most telling bits of evidence against Microsoft turned out to be its own internal e-mail. As a number of embarrassing Microsoft messages emerged, e-mail revealed the monopoly-building practices that led to Microsoft's dominance in its field. In one e-mail message, Bill Gates wrote, "Do we have a clear plan on what we want Apple to do to undermine Sun?" A note from another Microsoft executive to Gates said, "The threat to cancel Mac Office 97 is certainly the strongest bargaining point we have, as doing so will do a great deal of harm to Apple immediately" (Wilson, 1999).

Set an automatic message if a person cannot respond. Explain when travel or holidays prevent a quick response.

Use a signature. In order to ensure that people know who wrote the message, be sure to include a signature—a line or two at the end of the message with contact information. Most programs make it easy to create a ".sig" or "signature" file.

Do not change another person's message. In forwarding or re-posting a message, do not change the wording. If the message was a personal message, ask permission first.

Remember copyright. Respect the copyright on material that you reproduce. Almost every country has copyright laws.

Privacy. Unless using encryption, assume that mail on the Internet is not secure. Never put in an e-mail message anything that is unsuitable for a postcard.

Chain letters, *urban legends*, *phony virus alerts*, and *appeals for help* deserve special mention. Be wary of any e-mail that asks a person to forward it to friends. These messages are not legitimate. Know how to get help with e-mail that is questionable or illegal. Most businesses have a knowledgeable tech support person.

Disclaimers. If a business wants to add a disclaimer to its e-mail messages, brevity and reality ought to rule. The shortest and most cogent disclaimer would read something like this:

E-mail from people at your.domain.here does not usually represent official policy of Your-Organization-Here. See URL-Of-Policy-Document-Here for details (Stupid Email Disclaimers, 2003).

Voicemail Netiquette

Voicemail is e-mail in a spoken version. Voicemail is a message left in a digital "mail box" for later retrieval. The purpose behind voicemail technology is to avoid the restrictions of real-time, simultaneous telephone communications, where two people must be physically present at each end of the phone line for communication to take place.

When given a new voicemail account, a worker learns how to dial in to retrieve messages, how to delete them or replay them, and how to change the greeting. However, the etiquette of actually using voicemail is largely untaught. Employers assume that because people use telephones, they know how to leave a voice message. That is too optimistic.

Leaving a Message on Someone's Voicemail Account

Keep it short. No one wants to arrive at work in the morning and spend the first 20 minutes playing long, wordy, overly detailed messages.

Who is calling and why? Give name, phone number, and the subject of the call. Record a concise message, then, at the end of it, clearly repeat the name and the contact information such as a phone number.

Speak clearly. Also, if the location is noisy, such as a restaurant or on a street, find a quiet place to call from. Background noise can drown out the message.

Only leave one message. Do not repeatedly leave messages with the same information.

State's evidence. A phone message could come back to haunt a person, just as did President Clinton's phone messages to Monica Lewinsky that were found on her home machine. Business voicemail messages are stored on a computer, and other people can retrieve them accidentally, intentionally or legally through government subpoena.

Lack of privacy. For all the reasons above, a voicemail message is less private than a normal phone call. The business records and stores it. Remember that.

Handling the Voicemail Account

Change the greeting often to reflect location and availability. If someone will be out of the office on a course for three days, let people know. One year a major software firm shut down for Good Friday before Easter, yet the voicemail greetings failed to explain why no employee returned calls. That lack of response irritated many clients who the company left hanging.

Use the greeting to give alternate contact information. That includes e-mail, pager, or fax numbers. If someone has a lengthy welcoming message, save people the pain of hearing all that information repeatedly. Tell them at the start to hit "#" (or whatever the system requires) to bypass the greeting.

Do not forward calls to friends or co-workers without their permission. Practice common courtesy by asking for their permission beforehand.

Try to return all voicemail messages within 24 hours. At least, phone people to let them know that the message arrived and someone is working on the problem.

Delete unwanted messages. First, check with the employer to be sure that voice messages are not considered important company records.

Cell Phone Netiquette

The best way to cooperate with the people around us in the physical world is to follow a few simple rules:

Show consideration. In an office, make sure the device does not disturb others. Turn the ringer as low as possible. Use caller ID, voice messages, or if people must have the phone on, set the phone to vibrate.

Show consideration in public places. Move away from other people when talking on the phone. Exit concert halls or theaters before having an animated conversation.

Meetings and appointments are for being with people. Turn the cell phone off. The other people have dedicated that time to the event, and so should you. If you simply cannot devote your full attention to those present, quickly return the call, tell the caller that you are busy and will soon be available, and continue with the people in front of you. If handling the call is essential, leave the room to communicate.

Be safe when in motion. When driving cars, people are far more likely to harm others if they are using a mobile device. Please be responsible to and for others.

International Communication

Societies create cultural norms that the members grow up immersed in, so these habits become second nature. Workers from the U.S. are known for their individualism, directness, egalitarianism and relentless fast-pace. They are short on patience and theorizing, preferring to waste money rather than time.

Here is a simple intercultural difference. In the U.S., people often have randomly assigned identification numbers, such as 789456. However, in Japan and parts of China, "4" is a homonym for death, and a person might refuse any random number with a "4" in it. Likewise, in the U.S., businesses often strive to empower workers, designing their computer systems so that even entry-level people can exercise some judgment and individuality. Yet, in a Chinese organization, workers at the bottom of the organizational hierarchy feel much safer if managers tell them exactly what to do (Davidson, 2002, pp. 109-111). Such differences can also interfere with electronic communication.

Around the globe, in a matter of seconds, people contact others from a variety of cultures and traditions. People ought to be vigilant about how they communicate. A person from the U.S. will have methods and ideas that might jar the ears and hearts of those who differ deeply in their customs, ideas and the manner of expression. People do not have to agree with each person they communicate with, but they should at least be able to discuss any matter open to controversy, and always in a manner that is respectful of the other's background.

Some Suggestions to Help Us Interact Electronically

Remember that people with whom you communicate are located in different time zones across the globe. If you send a message, and you want an immediate response, the person receiving it might be at home asleep when it arrives. Give them a chance to wake up, come to work and login. Do not assume the mail did not arrive or that they do not care. Often people in other countries do not communicate via e-mail over the weekend or while on vacation. In truth, with all e-mail you should be patient.

The recipient is a human being whose culture, language and humor have different points of reference from your own. Remember that date formats, measurements and idioms may not travel well. Be especially careful with sarcasm.

ACCEPTABLE USE POLICIES

Having discussed the day-to-day practices that a business should encourage, companies should next codify their standards into an acceptable use policy. Employers should recall that the average person is only mentally productive for a few hours a day, regardless how many hours are "worked." Any e-mail and voicemail policy should endeavor not to kill happiness and creativity. In other words, the policy should allow time for gossip and throwing spit wads, calling home to check on the children and receiving an e-mail message from a long-lost friend (Adams, 1996, p. 317). Still, companies need to be explicit about some guidelines. They should be ready to answer questions such as: Can an employee download a freeware program and load it on a work computer?

There are many vexing questions still to be decided. Who is responsible for slanderous e-mail sent from a company's e-mail system? Does a disclaimer absolving the company of responsibility tacked at the bottom or top of message really mean anything? Exactly when can company officials read employee e-mail? At what point does an employee abuse the purpose of online communications provided by the company?

Concurrently—and sadly—insider crime poses the biggest computer threat to companies (Computerworld, 2003). Just as a cybersex addiction by one partner can tear a couple apart, misuse and mismanagement of the newest electronic tools can rip holes in a business organization.

How widespread are viewing pornography, shopping during working hours and other "off-task" activities? The home page of Websense Inc. can spread fear. Websense is a firm selling software that enables businesses to monitor, report and manage how their employees use the Internet, and it advertises to companies that their software will improve employee productivity, conserve network bandwidth and mitigate legal liability. According to the Websense, "During the nine-to-five workday: 70% of all Internet porn traffic occurs; 30% to 40% of Internet surfing is not business-related; more than 60% of online purchases are made" (Websense, 2003). Naturally, the Websense solution is to install tracking software that can pinpoint the employees who are abusing their network privileges.

Employees can cause other vulnerabilities for business. For example, downloading unsolicited e-mail is dangerous because some attachment files can contain a virus that can wreak havoc on a hard drive and spread through a business network. Right now, there are few laws that control workplace surveillance technology or abuses of what passes for the "normal" respect for any individual. Both employees and employers can behave unethically, and the problem appears to be the addictive nature of the Internet.

Employees have spent hours of their workday playing games on their computers, sending personal e-mail or gambling. The two biggest problems are day trading (or simply checking the stock market) and shopping online (Dvorak, 2000, p. 58).

What Makes an Acceptable Use Policy Work?

At the U.S. Internal Revenue Service, unauthorized access by IRS employees to tax returns and taxpayer records demonstrated how easily employees could use their desktop computer to link to a main database and then sift through private records, even when policy specifically prohibits them from doing so. The violations of policy probably come from the fact that the employees have not "bought into" the policy, that they had no part in making it, and that they have not realized how unethical their behavior is. In other words, the policy is not a reflection of the business culture, and vice versa.

Having a policy imposed on people without their "buying in" or active support is like having road rules that people ignore. Some drivers will run a red light unless they can see a reason why they should not. Therefore, a policy must be integral, a part of the organization and its ethic.

Once such an agreement is codified, people have clear information about what types of behaviors are not permitted, and they agree to accept responsibility for their actions. By spelling out the rules, the system administrators make it clear how to use e-mail and voicemail.

Of course, no one can anticipate all the actions that people will attempt. Most businesses have at least informal policies dictating that employees should not use information technology resources for noncommercial purposes or personal benefit or gain. At the minimum, a policy will acknowledge the employer's ownership of the system and announce the lack of privacy on company or government systems. A policy would state the permissible and impermissible uses of telephones, pages, e-mail, instant messaging, and so on.

LEGAL AND ILLEGAL ACTIVITIES
E-Mail and Voicemail as Business Documents

People sometimes think of e-mail as they do an informal telephone conversation, but e-mail (and now even "chat" on IM software) is of course, recorded. E-mail and voicemail are stored and saved, and they are discoverable in a court of law. In some businesses, the law dictates that they are stored for a set length of time. Government agencies, law firms and stock traders, for example, cannot delete messages freely. For example, in the U.S., the Security and Exchange Commission fined five Wall Street brokerage firms more than 8 million dollars for not preserving e-mail communications. The commission discovered that the firms purged the e-mail during a probe of business activities (Associated Press, 2002).

In her book, *Who Owns Information*, Anne Wells Branscomb devotes an entire chapter to *Who Owns E-mail*. Branscomb begins with the story of a female administrator who was horrified to find her boss reading printouts of employee e-mail. The administrator lost her job for her protest, and then tried to sue her employer, but there were no laws guaranteeing the confidentiality of e-mail at the workplace, so she lost her case (Branscomb, 1994).

There is obviously a tension between the employee's right to privacy and the business' right to control what goes on in the workplace. Every employee needs to know what degree of privacy she or he can expect on the business communication system. Wanting privacy is not an admission of guilt; it is simply a natural desire. For example, suppose an employee is working on a draft of a proposal. She does not show her co-workers the document while she composes it—how would she feel if someone judges her on the draft before she wants it reviewed? As for personal matters, if a child e-mails a mother at work, is it not natural to expect privacy in that transaction?

At the same time, the business needs to protect itself when a court order forces it to invade the privacy of the user (Scott & Voss, 1994, p. 61). Law offices in particular struggle with these issues. What should lawyers do about client-lawyer privilege and confidentiality? Their e-mail and voicemail communications may have special restrictions, because encryption may not be optional; it may be essential.

Monitoring Employees

Employers find it prudent to have employees sign a written agreement as a prelude to active monitoring. Simply installing the monitoring system and letting employees know about it seems to be enough to cut down enormously on bandwidth use (Scott & Voss, 1994).

In one survey, at least 45% of employers said they monitored their employees' phone calls, computer files or e-mail messages. The monitoring is necessary, employers argue, because of the networked nature of the workplace (Guernsey, 1999). One survey found that people spend more than twice as much time online at the office as they do at home, and most of that time they spend at sites such as eBay and Yahoo (Fox, 2000, p. 9).

Xerox installed software that recorded every web site employees visited while "at work." The software tracked the time spent and the type of site. Employees clocked up to eight hours a day shopping or viewing pornography during their inappropriate visits to web sites, and 40 Xerox employees nationwide lost their jobs. Under current law, employers are potentially liable if the employer's agents or employees use the employer's computers for improper purposes, such as sexual harassment, defamation and the like (Cotton, 2000).

Thus, any employer has a legitimate need to monitor, either on a spot basis or at regular intervals, company property, including e-mail and computer files stored on company hard drives, diskettes or CD-ROMS.

One example of the tricky situations that arise occurred when the Central Intelligence Agency (CIA) discovered that 160 employees exchanged off-color messages on a private chat room. The chat room had been part of a sting operation, established secretly on the CIA's top-secret network. The chat room, hidden from the agency's management, surfaced during routine computer security checks (Associated Press, 2003). When e-mail or voicemail is an integral part of an occupation, then a manager will look at these communications in order to evaluate the quality of work. For example, a customer service representative uses e-mail and voicemail in customer transactions; the employer has to review those messages.

Otherwise, when should the employer or manager look at e-mail? Ideally, managers would scrutinize e-mail and voicemail only for "duly authorized investigations" sanctioned by the Director of Human Resources or higher authority, or to obey a lawful subpoena (Barry, 1997). What happens if someone else, a system administrator or fellow employee takes a curious peek? Should there be a reprimand?

These questions are challenging. Laws about the ownership of electronic communication vary from company to company and from state to state. If a firm is developing its own e-mail policy, there are samples available to highlight possible concerns, such as guaranteeing the right to communicate about labor union affairs, penalties for system administrators who abuse their power, and so on.

Keystroke Monitoring

From the employee point of view, businesses might act unethically while monitoring keystrokes or providing inadequate equipment that leads to vision, neck, hand, wrist, or arm damage. The keystroke monitoring is particularly invasive, because any time an employee rests, perhaps to stretch for health or have a short chat for sanity's sake, the person is off task. In addition, keystroke monitoring allows system administrators to learn employee passwords. Although a systems person can break through password security, in general, employee passwords are encrypted and kept from prying eyes, and keystroke monitoring breaks the informal understanding between user and technical support person.

The newest version of software that monitors employees' every keystroke will add an optional banner alerting users to the presence of the system and telling them they are consenting to its use by operating the computer. Previous versions had been difficult to detect, leading some privacy advocates to complain about its sneaky intrusiveness. The company president said of the new version, "I heard a lot of concerns about the invisibility of the program. It had a splash screen that was just momentary, but this requires the user to acknowledge the message by clicking on a button before it goes away" (Glascock, 2000).

Records Management

A company focuses so narrowly on privacy or other concerns that it overlooks the value of preserving information as an organizational asset. Many firms no doubt want to destroy e-mail and voicemail records to keep these from turning up in a court of law. However, the business needs its records to maintain a coherent picture, such as saving the contacts it has with a potential customer.

The people responsible for the administration of e-mail systems often set e-mail destruction dates (known in the records management world as retention schedules) on the basis of purely technological considerations, such as to avoid the disk exceeding 80% of capacity, rather than on the value of the information as an organizational asset (Glascock, 2000). This could be a mistake if it later needs those records.

Security and Passwords

Another headache for the workplace is security. Security systems fail because users are human.

How many passwords can a person remember? Do workers know how vulnerable their system is? Who is responsible for network security? What motivates people to keep their passwords secret? Does force or threat of punishment work? Are systems used as they are designed to be?

When an employee chooses a password on a multi-user system, she has an obligation to her company and her co-workers to choose one that is hard to guess. However, many employees suffer from "password overload," trying to remember ten or twenty different passwords. Often a worker will have her password on a "sticky note" attached to the computer monitor. Later, another person might walk in and see the password. Workers might blame the system administrators for security problems, while the "techies" are tearing their hair out because of the lack of care and concern from their users. These are problems to keep in mind when designing and running a system.

Business Network Driver's License Test

It is odd that people need a license to drive; yet, they can jump onto the business network and the Internet with no training or socialization process. Rather than thinking of it as a privilege, they assume it is a right. One of the co-inventors of the Internet proposed that all users should be licensed, so that surfers on the information highway are as accountable as are drivers on the road (Reuters, 1999). There are basic skills and topics for each person in a work community to learn, and perhaps pass a test on. Here are a few items that could be on a company's Driver's License Test:

* Courtesy and netiquette
* How to verify information
* How to discern who really sent an e-mail message
* What is plagiarism?
* What information to give and to withhold on forms
* How to create a short signature

- Where and how to get help
- Allowable use of the network
- Forbidden use of the network

SUMMARY

With access to the Internet, and as members of the work force, people have responsibilities to both the world community and to their business. How can people know what to do if no one trains them? Modern institutions would do well to provide such guidance, as well as set policy for issues such as putting personal web pages on company-owned machines or displaying offensive images on computer monitors. The implications for information technology professionals seem obvious. Training, and constant reinforcement of principals, is the answer.

This chapter reviewed basic instant messaging, voicemail and cell phone etiquette. In order for business people to communicate successfully, they need acceptable use policies. No doubt, people will be reminded from time to time if they overstep the usage boundaries. Society will grapple with these issues poised by technology as long as people keep devising new artifacts. Cultures are still adjusting to the automobile, more than a century after its introduction, for, along with the ease of personal transport, cars brought an unwelcome plethora of environmental and social consequences, including more than 40,000 road deaths in the U.S. each year. People should take charge of new technology so they do not lose more than they gain.

REFERENCES

Adams, S. (1996). *The Dilbert Principle* (p. 317). New York: Harper Business.

Associated Press. (2000). *CIA investigates 160 for 'inappropriate' computer chat*. Retrieved May 23, 2002 from the World Wide Web: http://www.cnn.com/2000/US/11/12/cia.naughtychat.ap/.

Associated Press. (2002). *Tossed e-mails cost Wall Street*. Retrieved March 25, 2003 from the World Wide Web: http://www.wired.com/news/politics/0,1283,56692,00.html.

Barry, R. (1997). *Email messages ARE organizational records*. Retrieved November 9, 2002 from the World Wide Web: http://www.cpsr.org/program/addition.html.

Branscomb, A. W. (1994). *Who Owns Information?* New York: HarperCollins Publishers.

Cotton, C. (2000). *Electronic mail in the workplace: Employer monitoring vs. employee privacy*. Retrieved March 5, 2003 from the World Wide Web: http://library.lp.findlaw.com/constitutionallaw_1_91_1.html.

Davidson, R. (2002). Cultural complications of ERP. *Communications of the ACM, 7*(45), 109-111.

Dvorak, J.C. (2000, May 1). Narcware. *Forbes*, 58.

FBI spy case highlights insider threat to corporate data. (2001, February 21). *Computerworld.* Retrieved on March 6, 2003 from the World Wide Web: http://www.itworld.com/Man/2696/CWSTO57889/.

Fox, R. (2000). Logging online hours at work. *Communications of the ACM, 43*(5), 9.

Fried, I. (2002). *Fiorina voicemail: 'We're nervous.'* Retrieved November 24, 2002 from the World Wide Web: http://news.com.com/2100-1001-879863.html.

Glascock, S. (2000) Email with eyes; Internet users get a warning. *TechWeb.* Retrieved March 6, 2003 from the World Wide Web: http://www.techweb.com/wire/story/TWB20000121S0014.

Guernsey, L. (1999). *Surfing the Web: The new ticket to a pink slip.* Retrieved May 23, 2002 from the World Wide Web: http://www.nytimes.com/library/tech/99/12/circuits/articles/16spy.html.

Johnson, J. (1998). Netiquette training: Whose responsibility? *CPSR Newsletter, 16*(3), 14-18. Retrieved March 6, 2003 from the World Wide Web: http://www.cpsr.org/publications/newsletters/issues/1998/netiquette.html.

Netiquette Guidelines. (1995). Retrieved March 6, 2003 from the World Wide Web: http://www.faqs.org/rfcs/rfc1855.html.

Reuters. (1999). Web pioneer recommends license to drive online. *CNET News.com.* Retrieved March 6, 2003 from the World Wide Web: http://webreference.com/new/991129.html.

Scott, T. J. & Voss, R. B. (1994). Ethics and the 7 "p's" of computer use policies. In *Ethics in the Computer Age* (p. 61). ACM.

Stupid email disclaimers. (n.d.). Retrieved March 6, 2003 from the World Wide Web: http://www.goldmark.org/jeff/stupid-disclaimers/.

Websense (n.d.). Retrieved November 9, 2002 from the World Wide Web: http://www.websense.com/company/index.cfm.

Wilson, D. (1999, January 1). Delete that email. *Business 2.0.* Retrieved May 23, 2002 from the World Wide Web: http://www.business2.com/content/magazine/ebusiness/1999/01/01/13345.

Woodbury, M. (2000). Email, voicemail, and privacy: What policy is ethical? *Science and Engineering Ethics, 6*(2000), 235-244.

Chapter V

Managing Workplace Privacy Responsibly

Richard A. Spinello
Boston College, USA

John Gallaugher
Boston College, USA

Sandra Waddock
Boston College, USA

ABSTRACT

This chapter presents an ethical case for strong workplace privacy rights, which have been jeopardized by the proliferation of monitoring systems and surveillance architectures. After explicating the functionality of those technologies and tracing the history of workplace privacy concerns, we analyze key statutory frameworks and provide some grounding for the ethical imperative to protect workplace privacy rights. But privacy rights must be balanced with the corporation's legitimate need for employee information. To achieve this balance, privacy-related issues must be diligently managed, and we recommend reliance on the Total Responsibility Management model. With the aid of that model, we identify and defend five operative principles for ensuring that monitoring technologies are deployed in a fair and responsible manner. In addition to underscoring the importance of privacy rights, our objective is to demonstrate that workplace privacy is an organizational issue that must be prudentially managed by corporations aspiring to be good corporate citizens.

INTRODUCTION

Thanks to the ubiquity of networked digital technologies, privacy rights in the workplace have been under severe pressure for the last decade. There are numerous privacy-invasive technologies that corporations rely upon to monitor their workers in order to help ensure employee productivity or prevent the theft of trade secrets. These technologies range from web site surveillance software to Instant Messaging (IM) monitoring systems that take periodic screen shots of a user's messages. Some monitoring systems, such as SilentWatch™ surreptitiously capture keystrokes, including those that are instantly deleted. If an employee types an angry e-mail message but deletes it before issuing the **SEND** command, every keystroke is still recorded and available for inspection.

Despite the fact that these technologies are reconfiguring the workplace and are often embedded in the worker's tools without knowledge or consent, inadequate attention has been paid to the ethical responsibilities associated with their use. Workers become accustomed only to the level of privacy which these tools and instruments allow. According to J. Cohen (2001), in this new world "rights (and thus expectations) are defined by instrumentality…and by (fictional) consent rather than by any sense of the inherent inviolability of private papers and thought processes" (p. 34).

For many companies whose reputations have been sullied by activist and media criticisms of their corporate practices, explicitly managing these responsibilities should be a major concern. Indeed, responsibility management, which is akin to quality management, is potentially a "new business imperative" of the 21st century (Waddock, Bodwell, & Graves, 2002). Many companies, particularly multinationals with extended supply chains, are developing "total responsibility management" (TRM) approaches resembling total quality management (TQM) (Waddock & Bodwell, 2002). Below we will attempt to illustrate how a similar approach might be put in place in domestic companies with respect to the implementation and use of privacy-invasive digital technologies.

There is good reason to be concerned about privacy. Abuse of employee privacy by companies has the potential to emerge as an embarrassing public issue for companies that have not thought through their rationale for using monitoring systems. Reliance on sweatshop suppliers along with child labor abuses exploded as corporate responsibility issues during the 1990s. Developing a responsibility management approach to those issues has helped some companies cope with the criticism directed at them. Arguably, similar approaches to managing employee privacy could help companies avoid negative critiques of their policies and practices. Deployment of potentially intrusive digital technologies, we will argue, requires explicit management attention, engagement with stakeholders, and a systemic approach to managing the ethical responsibilities associated with those technologies (Waddock & Bodwell, 2002).

Briefly, responsibility management approaches (called "total" responsibility management or TRM) involve systematic efforts to manage stakeholder and environmental responsibilities through three related processes: inspiration, integration and improvement/innovation. Inspiration involves the vision setting process and is based on global standards or foundational values. These foundational values, often found in codes of conduct, set a minimum level of responsible corporate behavior. The other element of the inspiration process involves stakeholder engagement through which dialogue on important issues is facilitated and mutual relationships are developed.

Once a vision for responsible conduct is articulated, it needs to be explicitly integrated into employee policies and into management systems. For example, with respect to privacy-invasive technologies, there must be policies determining which monitoring technologies will be deployed in the firm, what kinds of information will be gathered, and how that information might be used.

The final element of TRM approaches is innovation and improvement, supported by relevant indicators that make up the measurement system. By measuring responsibility-related issues such as assessment of the types of technologies in use, the number of employees affected, and the ways in which data is gathered and disseminated, companies can then focus on innovations and improvements, where necessary (Waddock et al., 2002; Waddock & Bodwell, 2002).

The deployment of intrusive technologies in most organizations does not appear to conflict with privacy laws such as the Electronic Communications Privacy Act. We argue in this chapter, however, that the indiscriminate use of privacy-invasive technologies violates important ethical norms and is an affront to human dignity. We further argue that companies striving for reputations as good corporate citizens should *manage* their responsibilities for preserving employee privacy, human dignity and related values just as they now manage product quality. Managers must take notice of the pronounced discord between law and morality; they cannot take refuge in the deficiencies of the legal system if they are to sustain the quality of their employee relationships.

Most managers will probably concede that their workers deserve some privacy rights within the workplace, so the real question concerns the degree of monitoring that should be tolerated. We contend that because privacy is an intrinsic human good a worker's right to privacy should be as robust as possible. At the same time, we cannot neglect the employer's legitimate business interests. The right to privacy cannot be absolute, since the employer needs information for hiring, performance evaluation and so forth. Thus, the most contentious issue in this debate centers on achieving a proper balance between these two conflicting demands—management's need for knowledge and the moral imperative to preserve a worker's privacy rights. Achieving that balance, however, is unlikely to happen through unilateral or Draconian corporate solutions. TRM, on the other hand, enables a more prudent approach along with stakeholder engagement; that is, open dialogue between management and employees.

Our ultimate objective in this chapter, then, is to present the ethical case for strong workplace privacy rights, while demonstrating that companies can avoid infringement of those rights and still fulfill their information needs by adopting the methodology of TRM.

CONCERNS ABOUT WORKPLACE PRIVACY

Despite the rapid adoption of these new technologies and the shrinking privacy zone of many workers, this issue has received only modest attention in scholarly literature. Brown (1996) traces the genesis and gradual expansion of workplace privacy rights. While those rights have always been tenuous, they received prominent support during the 1970s and 1980s, when a more liberalized attitude about employee privileges began to emerge. Much was written at the time about the need to extend civil liberties to the workplace, and this prompted conscientious corporations to regard those liberties more seriously. Business writers such as Ewing (1982) and philosophers like Werhane (1985) argued vigorously for a broad spectrum of workplace rights including privacy and even more dubious ones such as "meaningful work." There was a general consensus in business ethics literature (DesJardins, 1985; Velasquez, 1992) that workers deserved privacy at work and that privacy would be safeguarded if employers gathered only *relevant* information about their employees through *ordinary* and common data collection methods. Employers should not routinely use extraordinary data collection methods such as hidden surveillance devices and polygraph testing, "unless the circumstances themselves [we]re extraordinary" (Velasquez, 1992, p. 400). This literature speaks to the need for openness in corporate privacy policies, as it also builds a case for management accountability.

In the mid-1990s the momentum for workplace rights was sidetracked thanks to the diffusion of networked digital technologies in the work environment. The modern workplace, where employees are always connected, lends itself to an unprecedented level of transparency. This situation imperils fragile privacy rights, prompting great alarm among ethicists. As Brown (1996) remarks: "if care is not taken in the ethics of the informed workplace, technology will divide and remove the individual from her authentic self" (p.

1243). Other ethicists writing about this topic express the same concern. Sewell and Barker (2001), for example, argue that we cannot be indifferent about this matter. Rather, we must adopt a "critical disposition towards workplace surveillance that can be used to engage with its 'dangerous side'" (p. 194). In addition, Introna (2001) contends that a reasonable level of workplace privacy is a matter of justice and that a "fair regime of workplace surveillance would tend to avoid monitoring unless explicitly justified by the employer" (p. 427).

Legal scholars have a different perspective on this issue, since they consider how employers monitoring their workers can avoid liability, given that the law is so unsettled (Ciocchetti, 2001). But many of these scholars are not blind to the dangers of widespread employee monitoring, and consequently they highlight the failure of the legal system to provide adequate protection for workers, particularly if workers are unaware of what the company is doing. Rodriguez (1998) concludes that the law unjustly prioritizes business interests to the detriment of employee privacy. Gantt (1995) echoes this claim, concurring that too much weight is ascribed to these "business interests" in a way that marginalizes privacy rights. Similarly, Rothstein (2000) contrasts the poor record of employee privacy protection in the United States to countries such as France and Germany. Those countries are more willing to support legislation mandating respect for privacy rights, which are not regarded as subservient to vested economic interests.

While the many works we have cited provide a coherent theoretical rationale for buttressing employee privacy rights, they lack a practical orientation. They fail to provide specific guidelines or a workable action plan for managers who are grappling with the problem of balancing those privacy rights with business interests. Conscientious managers who aspire to develop fair information policies for their organizations must approach the implementation of employee monitoring technologies much as they would any other management problem. Yet little has been presented about *managing* workplace privacy. In addition, the current literature does not take into account the newest wave of technological innovation in this area, which greatly magnifies the scope of the problem.

This chapter seeks to remedy these deficiencies. After reviewing the state of the art technologies available for monitoring and surveillance, we will discuss the apposite privacy legislation and present arguments on behalf of strong workplace privacy rights along with the need for explicit management of responsibilities associated with privacy. In order to assist managers in striking a prudent balance between the corporation's information needs and employee privacy rights, using the TRM framework we will provide several broad principles along with a plan of action for collaborative decision-making. The key issue here is achieving mutual accord between employers and employees on the right technologies and the right conditions for monitoring. But before we turn to those matters it is instructive to begin this analysis with a cursory survey of the available monitoring technologies and their impact on the privacy of workers.

OVERVIEW OF MONITORING AND SURVEILLANCE TECHNOLOGIES

The Employee Internet Management Industry

Both monitoring and surveillance technologies have rapidly proliferated throughout most work environments. There are often hidden cameras, electronic recorders, wireless location systems, and so on. For the sake of simplicity we will focus on tools used for monitoring an employee's personal computer (PC) and network use. These technologies enable companies to check on web sites visited, e-mail transactions or even online chatting. The broad category of tools that can be used to filter and monitor employee Internet usage is known as EIM, or Employee Internet Management software. More than half the Fortune 500, as well as roughly 17,000 companies use some form of EIM software (Stone, 2002). Trends also suggest that the number of firms monitoring employee Internet use is on the rise. For example, the American Management Association has regularly surveyed thousands of large and mid-sized firms regarding the use of electronic surveillance methods. While the percentage of companies recording and reviewing employee phone conversations and voicemail has remained steady at around 10% and 6% respectively, the number of firms reporting the use of e-mail monitoring exploded from 15% in 1997 to 46% in 2001 (A. Cohen, 2001). The AMA also suggests that 63% of large and mid-sized businesses monitor employee Internet use, with 40% of respondents reporting that they blocked access to certain web sites (Carter, 2001). Despite the apparent widespread use of monitoring technologies, Schulman (2001) notes that the AMA report reveals most firms employ such monitoring software only for spot-checks, rather than for constant surveillance, and suggests that the actual percentage of regular and systematic employer monitoring is closer to 25%.

Organizations are motivated to monitor employees for a variety of reasons, including curtailing workplace harassment (for fear of legal liability), minimizing nonproductive computer use (cyberslacking), and reducing the demands on bandwidth, storage and other computing resources. Many are prepared to take aggressive action against violators. Companies that have fired employees for inappropriate Internet use include Dow Chemical, *The New York Times* and Xerox (A. Cohen, 2001).

In certain industries some level of monitoring may even be required by law. For example, in the United States, the Health Insurance Portability and Accountability Act (HIPPA) mandates the use of audit trails to protect the privacy of patient data, in effect requiring that some employee system use be monitored.

Also, the U.S. Securities and Exchange Commission (SEC) record-keeping rules prohibit certain electronic correspondence with customers unless the firm is capable of monitoring such communications (Schulman, 2001).

The growth of the EIM business has attracted more than 50 vendors offering products that allow employers to monitor Internet and personal computer (PC) usage. These tools can be used for constraint, that is filtering and blocking web sites, as well as for generating reports consisting of detailed audits of employee Internet use. Although most vendors advocate that employees be informed about the installation of EIM software, it is possible to deploy these tools covertly. Further, U.S. law does not require that organizations notify employees that EIM software is being used.

Two basic technologies can be leveraged in EIM software—network/ server monitors that track information as it flows through an organization's networks and central servers, and client monitors that exist on the user workstations to track local PC use.

Network/Server-Based Tools

Products installed at the network or server level include filtering software such as SmartFilter™ and Websense™ These tools are largely targeted at employee web surfing and enable the restriction or monitoring of Internet activity throughout the organization. Most tools are administered at a central location and are customizable. For example, Websense™ permits policy-based rules that let administrators set which web site categories and access times are permitted for particular categories of employees. Browsing time quotas can be set for each category, and certain web sites can be restricted to after business hours surfing. These tools can block content outright and generate detailed reports on web site visits.

In addition to network filtering, server-based e-mail solutions such as MIMEsweeper™ may be employed to specifically examine and respond to e-mail traffic. All e-mail traffic travels through central corporate servers, so any messages sent or received through corporate accounts can be examined and archived. These tools can monitor and restrict internal and external messages, and can screen e-mail for viruses, malicious programs or attachments that violate file size limits. For example, they can be used to review e-mail content based on keyword searches, checking for objectionable content such as obscene words. Many companies that utilize such software are trying to enforce their various e-mail policies, such as those specifying the permissible size of e-mail files. The rationale for such policies is simple: if employees are sending snapshots or digital games as e-mail attachments, the network's performance will quickly deteriorate.

Moreover, in addition to real-time monitoring of e-mail communications virtually all computer systems keep a record of incoming and outgoing e-mail messages for security reasons in case of system failure. This is part of routine backup procedures. Some companies do the same for other communications as well. Corporations therefore must craft careful access and disclosure policies for this archived data.

Client-Side Tools

The vast majority of EIM software installed in organizations today is network or server-based. However, a number of client-side tools allow for an even deeper level of activity monitoring. Client-side tools (sometimes referred to as desktop monitoring systems) work differently from network filters in that these programs can monitor every action initiated at a particular PC. Most of these products work by examining the portion of the operating system known as the "event queue." The event queue is a sort of clearinghouse for all interaction with the PC—move your mouse, right click, type some characters and it is all captured in the event queue. This information is funneled through the operating system so that programs can respond to a user's actions. However, desktop monitoring software can plug into the event queue, capturing almost all of what a user is doing on the desktop, even if these activities don't result in network traffic. A variety of software products, including SilentWatch™ WinWhatWhere Investigator™ and WinGuardian™ can capture every keystroke (even deleted ones) that an employee types. Products that capture keystrokes can be particularly invasive, gathering data entered into secure web sites (e.g., credit card numbers at a vendor) or the contents of e-mail messages that were composed, but never sent. If one agrees that privacy is a foundation value, then employing such technologies may well go beyond the boundaries of responsible management.

Many tools that provide client-level monitoring through software installed on the PC are really hybrids that offer "agents," sitting on an employee's PC and reporting back to a central administrator. Such products include Game Warden™ that monitors and enforces policies regarding the playing of PC games. WinGuardian™ can be configured to capture "screen shots" at regular intervals, allowing remote monitors to view slides shows that illustrate what users are doing on their systems at particular intervals. Finally, products such as BeAware™ or IM Auditor™ can "watch" online chat sessions and monitor Instant Messages. BeAware™ can capture what is on the screen as frequently as every 10 seconds (Schoenberger, 2002). It too can be configured to look for keywords and phrases (such as "drugs" or "gambling") that will automatically trigger a screen shot of the monitored computer. IM Auditor™ can be used to review and store all of an organization's incoming and outgoing instant messages.

These more invasive client-side monitoring tools present an interesting management problem unrelated to the ethics or responsible use of such tools: capturing every employee keystroke along with a rich assortment of screen shots requires substantial storage. Accurately sifting through the data to discover usage patterns is also difficult and costly; human review of usage logs is time consuming and error prone, while system-based monitoring can be inaccurate, creating unnecessarily "flagged" occurrences while others slip through the system. In fact, monitoring may increase a firm's liability if it has instituted monitoring software, but did not act after illegal behavior had been detected.

Finally, it should be noted that in several cases where employees were fired for inappropriate Internet use, systematic employee monitoring using third-party tools was not employed. Log files and other features built into operating systems and applications present mechanisms for employee monitoring that may not involve installing software. Users regularly leave a bit-trail that can be tracked, provided an organization has access to the PCs or servers that a user interacts with. E-mail records may be archived through regular backups and, depending on the configuration, firms may store sent, received and even deleted e-mail at the server level. Operating systems such as Windows™ maintain lists of most recently accessed files, while Unix tools such as syslog can record program activity. Further, the default setting on most web browsers caches the graphics of visited sites and maintains a history of items viewed through the browser. By default, web browsers also support the receipt of "cookies" offered (and sometimes required) by web sites to assist with everything from tracking shopping carts to saving passwords. Examining cookies saved on a PC may indicate whether certain web sites were visited. While some of these features can be overridden or deleted if users are allowed to access preference settings and certain file locations on their desktop, the vast majority of users are unaware of the bit trail left by their activity.

Issues/Caveats

Company leaders need to realize that monitoring tools are not a panacea or an easy solution for low productivity; developing better relationships with employees through managing responsibilities, however, may be a far better means of realizing productivity gains. Trust and engagement can result in satisfaction, while invasive technologies only alienate those people on whom they are used. Additionally, using invasive digital technology irresponsibly can endanger a firm's reputation for being a good corporate citizen and create a climate of intimidation that does not lend itself to positive relationships between employees and the corporate hierarchy. In a knowledge-based economy, employee recruitment and retention can be significant sources of competitive advantage. Many potential employees indicate that they base decisions on where to work on the company's reputation for corporate citizenship (Rochlin & Christoffer, 2000). If a firm has employees who waste time, cyber-monitoring does not necessarily guarantee that those employees will be more productive, just that they will shift activities off-line or to personal networks that cannot be monitored (such as those subscribed to as part of cell phone service and accessed through mobile devices). Critics see this software as part of a flawed management philosophy that measures productivity by hours worked, rather than the quality of products produced (see, e.g., Pfeffer & Viega, 1999; Dessler, 1999). Web access can potentially make employees more productive—certainly five minutes spent surfing on amazon.com beats a two-hour lunch searching for a book at the local mall. Overly Draconian approaches can alienate employees, suppress morale and drive good workers away. There are high costs associated with the loss of skilled and knowledgeable employees, particularly in competitive labor markets.

Yet Websense's own research shows that most of its customers lean towards more heavy handed approaches with their workers, despite the fact that this represents flawed management thinking (Pfeffer & Veiga, 1999). Of the dozens of Websense™ web site categories, only a small number directly raise legal concerns, such as those featuring adult content, gambling, illegal activities, racism, hate, and violence. Employees may bristle if they become aware that through key word searches firms are tracking their visits to other web sites dealing with matters such as abortion advocacy, gay and lesbian rights, health, politics, religion, or sex education. When Websense™ surveyed its customers, it found that more than 75% managed more than 40 web site categories, either blocking them outright, allowing access only after a warning appears onscreen, or limiting access to certain users or times of day (A. Cohen, 2001).

LEGAL AND ETHICAL ANALYSIS

This enumeration of privacy-invasive technologies suggests the scope of the problem: workplace privacy is under assault from many directions and the workplace is on the brink of becoming a virtual panopticon where the worker becomes a "naked object of assessment" (Finkin, 1996, p. 267). These technologies offer the "possibility of total surveillance and control" (Borgmann, 1992, p. 103), yet their detrimental impact should be evident. The most adverse effects are the steady erosion of any semblance of privacy rights along with various dignitary harms that accompanies such erosion. In such an environment the bonds of trust become easily dissolved and employees are apt to become demoralized, making retention more difficult. Nonetheless, many employers see no problem with the open or clandestine deployment of these intrusive technologies, arguing that employee privacy rights must be overshadowed by competing interests, such as the need to protect corporate secrets, prevent illegal conduct and safeguard quality control standards. These employer demands contribute to the lowering of expectations for privacy, and, in a perverse leap of logic, corporations cite those diminished expectations as a justification for even more intrusive activities.

Moreover, current U.S. law offers little privacy protection for employees, while it similarly "provides employers with little guidance concerning the permissible depth of their intrusions" (Boehmer, 1992, p. 740). Aside from some narrow federal statutes, the basis of our legal right to privacy is found in the Fourth Amendment to the Constitution, the Electronic Communications Privacy Act (ECPA), and in the common law. The Fourth Amendment protects citizens from unreasonable search and seizure. It asserts "the right of the people to be secure in their persons, houses, papers, and effects, against unreasonable searches and seizures." The Supreme Court has ruled that the Fourth Amendment does pertain to employees and employee information (*O'Connor v. Ortega*, 1987). This amendment, however, applies only to the actions of the government and not to the actions of private organizations. Thus, while it may offer some safeguards for government workers, it offers no protection from the prying eyes of private corporations.

The Electronic Communications Privacy Act (ECPA), which was reformulated by Congress in 1986, imposes liability on any individual who "intentionally intercepts, endeavors to intercept, or procures any person to intercept or endeavor to intercept, any wire, oral, or electronic communication." There is also a provision pertaining to communications maintained in "electronic storage," which are off limits to anyone without proper authorization. The ECPA seems to have a special relevance for the monitoring of phone calls or e-mail in the workplace. But employers are largely exempt from the ECPA thanks to several major exceptions. The first of these is the "provider" exception. Corporations functioning as service providers of the equipment and network are not prohibited from monitoring the use of that equipment. Second, the consent exception means that the ECPA does not apply when communications are intercepted or recorded with the subject's permission. Finally, there is the "business extension exception," which permits network providers to access electronic communications as long as "(1) the intercepting device is part of the communications network and (2) the device is used in the ordinary course of business" (Rodriguez, 1998, p. 1453). Thanks to these generous exceptions the ECPA does little to protect the rights of most employees in the private sector.

Finally, common law protection offers little help in this context. There is a widely recognized right to privacy in the common law tradition that can be traced back to Warren and Brandeis (1890), who argued for the expansion of tort law to protect "the right of determining to what extent [one's] thoughts, sentiments, and emotions shall be communicated to others" (p. 205). There are several different torts that protect one's right to privacy, but the most relevant one for workplace privacy is unreasonable intrusion upon the seclusion of another. In order to prevail with a privacy infringement claim, however, there must be a "reasonable expectation of privacy," and if such an expectation is established, the intrusive activity into one's private affairs must still be "highly offensive."

According to Gantt (1995), "courts require not only that the employee have a subjective expectation of privacy but also that the expectation be objectively reasonable" (p. 376). As Finkin (1996) points out, "to the extent the reasonableness of the legitimate expectation of privacy is determined on objective grounds, it would rest upon employer policies [and] practices" (p. 226). Most employers are cognizant of this and so they craft policies minimizing privacy rights, which has the effect of diminishing subjective expectations. As a result, it is difficult for employees to obtain legal remedy for privacy invasions.

Consider the precedent established in *Smyth v. Pillsbury* (1996). In this case, Mr. Smyth transmitted several e-mail messages referring to his managers as "backstabbing bastards." Unbeknownst to Mr. Smyth, his e-mail messages were being intercepted and he was abruptly terminated for sending "inappropriate and unprofessional comments" over the Pillsbury e-mail facility. Smyth argued for wrongful discharge, claiming that Pillsbury had informed employees that e-mail communications were confidential and would not be used as a basis for reprimand or discharge.

The United States District Court for the Eastern District of Pennsylvania ruled in Pillsbury's favor. The court stated that company e-mail does not warrant privacy protection because e-mail by its very nature is a public form of communication, i.e., messages are transmitted over the network in an open, insecure fashion. As a result, employees should have no reasonable expectation of privacy in their e-mail messages. Also, according to the Court, Pillsbury had a legitimate need to monitor its e-mail communications in order to protect its assets and to ensure worker productivity. This interest overrides any privacy rights even if the employer did characterize its e-mail messages as confidential. Thus, "the company's interest in preventing inappropriate and unprofessional comments" outweighs any employee privacy interest, and, as a result, the interception of these messages was not highly offensive given that corporate interest (*Smyth v. Pillsbury*, 1996). This and similar cases have given employers legal protection to engage in e-mail monitoring and other forms of surveillance with relative impunity.

However, the law's permissiveness in no way implies the moral propriety of practices that negate worker privacy rights. When this issue is scrutinized through the lens of moral values it becomes evident that in this regard the law is not reflective of key moral principles and is inconsistent with internationally agreed upon foundational values, sometimes termed hypernorms (Donaldson & Dunfee, 1994, 1999). In order to prove this point we must demonstrate why privacy is such a critical moral value that deserves respect in all venues, including the corporation.

A good starting place for this investigation is Moor's (2001) general analysis of privacy, which asks whether privacy is a core moral value. If so, it would be easy to reach the conclusion that privacy must also be a right or entitlement.

Moor argues that the core values, those considered absolutely essential for human fulfillment, are life, happiness, freedom, knowledge, ability, resources, and security. He concludes, however, that while privacy is not a core value (since one can envision cultures that flourish without privacy), privacy is an articulation of security in some cultures. According to Moor (2001), "As societies become larger and highly interactive, but less intimate, privacy becomes a natural expression of the need for security" (p. 353).

In most advanced, computerized societies, therefore, privacy is a critical prerequisite for our security. How could one be "secure" if one's social security number or confidential financial information were openly revealed on the Internet for all to see? Thus, if we accept Moor's analysis, we must value workplace privacy not because privacy is a core value. Rather, we esteem privacy because of its indispensable role in guaranteeing a reasonable level of security, which is a core value, in our industrialized, information-intensive economy. According to Moor (2001), privacy should therefore be considered the equivalent of an intrinsic good "in the context of a highly populated, computerized culture" (p. 354) because of its inextricable link with security.

It stands to reason that if privacy is an intrinsic good in that context, a basic requirement for human beings who want to be secure, then individuals have a right or claim to privacy. Privacy is an entitlement because it would be unjust to deprive a person of his or her privacy for arbitrary or baseless reasons. According to Finnis (1980), the language of rights permits us to focus on the question of what is just or unjust from the other person's perspective: "the viewpoint of the 'other(s)' to whom something is owed or due and who would be wronged if denied that something" (p. 205). Since the benefit of privacy is essential for the individual's security and well being in community, it is a right because it is required of others in justice (Finnis, 1980).

And, if privacy is a basic human right required by the demands of justice, it cannot be casually suspended or ignored in the environment of the workplace. Disrespecting the right to privacy in that venue would be tantamount to disrespecting employees as persons, ignoring the requirement of privacy for a worker's well being.

Moreover, the efficacy of this argument is substantiated when we consider the ramifications of privacy's abnegation in the workplace. Without a reasonable level of privacy employees cannot be secure in this environment. Genetic testing, constant surveillance by hidden cameras, the monitoring of clickstream data, and so forth, are intrusive activities that ultimately reduce an employee's security, i.e., the employee's ability to protect herself from undue harm. This data, often taken out of context, can lead to adverse judgments and the possibility of manipulation by one's supervisor or others who might have objectives opposed to the employee's welfare. This problem is made worse by the asymmetry of power in most workplace relationships (Introna, 2001), by lack of openness about the privacy issue itself, and by companies' reluctance to engage with employees about the issue.   For example, if genetic testing became more rampant, employers might arbitrarily dismiss certain employees for genetic traits and the remote possibility of future health problems. Unless the employee can protect such data, he or she is vulnerable for the possibility of unwarranted discharge or other abuses.

In addition, what is at stake in the debate over electronic monitoring and other invasive technologies is the closely related value of human dignity, which is clearly a foundation value articulated in numerous international agreements, the most notable of which is the United Nations' Declaration on Human Rights and the Environment. The inessential and perpetual encroachment upon one's personal space is an affront to one's human dignity. The Kantian philosophical tradition dwells extensively on this topic. Kant's notion of personhood is predicated on the connection between autonomy and dignity. Human beings have dignity because of their autonomy, the capability of directing their lives and governing their actions in accordance with the moral law. According to Kant (1990, p. 52):

Morality is the condition under which alone a rational being can be an end in himself because only through it is it possible to be a lawgiving member in the realm of ends. Thus morality, and humanity insofar as it is capable of morality, alone have dignity.

When this power of normative self-determination is threatened or debili tated for an invalid purpose, so is one's dignity. Surveillance technologies often undermine our freedom, which is the basis of our dignity. It is common knowledge that most people will behave differently when they are being watched or monitored by others. In these circumstances it is normal to feel more inhibited and tentative about one's behavior. According to Zuboff (1988), it is not uncommon to find "anticipatory conformity" (p. 344) among those who are constantly observed in the "informated" workplace. Or consider once again the use of genetic testing which transforms the human self into a passive object open to a level of scrutiny that is beyond that self's ability to control. The human subject is objectified in search of data that can predict future health and serve as the basis for decisions about that individual's future. Such testing without a valid and morally sound purpose is an affront to the individual's basic dignity because it manifests a lack of respect for that person as an autonomous being who alone should control his or her destiny.

Rothstein (2000) suggests that Americans would be better off following the lead of continental Europe, which derives its protections against electronic monitoring and other intrusive technologies "from a concept of 'human dignity' rather than 'privacy'" (p. 381). He argues that the worker's dignity is denied "when she is treated as a mechanism transparent to the view of others at a distance and manipulable or disposable without the ability to confront the observer" (p. 381).

In summary, we conclude that workplace privacy rights are grounded in the requirement for the preservation of each worker's security and dignity in the workplace. We have demonstrated that security is a core moral value necessary for human flourishing and impossible to attain in certain contexts without some level of privacy. Furthermore, there is a moral imperative to respect the human dignity of one's workers, and that dignity is violated by the imprudent use of privacy-invasive technologies, since those technologies undermine autonomy, which is the source of that dignity. Good employee relationships and good corporate citizenship are not built on violations of human rights or human dignity, but on positive corporate practices that manifest respect for an employee's rights and his or her basic dignity (Waddock, 2001).

This right of workplace privacy, however, is a prima facie right; it is not absolute, since it must be balanced by the employer's rights to acquire relevant information and to protect its property. Corporations need to collect and process certain data about their employees for the good of the organization. No company can make sound hiring decisions without the proper amount of information regarding candidates for a given job. And it may be necessary for quality control purposes for corporations to engage in limited monitoring of phone calls answered by service representatives. Security needs might also demand some level of monitoring.

As we intimated earlier, another important rationale for e-mail monitoring or worker surveillance is the employer's imperative to shield its employees from sexual harassment, defamatory statements or other abuses, which can also expose a corporation to liability claims. Federal and state regulatory agencies responsible for enforcing racial and gender equality statutes put pressure on companies to have systems in place that can swiftly identify expressions of bias (or harassment) and effect necessary remedies. If harassment is taking place through the electronic mail system, monitoring software might be able to intercept the harassing messages or at least curtail the harassment before it escalates. The problem is that sexual harassment law under some circumstances imposes more liability on the employers than on the harasser.

However, if employers demonstrate swift and decisive response to the harassment complaint, they can usually avoid a lawsuit for negligence or other liability claims. Although there is some legal ambiguity about this matter, it does not appear to be the case that employers are required to take proactive steps such as the deployment of surveillance technologies in order to prevent harassment before it occurs and thereby protect themselves from liability. Since most employers are service providers, they should enjoy immunity from liability for "information provided by another information content provider" according to the

Communications Decency Act (1996). According to some legal scholars, based upon two precedent setting cases, *Zeran v. America Online* and *Blumenthal v. Drudge*, "the employer is not liable for the employee's statements" (Spencer, 2000, p. 33). Nonetheless, the CDA could be subject to reinterpretation, so employers cannot neglect the possibility of liability for those statements in the future. Hence they must factor in this possibility as they seek to balance employee privacy rights with the need to foster an environment free of harassing or defamatory statements.

Finally, a more questionable motivation to collect information is based on the need to predict human behavior, even in the workplace. Companies believe that the more detailed the profiles of their workers, the greater their ability to predict the probability of their long-term success within the organization. As Borgamnn (1992) writes, "the distinctive discourse of modernity is one of prediction and control" (p. 2). But where does one draw the line with this need to collect employee information? When do monitoring or data collection practices become intrusive and irresponsible because they exceed that hard-to-define boundary of the corporation's need to know? What are the limits to the corporation's insatiable demand for predictability and control? Responsibility management (TRM) approaches with their emphasis on stakeholder (employee) engagement and attention to foundation values can provide some help in addressing these questions.

RESPONSIBILITY MANAGEMENT APPROACHES AND PRIVACY POLICIES

As we have seen, the current law gives employers great latitude in the information that they can collect. But this state of affairs seems inconsistent with the value of human dignity and the need for privacy as a condition of one's security. What must be avoided is monitoring or surveillance that is intrusive and dehumanizing, that cannot be justified by the employer's need for knowledge to operate the business. Thus, our main argument is that a presumption should be given to a prima facie right of workplace privacy as a foundation value that should be incorporated within company codes of conduct and in other value statements that guide decision-making. It is the burden of the employer to demonstrate why this prima facie privacy right should be overridden and to justify the deployment of any particular monitoring technology endangering that right.

Obviously it will be difficult in some cases to make the determination of whose claim takes priority—the company's need to know or the employee's right to privacy. A justification for overriding this privacy right must be clear and convincing to a corporation's various constituencies. Relying on TRM, we offer some practical guidance for how the corporation can make the determination about when and how it should monitor its employees.

First, the unfair advantages stemming from corporate power asymmetries should be mitigated by allowing employees or their representatives to have a major role in determining policies for monitoring through a process of dialogue and openness about both the need for information gathering and the tools to be used. This collaborative effort will help set reasonable privacy expectations so that workers are not unduly compromised. As Westin (1989) observes, "employee involvement in the initial design, testing, implementation and continuing adjustment of work monitoring is critical to a successful process..." (p. 167). Companies using responsibility management (TRM) approaches recognize the need for engaging with employees on important issues like privacy, rather than management's simply taking its prerogative to impose decisions. Stakeholder engagement is a core element of the vision-setting (inspiration) process in TRM approaches, because it allows input by key constituencies into the development of corporate vision, values and, ultimately, practices. Dialogue provides a *means* for employee input on the touchy issue of privacy that might otherwise be lacking. It also has the potential to create a knowledgeable employee base, generating loyalty and trust. In a world where activists on a wide array of issues can create serious reputational difficulties for a firm, an informed employee may be a company's best defense.

Second, certain principles derived from the imperative to respect and institutionalize the foundation value of privacy should be adopted to offer the employee protection when monitoring technologies need to be used. We identify five operative principles for ensuring that monitoring technologies are being adopted and used in a fair manner. These principles provide a basis of managing responsibly in a difficult context and are built on the need to develop trusting relationships with employees, mindful about the impact of corporate actions on openness, accountability and trust, core aspects of good corporate citizenship (Waddock, 2001):

1.   The employer's justification for the adoption of monitoring technologies or the collection of employee data must be based on a well-grounded, cogent business need (accountability).

2.   If employers make the decision to monitor a particular activity or set of transactions they should utilize the least intrusive means possible (trust).

3.   Employers must develop strict access policies and ensure that all collected or archived electronic employee data is kept secure and confidential (accountability).

4.   All personal communications intercepted by monitoring technologies should be promptly disregarded by those scanning for content (trust).

5.   Employers have a prima facie duty to *inform* employees about the monitoring tools being used in their work environment (openness).

Let us elaborate on these five guiding principles. First and foremost, in any given situation where monitoring technology is being considered, a company must establish the presence of a cogent and well-founded business need. The employer must demonstrate that monitoring is essential for advancing its business interests and that no other alternative is viable, and it must be willing to be held accountable for any adverse impacts of such monitoring. For example, a securities firm may have a strong need to monitor e-mail if its brokers use the e-mail facility to communicate with customers. But another employer may have no such need "if it solely desires to minimize workplace gossip occurring within a purely intra-office e-mail network" (Gantt, 1995, p. 417). In making this determination companies should work out an objective cost benefit analysis, and allow employees significant input into the decision. Unless that analysis shows that the benefits decisively outweigh the costs, monitoring tools should be avoided. They should not be adopted for marginal gains in security or productivity.

This principle requires that all information collected or behavior monitored satisfy the condition of *relevance*, also related to accountability. For example, routine surveillance cameras in employee lounges will not yield substantial relevant information. There may be unusual circumstances or suspicions that justify the use of such a technology in extreme situations, but the burden of proof is on the employer to offer a persuasive justification for use in these ad hoc situations. In addition, while employers have a legitimate right to know about the general health of their workers, they do not need to be privy to the genetic composition of those workers. It's one thing for an employer to demand a medical examination but quite another to insist that workers submit to genetic testing.

Second, if the condition of a cogent business interest is satisfied and a decision is made to monitor, the least intrusive means consistent with those interests should be utilized, so that trust between the firm and its employees is not destroyed. This implies that companies should make every reasonable effort to minimize the monitoring or interception of content, that is, the substance of phone calls, faxes, e-mail communications, and instant messages. It is far less intrusive to track transactional data than *content*. It may be acceptable, for example, to track outgoing and incoming phone numbers to search for calling patterns that might prevent abuses (such as the illegitimate use of long distance lines), but this purpose can be achieved without listening in on the actual phone conversations. Likewise, in order to prevent abusive personal use, corporations may have a legitimate interest in monitoring transactional information of e-mail messages; they also may have an interest in checking attachments to screen for viruses and to ensure that file size limits preventing network congestion are followed. In all likelihood, however, these objectives can be met without routinely intercepting and reading the content of employee e-mails, an initiative likely to corrode trust and disrupt relationships. There may be times when a cogent business interest requires that content as well as transactional data be monitored, but in many cases that level of intrusiveness is unnecessary.

The application of these first two principles would also seem to preclude the deployment of certain technologies such as SilentWatch™ that track a worker's every single key stroke. That software is highly invasive, since it blatantly intrudes upon an employee's thoughts or "inner space." It is difficult to conceive of a cogent business interest that would justify this level of monitoring and the fine-grained data that it yields. Particularly for companies that have established good working relationships with employees, such invasive monitoring is unlikely to be necessary since the employees' and companies' goals are more likely to be congruent.

Third, the data collected through these monitoring technologies along with other archived digital information must be kept secure and confidential, another core aspect of building trust between employees and the firm's managers. For example, archived e-mail messages should not be available for routine or casual inspection by the employee's supervisor or others in positions of authority. It should be made accessible only for a justifiable cause such as maintaining system security, investigating allegations of improprieties, or meeting legal obligations. The more restrictions placed on access to employee data within the organization, the better a company can safeguard the privacy rights of its workers. Also, it is hard to imagine a tenable rationale for providing this information to those outside the company. For example, under ordinary circumstances prospective employers or other outsiders should not be informed about an employee's penchant for visiting certain types of web sites.

Fourth, if companies choose to monitor in real time, they will on occasion intercept communications that are clearly of a personal nature. Once it is determined that an e-mail, instant message, or phone call is dealing with personal matters, the monitoring must be terminated to safeguard the employee's personal privacy. Employers are accountable to employees for overstepping the boundaries of legitimate privacy, which involves irrelevant details about an employee's personal life. For example, supervisors who might be monitoring phone calls for quality assurance purposes must stop listening to any conversation once it becomes personal. Even the courts seem to embrace this principle. In *Watkins v. L.M. Berry & Co.* (1983) the court held that the monitoring of an employee's personal calls is impermissible, since it is not "in the ordinary course of business."

Finally, it is incumbent upon the employer to inform employees about all monitoring policies and surveillance technologies in use. Employees should not be subjected to covert surveillance or unexpected intrusions, unless the circumstances are extraordinary (such as an undercover criminal investigation). Central to the TRM approach to managing responsibilities is clear communication and openness about the policies and practices that are in place. This notification will eliminate confusion and help properly establish privacy expectations. In many situations employers have manipulated those expectations, but if the other conditions delineated here are dutifully followed, each employee will be assured a reasonable level of workplace privacy. In addition, employee development and training programs need to emphasize those privacy policies and to explain the purpose and functionality of the monitoring tools that are in use.

These are admittedly broad principles open to a certain level of interpretation. Employers and employees will most likely have different conceptions of what constitutes "a cogent business interest." But these principles can form the basis for fair policies and practices that realize the vision of a workplace that respects worker privacy rights.

Of course, as we have been at pains to insist here the need for a collaborative effort is acute. The TRM approach of "stakeholder dialogue" will surely help determine coherent and fair privacy policies. In such a dialogue differences can be explored and compromises negotiated. Without such a process of engagement through dialogue in place, it is easy to conceive that the more talented employees will seek employment elsewhere should they learn that their personal boundaries have been breached.

Finally, in accordance with TRM, the entire monitoring and surveillance infrastructure (including technologies in use, policies, archived data, and so forth) must be subject to ongoing evaluation through various metrics agreed upon by employers and workers. This will ensure that there is ongoing improvement and innovation in how these technologies are used in the workplace and how information collection and disclosure policies are implemented.

Privacy is only one of many complex issues that emerges in today's technologically sophisticated world. Like other issues that raise ethical concerns, the privacy issue is best approached explicitly, using many of the same management skills and techniques that have been successful in managing other responsibilities. Management systems are rapidly evolving to cope with labor and human rights, the natural environment, or quality (Waddock & Bodwell, 2002; Curkovic, Melnyk, Handfield, & Calantone, 2000; Evans & Lindsay, 1999); the ethical concerns raised by technology deserve equal management consideration.

CONCLUSIONS AND A LOOK AHEAD

The erosion of workplace privacy rights is likely to worsen unless companies begin to take their ethical obligations more seriously and adopt approaches such as TRM to deal with this management problem. The evolution of sophisticated and officious monitoring technologies will undoubtedly continue, and employers searching to enhance their predictive powers will be hard pressed to resist the temptation to deploy such technologies. As we observed earlier, despite the controversy over the extent of EIM use, trends suggest substantial future growth.

Other forms of workplace monitoring through video equipment, digital cameras, pen register devices, and similar mechanisms are also quite likely to proliferate. Prices on these surveillance devices are steadily declining, making it more cost effective for companies to bolster their security at the expense of workplace privacy rights.

At least in the U.S., the law has been impotent, unable to reverse the deterioration of worker privacy rights. Further, there is little sign that federal legislation will be enacted anytime soon to make those rights more secure. In the wake of terrorist attacks and threats, the U.S. government and major corporations are even more obsessed with security and less inclined to worry about privacy rights.

Regrettably, there are few initiatives that an employee can take in order to protect his or her privacy. Given each company's tight control of its technology, workers are usually constrained from using privacy-enhancing code (such as encryption programs) to safeguard their communications. Even if such code is not formally forbidden, its use often engenders suspicion and this could mean unwanted attention and other potential problems for employees who adopt these technologies.

Finally, the dynamic of market forces might force attention to this issue, but only when the labor market is competitive and companies are compelled to attract workers with the promise of a firmer commitment to privacy rights. The market, however, has generally been an inadequate forum for resolving such social issues. Without law, technology or the marketplace to constrain employers the only recourse is self-regulation through the swift embrace of ethical standards and management philosophies such as TRM. As we have sought to demonstrate here, privacy is a basic human entitlement, necessary for security in our computerized, networked society. Unwarranted surveillance and monitoring in the workplace disregards the pivotal nature of privacy as a value of great social importance; the indiscriminate use of these technologies also represents an affront to human dignity. American companies, therefore, should emulate their European counterparts and formulate policies that manifest more sensitivity to the privacy rights of their workers.

We have also insisted on the need for moral pragmatism in defining the scope of privacy rights, since the corporation's information needs cannot be casually ignored. As with most moral or social problems, it is critical to find the proper equilibrium between several conflicting demands. In this case it is essential to balance the employer's need to know with the worker's right to privacy. With this in mind, we have proposed several principles that will enable responsible corporations to achieve that precarious balance. Foremost among these principles is the requirement of a cogent and well-grounded business need as the basis for monitoring. In accordance with TRM, we have also maintained the need for worker participation to ensure fair information policies that will set reasonable expectations that are not subject to corporate manipulation.

REFERENCES

Boehmer, R. (1992). Artificial monitoring and surveillance of employees: The fine line dividing the prudently managed enterprise from the modern sweatshop. *DePaul Law Review, 41*, 739.

Borgmann, A. (1992). *Crossing the Postmodern Divide.* Chicago, IL: University of Chicago Press.

Brandeis, L. & Warren, S. (1890). The right to privacy. *Harvard Law Review, 4*, 193.

Brown, W. S. (1996). Technology, workplace privacy, and personhood. *Journal of Business Ethics, 15*(11), 1237-1248.

Carter, T. (2001). *ABA Journal, 87*(9), 28.

Ciocchetti, C.A. (2001). Monitoring employee e-mail: Efficient workplaces vs. employee privacy. *Duke Law & Technology Review, 26*, 102.

Cohen, A. (2001). Worker watchers. *Fortune, 143*(139), 70-75.

Cohen, J. (2001). Privacy, ideology and technology: A response to Jeffrey Rosen. *Georgetown Law Review, 89*, 17.

Communications Decency Act. (1996). Pub L No 104, 47 USC Statute, § 230(c).

Curkovic, S., Melnyk, S.A., Handfield, R. B., & Calantone, R. (2000). Investigating the linkage between total quality management and environmentally responsible manufacturing. *IEEE Transactions on Engineering Management, 47*(4), 444-464.

DesJardins, J. (1985). *Contemporary Issues in Business Ethics.* Belmont, CA: Wadsworth.

Dessler, G. (1993). How to earn your employees' commitment. *Academy of Management Executive, 13(2),* 58-67.

Donaldson, T. & Dunfee, T. (1994). Toward a unified conception of social contracts theory. *Academy of Management Review, 19*(2), 252-284.

Donaldson, T. & Dunfee, T. (1999). *Ties that Bind: A Social Contracts Approach to Business Ethics.* Boston, MA: Harvard Business School Press.

Electronic Communications Privacy Act. (1986). 18 U.S.C. §§ 2510-2520.

Evans, J. R. & Lindsay, W. (1999). *The Management and Control of Quality* (4th ed). New York: West.

Ewing, D. (1982). *Do It My Way or You're Fired.* New York: John Wiley & Sons.

Finkin, M. (1996). Employee privacy, American values, and the law. *Chicago-Kent Law Review, 62*, 221.

Finnis, J. (1980). *Natural Law and Natural Rights.* Oxford: Oxford University Press.

Gantt, L. (1995). Electronic mail monitoring in the private sector workplace. *Harvard Journal of Law and Technology, 8*, 345.

Introna, L. (2001). Workplace surveillance, privacy, and distributive justice. In R.A. Spinello & H. Tavani (Eds.), *Readings in Cyberethics* (pp. 418-429). Sudbury, MA: Jones & Bartlett.

Kant, I. (1990). *Foundation of the Metaphysics of Morals.* New York: Macmillan. (Original work published 1785).

Kolk, A., van Tulder, R., & Welters, C. (1999). International codes of conduct and corporate social responsibility: Can transnational corporations regulate themselves? *Transnational Corporations, 8*(1), 143-179.

Moor, J. (2001). Towards a theory of privacy for the information age. In R.A. Spinello & H. Tavani (Eds.), *Readings in Cyberethics* (pp. 349-359). Sudbury, MA: Jones & Bartlett.

O'Connor v. Ortega (480 U.S. 709). (1987).

Pfeffer, J. & Veiga, J. (1999). Putting people first for organizational success. *Academy of Management Executive, 13*(2), 37-48.

Rochlin, S. A. & Christoffer, B. (2000). *Making the Business Case: Determining the Value of Corporate Community Involvement.* Chestnut Hill, MA: Boston College Center for Corporate Community Relations. Unpublished manuscript.

Rodriguez, A. (1998, Fall). All bark, no byte: Employee e-mail privacy rights in the private sector workplace. *Emory Law Journal,* 1439.

Rothstein, L. (2000). Privacy or dignity?: Electronic monitoring in the workplace. *New York Law School Journal of International and Comparative Law, 23,* 379.

Schoenberger, C. (2002, May 27). The monitors have eyes. *Forbes,* 138.

Schulman, A. (2001). *Computer and Internet surveillance in the workplace: Rough notes.* Retrieved from the World Wide Web: http://www.sonic.net/~undoc/survtech.htm.

Sewell, G. & Barker, J. (2001). Neither good nor bad, but dangerous: Surveillance as an ethical paradox. *Ethics and Information Technology, 3*(3), 183-196.

Smyth v. Pillsbury (914 F. Supp. 97, E.D. Pa.). (1996).

Spencer, M. H. (2000). Defamatory e-mail and employer liability: Why razing Zeran v. America Online is a good thing. *The Richmond Journal of Law and Technology, 6,* 25.

Stone, B. (2002, September 30). Is the boss watching? *Newsweek,* 38.

Velasquez, M. (1992). *Business Ethics: Concepts and Cases* (3rd ed.). Englewood Cliffs, NJ: Prentice-Hall.

Waddock, S. (2001). Integrity and mindfulness: Foundations of corporate citizenship. *Journal of Corporate Citizenship, 1*(1), 25-37.

Waddock, S. & Bodwell, C. (2002). From TQM to TRM: The emerging evolution of Total Responsibility Management (TRM) systems. *Journal of Corporate Citizenship, 2* (7), 113-126.

Waddock, S., Bodwell, C., & Graves, S. (2002). Responsibility: The new business imperative. *Academy of Management Executive, 16*(2), 132-148.

Watkins v. L.M. Berry & Co. (704 F. 2d 577, 11th Cir). (1983).

Werhane, P. (1985). *Persons, rights, and corporations.* Englewood Cliffs, NJ: Prentice-Hall.

Westin, A. (1989). Monitoring and new office systems. In *Proceedings of the Forty-First Annual Meeting of the National Academy of Arbitrators* (pp. 165-173).

Zuboff, S. (1988). *In the Age of the Smart Machine: The Future of Work and Power.* New York: Basic Books.

Chapter VI

Virtual Harms and Real Responsibility*

Chuck Huff
St. Olaf College, USA

Deborah G. Johnson
University of Virginia, USA

Keith W. Miller
University of Illinois-Springfield, USA

ABSTRACT

In traditional communities, some actions are widely regarded as bad and unethical. But in online "communities," the virtual analog of those actions may not be regarded with the same clarity. Since "virtual" behaviors are distinct from ordinary acts, they require further analysis to determine whether they are right or wrong. In this chapter we consider an incident on the Internet that illustrates this confusion. The incident centered on a virtual act of sexual violence. This "rape in cyberspace," reported by Julian Dibbell in 1993, has generated questions about the significance of behaviors in virtual reality environments. We use the case to explore the moral nature of actions in virtual environments, emphasizing the themes of harm and responsibility. We then offer some tentative lessons to be learned and, finally, apply the lessons to virtual sex and to first-person shooter computer games.

INTRODUCTION

As people spend more of their time online, it becomes increasingly important to better understand the relationships between people that meet only (or most frequently) in cyberspace. In our traditional communities, some actions are widely regarded as bad or unethical. But in online "communities," the virtual analog of those actions may not be regarded with the same clarity. Since "virtual" behaviors are distinct from ordinary acts, they require further analysis to determine whether they are right or wrong. In this chapter we consider a relatively early incident on the Internet that illustrates this confusion. The incident centered on a virtual act of sexual violence by a sordid character called Bungle.

The incidence of a "rape in cyberspace" reported by Julian Dibbell in 1993 has generated a good deal of attention and a good many questions about the significance of virtual behavior in virtual reality environments. In this chapter we use the rape in cyberspace case as a focus for exploring the moral nature of actions and interactions in virtual environments. We emphasize, in particular, the themes of harm and responsibility. We conclude with some tentative lessons to be learned from the case and then we extend the analysis to virtual sex and to first-person shooter computer games.

BACKGROUND: THE BUNGLE AFFAIR

It happened in the living room in LambdaMOO. LambdaMOO is a multi-user dimension (MUD) object oriented program, a complex database maintained inside Xerox Corporation in Palo Alto and open to public access via the Internet. The program allows users to create and design the interaction space and context; a user can describe his or her own character any way they like, and can build new objects, including rooms and furniture. While users interact with one another as the characters that they have created, they see a stream of dialogues and stage descriptions.

One night a character, Bungle, entered LambdaMOO. Bungle had designed a subprogram, Voodoo doll, which could attribute actions to other characters. Using the Voodoo doll subprogram, Bungle took control of two other characters Legba (we capitalize this for clarity, although Dibbell used "legba") and Starsinger, and manipulated these characters to appear to engage in sadistic and sexually explicit actions. These actions were understood to constitute (and we refer to them as) rape. Legba and Starsinger were helpless throughout the entire incident. The episode ended when another character, Zippy, used a subprogram to freeze Bungle's commands.

*The virtual rape caused enormous ripples across the community of
LambdaMOOers. One of the victims, Legba, wanted Bungle to be
"toaded"—that is, to have his account removed from LambdaMOO.
Opinion was divided over what should be done to Bungle. On the
evening of the third day after the incident, the users gathered in
LambdaMOO to discuss Bungle's fate. There were four arguments: (1) The techno libertarians argued that rape in cyberspace
was a technical inevitability and that a solution would be to use
defensive software tools to filter out the offender's words. (2) The
legalists argued that Bungle could not legitimately be "toaded"
since the MOO had no explicit rules at all; they proposed the
establishment of rules and virtual institutions to exercise the
control required. (3) The third group of users, believers in
meritocracy, believed that only the programmers, or wizards as
they are known in MOO, have the power to implement rules. (4)
The anarchists, on the other hand, wanted to see the matter
resolved without the establishment of social control. There was no
agreement between these groups. To Bungle, who joined midway
through the conference, the event was simply a sequence of events
in virtual reality that had no consequences for his real life
existence.*

*After weighing the arguments, one of the programmers, the
Wizard JoeFeedback, decided to "toad" Bungle, banishing him
from the MOO. As a result of this incident, the database system
was redesigned so that the programmers could make changes
based on action or a petition of the majority of the LambdaMOO
community. Eight months and 11 ballots later, widespread participation produced a system of checks and capabilities to guard
against the type of violence that occurred. As for Bungle, he is
believed to be reincarnated as the character Dr. Jest.*

(Excerpt adapted from *Computer Ethics, 3rd Edition,* by Deborah
Johnson, based on "A Rape in Cyberspace: How an Evil Clown, a
Haitian Trickster Spirit, Two Wizards, and a Cast of Dozens Turned
a Database Into a Society," by Julian Dibbell, first published in *The
Village Voice*, December 23, 1993, pp. 36-42.)

This case has been widely discussed in a diversity of literature including
Lessig's *Code* (Lessig, 1999) and Sherry Turkel's *Life on the Screen* (Turkle,
1996). When Julian Dibbel first presented it to the world in a *Village Voice* piece
in 1993, he seemed as fascinated with the reaction of the LamdaMOO participants as with Bungle's behavior. He noted the shock and outrage of participants
who expressed feelings of being violated and engaged in emotional discussion of
how to respond to Bungle's behavior. This raised the question of the differences

between virtual reality (VR) and real life (RL), or more specifically the difference between behavior in VR and behavior in RL. The fact that the VR behavior was sexual and violent makes the question more salient and it also makes it more complex since virtual reality behavior and sexual behavior both carry heavy symbolic weight. In the case of virtual behavior in a text environment, the reality of text has behind it the power of imagery and imagination. Sexual violence is often described as symbolic of the dominance of the attacker and the humiliation of the victim.

Indeed it is because of the highly symbolic meaning of the act of rape that one can react to the "rape in cyberspace" with contradictory thoughts. On the one hand, it seems inappropriate and disingenuous to think of what happened as comparable to rape. It seems unfair to real rape victims to equate what happens to them with the experiences of LamdaMOO participants who witnessed a representational rape, albeit a representational rape that involved characters they had created and were supposed to be able to control. On the other hand, it does seem appropriate to say both that Bungle did something wrong (bad) and that the real person who was controlling Bungle did something wrong (bad). Both, it would seem, engaged in a form of violent sexual behavior. (More on this later.) So, the case is worth exploring, especially with an eye to understanding the moral status of virtual behavior, but also simply to find a language for talking about virtual behavior in moral/ethical terms.

ANALYZING THE PLAYERS/ACTORS

A good way to begin is by identifying the stakeholders in the Bungle incident and, by generalization, stakeholders in other virtual encounters. LamdaMOO participants only knew the names of the virtual characters: Bungle, Legba, JoeFeedback, and the rest. The usual assumption is that each virtual character is controlled by a flesh-and-blood person, and that is probably correct most of the time. However, other possibilities exist. For example: a single virtual character could be controlled by more than one flesh person (by committee); a virtual character could be controlled by a program simulating keyboard commands from a LamdaMOO participant; or a virtual character could be a program that was part of the LambdaMOO interface, written not by a normal participant, but by the LambdaMOO wizards. There are other possibilities, but these are suggestive.

In addition to these possibilities, we have to remember that the flesh controllers of virtual characters are acting in an environment created via software. Hence, the interface mediates the actions of virtual characters and flesh controllers. Figure 1 illustrates how these entities are related. In Figure 1, circles represent virtual characters, ellipses represent software, and squares represent flesh people; solid straight lines represent real time control, and dotted

Figure 1. Virtual Characters, Their Controllers, and the Interface Between Them

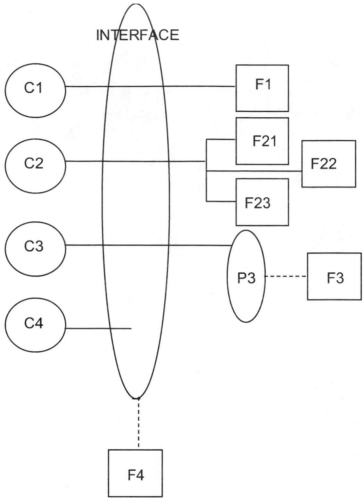

lines represent asynchronous control (such as a programmer has over object code that runs without direct supervision). Thus, C1, C2, C3, and C4 are virtual characters. Each F is a flesh person. F1 controls C1. F21, F22, and F23 are a committee that controls C2. P3 is a program, written by F3; P3 controls C3. F4 is a "wizard" who developed the interface; the interface controls the virtual character C4. (Note that F3 and F4 could be a group of programmers as well as an individual.)

So, who are the stakeholders in this case? This is not a simple question. Do we say that the virtual characters are stakeholders? Or do we say that only the flesh-and-blood controllers of the virtual characters are stakeholders? Morality is generally confined to flesh-and-blood individuals. That is, morality is confined to moral agents and generally human beings are the only beings we know of that qualify as moral agents. (This view is not universal; for example, see Friedman & Miller, 1995.) Hence, only the behavior of the flesh-and-blood controllers can probably be thought of in moral terms, but let us leave this question open for the moment. The case is interesting in part because it seems to challenge this idea of restricting morality to flesh-and-blood persons; after all, Bungle raped Legba and Starsinger.

Nevertheless, even if we restrict our focus to the flesh-and-blood participants in the LamdaMOO, there are other actors in addition to participants in the game. As mentioned in reference to Figure 1, the software system itself and the designers and controllers of the software system are agents/actors in the activities that take place in the virtual environment. Here there may be several types of actors, including most prominently the software designers and the wizards who run the game. We have to make a decision parallel to the one we made about virtual/real participants: should we say the software interface is an agent or restrict ourselves to flesh-and-blood persons who design or control the software interface? These flesh actors are stakeholders in the case insofar as they may or may not be harmed by the actions of Bungle or his flesh controller. They are also involved in the case because even if they are not harmed by the incidence of rape, they may be implicated in accountability for the incident.

HARMS TO THE PLAYERS
Three Dimensions of Harm

The case falls into the arena of the morality because it seems to involve harm. The act of rape is a heinous act. It involves coercion, it violates the autonomy of the victim, and it is an exercise of power that demeans and denigrates the victim. Our ideas about both sex and harm are deeply tied to flesh and blood. The rape in cyberspace is puzzling then, because, initially at least, it seems to suggest that rape can happen to virtual (non-flesh-and-blood) characters. While there was not a real rape because no physical contact was involved, it is interesting that LamdaMOO participants were upset and distressed about what happened to the virtual characters, Legba and Starsinger. Bungle's actions affected and may have harmed the flesh-and-blood LamdaMOO participants. What can we say about how they were affected?

The case is intriguing because it makes us aware of the symbolic nature of rape. Even a representation of a rape can have powerful effects. Moreover, in the virtual environment there is some physical behavior that does not equate to rape but parallels the coercive aspect of rape. Johnson (2001) argues that the flesh-and-blood controller of Bungle did two things wrong. First, he/she took control of characters he/she had no right to control, that is, he/she took control away from the controllers of Legba and Starsinger. Second, the flesh-and-blood controller of Bungle exposed all of the participants in LamdaMOO to a level of violence and pornography to which they did not choose to be exposed.

Given the nature of virtual reality software and hardware, there are a limited number of ways that a virtual character can rape another virtual character. (1) One flesh controller must control two characters; (2) two flesh controllers (each controlling a separate virtual character) agree to act out a rape; or (3) what happened in the Bungle case. Bungle broke into the software and took control of virtual characters that were not his (not his according to the rules of the MUD). If either (1) or (2) had taken place, the participants in LamdaMOO might have been upset, but what actually happened seems more parallel to rape because it involved a physical coercion. The flesh controller of Bungle broke into the system and in so doing violated the autonomy of the flesh controllers of Legba and Starsinger. So, while the flesh controller of Bungle did not commit real rape, he/she did something real and the something real involved coercion and the violation of the informal rights of individuals.

The second wrong according to Johnson is that the flesh controller of Bungle exposed participants in LamdaMOO to a level of violence and pornography to which they did not choose to be exposed. Here the physical activity involved in creating a representation moves to the background and the fact that participants were visually exposed to something comes into focus. Immediately, however, we have to be careful for there is nothing intrinsically wrong with exposing other individuals to visual representations. Rather it is the nature of the representations, and the fact that generally when it comes to explicit sexual content, consent is sought before exposure. This moral principle is based on the idea that explicit sexual content will have an effect and individuals should be allowed to choose whether to be exposed or not.

In exposing participants to representationally violent acts without their permission, we might think of the harm done as merely psychological harm. But psychological harm is a real harm, and it should not be dismissed or trivialized. It is commonplace to separate psychological harm and physical harm, but the distinction can be overemphasized. Doing harm to a person's mind is in many respects similar to doing harm to some other part of the body. An extensive discussion of the issue of mind and brain (Churchland, 1996) is outside the scope of this chapter. Instead we will include psychological harm as a "physical harm" for the purposes of our exposition. Those unconvinced that psychological harm qualifies as physical harm can imagine that one of Bungle's virtual victims was controlled by a flesh-and-blood person who developed ulcers after Bungle's attacks. Or perhaps another flesh-and-blood person got so incensed by the Bungle affair that she had a heart attack. These effects would be physical even though Bungle is virtual. Although such a physical manifestation is not, in our opinion, required for the classification of psychological harm as "physical," it is certainly sufficient.

Figure 2. Examples of Actions and Harms

	Source	Action	Target		Harm
1	C1	shoots	C2	▶	direct virtual harm to C2
2	F1	shoots	F2	▶	direct physical harm to F2
3	F1	manipulates	C1		
		and			
	C1	shoots	C2	▶	direct virtual harm to C2
		and			and
	shooting	offends	F2	▶	indirect physical harm to F2
4	F1	controls	C1		
		and			
	C1	controls	C2	▶	direct virtual harm to C2
		and			
	C1	offends	F2	▶	indirect physical harm to F2
		and			
	C1	offends	F3	▶	indirect physical harm to F3

So, virtual behavior can have effects both on virtual characters and on flesh and blood persons. Moreover, virtual characters do not act unless flesh-and-blood individuals act. Thus, even when there are flesh-and-blood effects from virtual acts, there are also flesh-and-blood acts controlling the virtual acts. Using the notations suggested in Figure 1, we can think of direct, indirect, physical, and virtual harms. Here are four examples: first, if a virtual character C1 shoots another virtual character, C2, then there is a virtual harm to C2. Second, if F1, the flesh controller of C1, locates F2, the flesh controller of C2, and shoots F2, then there is a real (physical) harm to F2. Third, F1, the flesh controller of C1, can manipulate C1 in such a way that C1 does something to C2 and this in turn, harms F2, the controller of C2. Fourth, as in the Bungle case, F1, the flesh controller of C1, takes control of C2 through C1, and manipulates both C1 and C2 in such a way that F1 violates the rights of F2 and harms F2, and also offends other flesh controllers (shown as F3 in Figure 2).

Now, these types of behavior can be distinguished in terms of their culpability by drawing on the work of Harré and Secord (1972). Harré and Secord distinguish intentional harm, negligent harm, and accidental harm. Intentional harm requires a "guilty mind" in the form of foreseeing and planning for the harm; negligent harm requires that the harm be foreseeable by a reasonable person, and that the actor had some control to "do otherwise" and avoid the foreseeable harm; and accidental harm requires either that the harm

Figure 3.   A Scheme for Types of Harm

Physical Harm			Virtual Harm		
	Direct	Indirect		Direct	Indirect
Intentional			Intentional		
Negligent			Negligent		
Accidental			Accidental		

not have been foreseeable by the harm-doer or that it be unavoidable. In addition to this threefold distinction, the case we are addressing suggests a difference between direct and indirect harm. Direct harm is the result of the action or omission of the person. Indirect harm requires mediation through some third party or entity. For instance, I might kick my neighbor's dog as a way of insulting my neighbor. The table in Figure 3 represents the possibilities just discussed.

Combining Physical and Virtual Harm

Combining virtual and physical harm produces complex cases. If a virtual character C1 abuses a virtual character C2 and F2 takes offense, the harm to F2 is indirect but physical (a flesh person has taken offense). If F1 intended to offend F2 by abusing C2, then the harm is intentional. Note that we are using "physical" to distinguish the harm from "virtual." The "physical" harm might be described as psychological or emotional, but we use the word physical for all these harms if they are done to a flesh person. (It is interesting to note that this sort of case can take place outside of virtual reality. Suppose that F1 publicly spits on a picture of F2's mother to insult and infuriate F2.)

Now let us consider complexities. What if the controller of virtual character C1 is a program? Assume that C1 is controlled by P1, a program developed by F1, a flesh-and-blood system designer. If, as above, F2 takes offense at an action of the programmed C1, then the harm is indirect (mediated both by the program and by the abuse of C2). But perhaps F1 didn't know that the programmed behavior would be offensive to F2; or perhaps F1 made a programming error; or perhaps F1 programmed P1 with a random pattern of behavior that happened to produce something offensive to F2. To evaluate any of these possibilities requires us to analyze how a reasonable person might have been able to foresee the harm. In the latter case of programmed control, it would seem that a standard of the "reasonable programmer" is called for, a specification of what a reasonable programming expert could foresee and control about the likely effects of a program on users and participants.

But indirect harm does not have to be mediated by a program that controls a virtual character. The interface for the LamdaMOO is itself a program, and the program structures the interactions of the characters. The design and implementation of the interface has consequences for the virtual characters and for the entities that control virtual characters. For example, the interface (and the "wizards" who develop and control the interface) may allow or exclude characters and/or their controllers from the MOO. The interface can "change the rules" for virtual characters and/or their controllers. Much of the behavior of the interface in this respect will be intentional. The designers will have taken forethought and planned to structure the interactions in a certain way. But any reasonably complex program (and even some simple ones) can produce behavior that the designer did not intend, but might have (or might not have) foreseen.

Harms in the Bungle Case

Now let us return to the details of the Bungle case. Because the flesh controller of Bungle broke into the system controlling the parameters of the game, the system designer(s) and the wizard do not, on the face of it, seem blameworthy. On the other hand, they both had responsibilities that might have been ignored. For both there is the issue of security and whether security was adequate to prevent simple attempts at breaking in and seizing control. In the case of the wizard there is also the issue of whether the rules of the MUD were adequately promulgated. While these are issues to be raised, the fact that the flesh controller of Bungle broke in points to his/her blameworthiness. It seems reasonably foreseeable that participants would not want to be exposed to the level of violence this break-in caused since the MUD had been in existence for awhile and that level of violence had not occurred.

An important aspect of the Bungle case is the way Bungle's actions illustrate the layers of meaning in the MUD. For convenience, we will call Bungle's (apparently anonymous) controller F-Bungle (for Flesh Bungle). F-Bungle controls C-Bungle. But, using the Voodoo doll subprogram, C-Bungle controls C-Legba and C-Starsinger. Note that this adds a new layer of mediation: F-Bungle controls C-Bungle who in turn (through the subprogram) controls C-Legba and C-Starsinger. The controllers of C-Legba and C-Starsinger ("F-Legba and F-Starsinger") took offense and, seeing past the multiple layers of mediation, are rightly furious with F-Bungle. Despite the protestations of F-Legba and F-Starsinger, the majority of the MOO's participants did not favor any action that extended beyond the virtual world of the MOO. And after C-Bungle was removed ("toaded" is the term used in the MOO), it was generally believed that F-Bungle created a new character, Dr. Jest, who then joined the MOO.

Physical Harm and Virtual Space

The harms in the Bungle incident were both virtual and physical (using our definition of these terms). The physical harms are somewhat easier to understand. F-Legba and F-Starsinger felt violated, angry and agitated. Other

MOO participants were also upset about the incident and the ensuing contro-versy. Dibbel's article goes to some lengths to explain how flesh controllers become intensely involved in a MOO's virtual reality and personally invested in and identified with the character(s) they play. The more invested a flesh controller, the more damaging virtual violence can be. It may be that F-Bungle was also upset about C-Bungle being toaded, although his distress would probably have been mitigated by the fact that F-Bungle could reenter the MOO as a slightly different character.

The difference in intensity of feeling between F-Bungle and F-Bungle's victims is not an unusual thing in the world of sexual assault. In most cases of sexual assault, and most particularly in cases of date-rape, the victims see the incident as highly important, even life-changing, and the harm as intense. Perpetrators, on the other hand, minimize the offense, even to the point of forgetting it (see Baumeister & Tice, 2000, Chapter 9). There seems to be evidence that, in perpetrators, this effect is partly produced by a lack of empathy for the victim: sexual offenders are titillated equally alike by violent and nonviolent pornography and the sufferings of the victims do not reduce their arousal (Baumeister & Tice, 2000, Chapter 9).

But in the Bungle case we have an additional factor that may enhance this discrepancy: virtuality. The harm is done in a virtual environment in which individuals are never in the physical presence of each other. Research by Kiesler et al. (1984) suggests that this virtuality may make it harder for participants to understand each other, to have empathy for each other, or to come to mutual agreement. The research demonstrates that the effect is produced because the audience of one's communications is not as salient, not as three dimensional, not as "present" as in a face-to-face interaction. This attenuation of social impact would make it even more unlikely that the perpetrator would feel empathy for the victim, thereby increasing the gulf in perception of the crime. Thus, there appears to be a likelihood that virtual interaction reduces the social influence needed to control the behavior of people like F-Bungle. This will make it harder for virtual societies to come to agreement on the nature and extent of any physical harm that their members may suffer.

Virtual Harm and Virtual Space

Leaving their flesh controllers out of the picture for the moment, it appears that C-Bungle harmed C-Legba and C-Starsinger by controlling them against their will, a clear violation of autonomy. When in control, C-Bungle had the two virtual characters perform sexual acts. In this instance, the addition of sexual acts is likely an attempt to further degrade the individuals and emphasize C-Bungle's power, rather than being about sex per se. (See Palmer, 1988; Baumeister & Tice, 2000 for reviews of the empirical work on whether rape in the real world is about power or sex. Both conclude that rape is about sex, obtained by means of force if necessary.)

But can we leave their flesh controllers out of the picture and still feel as though a harm has occurred? This seems at least problematic. Imagine two virtual robots that were programmed by means of neural net techniques. We suggest this indirect technique to minimize the connection of the program/robot with any real creator. If we observed one of these agents attempt to disable the other, would we be justified in claiming that any harm had occurred? This question of harm is separate from (and possibly prior to) the question of blame. What might harm mean in this case? Must harm occur to a flesh human in order for us to credit it?

We do at least include other animals in the category of things that can be harmed. Beauty product manufacturers have now taken to printing: "This product was tested without harming any animals." We occasionally speak of "the environment" as something that could be harmed. In doing so, we mean that its pattern, development, or integrity might be diminished or interfered with. This may well cause harm to humans in turn, but we do occasionally speak as though the harm to the environment will occur without it being necessary to trace this back to harm for humans. Thus, we can tentatively think of harm as occurring when the integrity, wholeness, capacity, or goal of an entity is interfered with or diminished. This sort of harm brings with it decidedly less moral baggage than harm against humans. It is a description of a change in state that is thought of as a diminishment. At least in this nonmoral sense, we can speak of virtual entities being harmed.

If one has a dedication to this sort of wholeness, one could then attach a moral sense to this diminishment-harm. One might even incorporate in this approach a special status for living entities and more particularly for humans. So we now at least have an understanding of harm (called diminishment-harm) that could apply to our virtual entities with moral force. But we have only accomplished this by imbuing the non-virtual world (including trees and rocks) with an ability to be harmed in some moral sense. This sense of harm is not, then, peculiarly virtual. But this sense of harm does allow us to imagine a morally-loaded virtual harm occurring without connections to flesh humans.

LESSONS TO BE LEARNED
FROM THE BUNGLE CASE

We have been sorting out and analyzing the Bungle case in order to see what we might learn about the moral nature of actions and interactions in virtual reality environments. While the analysis is still quite preliminary, we can begin to draw some conclusions.

1.   Virtual behavior can have real psychological and physical consequences. Therefore, the controllers of virtual characters have responsibilities for those consequences. These responsibilities are similar to those that real people have when they interact with other real people in other contexts. In real interactions, responsibilities vary with context (from a poetry reading to a stock exchange to love-making). Responsibilities in virtual environments will also vary with the context.

We might speculate that virtual contexts will vary more than real environments because the medium allows for a wider range of features while the physical world limits the possibilities of real world interactions, e.g., I can't fly in the real world but I can in some virtual environments. However, we are not yet sure this is true. Virtual interactions are always representational and this may limit the types or range of responsibilities. The second lesson begins to generalize about responsibilities in virtual environments.

2.   The flesh controllers of virtual characters are generally unknown (or can be unknown) to the flesh controllers of other virtual characters and this affects the nature of responsibility in virtual environments. On the one hand, flesh controllers must play out their responsibilities through the actions of their virtual characters. At the same time, their ability to anticipate the reactions of the flesh controllers of other virtual characters is diminished. That is, the virtual nature of the interaction makes it more difficult for players to anticipate and recognize the consequences that may result from manipulations of their virtual characters.

This makes it important to have rules specifying the range of behaviors that are and are not allowable in a virtual environment. This is precisely what LamdaMOO participants tried to do after the Bungle incident.

3.   The developers and controllers of a virtual environment interface, as well as the developer of an automated player, have responsibilities to the flesh controllers of virtual characters. The software that controls the virtual world and virtual characters shapes the environment and determines the possibilities for consequences to virtual characters as well as indirectly to the flesh-and-blood participants in the virtual environment. Again, the virtual nature of the immediate effects of the software does not remove responsibility for consequences to people, indirect though they may be.

The responsibilities of software developers and wizards (controllers of virtual environments) are not limited to avoiding intentional harm-doing, for this would mean no responsibility at all. Rather, the responsibilities of software developers and wizards have to be thought of in terms of reasonably foreseeable consequences. This extension of the responsibility of a virtual designer is based on the recognition that the designer has power (however unintentional) over those who use the interface (see Huff, 1997 for a discussion of unintentional power in software design). This might mean, for instance, that designers of virtual systems ought to take into account the diminished social impact of virtual actions, and in response should design systems that enhance social impact and social control. The goal would be to make the virtual reality more *socially* real, and this may not require giving it more of a semblance to physical reality.

4.   If justice is to be a goal in computer-mediated environments, then rules should be explicit. When freedom becomes license, harm is more likely to occur. The idea that a virtual environment is "without rules" is false and misleading. Computer-mediated environments always have rules, if none other than the software that runs the interface. Software is "hard" and physical in the sense that it allows and disallows behavior of various kinds. The software grants rights and privileges to different virtual and flesh participants.

By insisting that rules be explicit, the role of the interface is made immediately clear and other rules, not enforced by the interface itself, can also be made explicit. These "extra-interface" rules have to be enforced in a different manner than the rules that are automatically enforced by the interface. Of course, not all rules can be made explicit without an interminable listing. But the fact that physical harm to real individuals can occur should make us aware of the need to more carefully specify conventions of behavior.

5.   Virtual harm seems insignificant on its own, without connecting it to some real-world understanding of harm. This connection is most easily made through analogy to real-world physical harm. Even our attempt to come up with a "diminishment harm" that would hold in virtual reality required an analogy to harm to the environment, and was thereby anchored in real world harm.

Therefore, the language of "virtuality" is misleading. It suggests that what we do in virtual environments is "almost but not fully" real. But we can see how physical harm is the paradigm case of harm, and that virtual harm depends on physical harm for its effects.

VIRTUAL SEX

Let us now take these lessons and see how they apply to virtual sex, for one of the reasons the Bungle case is so provocative is that it suggests something like virtual sex. We define "virtual sex" as computer-mediated-communication with the intentional, explicit purpose of sexual satisfaction of at least one flesh person. This definition includes a range of possibilities that involve text-based MOO exchanges, chat room exchanges, and Internet pictures and movies. It also includes more elaborate mechanical devices controlled by computers for human sexual gratification. As with the MOO described above, participants could be flesh or automated. Our definition only requires that at least one participant be flesh.

Generally it seems plausible to begin with the idea that if a flesh person is "coerced" into virtual sex, there is harm. The harm is a combination of the coercion and the exposure to sexual content. The responsibility for the harm belongs to the entity that coerces the encounter. If a flesh controller's character sexually assaults a virtual character that is controlled by a program, the matter is less direct. Presumably software that enables this kind of encounter was programmed in order to facilitate this acting out by the flesh controller. (We can devise situations that violate this presumption, but they would be exceptions that prove the rule.) If software is designed to allow the flesh controller to commit these virtual acts, then the software developer shouldn't take offense when the software is used "as intended." Thus, we do not see an indirect physical harm to the software developer.

However, the software that enables the assault, and the flesh participant who initiates the assault, still can do harm. The effects of encouraging the rehearsal of sexual assault may encourage the act to be repeated in the physical world. If that is a consequence of the virtual act, or if it is likely to be a consequence, then the software developer (and marketer, etc.) are responsible for a harm to the flesh person attacked, and to a society threatened by such attacks. However, some believe that allowing people to act out such an attack virtually will help these people avoid committing an attack in the physical world. If that can be demonstrated, then there is good in making this software available to such a person, perhaps by prescription. The crux of the ethical argument would again be empirical: trying to determine which of the consequences is more likely, increase or decrease of sexual attacks. The empirical literature on the effects of violent video games (discussed in more detail later) makes it clear that, on average, we should expect more violence when video games (and likely, virtual reality games) allow individuals to practice virtual violence.

There is also an argument that despite any possible benign or beneficial effects of such software, that there is a harm to people who are offended and threatened by the existence and use of such software. Since a physical assault is surely a harm, the argument goes, then the assault's virtual "shadow" is a glorification of that harm. In a culture like the U.S. in which free expression is highly valued, it is unlikely that this second argument will hold sway.

A different situation is consensual virtual sex, either between two flesh participants or between a flesh participant and an automated partner. Is there harm in this kind of encounter? Presuming that the physical act being simulated virtually is considered benign or beneficial, then the potential harm of rehearsing an attack is no longer an issue. Indeed one could argue that the benefits of rehearsing sexual encounters be considered healthy. But there is another, more subtle possibility of harm. If some flesh participants find that virtual sex is a substitute for, rather than a rehearsal for physical encounters with physical humans, then the encouragement of virtual sex may diminish healthy sex between humans. At least some would consider this a harm to individuals and to the society as a whole.

A pattern seems to emerge in our discussion of virtual sex. If the virtual encounter replaces a harmful physical encounter, then the virtual encounter is good. If the virtual encounter replaces a beneficial physical encounter, then a harm to humans results. If the virtual encounter encourages healthy physical encounters, then the virtual encounter is good. If the virtual encounter encourages harmful physical encounters, then the virtual encounter is harmful. In this way, then, we see all decisions about virtual sex will derive from decisions about physical harms or benefits. Although people differ in their opinions of the goodness of some physical acts (for example, homosexual sex), there is far more consensus on other encounters (such as rape). When the issue is which consequences will result, that question is best considered empirically.

FIRST PERSON SHOOTER GAMES

Separate from the sexual aspects of the Bungle case, we can also focus on the violent nature of Bungle's act. Computer-mediated violence is big business. At least one estimate suggests that interactive computer games are a 6.5 billion dollar per year business (Digital Media Wire, 2001), and many of these games feature violence. The most prevalent kind of violence in these games is controlled by a single flesh player against virtual characters in a stand-alone game. Another popular variation is played online, where teams of virtual characters, controlled by multiple flesh controllers distributed over the Internet, battle other virtual characters with flesh controllers, or against virtual characters controlled by the game, or against both.

The analyses in previous sections are largely appropriate for computer games that encourage players to rehearse violent acts. As in the case of virtual sex acts, if the virtual acts *replace* acts physically harmful to humans, then the games may be beneficial. If the virtual acts *encourage* physically harmful acts, then the games themselves are harmful. In the world of games, especially those sold chiefly to children, responsibility falls chiefly on those who put the games into the hands of minors. This includes the game developers, distributors and the children's parents.

If it can be determined empirically that violent video games have largely detrimental effects, then there is clear harm done. The empirical literature on the effect of violent video games on aggression has been reviewed carefully by Anderson and Bushman (2001). Their meta-analysis of the research shows that "exposure to violent video games increases aggressive behavior in children and young adults." This review of 35 research reports (including 54 independent samples of subjects) makes it clear that this effect of increased aggression is produced by an increase in what the researchers call "aggressive cognition": thoughts, daydreams, story scripts, and mental reactions to provocation. The studies were a mixture of experimental and field research, with the experimental work showing clear causal links between video game violence and aggression, and the field studies showing that this effect occurs "in the real world." Thus, rehearsing aggressive action in violent video games increases the likelihood that people will aggress in the physical world.

Note that the social context of a game and the sensory bandwidth of its implementation may be significant here. A computer game that simulates skeet shooting seems ethically distinct from a computer game that simulates killing realistic renderings of identifiable human beings. The strong offense taken by LambdaMOO participants was based on actions described in a textual interface. If Bungle's aggressive actions had been displayed in realistic interactive graphics, might the offense have been stronger? How would the LambdaMOO community have reacted if Bungle had captured those scenes on the Internet for public consumption?

Virtual characters controlled by a stand-alone game and flesh controllers in a violent game distributed over the Internet are present expressly to participate in violence. This is a major difference from the Bungle incident. The virtual harms to characters are expected in violent computer games. The indirect physical harms to the participants, such as psychological damage, are probably not visible to human players that "volunteer" for the games. If a participant harms another human in part due to the rehearsal of violent acts, then the human hurt is unlikely to realize the part played by the game. This lack of awareness of the game's effects is another aspect different from the Bungle case, in which the LambdaMOO environment was a factor obvious to all the participants.

CONCLUSION

This is a preliminary sort of the ethical and metaphysical issues arising from the Bungle case and in general from virtual reality environments. The lessons we have teased out of the case seem promising, though there is still further analysis to be done. Perhaps the most important lesson is the first and that is that virtual actions and interactions have consequences for flesh-and-blood persons and hence, the flesh controllers of virtual actions, whether they control directly (as in playing a character) or indirectly (even by designing the virtual world), have responsibilities for their actions.

REFERENCES

Anderson, C.A. & Bushman, B. (2001). Effects of violent video games on aggressive behavior, aggressive cognition, aggressive affect, physiological arousal, and pro-social behavior: A meta-analytic review of the scientific literature. *Psychological Science, 12,* 353-359.

Anderson, C.A. & Dill, K.E. (2000). Video games and aggressive thoughts, feelings, and behavior in the laboratory and in life. *Journal of Personality & Social Psychology, 78,* 772-790.

Baumeister, R. F. & Tice, D. M. (2001). *The Social Dimension of Sex.* Boston, MA: Allyn & Bacon.

Churchland, P. M. (1996). *The Engine of Reason, the Seat of the Soul.* Cambridge, MA: MIT Press.

Digital Media Wire (2001). Interactive games on the Internet: An industry poised for the future. Panel. Retrieved Nov. 5, 2001 from the World Wide Web: http://www.digitalmediawire.com/DCgames.html.

Dill, K.E. & Dill, J.C. (1998). Video game violence: A review of the empirical literature. *Aggression & Violent Behavior, 3,* 407-428.

Friedman, B. & Millett, L. (1995). It's the computer's fault: Reasoning about computers as moral agents. Retrieved Nov. 5, 2001 from *SIGCHI 1995* on the World Wide Web: http://www.acm.org/sigs/sigchi/chi95/Electronic/documnts/shortppr/bf2_bdy.htm.

Griffiths, M. (1999). Violent video games and aggression: A review of the literature. *Aggression & Violent Behavior, 4,* 203-212.

Harré, R. (1986). *Varieties of Realism: A Rationale for the Natural Sciences.* Oxford: Basil Blackwell.

Harré, R. & Secord, P.F. (1972) *The Explanation of Social Behaviour.* Totowa, NJ: Rowman and Littlefield.

Hart, H.L.A. & Honoré, A.M. (1959). *Causation in the Law.* London: Oxford University Press.

Huff, C.W. (1997). Unintentional power in the design of computing systems. In S. Rogerson & T.W. Bynam (Eds.), *Information Ethics: A Reader.* London: Basil Blackwell.

Johnson, D. (2001). *Computer Ethics* (2nd ed). Upper Saddle River, NJ: Prentice Hall.

Kiesler, S., Seigel, J., & McGuire, T.W. (1984). Social and psychological aspects of computer-mediated communication. *American Psychologist, 39,* 1123-34.

Lessig, L. (1999). *CODE and Other Laws of Cyberspace.* New York: Basic Books.

Palmer, C. T. (1988). Twelve reasons why rape is not sexually motivated: A skeptical examination. *Journal of Sex Research, 25*, 512-530.
Turkle, S. (1996). *Life on the Screen.* London: Orion Books Ltd.

ENDNOTE

*   This is a revised version of a paper that appeared in Technology and Society Magazine, Volume 22, Number 2, Summer, 2003.

Section II

Ethical Implications

Chapter VII

Ethical Challenges for Information Systems Professionals

Gerald M. Hoffman
Northwestern University, USA

ABSTRACT

This chapter examines the special ethical responsibilities of information systems professionals based on the fundamentals of ethics as commonly understood in the Western world. We start first with principles from religious texts and the codes of ethics included in them. We then examine codes of conduct promulgated by nonreligious institutions. We conclude that ethics is personal, situational and changes over time. Thus, it impossible to formulate codes of conduct that apply to all real life situations. We identify the special ethical responsibilities that information systems professionals face in their roles as custodians of information technology, as custodians of the information systems that use this technology and as custodians of the data and information that surround information systems. The situations we face from day-to-day as we deal with the ethical aspects of information systems will always require us to decide between ethical imperatives that are in conflict with one another.

INTRODUCTION

This chapter is written primarily for information technology (IT) professionals, including everyone from a chief information officer (CIO) to a data base administrator to a junior programmer. But it also applies to a much larger audience. In today's environment of desktop computing with ubiquitous access to the Internet and to private networks, every business executive and every working professional in every field performs some of the functions of an IT professional from time to time. The issues, guidelines, imperatives and strictures developed here apply to everyone who uses or controls information systems, regardless of primary occupation or job title.

A journey through several dictionaries finds that the term "ethics" refers to morals, standards of conduct, differences between right and wrong, and other similar constructs. The Oxford English Dictionary defines ethics as: "[t]he science of morals, the department of study concerned with human duty." Ethics is about the behavior of people doing their duty, doing things that are sometimes difficult, unpleasant or unrewarding. We take this as the starting point of our discussion.

A good deal of the confusion surrounding discussions of ethics lies in not making a clear distinction between law and ethics—between the illegal and the unethical. The two concepts overlap but are different in important ways. The law identifies certain types of behavior of which society disapproves and attempts to prevent by an orderly and consistent set of rules and punishments. Ethics is at once more personal and more general, dealing with right and wrong beyond what the law sanctions. Every unethical act is not an illegal act and every illegal act is not necessarily unethical. And, as we shall argue below, ethical standards change over time, which is one reason why we amend our laws from time to time.

For the purposes of this paper, we assume *a priori* that all illegal acts are unethical. An individual may feel on occasion that a particular law is wrong and that violating it is ethically permissible, or even compulsory. A potential whistle blower often finds himself in this position. He is ethically required to serve the interests of his employer, yet he feels that his employer is violating some law or ethical principle with respect to the community at large. The whistle blower must make the hard choice of which imperative to honor. This is a small example of the larger issue of Gandhian civil disobedience:

[Mohandas Gandhi, leader of the movement for the independence of India from Great Britain, developed the tactic of civil disobedience (massive non-violent protests) that ultimately forced the British to leave. In our terms, his actions (blocking streets, massive but quiet marches, etc.) were illegal but were by his standards ethical in that they were undertaken for the greater

good of national independence (Encyclopedia Britannica Micropedia 4). This is an issue much too large for this chapter. We leave it to others.]

In this chapter, we pose these questions: From the point of view of ethics—of right and wrong—what behavior can be reasonably expected of an IT professional by society, by his employer, by his staff, by himself? And what behavior should the IT professional expect of others?

We attempt to provide some answers to these and related questions by:

- Setting forth broad ethical principles that can guide all IT professionals.
- Identifying the special characteristics of information technology that generate ethical issues unique to IT.
- Recommending specific responses to these issues.

As we address these topics, we examine several collateral issues:

- Is ethics personal? Is it appropriate for two different individuals facing the same issue to reach different conclusions?
- Is ethics situational? Does the proper ethical response to a particular problem depend on the context in which the problem arises?
- Is ethics changeable? Might an action that was ethical yesterday be unethical today?

We begin with the basic statements of ethical principles that have guided mankind since before the beginning of recorded history. We move from these principles to specific directives and actions designed to help all people lead an ethical life. We then address the responsibilities of professionals in general, and finally, we apply what we have learned to the special problems faced by information technology professionals.

This structure is analogous to the common business planning structure consisting of goals (what we want to be), strategies (coherent sets of activities we plan to undertake in order to achieve our goals), and tactics (specific actions we will take in the immediate future).

WHY WE ARE
CONCERNED ABOUT ETHICS

At one level of awareness, ethics has been a preoccupation of mankind since the beginnings of civilization. Having an accepted ethical structure is an absolute necessity for any civilization to exist and may indeed be the definition of civilization. Our interactions with our fellow beings are based on the often unspoken assumption that most people "do the right thing" most of the time.

Somehow, this seems less true today than it was a few years ago, which is one of the motivations for the creation of this book.

Our concern about ethical issues has been heightened by a number of recent developments. These include:

- The current climate of scandal and public distrust that surrounds almost every institution in our society.
- Luddite fears of technology, cast as an ethical issue by those who prefer that we all regress to a pre-industrial society, or at least stop further economic development.

(The Luddites were bands of English handicraftsmen whose jobs were being displaced by machines, notably the power loom. In 1811-1812 they rioted and destroyed many looms in the vain hope that they could turn back the clock to a time of hand work [Encyclopedia Britannica Micropedia 6].)

- Genuinely new problems and issues raised by increasing capabilities of information technology and its increasing importance in our lives.

ETHICAL GOALS

We begin with a brief look at the great religions that have provided the ethical foundations for our societies. The goal of all of these religions is the same: to help each individual be an ethical human being, which at its religious core always means obedience to God. Here are some of the religious/ethical imperatives familiar to most of us.

- *Jesus:* "Do unto others as you would have them do unto you."
- *Hillel, Jewish scholar and teacher in the first century of the common era:* "Do not do unto another that which you would find hateful if done to you."
- *Mohammed:* "None of you truly believes until he wishes for himself what he wishes for his brother."

We limit our discussion to the Judeo/Christian cultures because these are the cultures in which information technology has arisen, and hence which are the locus of most of the ethical issues faced by IT professionals. Having said this, we note the rising numbers of IT professionals in India, China and Japan. These people come from different religious and cultural traditions. Will their ethical stance in IT be different from that of people of the west? In the short term, probably not: they are entering a large and well-established IT culture with which they will initially conform. We cited Mohammed above to suggest that these issues may not be very different in other cultures, even in the long term. But who knows?

We do not discuss the rich tradition of nonreligious ethical philosophy from 18th and 19th century Europe and America because although the goals are cast in different terms, the imperatives—the codes of ethics—are basically the same as those stemming from Western religious tradition.

CODES OF ETHICS

Codes of Ethics are strategies for achieving ethical goals. They can be divided into categories in terms of who promulgates them.

- Religious codes of conduct directed toward individual behavior. The Ten Commandments are the familiar example.
- Professional codes of conduct created by professional societies such as the American Bar Association, the American Medical Association, and the Association for Computing Machinery.
- Organizational codes, created by individual companies or organizations to govern their own organizational activities.

There are literally thousands of these and more are appearing daily. We will discuss a few representative examples.

1. To begin at (or near) the beginning, let us consider the Ten Commandments and the Scriptures that elaborate them. Each Commandment in itself seems clear, to the point and a useful guide to good behavior. But note the contradictions. "Thou shalt not kill" is hard to dispute, but how does it square with "an eye for an eye" in the event of a murder? How does it square with fighting a war, which every religion in history has done? "Keep holy the Sabbath" is interpreted by Orthodox Jews to mean doing no work whatsoever on the Sabbath, not even lighting a fire to cook or to keep the house warm. But these same Orthodox Jews allow physicians to do their healing work on the Sabbath as on any other day.

Observation: Religious teachings are often internally inconsistent. Picking the right Commandment to follow depends on the circumstances. Ethics is indeed situational.

2. An early example of ethical standards in the professions comes from Hippocrates (460-377 B.C.) Here is the Hippocratic oath in full (Bartlett, 1995):

"I swear by Apollo Physician, by Asclepius, by Health, by Panacea, and by all the gods and goddesses, making them my witnesses, that I will carry out, according to my ability and judgment, this oath and this indenture. To hold my teacher in this art equal to my own parents; to make him partner in my livelihood; when he is in need of money to share mine with him; to consider his family as my own brothers, and to teach them this art, if they want to learn it, without fee or indenture. I will use treatment to help the sick according to my ability and judgment, but never with a view to injury and wrongdoing. I will keep pure and holy both my life and my art. In whatsoever houses I enter, I will enter to help the sick, and I will abstain from all intentional wrongdoing and harm. And whatsoever I shall see or hear in the course of my profession in my intercourse with men, if it be what should not be published abroad, I will never divulge, holding such things to be holy secrets. Now if I carry out this oath, and break it not, may I gain forever reputation among all men for my life and for my art; but if I transgress it and forswear myself, may the opposite befall me."

The second sentence is extremely self-serving on the part of the physician-teacher; it seems to be largely lost from practice. Other parts of the oath have survived virtually intact for 2,500 years.

Observation: Codes of ethics sometimes include injunctions designed more to serve the interests of the authors of the codes than to influence behavior toward ethical actions.

3.   The American Psychoanalytic Association (APA) recently published an Ethics Case Book (Dewald & Clark, 2001) containing a statement of broad ethical principles and standards and a large number of case vignettes, each illustrating one or more of the principles. The principles are:

- Professional Competence
- Respect for Persons
- Mutuality and Informed Consent
- Confidentiality
- Truthfulness
- Avoidance of Exploitation
- Scientific Responsibility
- Protection of the Public and the Profession
- Social Responsibility
- Personal Integrity

These principles are spelled out in considerable detail in 15 pages of text. Yet the authors felt compelled to provide 104 pages of examples elaborating the principles. This should in no way be taken as a denigration of this work. Rather, it bespeaks the difficulty of applying sometimes conflicting ethical principles to real situations.

Observation: There is a recurring theme in the examples: an emphasis on consultation with others, who will be objective but who may not know anything more about the ethics of the situation than does the physician with the problem. The assumption is that a third party with no direct interest in the issue at hand may provide a different and useful perspective on the problem.

4.   The Association for Computing Machinery (ACM) has a set of ethical imperatives called its Canons of Ethics. These can be summarized as follows:

•   Canon 1: Integrity. This canon mandates that a member of the ACM shall not pretend expertise he does not have, shall acknowledge any partisan position he takes, and shall faithfully serve his employer.

•   Canon 2: Increase Knowledge. Members are required to increase their own knowledge of the field and the knowledge of the profession as a whole.

•   Canon 3: Accept Responsibility. Members shall take responsibility for their work both in the acceptance of assignments and in their execution.

•   Canon 4: Act With Professional Responsibility. A member should participate in setting professional standards, and shall not misrepresent his status in the organization.

•   Canon 5: Use of Skills for the Public Good. A member shall take account of the general welfare of the public as he does his work, with emphasis on data privacy, security and integrity.

Weiss (1990) has written a "Self Assessment" designed to help the members of ACM understand these issues. He states, "This procedure in not intended to change your ethical values, but to assist you in clarifying and applying them in the new, complex situations in your professional career." As with the American Psychoanalytic Society, it relies heavily on cases, which it calls "scenarios." And as with the American Psychoanalytic Society, the scenarios are focused on identifying and resolving the ambiguities and contradictions among various ethical standards.

We now have answers to the three questions posed earlier in this chapter.

•   Yes, ethics is personal. The three religious statements of ethical goals we discussed are all cast in terms of the individual: "Treat others as you would be treated" implies that personal values determine ethical judgments. These values are formed from a mix of religion, upbringing, culture, personal experiences and perhaps genes. Given the complexity of these influences, it is likely that no two people in the world have exactly the same ethical standards.

- Yes, ethics is situational. The resolution of conflicting ethical mandates requires compromises that always depend on the context of the issue. Thou shalt not kill, except in war. Keep holy the Sabbath, but continue to treat the sick.
- Yes, ethics is changeable over time. Practices concerning personal data that were once so routine that they were never viewed as ethical issues are now at the center of serious ethical controversies. On a more mundane level, personal use of company e-mail systems is so prevalent that some companies have simply bowed to the inevitable and given permission for this use. The ethics of personal use of company property (e-mail systems) are changing.

Broad ethical goals, such as those of Jesus, Hillel and Mohammed, are essential as guideposts to ethical actions. However, specific codes of ethics are often not useful as direct guides to action because of their (I suspect) inevitable internal inconsistencies. They are most useful as clear starting points from which to explore the consequences of proposed actions and decisions. The cases in the APA Ethics Case Book and the scenarios in the ACM Self Assessment provide excellent examples of ways to use a code of ethics to analyze real world ethical problems in terms of first principles.

Returning to the earlier analogy with business planning, we often see similar situations in business. A broad business goal, say "increase market share," is defined and widely accepted. Strategies are contrived to support that goal. One might be opening an Internet based marketing channel; another might be decreasing costs. Individually, each is a good idea, but they are mutually contradictory: building the new marketing channel is certain to increase costs, interfering with the strategy of decreasing costs. The business response is necessarily a compromise, not dissimilar to ethical compromises we have noted above.

UNIQUE ETHICAL PROBLEMS OF INFORMATION TECHNOLOGY PROFESSIONALS

We now turn to the ethical problems unique to IT professionals. They of course are bound by all the general ethical principles that govern our society at large as well as the general ethical standards governing the learned professions.

But there are areas where IT professionals have additional ethical responsibilities because of the history and the role of information technology in our society. We list them here and discuss them in detail below.

- Certain of the general ethical responsibilities of professionals are more important for IT professionals than for others.
- IT professionals are the custodians of information technology itself.
- IT professionals are the custodians of information systems.
- IT professionals are custodians of the data and information that surround information systems.

All professionals have the obligation to use their skills and knowledge for the benefit of their clients/patients/users, as well as for the benefit of the general public. This obligation is more important in IT than in many other professions because the users of information technology are less likely to understand IT than they are to understand other professions such as architecture and accounting. In addition, the relationships between users and IT professionals is less well defined than users' relationships with other professionals.

These ambiguities present IT professionals with opportunities and temptations to abuse their professional knowledge and the respect that it engenders in the user community. It is not unheard of for a CIO in a large decentralized organization to try to gain personal control over all of the information technology in the organization by claiming that the technology requires centralization, even when this is not true.

The ethical obligation of the IT professional is to put organizational benefits above personal agenda, and to argue his personal agenda openly without using his technical expertise as camouflage.

IT makes theft and unauthorized distribution of intellectual property both easy and inexpensive. IT professionals typically have custody of the information technology in an organization and therefore can exert some control of the uses to which it is put.

- Napster was a site on the Internet that made it extremely easy and inexpensive to copy songs. It provided a central directory service that enabled its users to find songs on one another's computers, and it provided software that enabled them to copy the songs without paying any fees or royalties to the owners of the copyrights. The courts decided that this was a violation of copyright law and forced Napster to shut down. Other sites are now offering similar capabilities but without the central directory service. These too are probably illegal, but they will be much more difficult to shut down because they do not have central directories.
- Unauthorized copying of computer programs is an ongoing problem to companies using purchased software as well as to the vendors. Sometimes

this copying is done to save money or to circumvent company purchasing policies. Quite often, it is done by an individual who is attempting to help his employer complete a project without the delay of going through a lengthy procurement process, with little thought about the ethical issue involved.

- Use of company information technology assets for personal purposes is easy to do and hard to detect.

The ethical obligations of the IT professional are to monitor what is happening, to control it where possible, and to report it to higher authority when it cannot be adequately controlled.

IT professionals have custody of the information systems that run the company. They build or otherwise acquire these systems, and they operate them on behalf of the company. These systems define the business processes of the company. In theory, the design of these systems is a joint effort between the IT professionals and the users of the systems. In practice, the IT professionals often have a controlling role.

The ethical obligations of the IT professionals in the design and implementation of an information system include:

- Assuring that the system reflects the business needs as seen by the user, not as seen by the IT professional.
- Assuring that the system meets the invisible requirements often not seen by the user/designer. These include auditability, security and disaster recovery, among others.
- Selecting a technology platform for the new system that strikes a fair balance between the needs of the user and the overall needs of the enterprise, suppressing any personal preference to use a new and exciting technology.

The IT professional faces a number of ethical issues in his role as custodian of data and information. This is the area in which he is most likely to encounter a direct conflict between his own ethical standards and the needs and desires of his users.

- Insuring that the personal privacy of customers, suppliers and others is not compromised by misuse of data collected during the normal course of business.
- Insuring the personal privacy of company employees.
- Insuring that company assets, integrity and reputation are not compromised by unauthorized dissemination of information.

The ethical standards for privacy of personal data have been evolving and will continue to change as database and data mining technologies become more powerful. The ethical standard that seems to be evolving is to use customer data only for the purpose for which it was collected unless the customer gives permission for further use. This seems to be appropriate. However, implementing this policy has often resulted in significant abuse. One abuse is to define "purpose of collection" so broadly as to be meaningless. For example, in the collection of medical data, the provider often demands, before providing care, permission to distribute the data to anyone involved in the health care system, including in some cases the patient's employer. The Health Information Portability and Accountability Act (HIPAA) attempts to deal with this in the realm of health care, but it is not yet clear how effective it will be.

It is tempting to believe that these issues can be handled technically, by passwords, access controls, and the whole panoply of IT security technologies and techniques. These things are clearly important—even essential—but they are only the means by which human beings enforce their intentions. If the intentions are unethical, technical means cannot prevent the unethical actions.

The ACM's Canon 5 adopts a position requiring minimum data collection, minimum access, provisions for data security, time limited data retention, and planned disposal of data no longer needed.

FUTURE TRENDS

The basic ethical imperatives (Jesus, Hillel, Mohammed, and others) will not change for a millennium or so, that being roughly the periodicity of such changes in human history.

Public concerns about personal safety and terrorism will converge in ways that will decrease the level of personal privacy of individuals that the public is willing to accept. Biometric identification systems such as facial recognition will make these intrusions less visible but they will be more pervasive. We are entering an uneasy period in which we will make many mistakes as we work out new ethical norms for privacy.

The concept of intellectual property will change in the direction of widening the actions considered fair use by the buyer of a periodical, a recording or a computer program. The vendors of music and software will build elaborate systems for copy protection. Some of these systems will work technically. All will fail in the marketplace. In the end, the owners of intellectual property will be able to command premium prices (substantially above the cost of reproduction) only by making the intellectual property a part of a larger service offering.

SUMMARY AND CONCLUSIONS

We have reviewed the great and enduring ethical principles that have guided mankind for at least 4,000 years, and some of the contemporary responses to them with respect to information technology.

IT professionals—as all professionals—have particular ethical issues associated with their profession. Their responses must be IT specific, but the principles that guide them must be the same as those that guide us all.

We have identified a number of IT-specific ethical issues that IT professionals are facing, and suggested guidelines for dealing with them.

We observe that although the technology will change, and the ethical issues will change, and therefore the ethical responses will change, the ethical principles underlying those responses will not change.

No Code of Ethics, no list of dos and don'ts, will ever provide an unambiguous answer to a serious ethical question. IT professionals must learn to reason from first principles to reach ethical decisions. Life is complex and people are imperfect. The best we can hope to do is make reasoned comprises among ethical mandates and get on with our lives.

Finally, let us turn to the question of ultimate conflict. What should an IT professional do if he cannot follow his own ethical standards because of the demands of his organization? He must act the same way as any other ethical citizen: resist, complain, go public. In the end, he must resign. Tough medicine, but who ever said life was fair?

REFERENCES

Bartlett, J. (1995). *Familiar Quotations* (13th and Centennial Ed). New York: Little Brown and Company.

Dewald, P. A. & Clark, R. W. (eds.) (2001). *Ethics Case Book of the American Psychoanalytic Association*. New York: American Psychoanalytic Association.

Encyclopedia Britannica (15th Ed). Micropaedia 4, 406-407.

Encyclopedia Britannica (15th Ed). Micropaedia 6, 375-376.

Weiss, E. A. (ed.) (1990). Self Assessment Procedure XXII. *Communications of the ACM, 33*(11), 110.

Chapter VIII

Living Within Glass Houses: Coping with Organizational Transparency

Victoria E. Johnson
Mercer University, USA

ABSTRACT

This chapter discusses the influence of technological systems on managing stakeholder relationships in the global environment. The information, immediacy and intimacy—the transparency—afforded by technological networks have transformed the nature and the strategic vantage point of these key relationships. Transparency is created and enhanced because of the public's capacity to know and its ability to navigate the technological terrain. The author argues that the modern prism of transparency can illuminate and enhance the sharing and disseminating of salient knowledge of communities of interest. Thus, the technological imperative and organizational transparency are complements in understanding and effectively responding to stakeholder environments.

INTRODUCTION

Two of the most significant socio-economic developments of the latter part of the 20th century are the dominance of complex corporations in, and the pervasive influence of technology on, almost every facet of modern life (Post, 2000). These trends have mandated more intense discussions and investigations of the relationship between society and big business in the global environment of the 21st century. Conceptions of this relationship have evolved and expanded over the past 50 years. Necessarily, however, the information, immediacy, and intimacy afforded by the technological superhighway have transformed not only the nature of the relationship, but also, the strategic vantage point from which that relationship is perceived. That vantage point can be illustrated by expanding the metaphors of glass ceilings and glass walls, which are used frequently in the management literature to describe and explain certain organizational structures and behaviors. In the modern, global environment, the metaphor of glass houses must be included. Technological sophistication has exponentially increased the nature and scope of organizational transparency, adding yet another complex layer to an already complicated relationship.

IN THE COMPANY OF STAKEHOLDERS

Historically, society has long expected organizations to recognize the rights of individuals and of other organizations. It also expects corporations to manage their assets and behaviors in an accountable manner. However, over the course of the past several decades, these expectations for responsibility and account-ability have increased unabated. Notwithstanding society's legitimate interest in the business/society relationship, the essence of that role—its nature and scope—remained elusive and temperamental. Some years ago, Preston and Post (1975) provided a useful framework for analyzing the partnership between corporations and their socio-political environment. This view contends that, "the very purpose of the firm is to serve as a vehicle for coordinating stakeholder interests" (Donaldson & Preston, 1995, pp. 102-103) and remains a prominent theoretical model for analyzing the nature and role of corporations within modern society.

Stakeholders are persons or groups that claim ownership rights or interests in a corporation and its activities. Primary stakeholders are market-driven participants whose continuing participation and support are vital to the firm's prosperity. Secondary stakeholders are groups who influence, or are influenced by, the corporation. Therefore, a central purpose of stakeholder theory has been to enable managers to understand their primary and secondary stakeholders and to strategically manage them. Freeman's (1984) *Strategic Management: A Stakeholder Approach* introduced stakeholder theory into mainstream management literature. As Freeman states, "The stakeholder approach is about groups and individuals who can affect the organization, and is about managerial behavior taken in response to those groups and individuals" (1984, p. 48).

There are numerous examples which illustrate both the positive and negative outcomes resulting from a company's response to its stakeholders. New England's Malden Mills is one positive example. The strong support and assistance from employees, community officials, the governor, state legislative leaders and business leaders resulted in the rebuilding of the company after a devastating fire. Vivid examples of the negative consequences of stakeholder mismanagement are typified by the initial product safety issues experienced by Dow Corning, A.H. Robins and Johns-Manville. Stakeholder outrage at these companies' responses to concern led to a loss of market position, class action suits and loss of reputation. More recently, stakeholder fear, anger and disapproval have been highlighted by Enron, WorldCom and Tyco scandals. These companies are struggling with severe financial, managerial and credibility issues. Corporate attempts to recover from these threats are occurring in a dramatic and emotionally charged atmosphere conducted on the world stage.

Extending the base of the stakeholder framework, more current scholarship suggests that instead of concentrating on *managing* stakeholders, organizations should concentrate on establishing and managing productive, interactive *relationships* with stakeholders who are key to continued success (Waddock, 2002) and on identifying and utilizing influence strategies. Knowing how stakeholders may try to influence corporate behavior is critical knowledge for strategic management. In other words, if managers are to plan and act strategically, then they should have some idea of who the stakeholders are, what they want, and how they will attempt to acquire their ends (Frooman, 1999).

TECHNOLOGY—
TRANSPARENCY'S HANDMAIDEN

It is indisputable that the application of technology is a necessary and integral component to creating and managing the relationships between and among stakeholders. The rapid and ubiquitous advance of the information superhighway facilitates immediate disclosure, easy storage and retrieval, and instant dissemination of massive amounts of data to a global audience, creating and supporting an extensive interdependence (Johnson & Brennan, 2002). Just as a prism breaks down white light into its component parts, the technological revolution provides a prism through which the heads, hearts and hands of corporate activity can be viewed as components of the whole by stakeholders.

Information, which was once collected and stored in desks, file cabinets, safes or personal memory banks, is today immediately available through broadcast media and, more specifically, the Internet. Stakeholders are no longer denied discovery and disclosure of pertinent information, as was the case regarding the danger of asbestos and nicotine and the subsequent cover-up conducted by industry officials. Technology has opened Pandora's box and allowed transparency and scrutiny to emerge as critical components in the corporate stakeholder relationship.

Access to multiple constituencies is but a mouse click away, illuminating the presence of myriad stakeholder interests and demands. Moreover, companies must also pay very close attention to how those demands shift over time. For example, in the past passengers had little impact on the behavior of the airlines, regardless of company mistreatment or apathy. Until the advent of the Internet, airlines blithely and routinely disregarded customers' influence; the situation has changed dramatically. Numerous web sites have been developed that create vehicles through which passenger complaints can be forwarded to the Federal Aviation Authority and to other potential passengers. In the present situation, these companies are unable to dismiss the claims of their stakeholders. Very quickly, stakeholders who have an urgent cause and the power to exert their will or make significant demands (e.g., an activist group picketing or boycotting) can quickly become dangerous or coercive stakeholders (Waddock, 2002, p. 11).

In 1988, a confrontation over the use of a method of tuna fishing called purse-seining erupted between StarKist and the Earth Island Institute (EII). At that time, EII produced an eleven-minute video full of gruesome scenes of drowning dolphins. Parts of the video were aired on all the major networks. The Institute then mass produced it and distributed it to schools around the country. Initially, it was just the environmental groups which were alerted. Then gradually, the general public became aware of the issue and the subsequent call for a boycott of StarKist tuna. By 1990, 60 percent of the public was aware of the issue and the call for the boycott (Ramirez, 1990). As a result, this effort ultimately was successful, with StarKist changing its policy to purchase only tuna caught by methods other than purse-seining. Nevertheless, the issue and resulting responses were affected by the time and effort it took to alert the various stakeholders. Today, an infinite number of constituencies would be familiar with the fishing method, its inhumane outcomes and the call to action for change with a keystroke. With transparency comes the end of conduct that can be safely oblivious or condescending to society's demands and interests.

The digitization of business platforms places technology at the heart of corporate models and strategy (Post, 2000). The relationships between corporations and their various publics are faster, more frequent and infinitely configured. In general, these system-level effects stem from how communication technology changes whom people know and care about, and in turn creates new system interdependencies (Sproull & Kiesler, 1991). In the modern networked organization, stakeholder communities are connected to multiple groups and, simultaneously, constituencies are linked to one another.

Therefore, networks facilitate the instant sharing of information within potentially infinite communities with shared interests. Conscious awareness of relevant issues and concerns is much higher online than it was, or is, with other forms of media (Locke, 2000). Millions of customers, activists, suppliers, communities, etc., may be linked to a shared issue, concern or interest, thus creating not only more interpenetrating, but also more transparent systems as well. The point of which Motorola was made painfully aware by a television documentary aired in Great Britain several years ago. Motorola, a leading manufacturer of telecommunications equipment, discovered that it was being criticized for being involved in the land mine business. The documentary showed the company's logo on a land mine used in Pakistan. Semiconductor chips manufactured by Motorola had been sold to a European dealer who, in turn, sold them to a third party who assembled the land mine components. Motorola immediately withdrew from the business relationship and instituted new oversight mechanisms to monitor its distribution channels (Post, 2000).

One definition of transparency refers to the availability of information for traversing and exploring a large-scale social system. It provides the layman with a basic map of the organization as depicted in the information available on search engines and web sites (Waddock, 2002). Transparency is created and enhanced because of the public's capacity to know and its ability to navigate the technological terrain. People in the post-modern world desire more individual self-expression (and exhibit more self-absorption) targeted at particular areas of interest. Transparency provides the public with information it can use to evaluate, and to expose, an organization's performance (Demarie & Hitt, 2000). This has led to greater awareness and involvement in social investment firms such as Trillium, Calvert Funds and the Domini Fund. Organizations involved with social mutual funds have multiplied from a dozen in 1990 to approximately 50 currently. Total assets committed to social investing have increased from $1.2 trillion to $2.2 trillion in the past few years. Socially conscious investment now makes up about one out of every eight dollars (13%) of all money under professional management (McVeigh, 2000).

According to the Social Investment Forum, social investing in the United States has been growing at twice the rate of all assets under investment (http://www.socialinvest.org). In addition, social pressure has also led to the development of rating systems rewarding proactive and progressive corporate behavior by organizations such as Kinder, Lydenberg, Domini and Co-op America.

Moreover, companies that understand the value of transparency are more likely to use the Sunshine Standards for Corporate Reporting to Stakeholders. These principles, promoted by the Center for the Advancement of Public Policy, provide guidance for corporations in communicating directly with their stakeholders. They read in part: "All information should be provided that stakeholders may need to make rational, informed decisions in the marketplace, and to protect themselves from negative consequences of corporate actions; this disclosure must be complete, accurate, timely, objective, understandable and public" (Estes, 1998). It also provides the organization with crucial information with which to anticipate social expectations and manage stakeholder interests.

THROUGH A GLASS DARKLY

All implements of change carry inevitable advantages and disadvantages. Cause marketing, public service information, and affinity groups are very much a part of the modern model. Media events, such as the NetAid global concert, illustrate how galaxies of myriad interests and practice coalesce without a physical place, or a particular space in time. Cyber-communities organize around issues such as human rights, environmental sustainability, and social equity in waves of influence affecting society and corporations. This transparency allows companies to manage risks, prepare for emergencies and to proactively design responses. However, that ability does not always translate into preparation or positive performance.

In 1999, protesters disrupted the meeting of the World Trade Organization in Seattle. A disparate group of activists marched on the streets of Seattle protesting trade deficits, job losses, international free trade agreements, labor, human rights, working conditions, sweatshops and the environment. General protests centered around the impact of globalizations on civil society—impacts viewed as being imposed by powerful corporations without the consent of the societies affected (Waddock, 2002). The protestors were seeking and demanding "a seat at the table." Their success prompted another disruption at the World Economic Forum meeting in Davos, Switzerland in January 2000. Then, in September 2000, World Bank and International Monetary Fund officials were forced to shorten their annual meeting by a week of vociferous protests. These examples were facilitated by the capacity to mobilize bias on a global level using what has been termed "hactivism." Hactivism is a method which blends Internet technology withy social protest, producing new tools and new methods that not only annoy their specific targets, but also, the more traditional rank and file activists (Waddock, 2002). These new tools and methods continue to change and enlarge the power of the prism of transparency.

THE MIRROR HAS TWO FACES

Transparency is, however, a Janus-headed creature. The amount and quality of information will increase, enabling individuals and communities to learn about firms and their activities with rapidity and simultaneity. Organizational boundaries will become ever more permeable, creating what Davis and Meyer (1998) call the blur of a connected economy. The balance of power becomes more shared, as does the cost of behavioral change. Social capital—the trust and alliances generated by the relationships people in a system have developed over time—can be expanded and improved. This tapestry of relationships among groups moves separate battles to one battle via leadership networks and Internet capabilities. Transparency should enable corporations to respond faster and better to stakeholders' expectations. Moreover, it is this web of connectivity which is critical to delivering value added outcomes to end consumers. Transparency illuminates the human, albeit fragile, face of organizations.

Nevertheless, the other side of the face is that these same characteristics and capabilities can be used to relay fraudulent and damaging information with the same rapidity and synchronicity. Web pages displaying suspect or incomplete information can become part of collective mind-set with no impunity. Online community forums and chat rooms can become the repository of vituperative messages with little or no validity, adding to the collection of unverified and unverifiable urban legends. Transparency invites scrutiny and the development of communities of relevance and resistance; it is also a driver of change allowing parties of interest an opportunity to revise and reinvent. Because reputation, image and corporate identity have become more important as price and quality become more consistent, management can no longer expect to be exempt from personal accountability. Once gathered, information can be used and disseminated by other interested parties. There is little regulation to assure the veracity of that information. Infotech increases vulnerability to abuse from "hackers, diddlers and spoofers" (Brown, 2001, p. 2). The "shelf-life" of information has been shortened because of Internet time. Therefore, the window of opportunity to act on incorrect or partial information is available only briefly. This creates no value, and in fact may become "negative information" and result in barriers than can be crippling to organizations and stakeholder communities alike (Brown, 2001).

TRANSPARENCY AND THE FUTURE

Information, and the technological ability to retrieve and use it, is at the very center of corporate strategy. There is no industry, nor any competitor, which is immune to its transforming influence. Companies that can harness this transformation will be able not only to survive, but also to thrive, in the 21st century. Those which cannot will become defensive, vulnerable and imperiled. As Kelly (1998) described, honeybees shift from individual to hive behavior when a critical mass is achieved. Broadband connections will allow the inevitability and possibility of similar behavior in humans. The power of this invisible web of relationships may be intangible, but it is nevertheless omnipresent (Senge, 1991). Circles of power and influence change. Demands for greater disclosure and transparency are increasing, spurred on by Internet-enhanced social activism.

Recent examples illustrate this omnipresence and the interdependence. Initially, broadcast and print media did not make note of Senator Trent Lott's comments praising Senator Strom Thurmond for his past stand on segregation until several days after he had made them. Those media comments pale in comparison to the buzz of Internet "bloggers" who posted their indignation and the list of previous similar comments made by Senator Lott. Only then did the other media outlets join the fray (*Time*, December 23, 2002).

Similarly, the clandestine attempts by several prominent organizations to thwart internal and external transparency led to devastating results. Specifically, the use of e-mails and other internal correspondence provoked a series of whistle-blowing by Amanda Bower, Coleen Rowley and Cynthia Cooper, at Enron, the Federal Bureau of Investigation and WorldCom, respectively (*Time*, December 30, 2002). And the New York Attorney General's office investigated stock analysts when the SEC would not, formulating its cases against Merrill Lynch and other Wall Street investment firms and banks by reading more than 94,000 pages of e-mails (*Time*, December, 30, 2002).

Information will continue to flow at cyber-speed. Managers must be able to co-exist in the glass houses created and illuminated by digitization. They must be able to manage and understand the new complex and emergent behaviors and methods because, in fact, the Internet is itself a manifestation of transparency. Thus, transparency can undergird the principle that "corporations must not harm the public good, that employees are part of the corporation, that wealth belongs to those who create it and that community wealth belongs to all" (Kelly, 2001, p 184) The technological imperative facilitates pragmatic, integrative relationships (Frederick, 1995). More specifically, technological expertise creates avenues for honesty, openness, participatory leveling, and democratic environments. Transparency creates global interdependence and new relationships among economic, civil and social sectors. Associations need to balance the organizational and social advantages of greater transparency with the legitimate concerns about its disadvantages and limits (Demarie & Hitt, 2000).

Technological innovation can thrive only in an environment that invites or at least tolerates dissent. It is a process of imagining radical alternatives to what is currently accepted and sharing these new possibilities with others. Transparency encourages and allows a sense of intimacy or familiarity (even if, in reality, it is a false sense) to exist between and among corporations and their stakeholders. The scientific, the managerial, the economic, the philosophical, the cultural, the political have a way of running into each other (Sproull & Kiesler, 1991, p. 105). Telecommunications not only incite unorthodox ideas, they also allow them to be exchanged instantly. They inspire communities of dissent, collaboration and centralization. Social control is intimately connected with a measure of participation. Thus, transparency becomes a touchstone when negotiating in, and across, new national and international frontiers.

Business is first and foremost a social institution, a social invention. Corporate citizens can use transparency for enhancing reputation and sustaining customer goodwill and brand loyalty, and also for being granted permission to operate by communities and governments. In an ever-shrinking global context, corporate leadership success will depend, in large part, on the use of a holistic systems approach to enhance competitiveness and profitability. Transparency globalizes information and concentrates and democratizes its use. As Josiah Quincy wrote in 1774, if democratic principles were made the "object of universal attention and study" then the rights of humankind could no longer "be buried under systems of civil and priestly hierarchy" (Kelly, 2001, p. 185). Legitimately, one could also add systems of organizational hierarchy to the list.

Citizen organizations have emerged as a third independent sector in world affairs—challenging the domination of global agendas and transnational organizations. Increasingly, these constellations of interests are interlinked by Internet networks and a plethora of newsletters and web sites. Nevertheless, it should be remembered that advocacy sometimes implies and necessitates adversarial postures. However, advocacy should encourage inclusiveness and eliminate defensiveness. Even if conducted in a spirit of enlightened self-interest, consciousness-raising rarely succeeds in an atmosphere of condemnation and force. Partnerships between corporations and these interests offer an opportunity for mutually supportive relationships—ones with strong bonds of reciprocity, accountability and trust. Perhaps the technological imperative, and its handmaiden, transparency, can alter the orthodox belief that what is good for business is good for civil societies to include the perspective of what is good for society is also good for business.

Transparency's prism can illuminate and distort just as a glass house can reveal and reflect. The patterns of lacework within which these webs of interaction are nested are highly complex and virtually infinite. However, looking at these networks through the prism of transparency can enhance the sharing of salient knowledge of relevant communities of interest. This informed awareness could greatly facilitate the shift of perspective, or metanoia, that will be crucial to success in the complex, dynamic and interdependent global environment. Metanoia, as described by Seng (1991), means a shift of mind and perspective which combines the visions and values that are meaningful to stakeholders in operating practices that add value in the by-product of wealth generation and profits (Waddock, 2002). This perspective, which incorporates openness, integrity and disclosure—in other words, attributes of transparency—asks that corporations, in conversation with their stakeholders, view decisions as integrated and interconnected. Thus, embracing this shift will allow organizations and stakeholders to perceive the metaphor of the glass house as an exemplar of success in the modern environment, rather than as a beautiful, but fragile, structure always in danger of the errant stone.

REFERENCES

Brown, A. (2001, September/October).   Sometimes the luddites are right. *The Futurist*.

Davis, S. & Meyer, C. (1998). *Blur: The Speed of Change in the Connected Economy*. Reading, MA: Addison-Wesley.

DeMarie, S. M. & Hitt, M. A. (2000). Strategic implications of the information age. *Journal of Labor Research, 21*(3), 419-429.

Donaldson, T. & Preston, L. (1995). The stakeholder theory of the corporation: Concepts, evidence and implications. *Academy of Management Review, 19*, 252-285.

Estes, R. (1998). *The sunshine standards and the stakeholder alliance: A Win3 program for business, stakeholders and society*. Annual Conference, Certified General Accountants, Accounting Research Center, University of Ottawa, Canada.

Frederick, W. C. (1995). *Values, Nature and Culture in the American Corporation*. New York: Oxford University Press.

Freeman, R.E. (1985). *Strategic Management: A Stakeholder Approach*. Boston, MA: Pittman.

Frooman, J. (1999). Stakeholder influence strategies. *Academy of Management Review, 24* (2), 191-205.

Goodgame & Tumulty, K. (2002, December 23). Tripped up by History. *Time,* 22.

Ignatius, A. (2002, December 30). Crusader of the year, Wall Street's top cop. *Time,* 64.

Johnson, V. & Brennan, L. (2002). Examining the impact of technology on social responsibility practices. *Re-Imagining Business Ethics: Meaningful Solutions for a Global Economy, 4*, 107-123.

Kelly, K. (1998). *New Rules for the New Economy: 10 Radical Strategies for a Connected World*. New York: Viking.

Kelly, M. (2001). *The Divine Right of Capital: Dethroning the Corporate Aristocracy*. San Francisco, CA: Berrett-Koehler Publishers.

Lacayo, R. & Ripley, A. (2002, December 30). Persons of the year: Coleen Rowley, Cynthia Cooper, Sherron Watkins. *Time,* 30.

Locke, C. (2000). Internet Apocolypso. In R. Levine, C. Locke, D. Searls & D. Winberger (Eds.), *The Cluetrain Manifesto: The End of Business as Usual*. Cambridge: Perseus Publishing.

Post, J. (2000). Moving from geographic to virtual communities: Global corporate citizenship in a dot.com world. *Business and Society Review, 105*(1), 27-46.

Preston, L. E. & Post, J. (1975). *Private Management and Public Policy*. Englewood Cliffs, NJ: Prentice Hall.

Preston, L E. & O'Bannon, D. P. (1997).   The corporate social-financial performance relationship. *Business and Society, 36*, 419-429.

Ramirez, A. (1990, April 16). "Epic debate" led to Heinz tuna plan. *New York Times,* D1, 8.

Senge, P. M. (1991). *The Fifth Discipline: The Art and Practice of the Learning Organization.* New York: Doubleday.

Social Investment Forum (2000). Introduction to socially responsible investing. Retrieved July 9, 2000 from http://www.socialinvest.org/Areas/SriGuide/Default.htm.

Sproull, L. & Kiesler, S. (1991). *Connections: New Ways of Working in the Networked Organization.* Cambridge, MA: MIT Press.

Waddock, S. (2002). *Leading Corporate Citizens: Vision, Values, Value Added.* New York: McGraw-Hill Irwin.

Chapter IX

Ethical Challenges of Information Systems: The Carnage of Outsourcing and Other Technology-Enabled Organizational Imperatives

David Wiencek
Mercer University, USA

ABSTRACT

This chapter reviews the historical, technological and economic factors driving IT organizational design and resulting staffing patterns within the IT organization as a backdrop to reviewing the ethical aspects of outsourcing and other technology-enabled organizational imperatives. It examines the effect of developing a business model based on core competency analysis and examines IT sourcing alternatives from the viewpoint of three groups of stakeholders: individuals, the corporation and society. The chapter demonstrates that sourcing choices an IT manager makes result in ethical dilemmas, delineates various aspects of the dilemmas and provides some simple but effective resolution principles. The author hopes that the IT manager reading the chapter will be better prepared to apply ethical decision principles when choosing how to staff their organization and be aware of the possible negative and positive results of their decision-making.

INTRODUCTION

Information Technology (IT) managers today face growing pressures to reduce costs, do more with less and eliminate non-value added activities within their operations. Outsourcing has become a widely applied strategy to meet these imperatives. While the justification for outsourcing is often based on a financial model, there are other nonfinancial costs to the organization, its employees, investors and the public. This chapter is not concerned with the legal aspects of outsourcing, but rather the ethical aspects. Ethics provides the IT manager with a means to evaluate choices between alternative courses of action all of which can in some sense be justified. Kidder (1996) calls these alternatives "Dilemma Paradigms" or situations that involve "Right versus Right" (p. 109). Kidder defines four paradigms that may clash in any ethical dilemma: justice versus mercy, short-term versus long-term, individual versus community, and truth versus loyalty. Analyzing the steps to be taken when facing an ethical dilemma, Kidder suggests that once all the facts are known and the alternatives have been identified, the person facing an ethical decision must identify a moral principle to apply before resolving the dilemma (p. 154). There are many moral principles that may be applied towards the resolution of an ethical decision. Kidder lists three that are familiar and often employed. Do what is best for the greatest number of people (*ends-based* thinking); Follow the highest sense of principle (*rule-based* thinking); Do what you want others to do to you (*care-based* thinking) (p. 154). The manager reading this chapter may wish to reflect upon the applicability of these paradigms and resolution principles to the issues presented.

In the attempt to meet organizational imperatives, to be cost effective and to be competitive, corporations have focused on their core competencies to the exclusion of all others. For core, mission critical processes, the corporation must look inward and determine whether the corporation itself is the best organization to perform the function.

"Outsourcing non-strategic processes has been an important trend in the U.S. in recent years. While IT transactions began prior to 1990, outsourcing has certainly been popularized in the last decade. Part of the explanation lies in the larger trends operating in the world economy—increasing

competition, rapid technological change, global integration of markets, deregulation, and privatization. On a more micro level, strategic concerns have steered management to exploit the benefits offered by focus and specialization. Outsourcing non-strategic processes eliminates a distraction, enabling management to focus its distinctive capabilities on areas critical to its strategic success." (Glassman, 2000, p. 3)

Even the corporation that is ever vigilant to identify core competencies may find them to be illusory or easily copied by competitors. Moore (2002) has pointed out the transitory nature of core competencies and the difficulties facing an IT manager when a core competency becomes widely known and imitated. What had been a key corporate asset becomes merely a cost to be minimized. Missing this inflection point causes an organization to incur unnecessary costs. Unless an organization has a carefully nurtured strategy of concentrating on core functionality, while protecting other assets, the organization is ultimately doomed to be less successful than more focused competitors.

Trends in the technology industry towards standards-based products, the rapid obsolescence of technologies, and the transformation of computer hardware into a commodity have reinforced this almost fatalistic logic in favor of outsourcing. Moving from proprietary technologies at the hardware and infrastructure levels to standards-based technologies and components has created pricing pressure on hardware manufacturers. In response, these suppliers have developed service organizations, which are typically more profitable than hardware sales and compete to provide functions previously done by in-house staff. Over investment in technology, first in response to the Y2K problem and then in the dot.com and telecom bubbles has created a drastically different technology cost structure within the firm. Reductions in the variable cost of a corporation's technology investment have fallen on the employee and society with negative implications because of the capital-intensive nature of many technology investments and the effects of multi-year depreciation and technological obsolescence. How much of the technology, intellectual capital and the skilled resources so carefully acquired for competitive advantage have lost their value to propel the company to world class performance and are no longer a good investment of scarce corporate resources?

Corporate IT managers may also perceive pressure to outsource from investors, who in the 1990s responded to corporate outsourcing announcements by driving up stock prices. Data gathered by Stern Stewart & Company analyzed 27 large deals in the U.S., UK, France, Japan, New Zealand, and South Africa from 1993 through 1999. The study found that following 62% of the outsourcing announcements there was "a positive impact on stock price from IT outsourcing. The average company in the outsourcing group outperformed the market by 5.7% from two months prior to two months after the announcement" (Glassman,

2000, p. 2). This perception may not be correct. More recently, Simons (2003) examined data from the first nine months of 2002. Simons found that companies which efficiently improved their bottom line by cost-cutting, defined as where revenues declined and profits rose, had a 20% lower average price-to-earnings ratio than those who were less efficient, defined as companies where revenue increased but profit fell. While outsourcing is perceived as a means to reduce costs and increase efficiency, Simons (2003) suggests that the reality may be that cost cutting has limits, and that the market rewards those companies with the most room for improvement. In the slow growth, low inflation economy of the last few years, with corporations' ability to raise prices limited, cost reduction and efficiency gains have been key contributors to bottom line growth. The IT manager should weigh carefully the positive implications of outsourcing for long-term survivability and whether investors will ultimately reward cost cutting or revenue enhancement.

ETHICAL IMPLICATIONS OF OUTSOURCING

Among the ethical implications of outsourcing are fairness and the short and long-term impact upon the individual and the community. Stakeholder analysis has stressed the importance of considering business decisions within the context of the economic, legal and social responsibilities of the corporation and their effect upon employees, individual consumers, investors, suppliers, and interest groups (Post, 2002). Evaluating the effect upon each group, weighing the alternatives and striking a balance between economic, legal and social responsibilities are a key challenge for the IT manager. Simply asking who bears the cost in outsourcing and who reaps the benefits opens questions about fairness. The individual, whose job is lost, clearly bears a significant cost. Should the savings go to corporate shareholders? What of the individual whose job is not lost, but rather preserved through the newly acquired competitiveness of his employer? Is the benefit to him fair when the cost to others is lost jobs? Is outsourcing on balance positive or negative for the person who is transferred to a technology company that provides technical opportunities that his previous employer could not? What will happen if the employee's salary, pension or healthcare providers change?

Individual Implications

Individuals experience organizational imperatives through their work. Workers evaluate assignments, the work settings, relationship to peers, and compensation against a personal frame of reference. Because of outsourcing and rightsizing, the employment contract between the technology worker and the organization has fundamentally changed. Shorter technology lifecycles have resulted in a much briefer time between technology installation, exploitation and retirement. The individual sees in this cycle a lowering of the value of their knowledge and experiences, changes to their self-image. Economic forces, such as globalization, have also changed the relationship of workers to their work and have weakened the bond between employer and employee.

Societal Implications

The wider society participates in this dynamic of technology enabled cost shifting. As the example of lower technology manufacturing jobs moving to lower cost locations is repeated in the information services industry, the effect upon societal key success factors, such as intellectual capital generation and retention, workforce skill development and the viability of economic growth have become fair game for ethical review. Companies easily make the small step from creating a factory for local consumption to designing the product locally for sale worldwide. In the manufacturing of electronics, for example, the end game of this trend is the development of specialized firms that move work across multiple societies depending on cost or politics. Do corporate decisions about outsourcing diminish the societies that create them or enable those societies to become more competitive worldwide?

Corporate Implications

Balancing economic imperatives is the need for the corporation to behave ethically. Beyond obeying laws, corporations are expected to behave fairly towards their shareowners, employees and customers. Corporations are expected to behave ethically within the standards of their own culture and to ensure that their suppliers behave so as well. This is not a simple matter, as Post (2002) says:

"The question is not, Should business be ethical? Nor is it, Should business be economically efficient? Society expects both at the same time. Ethical behavior is a key aspect of social performance. To maintain public support and credibility—that is business legitimacy—business must find ways to balance and integrate these two social demands: high economic growth and high ethical standards. When a company acts ethically towards stakeholders, it improves its contribution to society. When a company fails to act ethically, however, it faces the risk of losing the public support needed to be both credible and successful." (p. 19)

As stewards of a creation of society, IT managers need to take their responsibility to behave ethically seriously.

Implications for the IT Manager

In this context of corporate competencies, the importance of information technology has undergone substantial transformations with implications for determining the technology candidates for both rightsizing and outsourcing. In the pre-outsourced model, according to a study published by IBM Global Services (2002, p. 17), IT organizations were responsible for overall IT strategy and architecture, project and technology procurement and systems management. IT organizations also designed, built, enhanced and maintained applications. In contrast, the modern IT organization retains in-house control of architecture and project management, but a subtle shift toward a business perspective is apparent in other core tasks. Today, an IT organization is responsible for domain expertise and business process analysis. Critical to our discussion of outsourcing, the organization is also a global systems integrator, an IT strategic sourcing manager and responsible for supplier relationships.

The IT manager is forced to make ever finer technological assessments. Companies desiring to use technology for competitive advantage must apply appropriate sourcing strategies. Companies attempting to create new products through technology or to use technology to transform their business must carefully select technologies and their suppliers. According to a study by IBM Global Services (2001, p. 3):

"Once viewed as simply a tool for reducing IT costs, outsourcing is today evolving to encompass strategically focused comprehensive management of critical business processes, including the transformation of legacy systems and applications to support newly crafted e-business initiatives. This emerging outsourcing model is referred to as transformational outsourcing—a broader but highly refined group of competencies that combines proven technologies, expert skills and services with thought leadership, business and industry acumen and process knowledge."

Another driver of the use of outsourcing is found in the internal dynamics of the firm. The modern corporate manager wants a return on technology investments similar to any other purchase. Money allocated to technology competes with marketing or manufacturing investments of a company. In addition, the limited pool of skilled managers within a company forces senior management to decide whether this scarce resource should be used to manage technology or some more core activity. The agile organization is constantly attempting to employ only as much technology as can make a positive contribution to profitability using the fewest number of skilled managers. With the slowdown in technology purchases, alternative sourcing is seen as a way for a corporation to access hardware and software as needed, modernize without capital costs and gain access to technology without investing in identification, installation, operation and disposal of technology.   By carefully choosing outsourcing partners a firm may gain access to intellectual capital and best practices that would be expensive or impossible to develop on their own. "Outsourcers must provide thought leadership, a willingness to share both risks and rewards, a proactive approach, industry knowledge, a global presence, scalable, asset-based plug-and-play capabilities, proven skills, flexible financing packages" (IBM Global Services, 2001).

IT managers and their employers stand at the center of the sourcing decision and choose which functions and people are outsourced. These two decision makers choose suppliers and their locations. IT managers, though constrained by labor agreements, laws and public opinion, are facing a dilemma: what is the ethical balance between economic and ethical justifications for their sourcing decisions. The next section will discuss how technology sourcing has evolved and what the ethical implications of alternative sourcing practices are today.

EVOLUTION OF OUTSOURCING
First Generation Outsourcing-Extended Functionality

Early information services outsourcing focused upon extended functionality in the computer environment and cost management. The first commercially viable computer outsourcing opportunities resulted from the centralized nature of early computing and the existence of large, complex computers. As rudimentary terminal input devices were developed, and communications capacity between host and terminal increased, connections between a remote user and a central machine became possible. The speed of the mainframe and the relatively slow interaction rates between the user and the central machine meant that many users could share a single machine. Owners of centralized machines were able to sell access to their hardware and their computing resources through time-sharing. The effect of this early outsourcing upon the individual, corporation and society was relatively benign. Organizations were buying a service that could not easily be hosted internally. Staffing was not being reduced. Economically, assets were being better utilized.

Even in this early form of outsourcing, there were the seeds of an ethical issue that would grow over time. What responsibility does a company have for the quality of the work experience? Does the company have the right to determine working conditions and location? Time-sharing represented the automation of data entry work, eliminating the need for person-to-person contact, and dehumanizing the work. Eventually, time-sharing would lead to the movement of jobs offshore. Timesharing's need to maximize investment in computing hardware led to 24 by 7 operations, setting the stage for global operating models in which all ties to geography were eliminated. The lack of geographical ties effected the work hours and life styles of the employee. The decision to buy, not build also meant that the corporation was not investing locally, but transferring wealth and skills outside the immediate environment. These changes, which have a negative effect upon individuals and local communities, had their genesis in this early technological development.

Second Generation Outsourcing—Physical Outsourcing

Next on the path to the current sourcing situation was physical outsourcing. In response to the complexity of the support and specialized physical facilities needed to operate a computer or a network, corporations began outsourcing IT operations. Companies such as IBM and EDS were followed in the operational outsourcing of hardware and operations by large accounting and consulting firms and telecommunication suppliers. The deregulation of the telecommunications providers and the possibility for large organizations to develop private data and voice networks also contributed to making operational outsourcing acceptable. With the growth of distributed computing and the creation of telecommunications management challenges, operational outsourcing could be extended to include the entire computer infrastructure from desktop to mainframe. According to Overby (2002), operational outsourcing will continue to grow but at a decelerating rate through 2006.

Third Generation Outsourcing—Offshore and Process Outsourcing

Whether through infrastructure on demand, as a utility or application service provider (ASP), as a turnkey solution or software in a pay for usage model, the choice of implementation method raises questions about the impact on the employee, the company, the community and the wider society. Two current implementations are especially vexing: off shoring and business process outsourcing.

In off shoring, the development, maintenance or support of IT is given to a supplier doing business in a foreign country. Off shoring, originally popularized by Indian firms such as INFOSYS, TATA and WIPRO, and now available in other countries such as Ireland, Canada, Mexico, China, Israel Russia and the Philippines offers development and maintenance for 10% to 50% less than the rates in the United States. In addition, the breakup of the Soviet Union made available a large pool of skilled IT professionals within Russia and the other countries of the former Soviet bloc. The number of jobs sent offshore and the value of the work performed offshore are expected to increase dramatically.

"In Asia, countries like Singapore, the Philippines, and Malaysia have begun to attract IT projects that were once executed in the U.S. and other Western countries. Another hot market for back-office projects is India,

which has a large, English-speaking workforce. NASSCOM, India's main association for software and IT service companies, said in a report issued on June 10, 2002, that India will employ 4 million people and earn $30 billion from IT service exports by 2008" (Debate over Scarcity—and Skills—of IT Workers, para. 20).

With the drop in demand for computer skills following the year 2000, remediation work and the staff reductions because of the telecom meltdown, many of these firms compete on price, making them even more attractive to the IT manager seeking cost reductions.

The other implementation of outsourcing that has become popular is business process outsourcing (BPO). In business process outsourcing, an entire function is provided by a third party, this includes process expertise, technology, including IT technology, and operations. Relationship management and policy setting remain with the original organization.

Whether viewed from a functional or an implementation perspective, an IT manager considering outsourcing must realize that their chosen supplier can only be successful through providing the service at a lower cost than the company currently does or accepting a lower profit. Unlike the company, which treats IT as a cost center, the supplier must make a profit to stay in business. The ethical IT manager considering outsourcing must ask from where the profit will come. In the best case, the outsourcer will benefit from economies of scale, inefficiencies within the company or better technological exploitation. As Glassman (2000) makes clear, "On the other side of the transaction is a profit seeking specialist. The specialist often enjoys economies of scale in providing service, has greater expertise, and can mobilize quickly the diverse capabilities needed to provide technical solutions" (p. 1). Unfortunately, the simpler method is to use lower paid labor.

Evolving Standards—Outsourcing and the Company Responsibility for Third Party Behavior

One current ethical question with which the IT manager must deal is determining what should be the company's responsibility for outside workers, their work environment and their community. Is the outsourcing company solely responsible for the conduct of the outsourced employee? Should the outsourcing company ensure that the workers are treated fairly by the company's standards? Should the outsourcing company be responsible for employee safety and working conditions? Does the outsourcing company's location determine which labor laws apply? What environmental standards should be used? If the work is transferred across borders, which privacy laws apply? If a legal dispute arises between outsourced employee and their employer, should the outsourcing company intervene? Should contract law apply or are companies that outsource expected to meet a higher ethical standard? What are the implications for the company's brand if public perception of an outsourcing becomes negative?

This section has shown that the evolution from timesharing to the present day sourcing alternatives presents the IT manager who wishes to behave ethically while still guaranteeing the economic viability of their firm with several dilemmas. The next section will examine the effect alternative sourcing has upon the individual and society, as well as discuss dilemma paradigms.

INDIVIDUAL CORPORATION AND SOCIETY

The immediate impact of alternative sourcing is on the individual. From the individual's viewpoint, outsourcing is a constant mix of cost shifting to him and benefit sharing for the company that the employee seldom controls. In the worst case, outsourcing and rightsizing means the loss of employment. Even individuals placed with an outsourcing vendor face the stress of a job change and the need to prove their worth to a new employer. Following an outsourcing, individuals' perceptions of their work, compensation, assignments and work setting change. In addition, their view of their peers, of their community, of the employment contract and ultimately their self-image and identity are all affected by outsourcing. Underlying the negative perspective of outsourcing and rightsizing are the fear of change and the need of many people for emotional fulfillment through work. Even if during an outsourcing, the new employer has dealt with the pay, benefits and development concerns of the individual, the process must still overcome fear of the unknown. The individual is constantly asking what right has a company to impose these costs.

Compensation

Pay and benefits are tangible rewards for an individual's effort and imply the value of work. Lowering any part of the compensation package is perceived as negative. Alternative sourcing often lowers the pay, options and benefits of the individual. First, is the impact of pay scales. A company reviewing the decision to outsource may reason that an outsourcer specializing in a functional area should value individual skills in that function more highly and pay more for them. In addition, a functionally specific supplier should be more profitable and be more generous to the employee over the long-term. If true, then the ethical decision is simple, as both parties benefit when the decision is a good one. This is not always the case. Many Fortune 500 corporations benchmark their pay practices against their competitors. Because of the differences between the pay scales of technology and non-technology sectors, transferred employees can often find themselves with lower pay. This is clearly a cost shifting from the individual to the company shareholders or management, with the company gathering all the benefits. The worker receiving less pay would judge the fairness quite differently from the shareowner with the larger dividend.

There are similar concerns around benefits, options and especially pensions. Since most defined- benefit pensions increase with the length of service, the change to a new employer often decreases the payout, particularly for older, more highly compensated employees. In addition, the difference in severance policies, which are often based on years of service, can reduce the incomes of workers with no offsetting benefit. Severance and pension issues also affect society. The reduction of the standard of living of the elderly implied by the loss of pension income and medical benefits affects most citizens, either as contributors to the Social Security System or as taxpayers supporting Medicare. The IT manager needs to ask what are the company's obligations to support the standard of living of their current, previous and retired workers. How do these obligations balance against the need to have immediate and ongoing profits to survive and contribute to the economic growth of the society? What role should the government play through the legal system in creating a balance between workers' rights and company well-being?

Individual Development Opportunities

Employers pay for two types of knowledge: technical skill and company experience. To remain valued, an employee must have assignments that allow skills to be refreshed and developed. Challenging assignments that offer developmental growth are sought in either the personal or the professional spheres. Outsourcing may provide new opportunities with the outsourcing firm, especially if the outsourcer specializes in the field in which the worker is employed. On the other hand, if the employee values company experience more highly, the employee would choose to stay with his or her current employer. In most outsourcings, the employee is without the ability to make the choice. The direction of his personal and professional development is imposed upon the employee by the decisions of the company.

The Individual's Sense of Community

The quality of the physical work setting is an important component of the individual's assessment of a position. Changes to the office environment, disruption of the workspace, or changes of their status within the workplace negatively affect the perceived desirability of a position. At a minimum, being outsourced means that an employee may work in the same location but for a different firm. In the extreme case, an employee may be relocated to the new employer's facilities with the disruption and stress accompanying a move. The status as a contract or vendor supplied worker often means that the individual loses the use of company facilities and services and has differential access to the workplace. These dislocations are borne by the employee but the benefits are to the company. Does this represent ethical behavior on the part of the firm?

The value of proximity between knowledge workers has been a central tenet of regional economics. As Hoover (1971) has stated:

"A crucial function of cities is to make it possible for large numbers of people to make contact easily and frequently for work, consultation, buying and selling, negotiating, instruction, and other purposes. People are more expensive to transport than almost anything else because their time is so valuable." (p. 297)

This centralization tendency has been lessened by the growth of telecommunications and collaborative technologies. For the knowledge worker, the exchange of an idea whether by telephone, e-mail, teleconference, real-time collaboration, online discussion groups or messaging diminishes the need for physical proximity. Ideas can be exchanged, debated and improved in real time, passed between offices or labs across the globe or discussed asynchronously. As a result, the physical location of the worker becomes less important than the existence of a communications infrastructure and a common language.

Physical proximity is not only driven by logistics, but also serves a social function. Proximity facilitates the development of an intellectual community of peers. Colleagues, subordinates and managers provide social interactions and frames of reference for the individual. Particularly, for information workers, the availability of a common community of interests is important to their professional development. As the complexity of work increases and judgment-based work replaces fixed assignments, the employee finds the development of ideas in the casual interplay between similarly oriented professionals. The value to the individual of working with like-minded people is psychic as well as economic. The modern corporation provides this community for workers as reflected in the organizational structure of functional departments. Does alternate sourcing increase this sense of community through widening the number interactions or diminish the sense of community through lack of physical contact? Ethically, does the IT manager have a responsibility to the worker or to their community to facilitate intellectual exchange?

The Employment Contract

Individuals accept positions with expectations about the quality and duration of the relationship with their employer. Employment includes the possibility of development of the individual by experience in various jobs, training and assignments. In effect, the employee creates multiple careers within a large corporation. This cost is borne by the corporation as a long-term investment in workers, and only partially offset by lower recruiting costs. Both the employee and the employer make an ethical choice, favoring the long-term benefits over the short-term, and each bear some immediate costs. This employment pattern of multiple careers within a large organization is a recent phenomenon.

"The traditional system it turns out is not so old after all. Outsourcing and contingent work practices were common during the early years of industrial development in the U.S. For instance, under the putting-out system in the 19th century, work was routinely contracted out to workers who made products in their home. The need for more stable employment relationships emerged partly in response to the growing complexity of technology, which needed massive capital investments as well as longer planning horizons." (Welcome Aboard — For Now, *para. 5*)

With rightsizing, the company has changed the balance and assumed that preferred staffing is to have only those individuals whose skills are immediately useable. This not only shifts the cost of development to the employee, but also changes the trust relationship between the employee and the employer. Employment becomes a temporary exploitation of current skills with no promise of development to ensure future assignments, resulting in a change in the social contract between employer and employee. As Post (2002) states:

"Beginning in the late 1980s and continuing into the 1990s fierce global competition and greater attention to improving the bottom line resulted in significant corporate restructuring and downsizing (termination) of employees in many countries. With the trend came a new way of thinking about the employer-employee relationship, which some researchers call a new social contract. Bonds between employers and employees weakened. Companies aimed to attract and retain employees not by offering long-term job security but rather by emphasizing interesting and challenging work, performance based compensation and ongoing professional training." (p. 410)

From the individual's viewpoint, employment has changed from a traditional long-term contract, often seniority based, to one of temporary engagements. From the company's viewpoint, a short-term gain in efficiency has been balanced against the long-term value of employee loyalty. For example:

"The 'Bouncing Back' study itself points to a culture of poor techie retention. Surveyed companies said the 'average acceptable time to retain their IT workers is just over two years,' which is down from an acceptable tenure of 33 months the year before." (Debate over Scarcity—and Skills— of IT Workers, *para. 27*)

The employee traded higher salary for long-term employment. Companies implemented the project model and the employee involuntarily became a variable cost.

The Effect of Outsourcing upon the Corporation

The chapter to this point has focused upon the effect upon the individual. However, the company is not immune to the negative effect of alternative sourcing decisions. The introduction described how the focus on core competencies and the need to eliminate functions that can be more cost effectively performed by other suppliers predisposed firms to outsourcing. In addition, the introduction pointed out that the scarcity of management talent requires that organizations employ them in the best and highest use. What has been the result? According to Cramm (2001):

"Many organizations are a shell of what they once were or a shadow of what they could be, because they give their best work to outsiders. I don't think anyone intentionally outsources the best work - that is, the most important projects and the critical business relationships—but it happens all too often.

Correctly applied, outsourcing is a lifesaver in navigating the changing seas of business and technology. Fortunately, there seems to be an endless supply of contractors and consultants. My CIO clients have plenty of experience in outsourcing. In fact, about half of their personnel work for somebody else, on average. That last thought always gives me a chill. At the end of the day, half of their people don't work for them—they work for somebody else. Those employees are working to achieve another company's long-term vision and are part of somebody else's culture and career development plan" (para. 1-3).

In this section, the company's responsibilities to shareholders, the community and society are the backdrop against which ethical dilemmas play out.

The Fragmentation of the Customer Experience

Firms, which specialize in some core aspect of their business and leave lower value activities to outsiders, no longer own the end-to-end customer experience. Unless the employees of the vendor of outsourced customer service closely align with the expectations of the customer and the organization, the perception of the customer may be negative. Insofar as a satisfied customer is easier to sell to than a new customer is to recruit or an unhappy customer to placate, outsourcing that diminishes the customer experience is negative to the long-term growth and even survival of the firm. Customer contact also provides an important source of information about the success of existing products and customer ideas about future needs. Unless the outsourcing relationship includes mechanisms to capture and communicate these ideas, firms are losing a valuable source of information by outsourcing customer contact. Further, the corporation may find critical data and process information outside the company's control. As data about a customer is increasingly dispersed across suppliers, the relationship between the company and the customer is changed. Who has the right to store data? What is the effect of local laws upon the non-local storage of personal information? How will the data be matched and to what purpose? Besides conflicting legal requirements, the IT manager must deal with the ethical questions of the proper gathering and use of private information in an environment not totally in their control. As companies have a responsibility to their workers to provide employment and to their shareowners to provide income and capital growth, outsourcing which fragments the customer experience putting the firm's survival at risk does not seem to be an ethical response.

The Corporate Culture

Another aspect essential to the long-term success of the corporation is the corporate culture. Corporate culture is the result of many complex forces. Often, the firm's self-image and consumer image is driven by the perception that the corporation is best able to provide a service, perform a function, build a product or solve a customer's problem. Unless outsourcing is positioned within the organization as an improvement in critical aspects of this mission, the corporate culture may reject or undermine the process. According to Glassman (2000):

"Outsourcing requires, however, a willingness to nurture a partnership with another company. The culture of many successful firms is to perform all functions in house, if they can do it, they believe they should. This mindset is often a roadblock to new ideas and initiatives that create shareholder value. Yet the evidence from the marketplace is that IT services can often be best obtained through contractual arrangements with industry specialists, making outsourcing an important shareholder value strategy that warrants attention of executives at the highest levels." (p. 6)

Attempting to change a corporate culture is not a step to be taken lightly. The manager considering outsourcing needs to understand this and assess the likelihood of success against the costs to the workforce.

Geo-Politics and Globalization

Corporations with outsourced IT departments may become inadvertently involved with geo-politics and globalization. Ethically, is this an appropriate role for a profit-seeking firm? Does the firm have the right to interfere in the affairs of other locations, cultures or countries? When a remote worker replaces a local employee, the corporation is exposed to the politics, legal system and culture of the distant workplace. Foreign outsourcers are subject to local authorities. Does the original firm have a role in how the outsourcer conducts business? Outsourcing, rather than eliminating ethical dilemmas, can multiply them.

Public Perceptions

The company making inappropriate ethical choices creates for itself public relations problems. An outsourcing organization may be thought of as a less desirable place to work, as a failing company, or as contributing negatively to the larger economy. As a legacy of the experience with job dislocations in the textile, shoe and electronics industries, outsourcing is often perceived within the local labor market as a sign that a firm is in trouble or does not care about the local community. This limits the ability of the firm to attract potential employees, increases recruiting costs and raises the expense of keeping existing employees. An employer that outsources a significant number of workers may seen as damaging the community through the transfer of employment outside the immediate area. Finally, the existence of a large group of former employees, who left under trying circumstances, contributes to unflattering publicity.

Economic Effects

The corporation is a legal creation of society. As such, the corporation has an economic and a social function. Corporations exist to serve their stakeholders within the society that allows their existence. One critical ethical concern is whether, through outsourcing as a cost-cutting tool, corporations are limiting the economic recovery of the U.S. Economy. Hilsenrath (2002) in the *Wall Street Journal* summarizes:

"John Maynard Keynes, the respected Depression-era economist, worried about excessive thrift in an economy. Every penny consumers socked away was a penny of income lost for another individual hoping to sell some product or service. By increasing their own savings, he worried; they lowered the overall pool of income in the economy. He called it the "paradox of thrift" and warned that the process could feed on itself. Today, economists are becoming worried about a paradox of corporate thrift, not consumer thrift. By cutting costs, the worry goes; they are repairing their own bottom lines, but holding back the overall recovery." (p. A2)

How should the IT manager weighing alternative sourcing balance short-term internal cost reduction pressures against long-term societal need?

Intellectual Capital Creation

Corporations also contribute through their research and development expenditures to the creation of intellectual capital. Much of the value in the modern corporation is in intangible information assets. By transferring the creation of these assets to outsiders, outsourcing diminishes the accumulation of intellectual capital within a company. Companies take only a small step from making a decision to outsource the maintenance of software to outsourcing the creation of the product. The transfer of software design and engineering work, which was originally thought not susceptible to outsourcing, has increasingly migrated offshore. Developing economies such as India and China have targeted engineering work through incentives and investments in universities and infrastructure. Capturing the momentum in the creation of computer products and protecting existing intellectual capital may prove critical to economic growth. Considering the long-term effect upon society, should an ethical company choose to in-source or outsource the creation of intellectual capital?

Outsourcing also exaggerates economic and cultural differences between the purchasing and source country. As an example of the former, according to *Forbes* magazine, China is producing ten times the engineers as the U.S. and paying them substantially less. According to Karlgard (2002), the United States graduates only 150,000 electrical engineers each year, while 750,000 graduate from Chinese universities. Even in the most westernized of Chinese cities, those on the industrialized coast, a Chinese engineer will earn between \$4,300 and \$8,600 yearly. Beginning with a large concentration of IT professionals, the United States cannot help but be negatively affected by this trend. While a discussion of the complex issues of globalization is beyond the scope of this chapter, information technology is clearly an enabler of this trend.

CONCLUSION

In the drive to reduce costs and improve effectiveness, the corporation has responded to technology-enabled imperatives by fundamentally altering the relationship between the employee and the employer and, to a lesser degree, the relationship to the local culture, economy and society. In this chapter, the ethical questions facing the IT manager have been reviewed against the standards of individual versus company, company versus community and the short-term versus the long-term effects of choices. The IT manager stands at the center of these dilemmas with two major stakeholders, the employee and the shareowner, and two minor stakeholders, the customer and the public. This chapter has suggested ends-based, rule-based and care-based principles for evaluating the dilemmas, and focused on cost shifting and benefit capturing analysis as useful yardsticks for the IT manager facing ethical decisions. The overall theme is that technology has enabled alternative sourcing and altered the benefit distribution to the detriment of the individual worker and society. Decisions faced by IT managers responding to technology-enabled organizational imperatives present many choices between right and right.

REFERENCES

Cost-effective application management solutions and the effect upon on IT Organizations. (2002). Retrieved October 8, 2002 from IBM Global Services on the World Wide Web: http://www-1.ibm.com/services.

Cramm, S. H. (2001, November 15). The dark side of outsourcing [Electronic version]. *CIO Magazine.*

Debate over scarcity – and skills – of IT workers. (n.d.). Retrieved October 10, 2002 from Knowledge at Emory on the World Wide Web: http://knowledge.emory.edu/articles.cfm?catid=10&articleid=550.

Glassman, D. (2000). *IT outsourcing and shareholder value, evaluation.* Retrieved November 10, 2002 from the World Wide Web: http://www.eva.com/evaluation/082000.shtml.

Hilsenrath, J. E. (2002, November 1). Employees bear brunt of corporate thrift. *The Wall Street Journal,* p. A2.

Hoover, E. (1971). *An Introduction to Regional Economics.* New York: Alfred A. Knopf.

Karlgard, R. (2002, November 11). Buy the numbers, digital rules. *Forbes,* 39.

Kidder, R. M. (1996). *How Good People Make Tough Choices.* William Morrow & Company.

Moore, G. A. (2002). Core versus context: Managing resources in a downturn. *INFOCUS, 2,* 8-9.

Overby, C. (2002). *U.S. outsourcing decelerates.* Retrieved November 11, 2002 from Forrester Research on the World Wide Web: http://www.forrester.com/ER/Research/Report/0,1338,13161,00.html.

Post, J. E. (2002). *Business and Society: Corporate Strategy, Public Policy and Ethics* (10th ed.). New York: McGraw-Hill.

Simons, D. (2003, January 23). Downsizing deflated [Electronic Version]. *Forbes Magazine.* Retrieved January 23, 2003 from the World Wide Web: http://www.forbes.com/2003/01/23/cx_ds_0123simons.html.

Transformational outsourcing: Responding to change in the e-business marketplace (2001, May). Retrieved October 8, 2002 from IBM Global Services on the World Wide Web: http://www-1.ibm.com/services/files/transformational_outsourcing_whitepaper.pdf.

Welcome aboard – for now (n.d.). Retrieved October 11, 2002 from Knowledge at Emory on the World Wide Web: http://knowledge.emory.edu/print_version.cfm?articleid=9&catid=10.

Chapter X

A Contrarian's View: New Wine in Old Bottles, New Economy and Old Ethics—Can it Work?

Marianne M. Jennings
Arizona State University, USA

ABSTRACT

While the view that new technology, new ways of doing business and new avenues of communication require new ethical standards is a commonly accepted one, a closer look at the nature of these new developments in juxtaposition with history demonstrates that the notion of new ethics for new eras has been tried in other social and cultural revolutions. History teaches that old standards are easily applied to new technologies. While the expediency of evolving ethics is tempting, adherence to such a fluid standard limits progress because the activity of change is not grounded in values. We have been here before and can simply put this new technology into an old framework of values and still enjoy progress, but with the peace of virtue.

INTRODUCTION

The rise of the Internet, the growth of the dot-com bubble, and the advent of new technology were wonders to behold. During the time of the go-go growth, there was a bit of arrogance about ethics in this new world. "We're different," they assured. "The old rules can't apply anymore," the new ageists explained. "Old-fashioned virtue ethics simply won't work in a high-tech world," dot-com'ers counseled.

The bubble burst began with a slow leak in April 2000. Slowly, discoveries emerged: the Internet has its pitfalls; investments in air generally don't pay out much; and even new economies are subject to old cycles. Along with the burst bubble has been righteous indignation about the new technology, the new companies, and, certainly, the new accounting methods. Sorting through the rubble of the bankrupt companies of the new-age economies, experts find meaningless financial statements, wealth that was all too fleeting, and questions about old values vs. new values.

Throughout the economic boom of this new age, the conventional wisdom was that old notions of ethics required modification in an international economy with new technology, a faster pace and cultural diversity. A post-mortem on the new economy perhaps makes the case that the same ethical rules that have worked for centuries of commerce may still work and should still be applied in this the age of information and technology. The purpose of this chapter is to provide a look at the ethical standards used by those who built the new economy and through historical parallels offer resolutions for advancement of the cohabitation of ethics, technology and new-age business.

A LOOK AT THE PREVAILING VIEWS ON LEGAL AND ETHICAL ISSUES IN THE NEW ECONOMY

The new economy brought not just new technology, players and products. New ways of doing business and new forms of businesses and technology created new attitudes about and niches in operations, law and ethics. The allegory often cited for these new attitudes, new approaches and new values was that of the New Testament teaching: "Neither do men put new wine into old bottles; else the bottles break, and the wine runneth out, and the bottles perish; but they put new wine into new bottles, and both are preserved" (The Bible). The temporarily effective argument for ignoring the existing infrastructures in both law and ethics was that the high tech industry and the Internet brought changes that were so dramatic that forcing it to fit would destroy both the new economy and the old rules.

As the new economy folded and unfolded, the allegory did not provide a perfect metaphor because the wine was not so new after all and even when you issue new bottles, there are safety and quality concerns that still apply. The prevailing attitude in the initial days of the high tech economy and markets was putting new wine into hastily manufactured bottles. The following section documents the not-so-new nature of the wine, and the danger of new bottles built in haste.

THE "WE'RE DIFFERENT" COMFORT OF ALLEGING DISTINCT AND UNIQUE ISSUES, ACTIVITIES, AND PROCESSES

The companies of the new economy had a "We're different" attitude. Many founders and executives of the dot-com/information-age companies emitted a gunslinger-swagger. Jeff Dachis, the former CEO of Razorfish and one of the founders of the so-called Silicon Alley in the SoHo District of New York City said, "…this is a revolution; we're packing rifles; and this is going to be something that's going to change the course of the way the world is operating" (CBS News, 2000).

When they rolled into the securities market, the world of marketing, and even the worlds of accounting and financial reporting, the dot-com'ers projected a view to traditionalists that they were different, better and slightly above the letter of the law. Their feeling of distinctiveness has produced everything from laxness in following rules to the creation of new rules for what were quite mundane and indistinct business activities.

NEW RULES AND EXEMPTIONS ON ACCOUNTING AND FINANCIAL REPORTING

Perhaps one of the most entertaining of the new financial theories of the dot-com era was EBITDA—earnings before interest, taxes, depreciation and amortization. During its era that lasted for the length of the dot-com bubble, EBITDA was used as the means for evaluating the worth of a company. EBITDA became the figure on which analysts and investors relied despite this nagging question: How meaningful is an earnings figure that fails to take into account very real expenses that are part and parcel of doing business? Measuring earnings before taking into account expenses was a novel and different idea, born at the insistence of company founders and financial theorists because they maintained that these new companies required new views on valuation and new numbers for proper financial analysis.

But this new EBITDA measurement gave neither a complete nor an accurate picture of the company's status. EBITDA was a substitute for the old-fashioned business measures of cash flow, or earnings *after* expenses are deducted. For a time, this new rule was applied and the old business measures were tossed aside as inadequate and inaccurate reflections of a company's true financial picture.

For example, WorldCom was a high tech darling during the growth stages of the new economy. Begun as a long-distance start-up when telecommunications was first deregulated, WorldCom emerged as the leader in all forms of wire and wireless communications by 2000, having acquired 64 other companies along the way, including the unfathomable acquisition of the international long distance carrier, MCI (Eichenwald, 2002a). Bernie Ebbers, the founder of WorldCom, had a unique idea: buy long distance phone service at wholesale rates through volume discounts, and then resell it at the retail level at a price that made money but was still lower than all of his retail competitors (Feder, 2002). His strategy was new, different and earned WorldCom a first-class rating among business leaders and the stock market. Assuming that this new economy was all new and different, even financial analysts, paid to pick apart accounting and financial statements, looked at WorldCom as part of a whole new world with new rules. *The Wall Street Journal* described the deference to Mr. Ebbers and acceptance of new accounting practices as follows, "During the company's heyday, few analysts complained that the frenetic pace of acquisitions made it difficult to gauge the company's health, a task also complicated by WorldCom's reliance on confusing pro-forma figures in its financial reports" (Blumenstein & Sandberg, 2002). They described the business community as regarding Mr. Ebbers as an "icon" and "larger than life" (Blumenstein & Sandberg, 2002).

WorldCom took some on-the-edge steps in presenting its financial statements, fully capitalizing, as it were, on this newfangled notion of EBITDA. During its frenetic pace of new economy acquisitions, WorldCom was booking phenomenal restructuring charges. These are charges determined by management for what it will cost to do the restructuring of the company following a merger. Those charges could include everything from employee downsizing to getting out of leases on facilities that are acquired. There were no accounting rules violated in how WorldCom booked its restructuring charges; they were simply very large charges. The actual costs might never be incurred, and taking a large charge at the time of the acquisition means earnings grow at a phenomenal rate, especially those EBITDA earnings that have no charges against them. And taking large restructuring charges gave WorldCom reserves into which it could dip in order to meet earnings goals in future years. However, the trick was keeping the acquisitions and mergers going, something WorldCom was unable to do when its merger with Sprint was not approved by the Justice Department.

The result was WorldCom soon had no reserves, no more mergers, and no post-restructuring bounces. In short, WorldCom reached a point where it had to rely on the old aspects of business: making money as a provider of services and seller of goods. Those old bottles of doing business well emerged. However, WorldCom proved to be lacking in these basic business skills. In fact, it was not all that efficient as a company in terms of operations and even collection of bills (Eichenwald, 2002a). One analyst noted, "WorldCom wasn't operated at all, it was just on auto pilot, using bubble gum and Band-Aids as solutions to its problems" (Eichenwald, 2002a).

Unable to make earnings through the sale of services, WorldCom's managers began to boost earnings by using accounting methods that did violate existing standards, such as taking $3.8 billion as capital expenses when they were ordinary expenses that should have been deducted from earnings (Sandberg, Solomon, & Blumenstein, 2001). In fact, by the time WorldCom was done, it had to restate its financials by more than $9 billion because not only did this change in the character of expenses make net income higher, it meant that EBITDA, the new bottle measurement for these new companies, was not affected at all because EBITDA did not require depreciation for the $9 billion in capital expenses not really reflected anywhere as a result (Pulliam & Solomon, 2002b). It was all very new and very fancy accounting that failed to show a company was teetering. In between those stunning earnings restatement announcements, WorldCom would declare bankruptcy on July 22, 2002, and, if we can believe its numbers on its assets, it was the largest bankruptcy in the history of the United States (Romero & Atlas, 2002).

The lack of relevance of EBITDA dawned on the financial world after companies such as WorldCom failed and shortly after the dot-com bubble burst. One financial editor has written, in light of the realization that this new method for evaluating the value of companies, that EBITDA really meant, "Earnings Before I Tricked the Dumb Auditor" (Colvin, 2002). For example, during the era of the bubble, Mary Meeker, considered the premier new economy analyst, continued to tout companies that were collapsing within weeks of her continuing "buy" recommendations. However, the cover of *Fortune* magazine from May 14, 2001, features a picture of Ms. Meeker and a story about her collapsed companies and the caption, "Can we ever trust again?"

EBITDA was there for Meeker's companies, and she employed it as the analysts' preferred tool of the new economy, but EBITDA was meaningless in terms of predicting business success or failure. EBITDA was touted as a new bottle. It really was a very old bottle of deception. Painting a positive picture of earnings using self-screened numbers is a very old approach to hoodwinking investors. In fact, some of the officers at WorldCom were indicted for fraud (Eichenwald, 2002b; Solomon & Pulliam, 2002b). The old theories of earnings-expenses = revenues, without any caveats or numbers withheld, appeared to be, when all was said and done, the best predictor of success or failure for a company.

The folly of these new-economy theories of finance and accounting was largely ignored until the companies began collapsing. As that folly was exposed and discussed, there was an accompanying question of why no one raised the issue of EBITDA's obvious irrelevance as well as its inability to reflect the true condition of a business. The answer to the question, "How did this go on for so long unchallenged?" brings other examples of the "we're different" attitude.

HEDGING YOUR BETS
USING YOUR SHAREHOLDERS

Recently, information about Dell Computer, Microsoft, and other new economy companies using the strategies of trading in their own shares in order to hedge their earnings risk has emerged. In other words, these companies were betting on themselves and their share performance, hedging their losses by using contra investments in their own shares (Sparks, 2002; Morgenson, 2002). Known as "playing the put game," these companies would sell options in their stock to raise cash. For example, if a company's shares were selling at $80 each, it could sell puts at $10 per share, exercisable in one year. If, at the end of that year, the shares are selling for $80 or more, the put expires as worthless. The company made money on the puts. If, however, the stock price falls to $40, as was the case when the bubble deflated, the put holder can buy shares on the market at $40 each and exercise the puts, or force the company to buy those shares at $80 each. The company then loses $30 per share because it must honor the puts.

Not only was there the undisclosed risk of the company's exposure should the share price drop, there was the additional issue of those who had sold the puts being in charge of the accounting and financial statements that, depending on their revelations, would control the share price in the market. Those responsible for meeting earnings goals had undertaken a great deal of risk that would ripen into loses if they failed to meet those earnings goals. Some of the biggest and most respected companies of the new economy were engaged in leveraged and hedged market activity in their own shares.

These share-trading, hedging and investment programs were not entirely clear to those shareholders who had invested in the companies with the assumption that they were making money by selling computers and software. Most investors did not understand the exposure of the company in terms of where earnings were coming from, as well as what might happen to these stock purchase programs if there were dramatic swings in the share prices, as there was when the bubble burst. Microsoft's gains on its share purchase program during 1997-2000 were $1.8 billion, a great deal of earnings from non-software business (Sparks, 2002).

NEW RULES ON
CORPORATE GOVERNANCE

New economy companies not only had new theories for financial reporting, they lacked the management and experience depth required to spot and correct what were marginal accounting and financial practices. There was a certain arrogance on the part of "e-businesses" developed for the accounting and financial practices of "bricks-and-mortar businesses." The old rules of transparent financial reporting, as well as staffing management and boards with the depth needed, were dismissed as superfluous. The high-tech companies sought to reinvent much of the way business was done because they believed that their new products, attitudes and approaches offered better alternatives for doing business.

New economy companies ignored conventional wisdom and best practices with regard to board structure. To the extent that these new and inexperienced managers and owners of companies were making mistakes and offering odd measures of value such as EBITDA, there should have been boards in place with sufficient depth and experience to counterbalance the often rash decisions and sometimes deceptive disclosures of the less experienced new-age managers. However, convinced that best practices for the old economy were not transferable to their new ways of doing business, the dot com'ers reinvented the wheel. Their board structures, with distinctions from S&P companies, are profiled below:

BOARD STRUCTURE ISSUE	INTERNET COMPANIES	S&P 500
Average # of directors	7.3%	11.9%
Percentage of outsiders	53.0%	67.6%
Percentage with a nominating committee	28.2%	87.1%
Percentage with at least one female director	23.1%	88.5%
(Inter@ctive Week; Directors Alert, 2000)		

The companies of the new economy did not have as many outsiders on their boards, their board processes were not as rigid in terms of nominations, and even diversity was not a high priority for them. The new-age leaders not only marched to their own drummers, their companies' corporate governance did as well.

Jeff Dachis, the former CEO of Razorfish, a shooting star of a company that served as a consultant to companies in the broad field of information technology with a specialization in web sites, told *Fortune* magazine, in response to its questions about Razorfish's board's lack of independence asked at the height of the company's rise to Wall Street darling, offered, "I control 10% of the company. What's good for me is good for all shareholders. Management isn't screwing up. We've created enormous shareholder value" (Schonfeld, 2002). A great irony is that GM offered "What's good for GM is good for the country," when Ralph Nader raised product liability and environmental issues about the way GM was mass-producing cars (Shipper & Jennings, 1984).

Mr. Dachis thought his board structure, as well as his attitude, were new and unique, a reflection of the know-how of the new-age executive. Mr. Dachis explained his different board structure and unique approach to corporate governance: "We want aggressive, bright people who 'get it' on our board, not representatives of corporate America who are interested in protecting the status quo" (Schonfeld, 2000). That pervasive attitude of "getting it" was often referred to as "digital hubris" (Wooley, 2001). Mr. Dachis earned the honor of the *New York Times'* quote of the day for May 31, 1999, when he said, "I feel completely and utterly entitled to whatever success comes our way. Not everybody's good, not everybody has the winning idea, not every idea deserves to be funded or to be public. I'm sorry, but there are sheep and there are shepherds, and I fancy myself to be the latter" (*New York Times*, 1999).

GenX owners, executives and entrepreneurs were not the only ones advancing the theory that the dot-coms and new-age companies were different. Even academics felt that this new economy called for new forms of governance. Professor Joe Grundfest of Stanford Law School, and a former SEC commissioner, defended the dot-coms' board practices: "Who's complaining? All things being equal, an outside board is not a bad idea. But I'd rather have a bunch of smart, honest insiders than sleepy, stupid outsiders. Things are going swimmingly—you have to be careful not to overgeneralize. The largest fraud problems in the market are not in the dot-coms" (Schonfeld, 2000).

THE RESULTS OF THE NEW RULES

Actually, Professor Grundfest and Jeff Dachis were both wrong on the company, boards and things going swimmingly. Mr. Dachis's Razorfish was one of the early casualties of the dot-com era. More than 50% of the SEC's fraud cases for 2000 and 2001 involved dot-coms, a historical first in terms of one industry dominating the investigation process (www.sec.gov).

What Razorfish and the other information technology companies did was not unique. The product was different; the nature of business was not. As cofounder Dachis explained to Vault.com: "Razorfish's work is all things digital, not just the Internet or Web design. Whether it's helping transform a roadside service firm into a company that enables mobility, migrating the large and complex back end of a major financial institution into a more user-friendly, web-based commerce site, or showing the world how easy it is to trade stock online, Razorfish helps clients leverage digital technology to improve their business at the core. In all of its work, Razorfish creates intentional user experience—a sort of modern version of good old-fashioned customer focus" (The Vault, 2000, www.excite.com)

The traditional "customer focus" portion of the philosophy was lost in the technological wizardry. When Razorfish went public in June 1999, its stock premiered at $56 per share. On May 10, 2001, following ongoing market realizations that the company's numbers were inflated, those shares were worth $1.11. They would dip to $0.14 before climbing back up again to $0.21 on October 11, 2001 (www.sec.gov). By that time, Razorfish was reporting earnings of $47 million, but still booking losses of $25 million because of its high expenses. Razorfish was a phenomenon of the information age, a company poised to create, refine and expand the Internet. But it had no checks and balances in terms of its financial reporting and disclosures. Worse, it had lost sight of the basic rules of business, a lesson Mr. Dachis now acknowledges publicly as he looks back at the mistakes he made in running the company, "Lessons learned: the numbers are the numbers—they don't lie. The macro point on that one is: basic business sensibilities need to be adhered to 100% of the time. When you know your client has not paid after 30 days, you have to collect that money on the 31st day" (Wooley, 2001).

Another high tech company with the "we're different" attitude was PSINet, a firm run by William Schrader and one that had its shares on NASDAQ as high as $60. PSINet grew from a few phone lines to a multinational that provided Internet services to over 100,000 businesses. To be able to do so, Schrader had to make acquisitions at a feverish pace and in locations all around the globe. The acquisitions were often made without the board's knowledge and PSINet was using a sort of off-the-books strategy for infusing cash into the company that was similar to the tools Enron was also using. One board member referred to the methods of operation and lack of approvals as "cavalier." When questioned about the company's strategy, direction and debt, and doubting analysts, Schrader responded, "I don't give a rat's ass what Wall Street thinks. We run our company for our customers, not Wall Street. They know it, and they don't like it" (Wooley, 2001).

By May 2001, PSINET's share price had tumbled from a high of $60 per share to $0.18. The board dismissed Schrader as PSINet defaulted on $4 billion in debt. Its bankruptcy was one of the largest of the dot-com companies. Mr. Dachis learned that it was not EBITDA, but cash that mattered in running a business and both he and Mr. Schrader learned that processes and good boards can make a difference despite their views about their stodginess and Wall Street's insistence about them. In short, these two front-runners in the world of information technology learned that the basics of business mattered in running a company.

Enron, another company of the new economy, used the Internet and information about energy supply markets to develop new ways for trading power across the country and minimizing risk for utilities on power prices. Its voiced view was that it was different from all the energy traders, from all other companies, because it was using technical computer modeling to make its money.

Enron began as a purveyor of natural gas and was indeed the largest national gas purveyor in the United States by 1995 (McClean, 2001). However, not satisfied being an energy company trading in energy, Enron moved into trading anything that could use the Internet. It was trading everything from phone lines to hedges for weather and then billed itself as "the biggest e-commerce company in the world" (Eichenwald, 2002c). Enron's niche was that of a company using technology to unite buyers and sellers with products and prices. In the initial growth stages of the high-tech market, Enron was able to show remarkable growth. But when that growth slowed, and in some markets actually stopped, Enron was faced with the realities of business and business cycles.

However, rather than following the rules for honest disclosure regarding its financial position, Enron began using some very old-fashioned accounting tricks of moving debt off the balance sheet in order to enhance share price and mask what was the failure of its innovative computer models to generate the double-digit growth it had experienced and continued to promise (Emshwiller, Smith, Sidel, & Weil, 2001).

Enron soon realized, it taking only about two years of such a novel approach to business for a collapse to come, that there were no substitutes for products, service and sales, not even accounting tricks. Enron had to restate four years of earnings (1997-2001) and its share price of $83 on January 14, 2000, fell to $0.67 per share on January 14, 2001. Enron entered bankruptcy, its audit firm was indicted and convicted of obstruction of justice, one officer has entered a guilty plea and its chief financial officer, Andrew Fastow, has been charged with 78 felony counts (Weil, 2001). The company that fancied itself as different from the rest and above the financial fray exists no longer.

THE HISTORICAL PARALLELS IN THE LAXNESS OF THE RULES

All of these companies of the new economy claimed unique status in terms of their departure from traditional rules regarding earnings, corporate governance, and even financial reporting. They characterized their positions, strategies, businesses and products as different from existing companies and distinguishable from anyone or anything in business history. But picking up the pieces from the failed companies brings the realization that, fundamentally, business remains the same, regardless of the nature of the product or the approach taken to sales, marketing and packaging. There must still be earnings. Expenses must be kept low. Customers must be satisfied and shareholders must trust that management is forthright in its disclosures and accounting practices. Oversight from an effective board matters, and there is no substitute for experience in handling business development and the issues that arise. The claimed immunity from business fundamentals so widely touted by new economy companies did not exist. The road to economic collapse based on new ideas, new economies and new approaches has been traveled before.

THE TULIP MARKET COLLAPSE

The story of the founding and growth of the Holland tulip market is a remarkably similar one. When the tulip was developed, people were enamored of it. They began buying tulips, fields of tulips and developing tulips. When tulips were no longer available, they began buying tulip bulbs because they would have a tulip at some time in the future. When there were no bulbs left, they created a market for tulip bulb futures. At the height of the market, one tulip bulb future cost $10,000 in present-day dollars. There was a market of air with complete dependence on the creation of bulbs in the future; these were investments in air completely dependent upon the honor of those selling these derivative tulip instruments (Dash, 2000).

Eventually investors realized that those who sold the futures could not possibly deliver all that they had sold and the market collapsed. The impact on the Holland economy was centuries in length. The new economy companies were not much different. For example, AOL and other companies were permitted to book revenues in advance using a formula that was based on the amount of business each advertising dollar was expected to bring to the company. At some point, in the future, they assured, there will be revenues and you can invest in anticipation of such revenues and you should value our stock as if those revenues are real. But economies have always cycled and the ads may not always bring the revenue. And sometimes you cannot deliver the bulbs you contracted for when you had none to sell.

THE 1929 MARKET CRASH

In his book, *The Causes of the 1929 Stock Market Crash*, Harold Bierman Jr. documents the similarities between our burst bubble and the great crash (Bierman, 1998). He lists high price/earnings multipliers, insider trading, stock options abounding, speculation, optimism and others that characterized our market rise and decline. He even notes that insiders in companies were selling their shares at extraordinarily high rates, a phenomenon seen documented in virtually all the new companies of the new economy. For example, Ken Lay, the former CEO and chairman of Enron, entered into transactions to sell Enron stock 350 times, trading almost daily, resulting in receipts of $101.3 million in stock sales. Between early 1999 and July 2001, five months before Enron filed for bankruptcy, Mr. Lay sold 1.8 million shares (Wayne, 2002). The prices for Mr. Lay's sales ranged from $31 to $86 per share. Jeff Skilling, who served as CEO of the company for about six months, just prior to its collapse, sold his shares at a rate of 10,000 every seven days. A lawsuit filed against the officers for the share transactions shows what lawyers for the plaintiffs in the case call, "the most massive insider bailout that we've ever seen…[t]he overall size of this case is unprecedented" (Wayne, 2002).

As much as the "we're different" theory was floated throughout the development of new technologies, companies and economies, it simply was not so. New products, new technologies, youth, a lack of historical foundation and perhaps other factors contributed to a certain arrogance in the new economy as well as a disregard for fundamental rules of running a business along with the basics of ethical conduct, something explored in subsequent sections.

THE POSTPONEMENT OF GRAPPLING WITH ISSUES WHILE WAITING FOR NEW RULES

Another view that drifted into the decisions and conduct of those in the new economy was one of concluding that because they were so different from anything and anyone who had come before that no one could resolve ethical and legal issues until someone established new rules. The result was that those in the new economy simply proceeded at will without those rules, espousing immunity because the rapid pace of technology demanded choices in areas in which there were no rules. In reality, there were easily applicable rules, but those involved preferred to await new and different rules, with the hope that they would enjoy technological exemptions.

An example from Internet toy sales illustrates. During the Christmas season 2000, Internet retailers sold $11.5 billion in consumer goods (www.ftc.gov). A number of e-retailers failed to deliver the goods their customers had ordered online in time for Christmas morning. The companies perceived that there were no rules for delivery delays because the transactions were consummated over the Internet and there were, at that time, no applicable rules and regulations. Not only were the toys not delivered on time, the parents had no advance warning of the later delivery and were unable to make other plans, thus leaving thousands of parents with empty stockings on Christmas morning, The faulty assumption was that they needed to wait for someone to develop rules on delays in Internet transactions.

When the parents complained to the Federal Trade Commission (FTC), the agency stated the obvious, "The Federal Trade Commission is advising online merchants to review their obligations under the Mail or Telephone Order Merchandise Rule to better serve their customers this holiday season." There were already rules in place for companies to notify customers who had placed phone, fax and mail orders that there would be a delay. The FTC simply concluded, "Why should Internet transactions be any different?" The FTC applied existing laws to high tech transactions, noting that the rapidity with which business could be done and the surprising drains on inventory were not excuses for not complying with the existing rules. The agency even offered suggestions, in effect under existing rules for companies to deal with unexpected Internet sales demands:

Running Late? Overwhelmed with Orders?
The Rule gives you several ways to deal with an unexpected demand.
- You can change your shipment promises up to the point the consumer places the order, if you reasonably believe that you can ship by the new date. The updated information overrides previous promises and reduces your need to send delay notices. Be sure to tell your customer the new shipment date before you take the order.
- You must provide a delay option notice if you can't ship within the originally promised time. The Rule lets you use a variety of ways to provide the notice, including e-mail, fax or phone. It's a good idea to keep a record of what your notice states, when you provide it, and the customer's response (www.ftc.gov).

The same was true of privacy issues with regard to Internet site usage and the distribution of site users' names and addresses to marketing lists and other firms. Already in place were privacy regulations that were applicable to banks, credit card companies and others. Internet merchants were subject to the same standards, but waited until they were told to follow them. Legislation passed in 2001 simply extended the application of existing laws to Internet merchants (Gramm-Leach-Bliley Act).

THE "WE'LL NEVER FIND
A SOLUTION" COMPLACENCY

There was yet another form of rationalization that those using technology used to justify breaches. That attitude embraced the notion that the technology was so complex no one could ever find a solution, so a policy of "no rules" was the only functional approach. Napster, the copying and downloading of copyrighted music, and the entire evolving process of obtaining music for free was a years-long illustration of this approach to rules and notions of ownership in technology. Young Shawn Fanning had found a way to copy music through a process he referred to as "peer-to-peer file sharing" (*A&M Records v. Napster*). Those in the music industry used the term "copyright infringement."

The perception of those using the Napster technology was that because the music could be exchanged via technology that there were no longer copyrights or property ownership. The view from the music industry was that without such property rights, the incentives for the creation and production of music were removed. The view from the young technological geniuses who developed the downloading capabilities was that trying to halt technology to enforce intellectual property rights was akin to catching a tiger by the tale; it could not be done.

The youngsters—Mr. Fanning was 18 at the time he developed his product—failed to realize that we had been down this technological road once before. During the early 1980s, the film industry was coping with a new technology called the Betamax video tape recorder (VTR). Consumers around the world were taping television shows, movies and other programming right from their television sets. Those in the movie industry made the same arguments that the music industry made against Napster: without the intellectual property protection, creativity and production would end.

In a case that journeyed to the U.S. Supreme Court, the justices found that the home recording was "fair use," or a permissible method of using the VTR machines that did not infringe on the movie industry copyrights (*Sony v. Universal City Studios*). The interpretation was a narrow one that was not the death knell the movie industry predicted. In fact, the decision in the case represented the birth of Blockbuster. The film industry embraced the new technology and found ways to market its products for use with the new technology.

The issues surrounding music downloading and Napster are not fully resolved. A federal appellate court ruled that the downloading was an infringement and ordered the Napster services shut down because the activities went far beyond the VTR case of one recording from a television set at home. The downloading represented a pipeline around the world for universal downloading. However, there still remains the great potential for the use of the technology as a complement to the copyrights of the owners. The new services offer downloading for a fee, one that is less than the purchase of a full CD at a music store, but one that nonetheless provides compensation for the intellectual property of creators, artists and producers. The conflicts can be resolved with accommodation for all interests, while using the technology that created the issues. The record companies have discovered that perhaps their prices for artists' CDs were too high and that they were losing the opportunities for one-song purchases that can be accomplished via the Internet. Honoring the principles of ownership and the protections of the law actually afforded an opportunity for the use of technology at higher levels than it was being used during the Napster pirating period.

The formation of contracts over the Internet has been a point of contention and frustration for companies, consumers and courts. The prevailing view was that this new technology was too elusive in terms of proof and documentation to provide the type of permanent record needed to support the formation of contracts. The obvious solution was to use the technology to establish the verification rather than thinking along traditional lines of ink, paper and tangible documents. Companies began to create passwords for use of accounts so that there was a means for customers to identify themselves. Companies began to require double verifications of the point of contracting. Before they contracted, the software required them to click a box saying that they understood that they were contracting. While it is true that they could not solve the problem of proof of contracting in the traditional sense, they had additional tools that could be used to provide fairly solid proof of contracting.

A HISTORICAL LOOK AT THE LEGAL AND ETHICAL ISSUES THAT ARISE FROM TECHNOLOGICAL ADVANCEMENTS

New products and new technology have always instilled a desire for new standards, rules and values. But, progress and distinct products and industries should not be the impetus for new values, rules and laws. Distinctiveness does not mandate exemptions from basic notions of running a business or from virtue ethics.

A LOOK BACK AT THE
INDUSTRIAL REVOLUTION

The horseless carriage was frightening when it was first introduced, but those who still used horses and buggies quickly discovered that the simple rules of the road that they had always used would work just fine for these newfangled devices. Staying on the right, passing on the left, stopping to yield—all could be done in a Model T as easily as in a wagon. A new provision—"slower traffic stay to the right"—ensured the peaceful cohabitation of the new with the old.

When the economy shifted away from farms and small businesses, there was an increase in the distance between employer and employee as well as an increase in the number of owners of businesses. Most businesses behaved as companies in our new economy did. They treated themselves as immune from the rules, rationalized that the old issues of fairness and honesty were inapplicable in industrial giants and largely ignored the implications of their choices. The result was the expansion of existing agency law to provide larger numbers of agents (the massive groups of employees working in factories) with protections that were once ironed out one-on-one in smaller businesses. But the new structure of labor laws, wage laws and even safety protections were based on the fundamental ethical notion of fairness. That is, to the extent new laws and rules were needed, they were simply expansions of old principles and not new standards. The standards were buried in the explosive growth.

For example, Upton Sinclair's *The Jungle* is cited as evidence of the need for more regulation of food processing, plant conditions and employer/employee relations. Perhaps the book is better used as an example of what happens when business grows so rapidly and technology changes so quickly that those involved forget the ethical assumptions that were more easily confronted and handled in the one-on-one relationships that had dominated the economy previously. It was difficult for the owner of the local general store to terminate employees in order to gain more profit for himself. There was a sense of community that would have produced backlash against the storeowner causing a reduction in business for his shoddy treatment of loyal employees. Community acceptance served as the checks and balances for business conduct in an era when businesses were small, local and longstanding.

With the absorption of the small, community businesses into the large, impersonal industrial firm, that one-on-one and eyeball-to-eyeball social pressure did not have the same effect, if it was present at all. Technology and changes in the way businesses operated did not require new standards. However, with standards being ignored, laws and regulations became a substitute. In these dramatic economic cycles, the perceived need for new laws and regulations springs from the need for the codification of ethical standards.

THE PARALLELS IN LEGAL ISSUES: ANTITRUST, FRAUD AND PRIVACY

Antitrust legislation has long been perceived as "new" law adopted because of the nature of the companies and their ways of doing business in the industrialized United States. Power concentration in the hands of a few companies was, after all, a new phenomenon and "new" antitrust laws were passed to cope with this new power concentration and the resulting impact on the way business is done. Antitrust laws are the codification of the ethical notion of justice, or, in childhood lingo, playing fair. When businesses were smaller and highly visible in the community, any perception of unfair treatment or attempts to drive others out of business were handled with consumer dollars. A classic illustration is found in Frank Capra's 1946 film, *It's a Wonderful Life*. The dastardly Mr. Potter wants to be the only bank in town, but he faces competition from George Bailey and his building and loan association. When Mr. Potter causes a drain on the Bailey institution, George is able to stay in business by appealing to customers on the basis of "Old Man Potter's" unfair tactics, usurious loans and heartlessness in dealing with late payments. The customers know they don't want to be left with but one choice for doing financial business in their small town. With their dollars and accounts, they curbed anticompetitive behavior.

They were able to control business behavior because they were face-to-face with businesses and business owners on a daily basis. They lived on the same streets, shopped at the same stores and interacted in their social and religious events. Societal pressure enforced voluntary constraints, the sense of justice and fairness.

Antitrust laws were promulgated because the Potters became too distant from the customers, shareholders, and even board to feel the constraints of their pressures and judgments. Business became impersonal and it departed from the virtues community enforced. The standards did not change, only the willingness to honor them did. The Sherman Act codifies the George Bailey phenomenon. As business is more widely dispersed, sheer size makes it difficult for community controls to uphold ethical notions.

Similar patterns and issues exist with regard to fraud. Fraud is infinitely easier to execute in an anonymous society. Community forces also curbed fraud: the shunning that occurred when one member of that community heaped an injustice upon another. Anonymity makes community enforcement mechanisms ineffectual. However, the line has not moved. Fraud is still fraud. Impersonal transactions make community controls ineffectual and the law becomes the means for curbing fraud. What is perceived to be new law or changed rules is simply the codification of basic virtue ethics because of the need for different enforcement.

The anonymity of the Internet presents an even greater challenge to community enforcement. The Internet is international and identities are not only missing the face-to-face contact, they may never be known given technology's mask through the ubiquitous screen name. We contract from afar without ever knowing our sellers or buyers. There are no faces, bricks and mortar, or people to whom customers can turn. Likewise, those who would take advantage of others are not tethered by the pain of eye contact or the knowledge about the costs of their fraud. In addition, the Internet provides speed with a few strokes of the keys. A fraud can be perpetrated in a matter of minutes. Scams do not take the groundwork and community-faith building that Professor Harold Hill embarked upon in another era in order to sell band instruments. Fraud is infinitely easier via the Internet.

Therein lies the true issue of ethics in this technology age. Technology advances at a rate that astounds. We watch as a 16-year-old is able to hobble the computer systems of multinational corporations through a few simple computer commands and wonder what laws we can pass to deter such behavior. We see another teen able to charge hundreds of thousands of dollars of merchandise using credit card numbers he has gleaned from hacking into a bank's credit card center. And we are speechless as we see 15-year-old Jonathan Lebed parley $8,000 in savings into $800,000 by using 23 screen names to tout obscure stocks to those using Internet sites and chatrooms as investment guides (Morgenson, 2000). The lad was comfortable defrauding thousands of unknown souls in order to amass a fortune before he finished middle school.

Regulations and laws limp along trying to keep pace with every innovative use of the Internet and each new ability mastered by technological masters. Regulation cannot keep pace. Regulation codifies, after the fact, what are simply ethical parameters of behavior. To the extent ethical standards have changed in this era of technology, they have changed in the sense of abandonment. Peter Kreeft has summarized our quandary in eloquent fashion:

For exactly at the time when the fatal knowledge of how to destroy the entire human race has fallen forever into our hands, the knowledge of morality has fallen out. Exactly when the vehicle of our history has gotten a souped-up engine, we have lost the road map. Exactly when our toys have grown up with us from bows and arrows to thermonuclear bombs, we have become moral infants.

THE SIMPLE EFFICACY OF
OLD RULES FOR NEW TECHNOLOGY

The supposed complexities of the issues surrounding technology should be reexamined using one question: What *is* different?

What we learn from the discussion of past and present is that the basics of business, from cost management to true earnings, will always apply no matter how novel the product. Companies such as Razorfish, PSINet, Enron, WorldCom and others have taught us that we cannot ignore the fundamentals of accounting, financial reporting, customer service and the making and selling of a good product. Financial wizardry is not only deceptive, it does not work in terms of delivering either products or return for investors. Following the burst bubble, the *Wall Street Journal* offered an in-depth look at where investors were turning. Just the title of the piece is instructive and insightful: "Back to Basics: After Tech Bubble Bursts, Value Investing Suddenly Makes Sense Again" (Lipin, Scannell, & Spurgeon, 2000). And investors were back to the companies of the old economy for the very simple reason that they understood what the companies were doing and could make sense of their financial statements (Browning & Ip, 2000). Investors also knew the price would be fair. Billionaire Warren Buffett observed, "If it is a nonglamorous business then there is a reasonable chance that the price will be right" (Lipin, Scanell, & Spurgeon, 2000). Mr. Buffett, the man not taken with the high-tech economy, was featured on the cover of *Fortune* magazine with the following caption, "The Oracle of Everything" (Lipin, Scanell, & Spurgeon, 2000). The inside story featured the following introduction, "Warren Buffett has been right about the stock market, rotten accounting, CEO greed and corporate governance. The rest of us are just catching on" (Serwer, 2002).

What we also learn is the adherence to the basic virtues of honesty, fairness, and justice is the source of market trust. These rules have never been complex, but the search for loopholes has made them seem so. Creative capitalization on accounting loopholes or the lack of regulation in certain areas is a short-term method for doing business. The loss of trust and the resulting impact on the value of the company and the reputations of those who have found those loopholes are devastating. Those of the new economy fancied themselves different from traditional business, but even their unique products, engineering and strategy did not serve to create a niche that permitted them to operate without adhering to the basics of business and virtue.

Just a glance at the collapse of Adelphia, the giant cable company, provides insight into the idea that no one, no matter how different or how much foresight they have shown, is exempt from honesty in business and the sound practices of an independent board and solid external review. Adelphia was another wonder-age company that grew from several hundred cable subscribers in Coudersport, Pennsylvania, to a seven-state multibillion operation (Solomon & Frank, 2002). But its officers, who also served on a board that had no real outsiders, were borrowing money from the company so extensively to cover their stock trades and margin accounts, that the company was forced into bankruptcy (Markon & Frank, 2002). Universal cable service is the new technological wonder the company produced. Looting the company is really quite an old business trick, and constitutes a crime even when those who commit it are innovators in the industry (Markon & Frank, 2002). Five officers of Adelphia were indicted.

The rules creep that enters into the discussions surrounding technology and ethics is based on the faulty assumption that because of rapidity, new methodologies and approaches, rules must change. Indeed, the better proposition is that precisely because of those changes, the rules must remain the same. The increasing impersonal nature of doing business does not demand a lower standard for ethical behavior. That increasing impersonal nature simply introduces temptation because of the lack of community checks and balances on unfair and unjust conduct. That temptation exists and that opportunities for dishonesty and taking advantage of others are not justifications for abandoning the standards of fairness and honesty. They are reminders for increasing vigilance in a world with few enforcement mechanisms. They are also tests for success. To the extent that we continue to exercise control over the temptations for dishonesty and taking advantage of others, business flourishes because of the opportunities for technology to increase in a laissez-faire world. To the extent behaviors must be controlled, curbed and prohibited, the licenses for technological development become limited. Regulations hamper growth and progress; freedom given through virtue permits and nourishes them.

One final and simple rule that emerges from this discussion of new business and old rules is: history repeats itself. While we may wish to believe that ours is a unique age and that none who have come before have seen the likes of our newfound ways of doing business, such beliefs are wrong. Those who have come before us could not have even envisioned the technology we have created, but they have witnessed the damaging human behaviors that occur when we make the assumption that the traditional rules surely can no longer apply to such magnificent forms of progress.

Andrew Carnegie introduced the mass production of steel, sharing of profits for employees and even the philanthropic good that businesses can do (Novak, 1996). But he also struggled mightily with his treatment of his employees during labor protests. Enron introduced new ways of trading energy, new financial models and even new methods for reducing risk. But its accounting methods, while perfectly within accounting rules, did not provide investors, including its employees, with an accurate picture of its solvency. As a result, Enron's employees have worthless retirement accounts. The same was true for WorldCom and its employees.

There was outrage at Carnegie for his treatment of his employees and similar outrage at the Enron and WorldCom executives for their failure to take steps to preserve the value of employees' futures. The products and times may be different, but the ethical issue of treatment of employees remains the same, and the virtue of fairness was at the heart of Carnegie's labor dispute even as it is at the heart of Enron's and WorldCom's stock pension plan for its employees. From the discussions presented, it is clear that the lessons of history, the basics of business, and the virtue of ethical standards as a measure for business choices and behavior have come home to roost with the fallen shooting stars of the new-age economy. We have seen a few of them confess to their follies. However, the concern that arises, despite those acknowledgments and the simplicity of ethics in this new era, is that the damage has been done and that confessions and admissions carry "the attic odor of atonement come too late" (Novak, 1996).

There is nothing new brought to us via technology. We have a new economy that tried to sell itself as new wine that required different, somewhat cheaper bottles. As it turns out, old recycled bottles were a better bet because the new bottles burst before us as the flimsy framework of flexible rules in accounting, corporate governance and customer service and honesty collapsed. They were flexible, but they did not provide a solid container for the exciting nature of business. New and rapid does not require a revamping of the foundations of business. The old bottles of solid business practices proved better containment units than the so-called "new and improved" units.

The old bottles are comprised of history, good business practices and the basic virtues of fairness and honesty. To carry the metaphor a bit further, perhaps the new wine was not so new after all. We have been down this revolutionary road before when it comes to business and learned that there are new products and new ideas, but the wine must be made within certain standards in order to get good results. Skimping on the bottle proved disastrous. The new ideas will survive the bubble's crash, for surely there is much in the technological revolution that benefits all. These new ideas just need to be bottled more carefully, along with the wisdom of age and experience.

REFERENCES

A & M Records, Inc. v. Napster, Inc. (239 F.3d 1004). 9th Circuit Court. (2001)

Bierman, Jr., H. (1998). The causes of the 1929 stock market crash: A speculative orgy or a new era? In *Contributions in Economics and Economic History, 195*. New York: Greenwood.

Blumenstein, R. & Sandberg, J. (2002, April 30). WorldCom CEO quits amid probe of firm's finances. *Wall Street Journal*, A1; A9.

Browning, E.S. & Ip, G. (2000, November 27). Back to basics: After tech bubble bursts, value investing suddenly makes sense again. *Wall Street Journal*, C1; C4.

CBS News (2000). Retrieved from the World Wide Web: www.cbsnews.com/stories/2000/02/15/60II.

Colvin, G. (2002, November 11). Between Right and Right. *Fortune*, 66.

Dash, M. (2000). *Tulipmania: The Story of the World's Most Coveted Flower and the Extraordinary Passions it Aroused.* New York: Three Rivers Press.

Directors Alert. (2000). Data from "Board Structures and Practices In An E-Business Environment." *A Best Practices Panel,* 15.

Eichenwald, K. (2002a, August 8). For WorldCom, acquisitions were behind its rise and fall. *New York Times,* A1.

Eichenwald, K. (2002b, August 2). 2 ex-officials at WorldCom are charged in huge fraud. *New York Times,* A1.

Eichenwald, K. (2002c, January 13). Audacious climb to success ended in dizzying lunge. *New York Times,* A20.

Emshwiller, J.R., Smith, R., Sidel, R., & Weil, J. (2001, November 9). Enron cuts profit data of 4 years by 20%. *Wall Street Journal,* A3.

Enron's other strategy: Taxes; Internal papers reveal how complex deals boosted profits by $1 Billion. (2002, May 22). *Washington Post,* B1.

Excite.com. (2000). *The Vault: Company profile.* Retrieved from the World Wide Web: www.excite.com.

Feder, B.J. (2002, May 1). An abrupt departure is seen as a harbinger. *New York Times,* C1.

Federal Trade Commission. (n.d.). Products and Services. Retrieved from the World Wide Web: www.ftc.gov.

Gramm-Leach-Bliley Act (Called the Financial Privacy and Pretexting Act). 15 U.S.C. Section 6801; The applicable regulations are found at 12 C.F.R. Section 225.

The Holy Bible (King James Version). (1992). Matthew 9:17. *See also* Mark 2:22 and Luke 5:37.

Inter@ctive Week Internet Index, covering 39 companies including Amazon.com, Cisco Systems, eBay, Novell, Qualcomm, Yahoo! and Sunmicrosystems.

Lipin, S., Scannell, K., & Spurgeon, D. (2000, November 27). New Deal Era: Old economy gains attention of M & A Crowd. *Wall Street Journal,* C1:C19.

Markon, J. & Frank, R. (2002, July 25). Five Adelphia officials arrested on fraud charges. *Wall Street Journal,* A3; A6.

McLean, B. (2001, December 24). Why Enron went bust. *Fortune,* 59-60.

Morgenson, G. (2000, September 21). S.E.C. says teenager had after-school hobby: Online stock fraud. *New York Times,* A1; C10.

Morgenson, G. (2002, September 22). Infatuated investors may be missing Dell's flaws. *New York Times,* BU1.

New York Times. (1999, May 31). *Quotation of the Day,* A2.

Novak, M. (1996). *New York: Free Press* (pp. 58-63).

Pulliam, S. & Solomon, D. (2002, October 30) How three unlikely sleuths discovered fraud at WorldCom. *Wall Street Journal,* A1.

Romero, S. & Atlas, R.D. (2002, July 22). WorldCom files for bankruptcy; Largest U.S. Case. *New York Times*, A1.

Sandberg, J., Solomon, D., & Blumenstein, R. (2001, June 27). Inside WorldCom's unearthing of a vast accounting scandal. *Wall Street Journal*, A1.

Schonfeld, E. (2000, March 20). Doing business the Dot-Com way. *Fortune*, 116.

Securities and Exchange Commission. (n.d.). *Fraud Investigations*. Retrieved from EDGAR database on the World Wide Web: http://www.sec.gov/edgar/searchedgar/webusers.htm.

Securities and Exchange Commission. (n.d.). 10-K filings. Retrieved from EDGAR database on the World Wide Web: http://www.sec.gov/edgar/searchedgar/webusers.htm.

Serwer, A. (2002, November 11). The oracle of everything. *Fortune*, 68-82.

Shipper, F. & Jennings, M. (1984). *Business strategy for the political arena*. New York: Quorum.

Solomon, D. & Frank, R. (2002, April 5). Adelphia story: Founding family retreats in crisis. *Wall Street Journal*, B1.

Solomon, D. & Pulliam, S. (2002, August 29). U.S., pushing WorldCom case, indicts ex-CFO and his aide. *Wall Street Journal*, A1.

Sony Corporation of America v. Universal City Studios (464 U.S. 417). (1984).

Sparks, D. (2002, January 15). Options put giants in a jam. *Business Week*, 68-69.

Wayne, L. (2002, January 13). Before debacle, Enron insiders cashed in $1.1 billion in shares. *New York Times*, A1.

Weil, J. (2001, November 5). What Enron's financial reports did—and didn't—reveal. *Wall Street Journal*, C1; C14.

Woolley, S. (2001, May 28). Digital hubris. *Forbes*, 66-70.

Section III

Policy Implications

Chapter XI

Liability for System and Data Quality

Robert D. Sprague
Eastern New Mexico University, USA

ABSTRACT

This chapter discusses various theories of legal liability related to computer system and data quality. Contract-based theories are discussed in detail, as most computer systems are acquired and data are accessed through some form of contractual relationship. Additional tort-based theories of liability are also discussed, particularly relating to publication of inaccurate data. As presented in this chapter, purchasers of defective computer hardware or software and users of inaccurate data have very limited legal remedies available. Further, the legal remedies that may be available are typically severely restricted by the contract through which the computer system is acquired or the data are accessed.

INTRODUCTION

Accompanying the proliferation of computers in almost every facet of life is an underlying risk to financial and physical well-being related to computer system and data quality. Software errors have been directly linked to business disruptions, loss of services (such as metropolitan telephone services), plane crashes, and even deaths (Santor, n.d.; Elmer-DeWitt, 1990). The world's reliance upon computers was particularly demonstrated in the later years of the twentieth century when it was discovered that many older, critical software programs could not properly calculate dates after December 31, 1999. The concern over the Millennium Bug led directly to the expenditure of billions of dollars to update computer software to eliminate this problem (Dearlove, 2001). The viability of a business often depends upon the continual and reliable operation of its computer system. In addition, significant financial commitments are frequently made on the basis of computer-generated data.

The consequences of low-quality computer hardware and software are not infrequent or insubstantial. A recent report from the U.S. Department of Commerce states that total U.S. software sales in 2000 were approximately $180 billion (RTI, 2002). The report estimated that the lack of an adequate software testing infrastructure costs U.S. software users over $38 billion per year, principally through error avoidance and mitigation activities. The report also noted that these estimated costs do not reflect costs "...associated with mission critical software where the failure can lead to extremely high costs such as loss of life or catastrophic failure" (p. ES-3). The report further noted that roughly 22% of PCs break down every year—compared to 9% of VCRs; 7% of big-screen TVs; 7% of clothes dryers; and 8% of refrigerators.

In just about every instance, a computer system is acquired, software is used, or data are accessed through a contract-based commercial transaction. Therefore, whether a computer, software or data vendor will be held liable depends on the language of the contract itself and the law of contracts. As this chapter will discuss, most contracts impose scant liability for vendors. Aggrieved users have pursued other avenues of relief through noncontract-based legal theories, but with little success. For computer, software and data users, the Latin maxim of *caveat emptor* still applies—let the buyer beware.

BACKGROUND

Two of the principal sources of law in the American legal system are court decisions resulting from lawsuits and laws enacted by legislatures. A lawsuit is initiated by an aggrieved party—the plaintiff—filing a complaint with the appropriate court, which must be defended by the party or parties named in the complaint—the defendant (or defendants). Unless the case is settled by the parties, a trial is held at which evidence is presented and witnesses testify. Either party may appeal the decision of the trial to a higher court of appeals. The appeals court reviews the trial proceedings to determine whether the appropriate laws were applied correctly. No evidence or testimony is presented at the appeal.

This trial and appeal process creates what is known as "common law." Each ruling by a court of law creates a rule of law. At a trial, the judge's ruling applies to the parties appearing before that judge. In higher courts, such as courts of appeal and state supreme courts, each ruling creates a rule of law that must be followed by lower courts. For example, a ruling by the California State Supreme Court must be followed by all other courts in the State of California. The ruling is "binding precedent" on the lower California courts. However, the California State Supreme Court's ruling need not be followed by the courts in any other state. As a result, each state has its own specific rules of law that apply within that state. In theory, if a judge is dealing with a new issue, and there is no binding precedent (from a higher court within the state) which the judge must follow, the judge may follow the rulings of courts in other states, but only if he or she agrees with the reasoning and analysis of those other courts.

Although there are federal laws and federal courts, there is no "federal common law." In certain circumstances, federal courts can sit as state courts, and they will apply that state's applicable law. Likewise, the U.S. Supreme Court, which is the ultimate authority on the law in the United States, will only consider a case involving state common law if a U.S. Constitutional issue is involved (such as whether a state rule of law violates the U.S. Constitution).

Statutory law consists of laws (statutes) passed by legislatures, state and federal. Statutes are passed to address a legal need identified by the legislature. State statutes are often passed to "correct" or modify a particular common law rule within that state. A state statute takes precedence over a conflicting state common law rule.

In the United States, commercial transactions are governed by contract law. Since each state's common law evolves relatively independently within its own court system, the result is a patchwork of laws relating to contracts, known as the common law of contracts. In the latter half of the twentieth century, however, the legal community made an attempt to modernize and establish uniformity in contract laws through the Uniform Commercial Code (UCC, or "Code")—a uniform collection of laws relating to commercial transactions. Article 2 of the UCC applies to contracts—specifically to transactions in goods. (Section 2-105(1) of the UCC defines "goods" as all things which are movable at the time of identification to the contract for sale.) Each state has now enacted Article 2 of the UCC, putting in place the same basic rules of law relating to contracts for the sale of goods. While this has improved the uniformity of laws for certain types of contracts, it is still up to the courts in each state to interpret these uniform laws and determine how they should be applied. The law of contracts in the United States is therefore a collection of *general* rules of law that provide a basis for predicting whether a court will permit a certain contract provision to be enforced.

As previously mentioned, aggrieved computer and software users, and particularly users of inaccurate information, have sought redress through noncontract-based theories through a body of law known as torts. A "tort" is a civil wrong—i.e., one party causes harm to another party through unacceptable conduct. Rules of law relating to torts also evolve through the common law process. In the U.S. there is a state-by-state common law of torts just as there is a common law of contracts. Unlike the law of contracts, however, there is no uniform collection of tort statutes similar to the UCC for contracts.

CONTRACT-BASED FORMS OF LIABILITY
Application of the Uniform Commercial Code

Most courts and legal commentators now agree that in transactions in which an ultimate software product is to be delivered, the software is classified as a "good" and the associated contracts are governed by the UCC (Horovitz, 1985; Rodau, 1986). The courts recognize that an intellectual process can be transformed into a good. For example, music produced by the artistry of musicians is not itself a good, but when transferred to a laser-readable disc becomes a readily merchantable commodity. Likewise, when a professor delivers a lecture, it is not a good, but, when transcribed as a book, it becomes a good (Advent Systems, 1991).

Application of the UCC to software contracts means that the Code's provisions relating to warranties, consequential damages, and disclaimers of liability will also apply. Before discussing the application of specific UCC provisions to computer-related contracts, particularly software contracts, it should be noted that for purposes of applying the UCC, the courts do not distinguish between "sales" and software licenses.

Article 2 of the UCC applies to contracts for the *sale* of goods. In contrast, software is invariably "sold" through a license agreement—technically, the recipient receives a right to use the software, but never ownership of the software. By licensing the software, software publishers are able to maintain control over copying and later redistribution by the individual user. As far as the courts are concerned, however, software licenses are treated as ordinary contracts accompanying the sale of products, and therefore are governed by the UCC (ProCD, 1996). Although the software publisher is technically the "licensor" and those acquiring software are technically the "licensee," they are still generally referred to as the seller and buyer, respectively.

Warranties, Limitations of Remedies, and Consequential Damages

From the perspective of the courts, it is advantageous for the parties to a contract to have that contract governed by the UCC. As one court has noted (Advent Systems, 1991), the UCC offers a uniform body of law on a wide range of questions likely to arise in computer software disputes, such as implied warranties, consequential damages and disclaimers of liability.

A warranty is a representation by a vendor regarding the quality of the product. There are three types of warranties: express warranty; implied warranty of merchantability; and implied warranty of fitness for a particular purpose.

An express warranty is created when the seller makes any statement or promise to the buyer related to the goods and which becomes a part of the contract. Descriptions of the goods create an express warranty that the goods will conform to the description. In addition, a sample or model creates an express warranty that the goods will conform to the sample or model.

An implied warranty of merchantability automatically arises whenever goods are sold by someone who regularly sells goods of that kind (a "merchant"). The implied warranty of merchantability essentially ensures that the goods are fit for the ordinary purposes for which such goods are used.

An implied warranty of fitness for a particular purpose arises whenever the seller knows of a particular purpose the buyer has for the goods, and the seller knows the buyer is relying on the seller's skill or judgment in selecting the appropriate goods to fit the buyer's particular purpose. The implied warranty of fitness for a particular purpose ensures that the goods are fit for the buyer's particular purpose.

Warranties can provide legal protection to the buyer regarding the quality of the goods (such as computer hardware or software) that are the subject of the contract. The UCC, however, also allows the seller to limit or exclude any or all of the warranties. When a vendor does provide a limited warranty   for example, that a hard disk drive will function properly for one year after purchase or that a software program will carry out its basic instructions with minimal errors—it is usually accompanied by a limitation of remedies. By contract, the purchaser agrees that in the event the product does not live up to its represented quality, the purchaser's remedies (and, hence, the vendor's liability) will be limited by the terms of the contract's limitation of remedies clause—usually a repair or replace option for defective hardware or a refund of the purchase price of software.

Often a computer hardware or software customer suffers damages beyond the cost of the hardware or software if there is a problem. The customer's business may be effectively shut down, or severely curtailed, if the computer system is not functioning properly. This type of damages is known as consequential damages—occurring indirectly as a result of the problem with the product. The UCC provides that consequential damages may be limited or excluded unless the limitation or exclusion is unconscionable. Limitation of consequential damages for injury to the person in the case of consumer goods is *prima facie* unconscionable, but limitation of damages where the loss is commercial is not.

There are two types of unconscionability: procedural and substantive. Procedural unconscionability concerns the manner in which the contract is entered into. Courts consider such factors as the setting of the transaction, the experience and education of the party claiming unconscionability, whether the contract contained "fine print," whether the seller used "high-pressured tactics" and any disparity in the parties' bargaining power (Brower, 1998). Substantive unconscionability, in contrast, examines the terms of the contract to determine whether any are unduly harsh or one-sided.

The exclusion of consequential damages in commercial transactions under the UCC is considered merely an allocation of unknown or undeterminable risks and is almost always upheld. The attitude of the courts regarding limiting liability for defective software is exemplified by the Washington Supreme Court (M.A. Mortenson, 2000): "In a purely commercial transaction, especially involving an innovative product such as software, the fact an unfortunate result occurs after the contracting process does not render an otherwise standard limitation of remedies clause substantively unconscionable" (p. 315).

The courts take a similar approach to defective computer hardware. For example, in the case of *Transport Corporation of America, Inc. v. International Business Machines, Inc. and Innovative Computing Corporation* (1994), the hard drive failed in the computer used by Transport Corporation of America (TCA). As a result TCA could not operate its business for over one day and had to re-input data after the disk drive was replaced. The vendor, IBM, promptly replaced the defective hard drive. According to the contract between IBM and TCA, that was the extent of IBM's liability and therefore that was the extent of liability the court allowed, despite the fact that TCA claimed it lost over half a million dollars as a result of the disc drive failure.

It has become standard practice in the computer industry, particularly for software publishers, to provide very limited express warranties, disclaim all other warranties, and severely limit remedies in the event of a breach of contract. These disclaimers and limitations of remedies are invariably enforced by the courts.

The initial premise under which disclaimers and limitations are allowed is that the parties negotiate the terms of the underlying agreement. Indeed, the U.S. Supreme Court has assumed a buyer will trade the risks associated with limited warranties for a (presumably bargained-for) lower price (Saratoga Fishing, 1997). The rationale for permitting warranty disclaimers and limited remedies is to lower the cost of the product—that it would be prohibitively expensive for the manufacturer to insure against every disappointed buyer. And the courts do not necessarily require equal bargaining power in order for warranties to provide these lower prices. As the California Supreme Court stated: "The law of warranty is not limited to parties in a somewhat equal bargaining position. Such a limitation is not supported by the language and history of the sales act [UCC] and is unworkable" (Seely, 1965, p. 151).

When Article 2 of the UCC was originally drafted, the focus was on recurring transactions among relatively large, sophisticated businesses. Neither the buyers nor the sellers, as a class, were favored. As one commentator has noted (Alces, 1999), the drafters of the UCC had a real interest in enacting legislation that would provide certain, predictable results, rather than legislation that would accommodate one business interest at the expense of another. Shrinkwrap agreements, however, were not contemplated at the time of drafting the UCC.

Shrinkwrap Agreements

In today's software transaction, "bargaining," at least on the part of the buyer, often consists of clicking on an "I Agree" button during software installation. Modern software is acquired through a variety of "wrap"-type agreements. A "shrinkwrap" agreement derives its name from software contained in a box wrapped in plastic (shrinkwrapped) The agreement pertaining to the software is either printed on the box and readable through the plastic, or there is a notice that the agreement is contained within the box. In either event, opening the box and installing and using the enclosed software is considered acceptance of the terms of the agreement.

The shrinkwrap agreement has evolved into the "clickwrap" agreement. Software is often acquired without any packaging (e.g., when it is copied to a computer ["downloaded"] from a web site or is pre-loaded on a computer). When the buyer installs the software a dialog box is displayed containing the license agreement. The user is instructed to select a button to accept the terms of the license agreement and complete the installation. The latest incarnation of the "wrap"-type agreement is the "browsewrap" agreement, which generally pertains to accessing information on a web page. A notice is placed on the web site informing the user that continued use of (browsing) the web site constitutes acceptance of a license agreement (the terms of which are usually made available by the user selecting a link on the web site).

Under shrinkwrap (as well as clickwrap and browsewrap) agreements, the buyer has the choice of either agreeing or not agreeing—the only way the buyer has the ability to use the software (or access the information) is to accept the former choice, with no opportunity to negotiate. Despite the lack of bargaining power on the part of the purchasers, in nearly all cases, shrinkwrap agreements have been held enforceable. And, as noted by the Missouri Court of Appeals (Estrin Construction, 1981), shrinkwrap-type agreements are considered vital to the efficiencies of modern commerce:

...The contract where the parties choose all the terms of agreement...is no longer typical. The proliferation of business transactions from the mass production and distribution of goods made too costly—and otherwise impossible—a separate contract distinctive for each separate transaction, and made inevitable a form contract for a typical transaction. Once

formulated by the business enterprise, the form is used in every bargain involved with that product or service. These terms are not the result of formal assent but are imposed. ...The other party does not agree to the transaction, but only adheres from want of genuine choice.

The legitimacy of an adhesion contract derives, not from the social value of a transaction freely negotiated, but from the social value of goods produced more abundantly and cheaper from the reduced cost of legal and other distribution services. ... (p. 422)

Due to the prevalence and enforcement of shrinkwrap agreements, a vast amount of software is acquired through a form contract with no opportunity to bargain for warranties or remedies. The historic context of contracts was that the parties negotiated the terms of the agreement. In particular, it was believed that the purchaser was willing to assume some risk that the acquired product may not meet all expectations—through limited warranties and remedies—in exchange for a lower price. In the modern computer-related contracting scenario, however, the purchaser assumes all the risk. Despite the theoretical underpinnings surrounding the creation of the UCC to provide buyers and sellers equal protections, the reality is that the law of contracts, particularly the UCC, provides no protection against the substantial losses businesses may encounter, and have encountered, when they cannot operate their business because data are lost or the computer system fails to operate properly.

These types of losses are generally considered economic losses and are the almost exclusive purview of contract law. That is why, as discussed below, aggrieved purchasers who have sought relief through the law of torts have met with very limited success.

TORT-BASED FORMS OF LIABILITY

A tort is a civil wrong committed by another. Tort law recognizes that individuals or businesses may owe a duty of care to others with whom they have contact. If that duty of care is breached, and the breach results in damages, the party that owed the duty of care may be liable for the resulting damages.

Products Liability

Since software is generally considered a product for contracting purposes, it is logical to consider whether a vendor would be held liable for damages resulting from defective software under the doctrine of products liability. This logic would apply to computer hardware as well. Products liability law protects those who suffer injuries as a result of a defective product. The law imposes upon a vendor strict liability for placing a defective product in the stream of commerce. This liability applies regardless of the amount of care exercised by the vendor in the preparation and sale of the product.

However, the vendor of a defective product is only strictly liable for certain types of damages suffered by the product's users: personal injury or damage to other physical property. To date, there has been no reported successful products liability lawsuit regarding defective computer hardware or software. All courts which have directly addressed the issue of whether products liability applies to defective computer hardware or software have ruled against application on the basis that the damages sustained are categorized as *economic loss*—a remedy not available under products liability law. As recently summarized by the Texas Court of Appeals: "Under the economic loss rule, economic damages are not recoverable unless they are accompanied by actual physical harm to persons or their property" (Hou-Tex, 2000, p. 107).

There are recorded instances where software errors have directly led to personal injuries. Between 1985 and 1987, a computer-controlled radiation therapy machine, the Therac-25, overdosed six patients in the U.S. and Canada with radiation, directly causing the death of two of the patients (Leveson, 1995). All of the lawsuits filed as a result of the overdoses were settled, so no rules of law arose from these incidents. One court has, however, indicated that where physical injuries are involved, products liability law would apply to defective software. The U.S. Court of Appeals (Winter, 1991), in discussing the types of highly technical tools that could be considered a product that injures someone, stated: "Computer software that fails to yield the result for which it was designed may be another [type of product]" (p. 1036). Where there are no physical injuries or damage to physical property, products liability law will not apply due to the economic loss rule.

The Economic Loss Rule

The economic loss rule was first enunciated by the California Supreme Court in *Seely v. White Motor Company* (1965), an early products liability case. In *Seely*, the brakes failed on a truck purchased by the plaintiff for heavy-duty hauling. The plaintiff sought recovery for injuries suffered in the resulting crash of the truck, loss of value of the truck itself, as well as lost profits (since the plaintiff could not operate his business as a result of the loss of the truck). The *Seely* court discussed the distinction between tort-based physical injuries and contract-based economic injuries. The court noted that the distinction rests on an understanding of the nature of the responsibility a manufacturer must undertake in distributing its products.

In particular, a manufacturer can be held liable for physical injuries caused by defects by requiring its goods to match a standard of safety defined in terms of conditions that create unreasonable risks of harm. A manufacturer cannot, however, be held for the level of performance of its products in the consumer's business unless it agrees that the product was designed to meet the consumer's demands. The *Seely* court further stated that a consumer should not be charged at the will of the manufacturer with bearing the risk of physical injury when he buys a product on the market. The consumer can, however, be fairly charged with the risk that the product will not match his economic expectations unless the manufacturer agrees that it will. The *Seely* court concluded that even in actions for negligence, a manufacturer's liability is limited to damages for physical injuries and there is no recovery for economic loss alone.

The U.S. Supreme Court has held (East River, 1986) that where no person or other property is damaged, the resulting loss is purely economic. "...[T]he resulting loss due to repair costs, decreased value, and lost profits is essentially the failure of the purchaser to receive the benefit of its bargain—traditionally the core concern of contract law" (p. 870).

A few computer purchasers have argued that data lost due to defective hardware or a defective computer system constitutes damage to "other property." The courts that have considered this argument have uniformly rejected it. The courts consider the data as integrated into the computer system. "[W]here a defect in a component part damaged the product into which that component was incorporated, economic losses to the product as a whole were not losses to 'other property'" (Transport Corporation of America, 1994, p. 957). The *Transport Corporation of America* court noted, however, that had the disk drive started a fire that caused damage to property outside of the computer system, then the exception to the economic loss doctrine would be applicable.

Negligence

The economic loss rule provides a substantial barrier to any recovery for defective computer hardware or software, regardless of whether the purchaser pursues a claim for products liability or negligence. Negligence is a tort theory which applies to conduct that falls below the standard established by law for the protection of others against unreasonable risk of harm. An action for negligence must establish that: (1) the defendant owed a duty of care to the plaintiff; (2) the defendant's lack of care (negligence) breached that duty of care; and (3) the defendant's breach of the duty of care proximately caused the damages suffered by the plaintiff.

As noted by the U.S. Court of Appeals (Rockport Pharmacy, 1995), the existence of a contract between the parties does not, in itself, give rise to a duty in tort. And, as with any tort claim not involving personal injuries, there will be no recovery without at least damage to "other property." In *Rockport Pharmacy*, the purchaser argued that the loss of data it suffered as a result of a defective computer system constituted damage to "other property." The court rejected this argument, holding that such losses represent nothing more than commercial loss for inadequate value and consequent loss of profits.

The courts also require some sort of calamitous event cause the damage to the "other property." The plaintiff in *Rockport Pharmacy* argued that the "computer crash" it suffered constituted such a calamitous event. The court also rejected this argument, declining to give the term "computer crash" a literal interpretation implying a violent occurrence, as opposed to a simple computer malfunction.

Even when the software vendor knows of a defect in the software and fails to notify the user, if the damages suffered are limited to economic losses, a negligence action will still fail (Hou-Tex, 2000). And where a purchaser pursues a negligence action, not based specifically on the inadequacy of a computer system, but upon the negligence of those installing or servicing that computer system, most courts are still reluctant to find negligence. For example, Gus' Catering complained of damages, in the form of lost business and customers, as a result of an improperly installed computerized restaurant management system. In particular, the vendor was unable to get the system operating properly for over two years, yet an independent technician Gus' finally called in was able to correct all the installation defects in two hours. The Vermont Supreme Court (Gus' Catering, 2000) denied recovery for lost profits, emphasizing that negligence law does not recognize a duty to exercise reasonable care to avoid intangible economic loss to another unless one's conduct has inflicted some accompanying physical harm. Loss of business profits, customers, and time are economic losses, not physical harms.

Gus' Catering did claim there were damages as a result of physical damage—that the defendant caused physical damage to the computer system by improperly installing the program and causing it to malfunction, analogous to dropping the computer to the floor and rendering it inoperable. The court essentially ignored this claim by ruling that Gus' Catering had suffered only economic loss.

Computer Malpractice

When companies seek to acquire complex computer systems that will become an integral part of the operations of the business they often rely to a significant degree upon consultants or those selling the systems to make appropriate recommendations. When those recommended systems fail to live up to their expectations, the companies have sought to hold the consultants and system vendors to a higher—professional—standard of care. In effect, these companies have sought to create the new tort of computer malpractice.

Over time, legal experts publish summaries of the law known as "Restate-ments." While Restatements are not law in and of themselves, they are highly regarded summations of the current state of the law in various categories and are often relied upon by the courts. One particular section of the Restatement of Torts (Restatement [Second] of Torts, § 299A, 1965) discusses the standard of care expected within professions:

Unless he represents that he has a greater or less skill or knowledge, one who undertakes to render services in the practice of a profession or trade is required to exercise the skill and knowledge normally possessed by members of that profession or trade in good standing in similar communities.

Comment b to § 299A of the Restatement (Second) of Torts provides the following explanation of this particular provision:

This section...applies to any person who undertakes to render services to another in the practice of a profession, such as that of physician or surgeon, dentist, pharmacist, occultist, attorney, accountant, or engineer. It applies also to any person who undertakes to render services to others in the practice of a skilled trade, such as that of airplane pilot, precision machinist, electrician, carpenter, blacksmith, or plumber. This section states the minimum skill and knowledge which the actor undertakes to exercise, and therefore to have. If he has in fact greater skill than that common to the profession or trade, he is required to exercise that skill...

The standard of care required for a "professional" is higher than that of one practicing a "skilled trade." If a service provider is held to a higher standard of care it is, arguably, easier to show that the service provider has not performed to that standard. Holding a computer consultant or vendor to a professional standard means they are held to a higher standard—they owe a greater duty of care to their customers than someone practicing a skilled trade.

Elevating computer professionals to a higher standard of care—by creating the tort of "computer malpractice"—was first attempted in 1979 in a case involving the early use of storing data on a disc. The attempted implementation of the disc storage system by NCR essentially failed, with only two of six programs becoming operational before the purchaser company finally gave up. In the subsequent lawsuit, the purchaser advanced a legal theory of computer malpractice based on NCR's representations surrounding the abilities of the computer system. The purchaser attempted to equate the sale and servicing of computer systems with professional malpractice. In declining to create a new tort of computer malpractice, the court stated that "[s]imply because an activity is technically complex and important to the business community does not mean that greater potential liability must attach" (Chatlos Systems, 1979, p. 741).

The theory of computer malpractice was analyzed more thoroughly in a later case involving a customized hospital billing and accounting system that never became fully operational. The hospital's (SIH's) subsequent suit against the vendor included a claim for computer malpractice. In denying SIH's computer malpractice claim, the court (Hospital Computer Systems, 1992) noted that professionals may be sued for malpractice because the higher standards of care imposed on them by their profession and by state licensing requirements engenders trust in them by clients that is not the norm of the marketplace. However, when no such higher code of ethics binds a person, such trust is unwarranted. Accordingly, the court saw no reason to apply a professional standard of care to computer consultants.

One court has, however, recognized a professional standard of care related to computer consulting. In *Diversified Graphics, Ltd. v. Ray J. Groves and Ernst & Whinney* (1989), the U.S. Court of Appeals did hold the accounting firm Ernst & Whinney to a higher standard of care. In *Diversified Graphics*, Ernst & Whinney had agreed to help Diversified Graphics obtain a turnkey data processing system. The court determined that Ernst & Whinney's conduct fell short of the applicable standard of care.

It should be noted that in the *Diversified Graphics* case, Ernst & Whinney was an accounting and consulting firm. Its members were therefore subject to state licensure standards, as well as standards adopted by the American Institute of Certified Public Accountants. It was essentially these professional standards that the court determined Ernst & Whinney had failed to meet. In a later case involving Ernst & Whinney in a similar dispute (RKB Enterprises, 1992), however, a New York appeals court specifically found that Ernst & Whinney would not be held to a higher standard. While noting that "there is no cause of action for professional malpractice in the field of computer consulting" (p. 816), the court ruled that the fact that Ernst & Whinney was a certified public accountant firm had no bearing on the computer management consulting services it provided.

A more practical approach is reflected in the case of *Data Processing Services, Inc. v. L.H. Smith Oil Corporation* (1986), in which the court focused on the skill Data Processing Services, Inc. (DPS) represented it possessed, not necessarily whether those skills qualified for a profession or for a skilled trade:

Those who hold themselves out to the world as possessing skill and qualifications in their respective trades or professions impliedly represent they possess the skill and will exhibit the diligence ordinarily possessed by well informed members of the trade or profession. ...We hold these principles apply with equal force to those who contract to develop computer programming.

The trial court found: (a) DPS represented it had the necessary expertise and training to design and develop a system to meet the needs of Smith; (b) DPS lacked the requisite skills and expertise to do the work; (c) DPS knew it lacked the skill and expertise; (d) DPS should have known Smith was dependent upon DPS's knowledge and abilities; and (e) DPS should have foreseen Smith would incur losses if DPS did not perform as agreed. …These findings demonstrate DPS breached its implied promise of having the reasonable skill and ability to do the job for which it contracted (pp. 319-320).

It should be noted that, like the *Data Processing Services, Inc.* case, computer malpractice cases are a mixture of negligence and breach of contract actions. The plaintiffs argue that the defendants fail to perform to a professional standard (typically a negligence-based assertion) resulting in a breach of the contract upon which the services originated. The ultimate issue that should determine liability was addressed by the *Data Processing Services, Inc.* court: did the defendant breach its implied promise of having the skill and ability to do the job for which it contracted?

Fraud in the Inducement

Another category of tort is fraud in the inducement, which occurs when the defendant makes false representations of material facts which are justifiably relied upon by the plaintiff to the plaintiff's detriment. Therefore, if a vendor fraudulently misrepresents the capacity of a computer system or the quality of software, the purchaser may have a claim for fraud. However, as in the other types of torts discussed previously, if the purchaser claims nothing more than disappointment with the product(s) purchased, the terms of the contract will control whether the plaintiff can recover any damages. Once the contract has been made, the parties should be governed by it (Huron Tool, 1995).

As discussed by the Michigan Court of Appeals in *Huron Tool*, the complaining purchaser must establish a fraud claim which goes beyond just complaining that they did not receive what they bargained for. "Fraud in the inducement…addresses a situation where the claim is that one party was tricked into contracting" (p. 544).

While the courts are very careful to maintain the distinction between contract law and tort law—by not allowing tort remedies when parties are restricted to contract remedies—the end result is that tort law effectively provides no more relief than does contract law for aggrieved computer hardware and software purchasers. In exceptional circumstances, where a purchaser has been fraudulently induced into entering a contract, a tort remedy may be available. For the most part, however, courts require aggrieved purchasers to accept the risk of their bargain—that what they purchase may not have the quality they expected. In that event, they must rely upon the terms of the underlying contract for their remedies, and no more.

LIABILITY FOR PUBLISHING INACCURATE DATA

The Internet has revolutionized the mass delivery of information. However, information was delivered online long before the commercialization of the Internet. A critical dimension of online information delivery is the speed at which information is disseminated, not necessarily the extent of that dissemination. Due to the speed of dissemination, however, information delivered online is not always accurate. The legal issue that arises is whether someone who claims damages as a result of an inaccuracy can hold the electronic publisher of that information liable for those damages. As a general rule, they cannot.

Publishers of Non-Authored Information

Historically, the courts have generally not held publishers liable for inaccuracies in the information they have published. As discussed by the Supreme Court of Hawaii (Birmingham, 1992), there is an almost absolute immunity for publishers of information they do not author. Where the publisher does not author or guarantee the contents of the publication, it has no duty to investigate and warn its readers of the accuracy of the contents of its publications.

The *Birmingham* case involved personal injuries suffered by the plaintiffs as a result of what they alleged to be inaccurate information in a publication. Even where plaintiffs have suffered severe injuries as a direct result of inaccurate information, such as an incorrect description of mushrooms that are safe to eat (Winter, 1991), the courts do not hold the publisher liable for the injuries suffered, provided the publisher is not also the author.

Courts have, however, carved out an exception when the information involved is highly technical in nature. For example, some courts (Saloomey, 1983) have held a publisher liable for injuries suffered as a result of inaccurate aeronautical charts, considering the charts highly technical tools. Likewise, one legal commentator (Phillips, 1999) has argued that producers of Geographic Information System (GIS) mapping and database analysis may be under a similar threat of liability for inaccuracies. However, as with "traditional" products liability and negligence laws, without a physical injury or damage to other physical property, a publisher will not be held liable for inaccurate information, regardless of the type of information published.

Publishers of Authored Information

The laws relating to liability for inaccurate information are somewhat different when the publisher is also the author of the information. Restatement (Second) of Torts § 552 (1977) provides, in part:

One who, in the course of his business, profession or employment, or in any other transaction in which he has a pecuniary interest, supplies false information for the guidance of others in their business transactions, is subject to liability for pecuniary loss caused to them by their justifiable reliance upon the information, if he fails to exercise reasonable care or competence in obtaining or communicating the information.

Before § 552 liability will be imposed, however, it must first be found that the publisher owes a specific duty to the recipient of the information. This limitation was discussed by a New York City court (Elridge Daniel, 1987), which noted that a news service is not liable to its readers for negligent false statements unless a "special relationship" exists between the publisher and the subscriber which would give rise to a specific duty of care. While the *Elridge Daniel* court noted that technological advances must continually be evaluated and their relation to legal rules determined so that antiquated rules are not misapplied in modern settings, ultimately, if the substance of a transaction has not changed, new technology does not require a new legal rule merely because of its novelty. The fact that the subscriber obtains the information through an online subscription does not, in itself, create a special relationship, particularly where, as here, the court determined there was no functional difference between the defendant's service and the distribution of a moderate circulation newspaper or subscription newsletter.

Therefore, before a publisher of inaccurate information can be held liable for damages resulting from that inaccurate publication, a special relationship must exist between the publisher and reader—the publisher must owe a specific duty to the reader. The case of *Rosenstein v. Standard & Poor's Corporation* (1993) illustrates a situation where that special relationship may exist. In *Rosenstein*, Standard & Poor's (S&P) provided the official closing stock prices, which were used by the Chicago Board Options Exchange to settle options contracts. Therefore, option traders, such as the plaintiff Rosenstein, relied upon the S&P data to settle their accounts. The Illinois court of appeals determined in this instance there was a special relationship:

The entire transaction that we consider in the instant case is founded upon information provided by the defendant. Option traders are required by the license agreement, the terms of which are incorporated into the Exchange rules, to exclusively use that information to settle their option contracts.

Although S&P may suggest that it is merely selling a product, information is the product and it is clearly for the guidance of others in commercial transactions, and, in fact, the determinative factor in those business transactions (p. 669).

While the Illinois Court of Appeals in *Rosenstein* found that a special relationship existed between the publisher and the subscriber, the terms of the underlying subscription agreement still controlled. The subscription agreement contained an "exculpatory" clause, which provided that Standard & Poor's did not guarantee the accuracy or completeness of the information provided. In enforcing the clause, the court based its analysis on reasoning very similar to that used by courts when upholding limitations of warranties and remedies: "...[T]here is a broad public policy permitting competent parties to contractually limit their respective liability and to allocate business risks in accordance with their business judgment" (p. 671).

As with pursuing remedies for defective computer hardware or software, those who have suffered damages due to inaccurate information may find themselves without a remedy. Publishers of information enjoy a broad immunity for commercial losses suffered as a result of inaccurate information when the publishers are not the authors of the information. In addition, authors of inaccurate information that cause damages will only be liable for those damages if a special relationship exists between the author and the recipient. Finally, as seen in the *Rosenstein* case, courts will still honor any limitations of remedies contained in the contract underlying the transaction that formed the basis for supplying that information.

FUTURE TRENDS

An updated version of the UCC that specifically deals with computer-related transactions, the Uniform Computer Information Transactions Act (UCITA), is currently under consideration by state legislatures and the legal community (Murphy, 2000). UCITA is no panacea for computer hardware and software purchasers. UCITA is not without its critics, such as Kaner (1999): "UCITA changes the economics of defective software in ways that will encourage software publishers and large custom software development firms to deliver shoddier products faster" (p. 444). Indeed, UCITA assumes that "merchantable" software (i.e., software that is fit for its ordinary purpose) will contain errors: "The presence of errors in general commercial [software] products is fully within common commercial expectation" (§ 2B-403, Reporter's Notes, para. 3.a).

Although only two states (Maryland and Virginia) have adopted UCITA and the proposed Act has sparked a large extent of criticism (UCITA Facts), its current form indicates that any direction of change regarding computer-related contract law does not favor purchasers. Likewise, the type of damages a purchaser may suffer due to a lack of computer system or data quality—lost profits, business disruptions, lost time—are barred in tort-related legal actions. The courts have been so consistent in maintaining the dichotomy between contract damages and tort damages that no significant change is expected in the near future.

Time and again, courts recognize that the parties to a commercial transaction allocate risk, even when there has been no negotiation and the parties do not enjoy equal bargaining power. The result is that all of the risk for defective computer hardware or software or inaccurate data has been shifted to the purchaser. As long as the purchaser bears all the costs of these defects or inaccuracies, the vendor has no incentive to increase or guarantee quality. If the law were to impose more risk upon vendors, would quality improve?

Microsoft has been the subject of much criticism for producing shoddy software, particularly software with blatant security vulnerabilities (Menn, 2002). The issue of defective software has become so severe that commentators (Computer Science and Telecommunications Board, 2002; Sager & Greene, 2002) and legislators (Menn) have called for new standards of liability for software publishers. In early 2002, Microsoft Chairman Bill Gates published a company-wide memo outlining a strategic direction for Microsoft to produce software that is available, reliable and secure (Schneier & Shostack, 2002). In the memo, Bill Gates is quoted as saying: "We must lead the industry to a whole new level of Trustworthiness in computing." Bill Gates is also quoted in the memo as saying, "So now, when we face a choice between adding features and resolving security issues, we need to choose security."

If Bill Gates and Microsoft are reacting to the threat of additional liability for the lack of quality in their software, this supports the contention that computer hardware, software and data vendors, if faced with the potential of being held liable for the lack of quality in their products, will begin to assume more of the risks associated with defective hardware or software or inaccurate data.

CONCLUSION

The law allows computer system and data vendors, by contract, to disclaim any guarantee of quality, as well as prohibit any recovery for damages suffered by the purchaser where there is a lack of quality. The courts have consistently upheld such contract provisions. In addition, the type of damages usually suffered by disappointed purchasers or users are economic in nature—exactly the type of damages that are not recoverable in a tort action. The result is that between the contract and the courts, purchasers and users who suffer damages as a result of defective computer hardware or software or inaccurate data simply have no meaningful recourse. *Caveat emptor!*

SUMMARY

Defective Computer Hardware or Software

Legal Theory of Liability

- **Contract.** Vendor permitted to disclaim any promise of quality as well as severely limit any monetary damages arising from defects.
- **Strict Liability.** Only applies where there is physical injury to person or damage to physical property other than the product itself.
- **Negligence.** Does not allow recovery for "economic losses"— e.g., lost profits, business interruption, loss of value.
- **Computer Malpractice.** Courts have generally refused to acknowledge a professional standard of care for the computer industry.
- **Fraud in the Inducement.** One possible source of liability if the vendor has made false representations of material facts to induce the purchaser into the contract—however, representations must go beyond mere quality of the product.

Inaccurate Published Information

Legal Theory of Liability

- **Publishing Non-Authored Information.** Publishers enjoy near absolute immunity for inaccurate information of which they are not the author.
- **Publishing Authored Information.** Publishers of inaccurate information of which they are also the author will only be liable if a special relationship exists between the publisher and the subscriber/user.

REFERENCES

Advent Systems Limited v. Unisys Corporation, 925 F.2d 670 (3d Cir. 1991).

Alces, P. (1999). W(h)ither warranty: The b(l)oom of products liability theory in cases of deficient software design. *California Law Review, 87*, 269-304.

Birmingham v. Fodor's Travel Publications, Inc., et al., 833 P.2d 70 (Haw. 1992).

Brower, et al. v. Gateway 2000, Inc., 676 N.Y.S.2d 569 (N.Y. App. Div. 1998).

Chatlos Systems, Inc. v. National Cash Register Corporation, 479 F. Supp. 738 (D. N.J. 1979).

Computer Science and Telecommunications Board. (2002). *Cybersecurity today and tomorrow: Pay now or pay later.* [Prepublication Edition]. Retrieved January 16, 2002 from the World Wide Web: http://books.nap.edu/html/cybersecurity.

Data Processing Services, Inc. v. L. H. Smith Oil Corporation, 492 N.E.2d 314 (Ind. Ct. App. 1986).

Dearlove, D. (2001, January 18). The heavy price of fear and hype. *The Times (London).* Retrieved May 15, 2002 from LEXIS/NEXIS, Legal News.

Diversified Graphics, Ltd. v. Ray J. Groves and Ernst & Whinney, 868 F.2d 292 (8th Cir. 1989).

East River S. S. Corp. v. Transamerica Delaval, 476 U.S. 858 (1986).

Elmer-DeWitt, P. (1990, January 29). Ghost in the machine. *Time*, 58-59.

Elridge Daniel v. Dow Jones & Company, Inc. (News Retrieval Service), 520 N.Y.S.2d 334 (N.Y. Misc. 1987).

Estrin Construction Company, Inc. v. The Aetna Casualty and Surety Company, 612 S.W.2d 413 (Mo. Ct. App. 1981).

Gus' Catering, Inc. v. Menusoft Systems, 762 A.2d 804 (Vt. 2000).

Horovitz, B. (1985). Computer software as a good under the Uniform Commercial Code: Taking a byte out of the intangibility myth. *Boston University Law Review, 65,* 129-164.

Hospital Computer Systems, Inc. v. The Staten Island Hospital, 788 F. Supp. 1351 (D. N.J. 1992).

Hou-Tex, Inc. v. Landmark Graphics, 26 S.W.3d 103 (Tex. Ct. App. 2000).

Huron Tool and Engineering Company v. Precision Consulting Services, Inc. and Joseph B. Wulffenstein, 532 N.W.2d 541 (Mich. Ct. App. 1995).

Kaner, C. (1999). Uniform Computer Information Transaction Act: Software engineering and UCITA. *John Marshall Journal of Computer & Information Law, 18,* 435-546.

Leveson, N. (1995). *Safeware: System Safety and Computers.* Reading, MA: Addison-Wesley.

M.A. Mortenson Company, Inc. v. Timberline Software Corporation and Softworks Data Systems, Inc., 998 P.2d 305 (Wash. 2000).

Menn, J. (2002, January 14). Security flaws may be pitfall for Microsoft. *Los Angeles Times.* Retrieved January 14, 2002 from the World Wide Web: https://www.latimes.com/business/la-000003463jan14.story?coll=la-head-lines-business-manual.

Murphy, T. (2000). It's just another little bit of history repeating: UCITA in the evolving age of information. *Golden Gate University Law Review, 30,* 559-591.

Phillips, J. (1999). Information liability: The possible chilling effect of tort claims against producers of geographic information systems data. *Florida State University Law Review, 26,* 743-777.

ProCD, Inc. v. Zeidenberg, 86 F.3d 1447 (7th Cir. 1996).

Restatement (Second) of Torts. (1965). § 299A.

Restatement (Second) of Torts. (1965). § 299A, comment b.

Restatement (Second) of Torts. (1977). § 552.

RKB Enterprises, Inc. v. Ernst & Young et al., 582 N.Y.S.2d 814 (N.Y. App. Div. 1992).

Rockport Pharmacy, Inc. v. Digital Simplistics, Inc., 53 F.3d 195 (8th Cir. 1995).

Rodau, A. (1986). Computer software: Does Article 2 of the Uniform Commercial Code apply? *Emory Law Journal, 35*, 853-920.

Rosenstein v. Standard & Poor's Corporation, 636 N.E.2d 665 (Ill. Ct. App. 1993).

RTI. (2002, May). *The economic impacts of inadequate infrastructure for software testing.* U.S. Department of Commerce, National Institute of Standards & Technology. Retrieved June 18, 2002 from the World Wide Web: http://www.nist.gov/director/prog-ofc/report02-3.pdf.

Sager, I. & Greene, J. (2002, March 18). The best way to make software secure: Liability. *BusinessWeek*, 61.

Saloomey v. Jeppesen & Co., et al., 707 F.2d 671 (2d Cir. 1983).

Santor, G. (n.d.). Famous bugs. *Infotech.* Retrieved February 15, 2003 from the World Wide Web: http://infotech.fanshawec.on.ca/gsantor/Computing/FamousBugs.htm.

Saratoga Fishing Co. v. J.M. Martinac & Co., 520 U.S. 875 (1997).

Schneier, B., & Shostack, A. (2002, January 24). Results, not resolutions: A guide to judging Microsoft's security progress. *SecurityFocus Online.* Retrieved January 22, 2002 from the World Wide Web: http://online.securityfocus.com/news/315.

Seely v. White Motor Co., 403 P.2d 145 (Calif. 1965).

Transport Corporation of America, Inc. v. International Business Machines, Inc. and Innovative Computing Corporation, 30 F.3d 953 (8th Cir. 1994).

UCITA § 2B-403, Reporter's Notes, ¶ *3.a.* (2002, October 15). National Conference of Commissioners on Uniform State Laws. Retrieved February 15, 2003 from the World Wide Web: http://www.law.upenn.edu/bll/ulc/ucita/2002final.pdf.

UCITA Facts. Retrieved February 15, 2003 from the World Wide Web: http://www.nccusl.org/nccusl/ucita/UCITA_Facts.pdf.

Winter v. G.P. Putnam's Sons, 938 F.2d 1033 (9th Cir. 1991).

Chapter XII

Software Engineering as a Profession: A Moral Case for Licensure[1]

J. Carl Ficarrotta
United States Air Force Academy, USA

ABSTRACT

This chapter makes the argument that software engineers, as part of a program of moving toward more formal professionalization, should be licensed. It outlines the nature of the profession and the arguments that justify licensing in professions other than software engineering. It then traces the initial steps the software industry has already taken towards professionalization, including codes of ethics and educational standards. There are morally and practically compelling arguments, rooted in the professional's obligations to society, to do more: licensing, or some other sort of formal, binding and revocable certification, is also necessary. The chapter considers but rejects a number of reasons one might resist this as a goal.

INTRODUCTION

Software engineers should be licensed. Many other lines of work, especially traditional professions like law and medicine, justifiably require licenses and other sorts of professional certification of their practitioners. The software industry has already taken some initial steps towards professionalization, including codes of ethics and educational standards sponsored, developed and endorsed by the Institute of Electrical and Electronics Engineers, Inc. (IEEE) and the Association for Computing Machinery (ACM). But these initial steps, while salutary, are not sufficient. For the same reasons so many other fields have more or less strict licensing requirements, the software industry should adopt analogous processes and procedures. It should move toward, even if incrementally, more formal professionalization, to include licensing or professional certification.

BACKGROUND:
WHAT MAKES A PROFESSION?

Consider the following argument.

Premise 1: Broccoli is better than nothing.
Premise 2: Nothing is better than sex.
Conclusion: Broccoli is better than sex.

The joke turns on an ambiguity in one of the key terms in the premises. The word *nothing* means something different in Premise 1 ("not having anything") than it does in Premise 2 ("there is no thing that"), allowing us invalidly to reach the (presumably) false and comical conclusion. Ambiguity in our terms can, apparently, get us into trouble.

Professional is another term fraught with ambiguity. It might describe nothing more than taking money for one's services. It has also been used to denote a certain high level of proficiency, as in "Joe's a real pro." One professional engineer, when pressed for what he thought made a professional, claimed (tongue in cheek) that professionals wore neckties.[2] And of course, there is the commonly held idea that professionals, whatever they turn out to be, are more esteemed in society than those in other lines of work, and are typically more highly paid. We want our children to be, or at least to marry, one.

There is a more focused and interesting sense of the term *professional*. It is the sense attached to a number of paradigm institutions and callings, which together seem to provide examples that answer to this more interesting conception of *profession*: law, medicine, the clergy, the military officer corps, teaching, public accounting, and many types of engineering, to name a few. There are no doubt other occupations that answer to this sense of being a professional—an exhaustive list is not needed for our present purposes. But it is important to make clear, beyond simply pointing to examples, what makes for membership in this group, because professionals in this sense, as we shall see, have special legal and moral obligations to uphold. If there are other lines of work, hitherto not included in our ready lists (more specifically, software engineering) that actually belong, then it will be important to acknowledge their special status, and recognize and act upon the concomitant special legal and moral obligations.

Huntington (1957) famously suggested that professions of the type toward which we are gesturing are characterized by three primary features: expertise, responsibility, and corporateness (pp. 8-10). As an expert, the professional has specialized knowledge "in a significant field of human endeavor" (p. 8). Professions of the sort we are examining, in Huntington's view, all provide a service "which is essential to the functioning of society" (p. 9). The essential nature of the service provided creates a special responsibility, a responsibility to deliver the service well and whenever needed. As for corporateness, members of professions form "an organic unity and consciousness of themselves as a group apart from laymen" (p. 10).

Using Huntington's model, we must notice that he expects no profession, even the benchmark examples of medicine and law, to have "all the character-istics of the ideal professional type" (p. 11). Not all of these three traits are present in equal degrees even in lines of work that we take as clear exemplars of professions. In fact, in some cases, one of the traits could be missing altogether. For example, architects may not answer strongly to the corporateness criterion, but we do not doubt they are professionals. Moreover, there may be lines of work that possess all three of the characteristics, yet which we would hesitate to label a profession. Plumbers clearly engage in important work and seem to answer in some way to all three of Huntington's criteria, but are not professionals in the sense we are exploring. Nevertheless, Huntington points to these three characteristics as the core of what generally makes the professions special and important.

Harris, Pritchard and Rabins (1995, p. 11), in addressing this same problem, list the following characteristics as markers of a profession:[3]
1.   The professional undergoes training of an intellectual character, to include exposure to theory and the practice of professional judgment. More than this, the professional requires knowledge and appreciation of the broader culture in which the profession is embedded.
2.   The professional's skills are vital to the well-being of the larger society; we rely on professionals for the provision of important needs. Law, in the ideal, serves justice. Medicine safeguards our health. The military provides security. Public accountants are essential, in a modern economy, to our financial well-being. This service to society is an important part of why the professional needs the broad education called for in (1) above. Since the profession provides a service vital to the overall functioning of society,

providing it well and effectively requires overall knowledge of society, basic human needs, culture and how they work.

3. The profession enjoys autonomy, which is justified because of the professional's specialized knowledge and judgment. No other body or agency would be competent to regulate or monitor the target professional activity, so self-regulation is necessary.

4. Ethical standards are proclaimed by the profession, usually through more or less formal codes of ethics. A number of factors make these codes and their enforcement important. We have already seen that the professions provide vital services. So the consequences of professional failure and incompetence are typically very serious. There is a public vulnerability created by the radical asymmetry of knowledge and expertise we see between the professional and the laity. These (and perhaps other) factors make it essential that professionals be conscientious, competent, trustworthy, and committed to serving the public good. These functionally driven moral duties are recognized by the professions, and formalized in the codes of ethics they promulgate.[4]

5. Professionals have a monopoly over what they do, or nearly so, via professional schools, certification and licensing. Given the overall understanding of the professions already spelled out, we can immediately make a simple, but I think strong, moral and prudential argument for the practice of licensing or certifying. The work being done is extremely important to society as a whole and in particular the individuals or organizations who rely on the professional. The consequences of professional failure are serious. Indeed, Malham Wakin was moved to claim that "within the context of the professional ethic, it appears the line between incompetence and immorality is a very thin one" (1986, p. 211). The majority of those who rely on professionals are not normally in a position to judge whether the professional is truly well-qualified or even competent to do the work; nor can they tell if the professional is in possession of the functionally required professional moral virtues.

In light of all this, we can see the moral and prudential necessity for publicly certifying or licensing professionals to practice. And this necessity could explain why so many of the professions we previously identified already have such procedures. Lawyers, physicians and public accountants are certified and licensed by their own governing professional bodies and the state. Military officers are commissioned, and clergy are ordained. Before professional status is conferred in any of these fields, the proper education and judgment must be demonstrated; moreover, technical or moral failure may and often does result in being stripped of previously earned professional status.

This list of characteristics is very close to Huntington's, and indeed, were we to consider Huntington's full discussion of the issues, completely compatible with it. The big picture painted in both of these analyses (Huntington, 1957; Harris et al., 1995) captures well the salient features of the professions, and we will use it for the purposes of this chapter. Also note that they both opt methodologically to identify not a "strict" definition, but rather a weighted set of characteristics which, when considered holistically, assist in rendering a sound judgment as to whether a line of work is a profession (p. 11). For understanding the concept of a professional, this weighted set approach seems preferable to a non-weighted set of necessary and sufficient conditions. Some philosophers think, roughly, that *all* concepts are best understood as sets of weighted characteristics. But we need not make a commitment here to that more thoroughgoing view—suffice it that the concept of a profession, because of its complexity, is best approached using the weighted set approach.

SOFTWARE ENGINEERING AS A PROFESSION

The role that software engineering plays in society has changed radically over the last 50 years. In its early stages, automation was a mere curiosity to everyone except those engaged in its development. But eventually, its amazing utility was understood, and the business of software engineering rapidly expanded as an expert service provided for a (handsome) fee. The number of jobs grew, from the 1970s on, more quickly than schools could develop and implement training programs to supply workers. Now, after the turn of the century, we are coming to understand the full effects of what has amounted to a profound technological revolution. Automation and the software that makes it work are now an inextricable part of business, law, medicine, transportation, public safety, defense, government, and indeed, every major human enterprise. It touches every aspect of our lives. No less than fire did in another epoch of our history, automation now serves as an essential tool for the provision of basic human needs.

Given this state of affairs, should we consider software engineering a profession? Obviously, not everyone occupied with automation is a good candidate. Data entry clerks clearly are not engineers. Nor are entry-level coders, closely supervised and responsible for only a small portion of a programming project (though we might think of these programmers as software engineers in training). Indeed, no one focused on only a narrow area of competence, whether they are a programmer, an analyst, a tester, etc., should automatically be thought of as a software engineer. Granted, it is notoriously difficult to provide a precise set of criteria for identifying software engineers (Software Engineering

Defined, 1997). But for now we can make do with the rough idea that there is a subset of people in the industry that have broad expertise, command of theoretical principles and ultimate responsibility for the quality and safety of software systems. Are *these* individuals part of a profession? Let us think of software engineering in terms of the model for the professions we have already developed, and consider each of the previously proposed criteria in turn. The model may be helpful for deciding whether software engineering is also a profession in the sense we have identified.

1.   Competent software engineers obviously undergo extensive technical training, and must pursue continuing education throughout their careers as developers. Seasoned professional judgment, and not just the following of mechanical rules, is required in all but the simplest of software projects. The engineer balances multiple considerations, to include performance, economy, safety, elegance, maintainability, and a host of other factors. In addition, most software, whether directly or indirectly, often has an important impact on the larger society and how individual human beings live their lives. Because of this, the best software engineers will, and should, have the broader education identified by Harris et al. (1995). So software engineering, like the other professions we have considered, requires a special sort of education. Of course, unlike the other professions we have considered, many practicing software engineers might lack all or part of this required education, and still be deemed software engineers. There are no formal mechanisms to prevent this from happening. The ACM has, however, undertaken to make recommendations for the appropriate content of curricula for preparing software engineers (ACM Curricula Recommendations, 2000).

2.   Just as obvious in this day and age, the software engineer's skills are vital to the well-being of the larger society. We rely on them for the provision of important needs and professional failure has serious consequences. An anecdotal survey of some software failures ought to persuade us informally what a careful study could demonstrate with certainty.

       The so-called Y2K problem was a well-known problem created by an industry-wide failure of software engineers. Besides the incredible economic impact the bug had on private industry, there were well-documented and serious effects on the U.S. Department of Defense, the U.S. Department of Energy, the U.S. Office of the Treasury, NASA, and a myriad of other government agencies (Lessons Learned, 2000). Software problems with the baggage handling system of the new Denver International Airport cost taxpayers and the flying public many millions of dollars (New Denver Airport, 1994). A payroll and personnel computer system recently purchased by the city of Atlanta (for more than 10 million dollars) "works so poorly that the city plans to abandon it" (Bennett, 2002, p. B1). A consultant to the city is quoted in a headline as advising the city to "Just shoot it and walk away." Space programs around the world have endured catastrophic losses of spacecraft and launch vehicles due to software malfunctions. A clear example: the Mars Climate Orbiter crashed into the surface of Mars because of a failure by programmers properly to convert metric to English values (NASA: Human Error, 1999). Consider security/crypto expert Bruce Schneier's reflections on the present state of computer security:

In security terms, he explained, cryptography is classed as a protective countermeasure. No such measure can foil every attack, and all attacks must still be both detected and responded to. This is particularly true for digital security, and Schneier spent most of his speech evoking the staggering insecurity of networked computers. Countless numbers are broken into each year, including machines in people's homes. Taking over computers is simple with the right tools, **because software is so often misconfigured or flawed** *[emphasis added]. In the first five months of this year [2002], Microsoft released five 'critical' security patches for Internet Explorer, each intended to rectify lapses in the original code (Mann, 2002, p. 96).*

And we should shudder to think of what might have happened if the following software failure had not, by luck, been detected when it was: "An early version of the [Ballistic Missile Early Warning System] mistook the rising moon for a missile heading over the northern hemisphere" (Myers, 1976, p. 4). If this brief survey is not convincing, Nachum Dershowitz (2000) of Tel Aviv University has collected and documented more than 100 software "horror stories" like these. And no single story captures the countless hours lost and dollars spent on the garden-variety problems caused by the poor production of software. Software projects being finished on schedule are a rarity (Brooks, 1995, pp. 14-15). The cost of repairing and maintaining millions of lines of badly designed and written code may be the hardest to see, but perhaps most spectacular collective failure for software engineers (Putnam & Myers, 1992, pp. 86-87). The exact impact these common problems have had on society would be hard to measure, but undeniably, the drain on society's financial well-being is significant.

Of course, we could easily produce such stories for other professions. But this is not the point. The question at hand is whether the consequences of professional failure (due either to incompetence, immorality or both) in the software industry are serious. These examples aim to show they are. That the consequences of failure are so serious demonstrates what a vital service software engineers often provide. Software engineering shares this important feature with the other professions.

3. Does software engineering enjoy professional autonomy, justified because of the practitioner's specialized knowledge and judgment? Or rather, do other bodies or agencies regulate, monitor and manage the activity? Here at least we see a difference between software engineering, how it is presently practiced, and the professions examined by Huntington and Harris et al. Software engineers, while they might belong to the ACM or IEEE, do not form a self-governing body anything like, for example, the various bar associations or the American Medical Association. Nor do they typically operate as independently practicing professionals. More often, software engineers are employees, ultimately managed and regulated by others outside the discipline. The source of many jokes, more than a little frustration, and perhaps a great deal of engineering failure, this state of affairs may not be ideal given what we have already noticed.

4. Ethical standards are already being proclaimed and promulgated by software engineers. Apparently moved by arguments that conceive of software engineers as professionals, the largest organizations of software engineers undertook publicly to articulate the ideal moral commitments of the groups. Committees composed of representatives of practicing engineers and academics have formulated two thoroughly worked-out ethical codes (ACM Software Engineering Code, 1997; ACM Code of Ethics and Professional Conduct, 1992). They have been formally accepted and published by the ACM and IEEE. The short version of the 1997 code, reproduced below, makes clear the moral thrust of these public documents.

Software Engineering Code of Ethics and Professional Practice
ACM/IEEE-CS Joint Task Force on Software Engineering Ethics and Professional Practices
Short Version

Preamble

The short version of the code summarizes aspirations at a high level of the abstraction; the clauses that are included in the full version give examples and details of how these aspirations change the way we act as software engineering professionals. Without the aspirations, the details can become legalistic and tedious; without the details, the aspirations can become high sounding but empty; together, the aspirations and the details form a cohesive code.

Software engineers shall commit themselves to making the analysis, specification, design, development, testing and maintenance of software a beneficial and respected profession. In accordance with their commitment to the health, safety and welfare of the public, software engineers shall adhere to the following eight principles:

1. Public: Software engineers shall act consistently with the public interest.
2. Client and employer: Software engineers shall act in a manner that is in the best interests of their client and employer consistent with the public interest.
3. Product: Software engineers shall ensure that their products and related modifications meet the highest professional standards possible.
4. Judgement: Software engineers shall maintain integrity and independence in their professional judgment.
5. Management: Software engineering managers and leaders shall subscribe to and promote an ethical approach to the management of software development and maintenance.
6. Profession: Software engineers shall advance the integrity and reputation of the profession consistent with the public interest.
7. Colleagues: Software engineers shall be fair to and supportive of their colleagues.
8. Self: Software engineers shall participate in lifelong learning regarding the practice of their profession and shall promote an ethical approach to the practice of the profession.

---

5. So obviously, software engineering has much in common with other professions and appears to answer well so far to the weighted set of characteristics in our model. Plausibly, software engineering should be thought of as a profession itself.[5] But there is a glaring difference, in this fifth element of the model, between software engineering as it is presently practiced and the other professions. Generally, software engineers do not need a general certification or license of any kind (even though some employers might ask for narrowly defined certificates of training on certain skills or products—these are not tantamount to a professional certification). While some kinds of engineers at least have the opportunity to earn a Professional Engineering (PE) license, in these fields it is estimated that only 15% to 20% of engineers hold such licenses, and the license is not a requirement for calling oneself an engineer or "plying the trade" (Professional Engineer License Requirements, 2001). The software engineer does not have even this or any analogous opportunity to obtain professional certification or licensure, and plainly, no such status is required to work. We should think back to the times when anyone could claim to be a physician or a lawyer. We are in a similarly unhappy situation these days with engineers of all kinds, but especially software engineers. The proof of their professional competence is in the pudding of their work; when damage

(sometimes grievous damage) is done in our process of discovery, it is too late. Even outside the professions, we cannot so much as get our plumbing done, our electrical wiring installed, or our hair styled without the practitioner having a certification or a license. And among the professions, doctors, lawyers, teachers, clergy, accountants, architects, military officers, and many others need difficult-to-obtain certifications and licensure, which can be, when performance falls short, taken away. That software engineering is approached differently should be cause for at least serious reflection. Indeed, it should be cause for more than that: the proper response is some kind of reform. For the same reasons we license other professionals, in some form or fashion software engineers ought to be licensed too.

REASONS TO RESIST LICENSURE

Of course, there may be arguments that would give us reasons to stop short of the demand that software engineers, like so many other professionals, should be licensed. In what follows, four basic reasons are considered, but rejected.

First, we might consider licensing or certifying not the professional, but rather the products they sell. Cars are required to meet certain performance and safety standards. Homes and commercial properties must be constructed in accordance with building codes. Our toasters might receive, if we care to check, a seal of approval from an organization like Underwriters Laboratories. Along the same lines, developing certain standards for software performance and reliability would certainly not be a bad thing.

But this approach, by itself, would not work well enough for software. It could not provide adequate assurances that the necessary and appropriate steps were taken for every software project. Certifying products (rather than those who make them) works best when the product has a fixed function, fixed sets of concerns about how it is made, and a way for us to say, in advance, exactly what those concerns are. In cases like these, certifying the product is all we need. Software is not like that. Each automation project is different, and the functions performed can differ radically. There is, to put it another way, too much custom work in software engineering: too many variables, too much complexity, too much need for particularized judgment by an individual with professional training. Even if we were to try the product certification approach, the full list of standards for grading each product could approach being idiosyncratic in each case. Similar reasons could be adduced for why we do not simply certify the product in many other professions. For example, the medical profession does not merely provide health care that meets certain itemized standards of delivery, similar to a building code (though a certain amount of this kind of certification is mandated, like in drug approvals by the FDA and in minimum standards of due care for doctors).   Instead, we realize that the minimum, list-like standards must be supplemented by someone with extraordinary training and experience, to account for the particulars presented by a given patient's case. The need for this kind of professional judgment generates, in part, the need for licensing physicians. Similar arguments could easily be made for most, if not all, of the other professions. Software engineering is in the same boat.

Second, we might want to argue that it is not the product or the professional that ought to be certified or licensed, but rather the company. Maybe something like ISO 9000 certification or the Configuration Management (CM) Model could be worked up, a set of standard practices that software companies should be required to implement. The widely-used Capability Maturity Model (CMM) might constitute a step in this direction (Carnegie Mellon, 2003). By certifying companies, we might be able to guarantee systematically that software products will be safe, reliable, or at least not inimical to the public good. But one of the problems that plagued our first suggestion (that we might simply certify products) will undermine this suggestion as well: one size will not, and could not, fit all. Different kinds of products and applications will have different, sometimes very different, production requirements. The testing, maintainability, reliability, etc., of a program developed to control our nation's air traffic should be handled much differently than the software for a new video game. Any attempt to substitute a standard industry-wide set of rules for real professional judgment will fail to provide what we need. And even if we were tempted by this approach, who but professionals would be competent to craft development standards and test procedures, etc., that would guide the certification of software companies?

Of course, this way of looking at things recognizes that software is most often developed in large organizations by teams of engineers.   Systemic, organizational practices will have a huge impact on the quality of the final product. But insistence on certain practices and organizational principles (even to the point of certifying companies), while it may be of benefit, cannot serve as an alternative to or substitute for certifying professionally qualified engineers. What we should prefer is some combination of professional judgment by engineers, along with some set of standards and constraints that regulate the development environment (which of course, we should notice again, properly would be crafted by software engineering professionals).

Third, we might just deny that software engineers are professionals in the requisite sense, and hence, a fortiori, do not need certification or licensing. This approach holds the least promise. Given the undeniable state of affairs we have already outlined in the previous section, how could one sensibly maintain this view? Does the fact that software engineers normally work in teams help to make this case? After all, doctors, lawyers and clergy do not always work in teams. But doctors, lawyers, clergy and accountants, any of the professionals really, often do work in teams. Military officers almost always do. They are all still professionals. Maybe our hypothetical objector has in mind what we noticed above: that data entry people, or even those restricted to producing just segments of code, do not make the kinds of decisions that would require special training, or professional judgment. This is a point we can take, but still insist that, somewhere in the process of software development, a professional software engineer needs to be in control over what is done. Perhaps it would be helpful to think in terms of a system of rank or grade, with levels of competency and professional status. However, thinking this way would not obviate the need for professional certification or licensure—it only works out in more detail how it might be done (which will be discussed again below). Another way to insist that software engineering is not a profession: focus on the fact that software is not always important. Not every project or every product has the impact on individuals or the society at large that would justify giving the developer the kind of special status normally reserved for a professional. But here again software engineering is no different than all the other professions. Sometimes a doctor is just lancing a boil, or prescribing an antibiotic, or any number of other minor things that a skilled health care worker could manage. A lawyer might be preparing only a simple document, one that a paralegal could easily accomplish. But of course, only the professional should be trusted to know when a trained employee can manage something, and when he cannot. Recognizing this continuum of importance and difficulty does not do away with the need for professional status.

Fourth, we might recognize the problems that lead to requiring licensure, but still think this solution to the problems would be impractical or ineffective. An ACM-chartered task force has published conclusions along these lines (Knight & Leveson, 2002). There is much in this report worth considering. However, as we shall see in what follows, we should not think their conclusions obviate the need eventually to certify or license software engineers.

The report in part considered whether software engineers should be licensed using some already existing procedures. As mentioned above, in every state there are laws that regulate granting the title of professional engineer (PE). These laws approximate, to varying degrees, a model law endorsed by the National Society of Professional Engineers (NSPE). The model requires a four-year university degree accredited by the Accreditation Board for Engineering and Technology (ABET); passing a thorough examination on fundamentals of engineering; four years of experience; a second examination on professional principles and practices; and letters of recommendation from practicing profes-sionals (Knight & Leveson, 2002, pp. 87-88). For the most part, engineers may not provide professional services directly to the public without attaining this PE status, though they may work for engineering firms or the federal government without it.

The task force was right to conclude that licensing software engineers under the auspices of this present system for licensing PEs would be impractical and ineffective (Knight & Leveson, 2002, p. 88). To begin with, the fundamentals of engineering (FE) examination presently given for those on the PE track is inappropriate for those receiving computer science degrees—largely it tests the wrong kind of background knowledge. Also, not all computer science departments are eligible for ABET certification—again, this is a matter of ABET looking for a different kind of curriculum than is appropriate for training the software engineer (see also Kennedy & Vardi, 2002, p. 95). Besides, even if this kind of license did make sense, there is a problem of venue. Large software projects often span many states, and might be sold in every state. So under the present PE licensing procedures, software engineers providing direct services to the public would often need to be licensed, and pay licensing fees, in every state in the union. And since most software engineers work for large firms or the government, most would be exempt from the licensing requirement anyway (see also Kennedy & Vardi, 2002, p. 94).

All this shows is that, if we wanted to license software engineers, it would not be advisable to use the system presently in place for PEs. The ACM agrees (White & Simons, 2002, p. 91). Rather, we would need to adjust the process, at the very least to address the problems the task force pointed out. Basic examinations would need to test material relevant to fundamentals of software engineering. Degrees would need to be evaluated not using standard ABET criteria, but instead using what makes sense for computer science departments that are preparing software engineers. Mutual recognition of licenses between states, or even a national licensing program, would be especially important for software engineers (and might even serve to improve all kinds of professional licensing—software cannot be the only profession that experiences these problems of venue). And of course, exempting software engineers from earning a license, simply because they work for a firm or the government, does not seem like a good idea for the reasons we entertained above—certifying the company rather than the employee just will not accomplish all the goals. Indeed, we should wonder if this sort of exception is sensible for any kind of engineer, or any other professional. For example, we should not feel comfortable being treated by an unlicensed physician simply because he is the direct employee of an HMO or the government.

Surprisingly, the task force did not conclude with a recommendation for special licensing procedures. In fact, they did not even entertain this possibility, and instead recommended against licensing software engineers at all. They produced yet more arguments, these arrayed against the practicality or effectiveness of licensure even if we *were* trying to produce a special system. Several of the arguments centered on the possibility of examinations (Knight & Leveson, 2002, p. 89). They claimed there is no generally agreed upon body of knowledge in software engineering to test. Even if there were such a body of knowledge, we could not put the tests in multiple-choice format. Also, software practices and procedures evolve so rapidly we could not update the examinations quickly enough to keep up. Moreover, if the tests were hard enough to be effective measures of competence, they would exclude too many aspiring engineers in a labor market mostly plagued by shortages; and if the tests were easy enough to pass in large enough numbers, they would not be effective.

These concerns about testing are spurious. We should be highly skeptical of the claim that software engineering has no body of theory and practical principles that could be taught and tested. Were this true to any serious extent, the granting of computer science degrees would be something of a pointless exercise. The format of the test would of course need to take whatever shape was appropriate to the material; professional examinations could easily contain mixes of multiple-choice questions and essays or exercises. And many professions (medicine comes to mind) manage, in their licensing examinations, to keep up with rapidly advancing knowledge in the field; it is hard to imagine why software engineering could not. Finally, the concern about excluding too many engineers from professional practice misses the mark. If we could demonstrate professional incompetence, either before entering practice or after undertaking it, why would we want to allow an engineer to keep working? The proper response to a shortage of competent people would be to train and educate more software engineers, not hide the problem by declining to test and license them.

The task force also worried about whom, exactly, should be licensed. Again, as we have already noticed, not everyone in the business of producing software seems to deserve professional status. So who needs a license? Requirements writers? Designers? Coders? Librarians? Quality assurance and test people? A person who uses a spreadsheet? "The breadth of people involved in the production of software would make licensing all of them impractical and not particularly helpful" (Knight & Leveson, 2002, p. 89). This is of course true. But it does not follow from this that *none* of the people involved in the production of software should be licensed. Many other professions have managed to work out who, of the many involved in delivering their professional service, needs a license. For example, in delivering health care physicians work with nursing and pharmaceutical professionals, and are assisted by aides, receptionists, technicians, and many others. There is no mystery in designating the doctor as an important seat of professional responsibility and a holder of professional status. Lawyers, accountants, architects, and the military have made similar distinctions. Software engineering could do the same.

The report also concluded that licensing software engineers would not assure public safety. As is now the case with the PE license, it would still be up to individual engineers to determine if they are competent to undertake a particular project (Knight & Leveson, 2002, p. 89). For similar reasons, McCalla calls the license a "blunt instrument" that will not truly identify those who have the requisite professional qualities (2002, p. 101). So why bother with the process in the first place? This objection overstates what any sensible person should expect a licensing process to do. Professional licenses do not, and cannot, *assure* safety in any profession. They only contribute to making public safety more likely, and tell us that the licensed practitioner has met certain minimum standards of professional competence. Further, licenses provide a mechanism (the option of removing professional status) for identifying those who have demonstrated incompetence or other kinds of professional failing. A mere certification (perhaps this is the ACM's preference—see White & Simons, 2002, p. 91), or worse yet no formal procedures at all, would leave us without this important mechanism.

The last argument the task force presented against licensing software engineers: "If software engineers are licensed, they will be subject to malpractice lawsuits" (Knight & Leveson, 2002, p. 90). Apparently, to the present date, "malpractice" lawsuits against incompetent software engineers have failed because there are no publicly endorsed standards of professional practice. If software engineers articulate such standards, and practitioners are licensed, then they will no doubt expose themselves to lawsuits when failure to live up to those standards causes harm. But is this a reason not to embrace professional responsibility? If the tort system is not fair in how it assigns damages, then this is where we should seek reform (in the tort system). But shielding software engineers from any blame whatever by declining to articulate standards is certainly to miss the high road.

So this fourth basic reason to resist licensure (that it would be impractical or ineffective) is no more compelling than the other three. We considered the many worries raised by the ACM task force, and found none of them completely persuasive. To summarize this section, while standards for products and companies would be good things, in something as complex as software engineering they could not serve as a substitute for the judgment of professionals. And even though not all members of the teams that make software share professional control, judgment and responsibility, *some* members of that team do. The same reasons that lead us to license other professionals make sense for software professionals, and there are no insurmountable bars to practical and effective moves in that direction.

FUTURE TRENDS:
HOW SHOULD WE PROCEED?

The world we occupy has, as it has so many times before, changed again. In the last century, our use and reliance on new technologies of various kinds has created new occupations. Some of these occupations should be re-conceptualized as professions, since, like the other professions, they also supply vital wants and needs to individuals and society. We should expect that software engineering, along with other types of engineering, will eventually respond to the pressures of this situation and come to resemble the other professions more closely. In the case of software engineering, we have recently seen slow but significant moves toward complete professionalization. What remains to be done is a more rapid, self-conscious and intelligently planned completion of what is already underway.

What would such a completion look like? At this point in the process, we should only make tentative suggestions. A first step would require that we decide who in the software industry, exactly, should carry professional status. The ACM task force was correct in noticing that not everyone would. Next, formalizing entry into the profession could take the same rough shape that we saw for the PE. Perhaps it will be possible to take what is good in the PE licensing process, and yet revise what is bad or not appropriate for software engineers. The state of Texas is trying something like this approach (Bagert, 2002). A four-year education (of the right sort), initial testing, an appropriate internship or period of experience, a final examination before full licensing, recommendations, and reasonable requirements for continuing education all seem important. We should move away from exceptions for those who work in firms or for the government. There would also need to be a standing body with the power to strip software engineers of their licenses should they fail to meet professional standards. But the details of this complete process, both in design and implementation, are far beyond the scope of this or any other small chapter. All this should be carefully worked out by a partnership of government, industry, academics, and practicing software engineers.[6] This is the work that remains to be done.

CONCLUSION

The central claim of this chapter is that the procedures, practices, institutions, and attitudes that govern software engineering as a profession have failed to keep pace with the reality of a radical and rapid change. Software now plays an important part in what it means to live a human life; and those who make software, because they are professionals, have had foisted on them (like it or not) professional responsibility. The fact that many engineers already know this is a fine thing, but not nearly fine enough. The ACM acknowledges that we have no assurance software engineers in general will make obligations of competence and public-minded moral virtue a part of their own professional identity: "Adherence of professionals to a code of ethics is largely a voluntary matter" (ACM Code of Ethics, 1992). The industry must find a way to raise the professional consciousness of software engineers, so that it will be a common, even universal, part of the software engineer's self-understanding. Failure to accept this mantle ought, finally, to be a bar to doing such important work. Toward this end, there should be a move toward professional certification or licensure.

REFERENCES

ACM Code of Ethics *and Professional Conduct.* (1992). Retrieved from the World Wide Web: http://www.acm.org/constitution/code.html.

ACM Curricula Recommendations. (2000). Retrieved from the World Wide Web: http://www.acm.org/education/curricula.html.

ACM Software Engineering Code of Ethics and Professional Practice. (1997). Retrieved from the World Wide Web: http://www.acm.org/ serving/se/code.htm.

Bagert, D. J. (2002). Texas licensing of software engineers: All's quiet, for now. *Communications of the ACM, 45*(11), 92-94.

Bennett, D.L. (2002, September 23). City fed up with computer system. *The Atlanta Journal-Constitution*, B1.

Brooks, F. P. Jr. (1995). *The Mythical Man-Month: Essays on Software Engineering* (Anniversary Ed.). Reading, MA: Addison Wesley Longman.

Camenisch, P. F. (1982). On being a professional, morally speaking. In B. Baumrin & B. Freedman (Eds.), *Moral Responsibility and the Professions* (pp. 42-61). New York: Haven Publishing.

Carnegie Mellon Software Engineering Institute: Capability Maturity Model for Software. (2003). Retrieved from the World Wide Web: http:/ /www.sei.cmu.edu/cmm/cmm.html.

CNN. (1999). NASA: Human error caused loss of Mars Orbiter. *CNN Reports*. Retrieved from the World Wide Web: http://www.cnn.com/TECH/space/ 9911/10/orbiter.02/index.html.

Dershowitz, N. (2000). *Software horror stories.* Retrieved from the World Wide Web: http://www.cs.tau.ac.il/~nachumd/verify/horror.html.

Harris, C. E., Jr., Pritchard, M.S., & Rabins, M.J. (1995). *Engineering Ethics*. Belmont, CA: Wadsworth Publishing.

Huntington, S. P. (1957). *The Soldier and the State: The Theory of Politics and Civil-Military Relations.* Cambridge, MA: Belknap Press of Harvard University Press.

Kennedy, K. & Vardi, M. Y. (2002). A Rice University perspective on software engineering licensing. *Communications of the ACM, 45*(11), 94-95.

Knight, J. C. & Leveson, N. G. (2002). Should software engineers be licensed? *Communications of the ACM, 45*(11), 87-90.

Mann, C. C. (2002, September). Homeland insecurity. *The Atlantic Monthly, 290*(2), 81-97.

McCalla, G. (2002). Software engineering requires individual professionalism. *Communications of the ACM, 45*(11), 98-101.

Myers, G. J. (1976). *Software Reliability: Principles and Practices.* New York: John Wiley & Sons.

National Research Council. (1997). *Software engineering defined.* Retrieved from the World Wide Web: http://wwwsel.iit.nrc.ca/sedefn/SEdefn.html.

National Y2K Clearinghouse, U.S. General Services Administration. (2000). *Lessons learned.* Retrieved from the World Wide Web: http://www.y2k.gov/lesslearn.html.

Parnas, D. L. (2002). Licensing software engineers in Canada. *Communications of the ACM, 45*(11), 96-98.

Professional Engineer License Requirements. (2001). Engineering Exam Resources. Retrieved from the World Wide Web: http://www.theinformant.com/require.html.

Putnam, L. H. & Myers, W. (1992). *Measures for Excellence: Reliable Software on Time, within Budget.* Englewood Cliffs, NJ: Prentice-Hall.

U.S. Department of Transportation. (1994). New Denver Airport: Impact of the Delayed Baggage System. *National Transportation Library, Report Number RCED-95-35BR.* Retrieved from the World Wide Web: http://ntl.bts.gov/DOCS/rc9535br.html.

Wakin, M. M. (1986). The ethics of leadership II. In M. M. Wakin (Ed.), *War, Morality, and the Military Profession* (2nd Ed, Rev. and Updated) (pp. 200-216). Boulder, CO: Westview Press.

White, J, & Simons, B. (2002). ACM's position on the licensing of software engineers. *Communications of the ACM, 45*(11), 91.

ENDNOTES

1   The ideas in this chapter found their inchoate beginning in, and will be further developments of, discussions conducted at a 1997 engineering ethics conference held at Duke University. I am especially indebted to Dan Gotterbarn, who spearheaded the IEEE and ACM efforts to develop a software engineering code of ethics. The ideas were first presented in a more developed form to a seminar I led later that year with the Colorado Springs, Colorado chapter of the ACM.

2   The engineer was Lieutenant Colonel Gregory Tarr, USAF. He made this helpful observation in a conversation with the author in Montgomery, Alabama in 1996.

3   Their original order of presentation has been changed.

4   Paul Camenisch (1988) presents interesting arguments in support of this general idea.

222 Ficarrotta

5   We might suspect that even using somewhat different models for the nature of the professions (there are many, though none are radically different from what we are using), we would still conclude that software engineering belongs in the group.

6   For an example of how *not* to proceed, consider the merely verbal disputes and turf battling that has transpired in Canada (Parnas, 2002).

Chapter XIII

Copyright Law in the Digital Age

Jordan M. Blanke
Mercer University, USA

ABSTRACT

This chapter discusses the current state of copyright law with respect to works contained on different media. It traces the history and purpose of the law, while focusing on how digital technology has shaped its evolution. It describes how recent legislation and court cases have created a patchwork of law whose protection often varies depending upon the medium on which the work lies. The author questions whether some of the recent legislation has lost sight of the main purpose behind the copyright law, the promotion of learning and public knowledge.

INTRODUCTION

As society has transitioned to a digital world, copyright has emerged as the most important area of intellectual property law. While the scope of patent, trademark and trade secret law has each greatly expanded in the last decade or so, copyright law has gotten the most attention. The popularity of the Internet and the digitization of information have strained traditional copyright principles and presented many difficult new questions. The law, which must and does evolve as society changes, is being forced, again, to address new technologies. It must either apply existing rules to these new technologies, or create new rules.

A BRIEF HISTORY OF COPYRIGHT LAW

In order to understand copyright law, as it exists today, it is important to understand its origins. The legal authority for copyright law in the United States comes from the Constitution itself. Among the enumerated powers granted the Congress in Article I of the Constitution is the power:

To promote the progress of science and useful arts, by securing for limited times to authors and inventors the exclusive right to their respective writings and discoveries. (U.S. Const. art. I, § 8, cl. 8.)

Like much of the language in the Constitution, this clause was the product of compromise. James Madison, the principal drafter of the language, believed that the copyright law should benefit both the author and the general public. The author would reap the rewards of his creative effort for a limited period of time, and thereafter, the public would benefit by receiving these works into the public domain. Thomas Jefferson was apprehensive of any type of monopoly, even a limited one granted to the author of a creative work. He finally acquiesced to the notion of a copyright, as long as it was for a limited period of time. Both Madison and Jefferson readily agreed that the primary purpose of the law would be to promote learning and the progress of public knowledge (Vaidhyanathan, 2001).

An author's copyright interest in a work is granted by statute for a specific period of time, as opposed to being a "property" right to be possessed indefinitely. British law, at the time, recognized both types of these interests, but the Constitution only granted Congress the authority to create a statutory right for a limited period (Patterson, 1992).

The first Copyright Act of 1790 granted a copyright to authors of maps, charts and books for a period of 14 years, renewable for one additional term of 14 years. Over the past 200-plus years, both the scope and duration of this copyright interest have greatly increased. As new media were developed, the law responded. During the 1800s, the copyright law was modified several times to expand its scope to include prints and engravings, musical compositions, public performances of dramatic works, photographs, paintings, drawings and statues.

In 1909, the copyright law was completely rewritten, granting copyrights for "all the writings of an author" (Copyright Act of 1909, § 4). Since that time, this language has been interpreted to include, among other things, motion pictures, sound recordings, radio and television broadcasts of sporting events, and computer programs. Principles that were originally intended to pertain only to books, maps and charts have been applied to new and very different media. As will be discussed below, this has often resulted in inconsistent application of the law.

The length of the first term of copyright was increased from 14 to 28 years in 1831, and the length of the renewable term was similarly increased to 28 years in 1909. In 1976 the duration of a copyright was expanded to the life of the author plus 50 years, or 75 years for a corporate author. The Sonny Bono Copyright Term Extension Act of 1998 increased those periods by 20 years. Thus the duration of a copyright today is vastly different from that envisioned by both Madison and Jefferson during the Constitutional Era.

BASICS OF COPYRIGHT LAW

Under the Copyright Act of 1976, which became effective on January 1, 1978, a federal copyright interest attaches from the moment that an original work of authorship is fixed in a tangible medium of expression. Works of authorship include literary works; musical works, including any accompanying words; dramatic works, including any accompanying music; pantomimes and choreographic works; pictorial, graphic, and sculptural works; motion pictures and other audiovisual works; sound recordings; and architectural works. A copyright interest attaches as soon the expression is written down, recorded, photographed, videotaped, digitized, or otherwise fixed in any tangible medium (Copyright Act of 1976).

The owner of a copyright has the exclusive rights to do and to authorize any or all of the following: to reproduce the copyrighted work; to prepare derivative works based upon the copyrighted work (such as foreign translations, sequels and spin-offs); to distribute copies of the copyrighted work to the public by sale, rental, lease or lending; and in the case of some of these categories of copyrighted works, to perform or display the copyrighted work publicly.

The owner of a copyright is free to enjoy these exclusive rights subject to a series of limitations or exceptions. Some of the exceptions are very narrow and specific. For example, the owner of a computer program may make a backup copy of the copyrighted work for archival purposes (Copyright Act of 1976, § 117).

The most important of these exceptions is "fair use." Section 107 of the Copyright Act provides that:

[T]he fair use of a copyrighted work…for purposes such as criticism, comment, news reporting, teaching (including multiple copies for classroom use), scholarship, or research, is not an infringement of copyright. In

*determining whether the use made of a work in any particular case is a fair
use the factors to be considered shall include:*

1.   the purpose and character of the use, including whether such use is of a
      commercial nature or is for nonprofit educational purposes;
2.   the nature of the copyrighted work;
3.   the amount and substantiality of the portion used in relation to the copy-
      righted work as a whole; and
4.   the effect of the use upon the potential market for or value of the
      copyrighted work (Copyright Act of 1976, § 107).

Not surprisingly, many court cases addressing "fair use" involve the
determination of whether a particular use of a copyrighted work is a "fair use."
Generally, a court will explore the purpose or nature of the use and apply the four
factors listed in the statute to the facts of the case. For example, if a professor
discovers a recently published copyrighted article, relevant to a topic she is
teaching that day, her photocopying and distribution of the article to her class is
a "fair use" of that copyrighted work. It is for a purpose specifically addressed
in the statute (i.e., teaching), done in a manner anticipated by the statute (i.e.,
multiple copies for classroom use), and consistent with most of the four factors.

It is often difficult to determine if the copying of a particular work is
appropriate or permissible under the copyright law. A good starting point is to
assume that a work is copyrighted. It is no longer required that a copyrighted
work contain a copyright notice, although it is still advisable to include one, in
order to preclude a defense of innocent infringement. One should not assume
that a work is not protected by copyright simply because of the absence of a
notice. Similarly, one should not assume that a work cannot be copied legally just
because it does contain a notice. Remember that an owner of a copyright may
grant whatever rights to copy the work to anyone he or she wishes. For example,
many scholarly journals specifically give permission to copy an article contained
therein for nonprofit, educational purposes. Furthermore, despite the fact that
a work is copyrighted, its copying may be a "fair use."

Copyright law protects expression. It does not protect the underlying idea.
One can obtain a copyright for a particular song, but not for the concept of mixing
lyrics with a background melody. One can obtain a copyright for a screenplay
involving six friends who live together in New York City, but not for the
underlying theme that would encompass any screenplay written about friends
living near each other in a big city. It is said that "imitation is the sincerest form
of flattery," but copyright law protects against only a very close imitation, not a
mere variation on the theme.

Another important principle of copyright law is that a copyright cannot
protect facts. The names of our presidents and vice-presidents, the dates of their
administrations, and their party affiliations are all facts. They are part of the

public domain. An author can write about history, and her specific expressive narrative will be protected. But the facts themselves can be used by anyone.

The Feist Case

In 1991 the Supreme Court decided a major copyright case involving facts and databases (*Feist v. Rural*). The case is important because it refocused attention on the basic constitutional requirements of copyright law. Feist Publications published a white pages telephone directory that included the names and addresses of all the listings contained in the directory of a competitor. Rural Telephone Service, the competitor, sued for copyright infringement. The lower courts found for Rural, holding that the telephone directories were copyrightable, that there was copying, and that, therefore, there was copyright infringement.

The Supreme Court reversed, finding no copyright interest in Rural's directory. The Court emphasized that *originality* is a constitutional requirement for copyright:

The sine qua non of copyright is originality. To qualify for copyright protection, a work must be original to the author. ...Original, as the term is used in copyright, means only that the work was independently created by the author (as opposed to copied from other works), and that it possesses at least some minimal degree of creativity. ...To be sure, the requisite level of creativity is extremely low; even a slight amount will suffice. The vast majority of works make the grade quite easily, as they possess some creative spark (Feist v. Rural, 1991, p. 345).

The Court held that Rural's selection, coordination, and arrangement of its listings, by alphabetical order of surname, could not have been more obvious, and accordingly, did not satisfy this minimum constitutional standard for copyright protection.

The Court discussed the interplay between two well-established propositions: that facts are not copyrightable, and that compilations of facts generally are, as long as there is some originality in the selection or arrangement of the facts. The Court cautioned that even if there were such originality, the copyright would in no event extend to the facts themselves. The Court made clear that under the Copyright Act of 1976, "originality, not 'sweat of the brow,' is the touchstone of copyright protection in directories and other fact-based works" (*Feist v. Rural*, 1991, pp. 359-360). The "sweat of the brow" doctrine had been judicially sanctioned in a number of cases over the years. The Court also held that "copyright in a factual compilation is thin. Notwithstanding a valid copyright, a subsequent compiler remains free to use the facts contained in another's publication to aid in preparing a competing work, so long as the competing work does not feature the same selection and arrangement" (*Feist v. Rural*, 1991, p. 349).

In commenting on the fairness of this result, the Court observed that:

It may seem unfair that much of the fruit of the compiler's labor may be used by others without compensation. As Justice Brennan has correctly observed, however, this is not 'some unforeseen byproduct of a statutory scheme.' ...It is, rather, 'the essence of copyright,' and a constitutional requirement. The primary objective of copyright is not to reward the labor of authors, but 'to promote the Progress of Science and useful Arts.' ...As applied to a factual compilation, assuming the absence of original written expression, only the compiler's selection and arrangement may be protected; the raw facts may be copied at will. This result is neither unfair nor unfortunate. It is the means by which copyright advances the progress of science and art (Feist v. Rural, 1991, p. 349).

The *Feist* case was decided in 1991, just as the digital world was beginning to take shape. Personal computers and audio CDs were commonplace, and CD-ROMs were beginning to become popular. The Internet was evolving quickly. By the mid-1990s, the technological landscape had changed. Computers were faster, more powerful, and could store greater amounts of data. Read/write CD drives became available, and most importantly, the Web grew exponentially. Anyone with a computer and a modicum of ingenuity could digitize, compile and copy (or copy and compile) almost anything. Cyberspace became an electronic trading post (Blanke, 2002).

DIFFERENT MEDIA

Largely due to fear of how easily this digital technology would facilitate copying, there is today a hodgepodge of laws that often provide different protection based upon the type of medium on which the copyrighted expression lies.

Books

It should not be surprising that the copyright law as it pertains to books is the most easily applied and best understood by the general public. After all, books have been the most common medium for centuries. Most people would readily agree that photocopying the pages of a copyrighted book would be an infringement. Most understand that a book usually contains copyrighted material for which the author should be entitled to benefit financially. Photocopying the book without permission and without legal right to do so amounts to infringement.

Computer Software

Computer software has been protected by copyright for a relatively short time, beginning in the 1960s, but not fully protected until the Copyright Act of 1976. It is somewhat surprising to see how quickly the public has learned that computer software is subject to copyright protection. Whether the software is contained on floppy disk or CD-ROM or is downloaded from the Web, most people would probably admit knowing that the software was copyrighted.

Two decades ago software publishers struggled to protect their product. Many consumers were unwilling to accept the notion that a copyrighted work on a floppy disk was as worthy of protection as a copyrighted work in a book. Publishers tried a variety of methods to protect the software, often using technology to prevent the act of copying. For example, a publisher might have sold its software on a floppy disk, which contained code preventing a user from reproducing the disk with a "diskcopy" command. Some enterprising person quickly discovered that the way to circumvent this software "lock" was to write a software "key." The publisher then created version two of the "lock" in order to thwart the "key." Soon thereafter came version two of the "key." And so on.

Eventually the software publishing industry decided that it might be more effective to educate the public, teaching it that the copyright law protects software. Anyone who has ever installed or downloaded software has faced a barrage of warnings and notifications clearly stating that software is so protected. Today, while certainly there are people who have no qualms about illegally reproducing copyrighted software, most people would have to admit that they know the software is protected by copyright.

Almost all software is sold by license agreement. The owner of the copyright can specify the terms of usage. The purchaser is free to accept these terms or buy a different piece of software. For example, a license may permit installation on one machine only, or it may permit installation on both a work and a home (or portable) machine, as long as the software is never used on the two machines at the same time. Different companies can have different license agreements. The terms of the licenses are entirely a matter of contractual specification. The owner of the copyright is free to sell, lease, rent or license his work however he chooses. It is not uncommon for software licenses to vary greatly from one vendor to another.

Videotape

The advent of the videotape recorder greatly concerned the television and movie industries. They feared that the average consumer would be able to record any copyrighted television show or movie broadcast over the airwaves without any compensation to its owner.

In 1982 several television and movie studios sued Sony for contributory infringement, seeking to stop the manufacture and sale of videotape recorders. The basis of their claim was that Sony provided the means by which other individuals could infringe the copyrighted works. In order to defeat a contributory infringement claim, one must show that there is a legitimate non-infringing use of the product. The Supreme Court examined evidence that showed that a typical user of a videotape recorder (in 1982) owned three or four blank tapes. It concluded that the taping over the airwaves of copyrighted programming amounted to a legitimate and common fair use called "time-shifting" (*Sony v. Universal*, 1984). For example, a person would tape a soap opera that aired during work hours and watch it at a more convenient time.

Somewhat ironically, in the aftermath of the case, a multi-billion dollar videotape sale and rental industry developed and flourished. However, the holding in the *Sony* is not as broad as many people might think. While it is a fair use to record a copyrighted work for later viewing (i.e., "time-shifting"), it is not a fair use to record for purposes of building a library of shows or movies. There is no exception for personal home use of videotaped materials. Furthermore, there is nothing that permits the use of a dual recorder to make a copy of another copyrighted videotape.

One of the reasons that studios like Disney were not as upset about the home taping of movies was because they learned to become masters at marketing and remarketing the sale of videotapes. With movies touting "never before seen footage" and "digitally remastered soundtracks," the studios were able to convince the public that is was much better to buy a copy of the tape than to merely record it off the airwaves.

This was largely due to the fact that analog technology produced an inferior copy. A home videotape recorder could never reproduce the clarity of the picture or sound of the original. The industry learned that many consumers would still buy an original copy of the movie in order to have the superior quality. The introduction of digital recording devices would present new problems.

Music

The effect that digital technology has had on electronic media and copyright law is best illustrated in the music industry. For a long time, while there was concern about the illegal taping of copyrighted music, it was tempered by the knowledge that the analog technology produced an inferior copy. The quality of the product deteriorated dramatically from copy to copy, whether the recording was made from a record, a radio transmission, or from another tape.

It was not until the advent of digital music, in the form of CDs and DATs (digital audio tapes), that the music industry became more concerned. While DATs became reasonably popular in Japan in the 1980s, the music industry successfully lobbied Congress to prevent the sale of the machines in the United States. It was not until the passage of the Audio Home Recording Act of 1992 (AHRA) that the manufacture or importation of DAT players was permitted.

The AHRA requires that every digital audio recording device contain a Serial Copy Management System that prohibits or impedes the copying of a copy. The AHRA also establishes a mandatory royalty scheme that authorizes a payment for the sale of each blank DAT, upon the assumption that eventually a copyrighted work will be contained on that tape. In return for this, the consumer gets the right to make analog or digital audio recordings of copyrighted music for his or her private, non-commercial use. Such copying is still considered to be a copyright infringement, but consumers are, in effect, immune from suit for this type of copying.

The copying of music again became a major issue just a few short years after passage of the AHRA because of more new technology. When the AHRA was enacted, files containing digital music were relatively large, and data transmission speeds over the Internet relatively slow. By the late 1990s, that had changed. Compression techniques reduced the size of music files over tenfold, and DSL and cable modems increased transmission speeds even more dramatically. Digital music could now be copied, stored and transmitted perfectly and quickly.

In 1999, the Recording Industry Association of America (RIAA) sued to enjoin the manufacture and distribution of the Rio, a portable music player capable of playing MP3 files downloaded by computer. A federal appeals court in California held that the Rio was not a "digital audio recording device" under the AHRA and, therefore, was not subject to the restrictions requiring a Serial Copying Management System. The court denied RIAA's request, favorably comparing the "space-shifting" nature of the Rio to the "time-shifting" of videotape recorders in the *Sony* case (*RIAA v. Diamond*, 1999).

Two years later, the same appellate court in California enjoined Napster from facilitating the distribution of copyrighted songs in MP3 format in a peer-to-peer network environment. The court analyzed the four fair use factors and held that Napster and its system's users were not engaged in a fair use of the plaintiff's copyrighted works. It specifically rejected Napster's defense that users were merely "space-shifting" or "time-shifting" (*A & M Records v. Napster*, 2001).

In the *RIIA* case, it was assumed that many users were merely condensing songs from their audio CDs into MP3 format, and storing them more compactly on the Rio. In *Napster*, it was clear that most users did not own copies of an original CD, but were making unauthorized copies of copyrighted works.

The music industry continues to battle the rampant swapping of copyrighted works over the Internet. With the proliferation of peer-to-peer networking and high transmission speeds, it is a near impossible task. Instead, we are beginning to see the production of copy-protected audio CDs that will not play on computer CD drives. It remains to be seen if the public will accept this technology.

DVD

Movie DVDs contain encryption code that prevents them from being easily copied. In 1998 Congress passed the controversial Digital Millennium Copyright Act (DCMA). Among other things, it provides civil and criminal penalties for distributing any code or device intended to circumvent the encryption code. When a web site posted a computer program containing such decryption code, several movie studios sued to enjoin the posting. In 2001, a federal appeals court in New York upheld the injunction issued by the trial court preventing the posting of the code. The court rejected arguments that the anti-circumvention provisions of the DCMA unconstitutionally prohibit fair uses of DVD content, and that the decryption code was entitled to First Amendment protection.

Lawrence Lessig wrote of the interplay between law and code in cyberspace (Lessig, 1999). He stated that, basically, the law attempts to regulate code, but as encryption technology and the DCMA illustrate, code can also regulate the law. For example, while it might be a fair use to copy a short clip from a movie on a DVD, if copy protection devices on the DVD prohibit such copying, that permitted fair use may be impossible. It may prove very dangerous to let code dictate the direction of the law.

The movie industry faces essentially the same problems as the music industry. With the advent of DVD recorders, perfect digital copies can be made in a matter of minutes. The Internet facilitates their almost instantaneous distribution. There recently have been reports of several movies being available on the Web even before their theatrical debuts.

CONCLUSION

There are those who believe that copyright has been extended in scope to cover subject matter that it should not reach (Patterson, 1992) and extended too far in duration (Lessig, 2001). They are probably right. However, rather than addressing these problems, the law has evolved such that much of the protection it provides depends upon the medium on which the expression lies.

Society needs to decide if the purpose behind the copyright law, the promotion of learning and public knowledge, should still be paramount. If so, the law needs to be updated to make its application more consistent, and less dependent upon the type of media upon which the expression is fixed. If the use of a copyrighted work is deemed to be a fair use, for example, it should not matter whether the work is contained on a videotape, a CD or a DVD, or whether code might exist for a particular medium that would prevent its copying.

REFERENCES

A & M Records, Inc. v. Napster , Inc., 239 F.3d 1004 (9th Cir. 2001).

Blanke, J. M. (2002). Vincent Van Gogh, "Sweat of the Brow," and Database Protection. *American Business Law Journal, 39*, 648-57.

Copyright Act of 1909, ch. 320, § 4, 35 Stat. 1076 (repealed 1976).

Copyright Act of 1976, 17 U.S.C. §§ 101, 102, 103, 106, 107, 117, 1008, 1201 (2002).

Eldred v. Ashcroft, 123 S. Ct. 769 (2003).

Feist Publications, Inc. v. Rural Telephone Service Co. Inc., 499 U.S. 340 (1991).

Lessig, L. (1999). *Code and Other Laws of Cyberspace*. New York: Basic Books.

Lessig, L. (2001). *The Future of Ideas. The Fate of the Commons in a Connected World*. New York: Random House.

Patterson, L. R. (1992). Copyright overextended: A preliminary inquiry into the need for a federal statute of unfair competition. *Dayton Law Review, 17*, 396-403.

Recording Industry Association of America v. Diamond Multimedia Systems, Inc., 180 F.3d 1072 (9th Cir. 1999).

Sony Corp. v. Universal City Studios, Inc., 464 U.S. 417 (1984).

Universal City Studios, Inc. v. Corley, 273 F.3d 429 (2nd Cir. 2001).

U.S. Const. art. I, § 8, cl. 8.

Vaidhyanathan, S. (2001). *Copyrights and Copywrongs: The Rise of Intellectual Property and How it Threatens Creativity*. New York: New York University Press.

Chapter XIV

"Digital Orphans": Technology's Wayward Children

Mark Kieler
Carnegie Mellon University, USA

Michael J. West
Carnegie Mellon University, USA

ABSTRACT

This chapter examines rapid technological obsolescence, and the potential impact on retrieval of intellectual creations by future generations. The authors define "intellectual creations" as human expressions embodied in text, music or art. Increasingly, we encode these creations in digital formats that have extremely short life cycles. Eventually, backward compatibility is lost. Thus, after very little time, a digital encoding format becomes obsolete, and intellectual works encoded in the format may become irretrievable. In contrast, the cultural worth of an intellectual creation may not be realized for generations. Additionally, future generations must access artifacts, including intellectual creations, to understand a culture in historical context. The authors contend that technology—intensive storage and manipulation of data may result in an inability to gain this access. Technology creators have some responsibility to facilitate future retrieval through careful documentation, and by selective maintenance of hardware that may be required to access archival media.

A SENSE OF HISTORY

Can progress exist without consciousness of the past? At first glance, such a question seems absurd. We like to think of ourselves as sophisticated enough to understand Ortega and Gasset's injunction that those who forget history are condemned to repeat it. In the realm of technology, particularly information and communication systems, we cannot ignore the present's debt to the past. However, as cultures represent themselves over time, cultural artifacts nearly always outlive the technologies that made them possible. How exactly were the Pyramids constructed? When no speakers of an ancient language exist, how do we know what it sounded like? If we consider software as an artifact of technological or digital culture, we encounter an analogous problem. Imagine the discovery, hundreds of years from now, of an eight-track tape or a floppy diskette containing a document written in WordStar. Once a code has been lost, have all texts written in that code been lost as well? This chapter explores some of the implications of technological evolution on the artifacts—texts, sounds, images—it leaves behind.

Marketing specialists have focused on Geoffrey Moore's concept of "the chasm" to explain the gap between the early market for a given technology ("visionaries," early adapters) and the mainstream market (pragmatists, conservatives) (Moore, 1991, 1999). Where most technology developers flounder is in this chasm between the early and mainstream markets. Financial success, and even viability, depends on reaching the mainstream market quickly enough to offset the costs of development.

At the other end of the cycle, we find the point at which a given technology is finally abandoned by a sufficient number of people that it is no longer supported or maintained. It ceases to exist except in archival form. The disappearance of eight-track tape technology is one example. As we reach the twentieth anniversary of the introduction of Compact Disc technology, we can already see it coming to be replaced by DVD (Digital Video Disc) technology, which will in time come to be replaced by another technology altogether. The editors of *Wired Magazine*, a publication devoted to presenting the cutting edge of technology, must face the reality that wireless technology is quickly overtaking the wired world.

Linguists stress the organic nature of language — that it is in constant evolution. What are grammars, after all, except codifications, constructed of "snapshot images" of spoken and written language usage. Dictionaries must be revised periodically to include neologisms; slang dictionaries have a notoriously brief shelf-life, sometimes finding themselves out-of-date by the time they are published. Despite the fact that both are considered examples of English, speakers of the vernacular of Shakespeare and the vernacular of current rap music would find each other mutually incomprehensible. With technology, as with language and culture, timing is everything, and context plays an important role in shaping how we interact both with each other and with technology.

HOW DO WE KNOW
ABOUT PAST CULTURES?

In engineering, a transmission path can be defined as requiring a transmitter, a receiver, a transmitting path, and an encoding/decoding method. One can think of the history of human communication in these terms. The transmitter is anyone who wishes to relate a piece of information, the receiver is anyone who intercepts the message, the encoding/decoding is any attempt to put the information into a format that others may understand, and the transmitting path (or medium) is the means for moving the information from place to place, over distance and through time. While the primary transmitter and receivers are almost always meant to be humans, all other parts of the transmission system have changed greatly over time. Linguists, beginning with Ferdinand de Saussure, established semiotics as a science of signs, which likewise focuses on the sender and the receiver of a message. Semiotics also posited the arbitrary nature of the sign and looked at the ways human languages encode and transmit messages.

From the distant past, we may uncover artifacts made from relatively durable materials, or we may find drawings or carvings in relatively sheltered areas, such as caves or large burial vaults. Artifacts reveal much about a culture, depending on their purpose, and the quality of materials from which they are made. Drawings form a type of language in their stylistic depiction of events and the way in which people and things are portrayed. Our record from ancient civilizations is far from perfect or complete, but archaeologists can construct some details about them from these clues.

Significant events have often been recorded in the living embodiment of a storyteller, and oral traditions still form an important part of many cultures. The historical record has often been related by language, as well as by performance, such as a ritual dance. Some of these oral histories survived long enough to be recorded in other more permanent media. However, not only have many oral traditions died with the last generation of storyteller, others assumed inaccuracies and exaggerations as a result of being passed serially through generations

As languages evolved and became standardized, it became possible to encode events in written form. Because writing has traditionally been the province of the learned few, written documents were recorded on long-lived media, and special care was accorded to their storage. Fortunately, many ancient documents have survived, although deterioration and time have often extracted great tolls. As we have noted, however, the encoding format, human language, is in a constant state of evolution, and when a culture dies, the language often dies with it. Language experts attempt to reconstruct meaning by looking for patterns that may establish types of words and contexts, and similarities to more modern languages.

In addition to printed text, human expression is also accomplished through artistic means, such as music, painting and dance. While it has been only relatively recently that we have been able to preserve musical and dance performances, it has been possible for quite some time to provide a written procedure for recreating music. The method of recording music on paper using notes, measures, and time definitions has remained unchanged for centuries. Thus a modern group of musicians can essentially recreate the intentions of the composer. The methods for recording dance instructions are much less standardized, and we frequently rely on interpretations and tradition to create dances from musical accompaniment.

Art works vary in durability depending on the types of inks/paints/dyes used, and the media on which they are deposited. Colors may fade or change with time, centuries of dirt and grime accumulate on the artwork, and the substrate may deteriorate. Sculpture is, likewise, not immune to damage from acid rain and other environmental factors.

THE INTRODUCTION OF TECHNOLOGY

The invention of the printing press made wide distribution of information possible, and mass production of paper goods made it affordable for the general public, particularly in the evolution from fiber-based paper to paper based on wood pulp. However, the transition from fiber-based media to inexpensive paper carried a price. Unlike fiber-based paper, pulp-based paper has been manufactured over most of its existence through an acid-based process. The acid remains in the finished paper product, and eventually causes its destruction. Thus, we have the paradoxical situation in which books from the 19th century are often more legible than books dating from the 20th century, due to the advanced state of deterioration of acid-based paper.

Text

Text was the first means of expression to be converted into electrical form. In fact, unlike other representations of human expression, text went "direct to digital." Morse code can be thought of as a duration-encoded digital signal. Text converted into these series of dots and dashes would be unrecognizable to anyone who did not understand Morse code. Storage of these signals was very primitive, and used mainly to "buffer" the information until a human could convert it back to text. Thus, long-term storage and archiving of Morse code traffic was not an issue.

The first modern bit encoding of text occurred in 1874. Emile Baudot, a French telegraph engineer, devised a five-bit code for each letter of the alphabet. Thus, unlike Morse code, each symbol had a fixed length representation, dependent only on the presence or absence of electrical current. The Baudot code had no provision for case representation; nevertheless, it was a durable standard, used by the news service teletypewriters through the 1970s (Freed, 1995, p. 77). In these applications, again, there was infrequent need for storage. However, many machines had recorders/readers that could punch the sequential codes as holes into a paper tape. Many early computer enthusiasts stored their programs in this fashion. The digital code can be read, albeit slowly, merely by holding the tape up to a light.

Representation of upper and lower case letters required more combinations than could be represented using five bits. ASCII (American Standard Code for Information Interchange) uses seven bits to represent not only upper and lower case letters, but also numbers, punctuation, and many other special characters. While Baudot could represent 2^5 or 32 characters, ASCII can represent 2^7 or 128 different characters.

ASCII remains the plain text standard. The rise of WYSIWYG (what you see is what you get) computer interfaces, and the availability of sophisticated word processing programs, made it possible to digitally encode additional expressions to text. Different art styles of text (fonts) could be used, and these fonts could be changed in style to be italicized, underlined, bold, super-and sub-scripted, and embody any other number of visual variations. It became necessary for word processing systems to evolve to encode these variations. This may be accomplished by adding bits to the original seven-bit ASCII data, or by software commands, placed before a section of text, that define the look of the section. At this point, we deviate from international standards into conventions of the word processing software itself. As the level of sophistication increases, we begin to lose the ability to universally understand an encoded section of text. In fact, the actual text becomes only a tiny portion of the code needed to reproduce the art of the text.

The following example shows the problem: We start with the following simple paragraph:

This is an elementary paragraph. It is a collection of thoughts arranged in a group of sentences. The word processor converts each letter to a digital representation and stores it.

This text can be encoded using nothing more than seven bit ASCII. However, we are generally unable to create any style to the basic text. Word processing software allows for this, but greatly affects the ability to recognize the basic text without the word processing software itself. Here is the same paragraph, encoded in a old, but sophisticated program format, WordPerfect® 5.1 for DOS:

```
ÿWPCž•   •
•ûÿ• 2 Ú ••• B • 4 J ••• ~ Z ••• | x  Times New Roman (TT)
Arial (TT) Courier New (TT)      •••ô•Cô•\•• •PŽ•6Qô•P
•••ô•J ä•2•¼• •P± Š•Q•••ô•P                        "•••ô•d
þ•6•X• ••@É D•Q•••ô@                              ûÿ• 2 î•
• ? ••• › K ••• æ ••• ì• Ù•• ÿôéÞphoenix • • •ÙÑ•# X•X
ä•2•¼• •P±    Š•Q•••••••X•P# •Ñ        This is an elementary
paragraph ÿÒ••, ÿ• • ûÿ• 2 ••°•••Ä Ú•        Default Paragraph
Fo •Default Paragraph Font        •1 1 Ñ•# X•P ô•\••    •PŽ
•6Q•••  ••X•P# •ÑÓ•• •• •ÓÓ•• • • •ÓÑ•# X•X
ä•2•¼• •P± Š•Q•••••••X•P# •ÑPlain Text      •Plain Text
•; 1 Ð•• ••ÐÑ•# ô•d þ•6•X• ••@É D•Q••••••ô•@#
•ÑÓ•• •• •ÓÓ•• • • •ÓÑ•# X•X ä•2•¼ •P±
Š•Q•••••••X•P# •ÑÐ• •°•°•L•L••ÐÛ •   •• Plain Text
• ÛÐ•• • • ÐÑ•# ô•d þ•6•X• ••@É D•Q••••••ô•@#
•ÑÓ•• •• •ÓÛ•• •• •ÛÑ•# &•J ô•\••          •PŽ•6Q•••
••&•P# •ÑThis is an elementary paragraph. It is a collection of
```
thoughts arranged in a group of sentences. The word processor converts each letter to a digital representation and stores it.

Notice that the text is now only a tiny portion of the bits that make up the "document." The additional command bits are not intended to be read as ASCII text. Thus, when printed by a program that expects ASCII codes, they are sometimes recognizable as text, and sometimes not. The basic text, however, is not modified in content. A more recent word processing program, such as Microsoft Word 2000®, results in considerably more non-ASCII encoding around the basic text.

The final step is a "universal" visual encoding of data that does not distinguish between text, graphics, and pictures. Adobe Acrobat® is an example of this type of program. We would like to show you the Acrobat® encoded version of the above paragraph, but it is more than six pages long! We hope you will trust us when we tell you that the result is all scripts, proprietary commands, and encoding of visual representations of the text. The ASCII-retrievable portion is completely gone!

Audio and Visual Technology

As the 19th century progressed, a new visual recording technology became available in the form of photosensitive plates and, later, film. Thus, it became possible, for the first time, to record actual images for future reference.

In the late 19th century, it became possible to record human activity in forms other than the written word and visual stationary images. The phonograph made audio recording possible, and motion picture film allowed preservation of moving images. For the first time, it became possible to record, not only words and music, but the nuances of the performers. Visual events could be recorded as they happened, in real time.

Conversion of sensory images into electronic form began in the 1800s for audio, and the late 1920s for visual images. Although the signal could be encoded, transmitted, and decoded in an electronic format, storage was still mechanical, by means of a vibrating stylus for audio, and mechanical/chemical, through use of photosensitive film for visual images. It also became possible to store electronic representations of audio information through modulation of a light beam stored on film. Of course, this development made sound motion pictures possible.

The electronic encoding of visual information is noteworthy because it is at this point in history that the original signal cannot be recovered merely by simple conversion of an electrical or magnetic impulse to light or motion. This is because the visual image is scanned with a series of lines. In the U.S. NTSC (National Television System Committee) one video frame consists of 525 such lines. Alternate lines are scanned 30 times per second to create a complete picture. At this point, it is not merely enough to just convert the signal back to a physical form; one must be able to recreate the various electronic levels and pulses used to correctly reconstruct the scanned image. Thus, video images created with the three major international broadcast encoding methods, NTSC, PAL (Phase Alternation Line) or SECAM (Sequential Color Amplitude Modulation) can only be viewed on equipment designed to specifically decode these signals.

By the end of the 1940s, it became possible to store data directly in electromagnetic impulses. Starting with audio signals, technology progressed to electronic storage of monochrome video in a commercially viable format by 1957 (Reitan, 1984, p. 60). At this point, the signal was no longer visible by direct inspection of the storage medium, although techniques were developed for viewing the electromagnetic data through the use of photomicrographs (Huang, 1957).

In the 1960s, conversion of audio and video data into digital signals became possible. By 1979, real-time digital audio storage was a reality, with digital video becoming practical in the mid 1980s. At this point, the observable representation of the signal is a stream of 1's and 0's, and is indistinguishable from any other stream of 1's and 0's unless one both knows what the data represents, and possesses the reverse algorithm through which the data was encoded. The significance at this point is that, not only is the data being broken into parts and encoded, it is also being processed through *mathematical algorithms* that can radically and irretrievably alter the original representative patterns of the data. So, in addition to the physical details of how the data was encoded, we also need *mathematical processing information* on how the data was changed after its conversion.

QUANTITIES OF DIGITAL DATA

One of the problems with direct digital encoding of any material is the sheer number of bits required to represent the information. For example, encoding two channels of audio at the "standard" Compact Disc sample rate of 44,100 samples per channel per second, with 16 bits per channel, requires 1.4 million bits per second merely to represent the audio data. Addition of data and control bits, and digital modulation for error detection and correction result in a net bit rate of 4.32 million bits per second (Carasso, Peek, & Sinjou, 1982, pp. 152-3). Thus 60 minutes of digital audio requires almost 2 billion bytes (remember that a byte is eight bits).

Of course, still and moving images require far more data. Consider that a stationary standard VGA resolution of 640x480 spots or "pixels," at current "typical" color space expectations, requires 24 bits of encoding per pixel. This translates to almost 7.4 million bits per screen. At a video rate of 30 frames per second, this translates to over 221 million bits *per second*.

Using the Compact Disc example, it is clear that we are already in trouble for retrieving data if we do not understand the encoding scheme. We must know how the data has been "interleaved" or spread out over the disc to minimize error effects due to damage. Moreover, we must know the digital modulation and coding scheme, how many bits have been added for data and control, and possibly the encoding of these bits. Clearly this is a trivial matter in the present: If you want to decode a CD, merely pop it in a CD player! But what about a century from now?

Lossy Encoding

In order to store and transmit the very large amounts of digital data required for large collections of audio, or any collection of still or moving images, it becomes necessary to employ data reduction schemes. Although we can accomplish some reduction in data by intelligently encoding it, we cannot make any real progress without actually losing or throwing out pieces of the original information (hence the term "lossy"). We determine the amount of data that we can discard based on our ability to reconstruct it from redundancies in the retained data, and/or from models of human perceptual limitations in discerning lost data. Thus, "lossy" encoding allows us to make tremendous gains in storage efficiency, but we further obscure the original signal being stored.

Audio Example

Recall that, in order to fully support human hearing's frequency response and dynamic range, we needed to encode audio at 44,100 bits per second, 16 bits per channel. Each individual 16-bit sample can be directly translated to a voltage level in standalone fashion. No "real" sound signal, however, goes through all 65,536 levels of loudness 44,100 times a second. They change smoothly and gradually. We might be able to represent the difference between successive samples using only four bits, or two, or maybe even one. So, if we translate the *difference* between the intensity of two successive samples, instead of the absolute value of each, we can achieve a substantial economy of storage. The only sample we need to encode fully is the very first one. We don't gain back all of those now-unused bits, however, because our samples now vary in length. Before we could just count off 16 bits; now we need at least four bits to tell us how many bits are assigned to each sample, plus some sort of unique "header" that tells us a new sample has started. So we have gained some economy, but must give back some of these gains because we have sacrificed the repetitive pattern of the original encoding.

We can gain additional efficiency through the following methods, in order of increasing complexity:

1. Process left and right stereo channels into a "sum" (middle) and "difference" (side) channel. The advantage is that redundant information from both channels is now mostly combined in the "middle" channel. The "side" channel, in comparison has much less data, only reaching its maximum when the audio information is entirely in one channel. It is very rare that significant information is only in one channel, so the "difference" channel carries much less information at a lower average level. In analog form, this encoding is used in FM stereo broadcasting.

2. Further combine channels, eliminating position information where the ear can't detect it, or possibly encoding positional intensity into discrete locations in the sound field, spaced closely enough that the ears interpret them as a continuous sound space. In this case there is really only one audio channel, with a few extra bits to determine where each individual sample is to be placed within the sound field. If the reproduced sound is in a frequency range in which the ear is relatively insensitive to spatial cues, the positional information can be entirely eliminated for these samples.

3.   Completely eliminate sounds the ear can't hear. For instance, a loud tone at a given frequency will "mask" the presence of a wide range of less intense frequencies near that tone. The ear functions as a group of filters, and a mathematical duplicate of these filters can successfully allow removal of non-audible sounds. Given the sophistication of current psychoacoustic models, most listeners will not find objectionable differences between the original audio and that re-created from the "simplified" data. Or, at least, they will tolerate the small differences, given the vast increases in storage density facilitated by the data reduction.

If we are willing to sacrifice audio quality, we can narrow the range of reproduced frequencies resulting in fewer samples per second, increase the noise/decrease the dynamic range of the signal requiring fewer bits per sample, or use only one (monaural) channel to completely eliminate the need for spatial information.

Flexible audio compression formats, such as Moving Picture Experts Group Layer 3 audio (MPEG 3 or MP3 as it is commonly known) accommodate all of the above modes of economy. MP3 is capable of a reasonably high quality of audio reproduction at a rate of 120,000 bits per second (Jack, 1996, p. 430) or a better than 10 to one savings from our original requirements. However it is obvious that the bit stream of the encoded audio signal now represents a set of mathematical manipulations, on top of the previously discussed interleaving, control, data, and error correction manipulations. It is impossible to reconstruct the data into anything resembling the original sounds without a full and complete knowledge of the encoding scheme.

Video Manipulation

Digital video formats also severely change the representation of the original information. It is clear that, if one looks at a still photo, many areas of the photo have little change from the areas that surround them. Still picture compression methods encode all of these areas as one set of bits. So, for instance, if an object is photographed against a single color background, a picture compression scheme would construct most of the background, and uniform color/intensity details of the object from relatively few bits, with only transition areas requiring large amounts of information. Additionally, it is clear that every single color/intensity combination that can be represented by 24 data bits is not used in most picture representations, so data can be further compressed by assigning all bit patterns used in the picture to a "look-up" table consisting of many fewer combinations. An example of a popular digital encoding format is the Joint Photographic Expert Group (JPEG) standard. Anyone who has ever scanned a photograph as raw data, and subsequently saved it in a compressed format is aware of the dramatic reduction in data made possible by these techniques.

Motion video uses these methods to store individual frames, but reduces data further by using motion prediction to create intermediate frames. So at 30 frames per second, on average only about two frames per second are fully characterized. Even these are compressed to an average of about one bit per pixel. In the MPEG standard, they are called "I" or "Intra" frames. The others are interpolated using mathematical prediction methods. Of these, the most detailed, "P" or "Predicted" frames are encoded at the rate of about 0.1 bits per pixel. They facilitate forward prediction. "B" or "Bi-directional" frames allow for backward prediction and are encoded at the lowest rate of 0.01 bits per pixel. Combinations of these frames form a "GOP" or "Group of Pictures"—a more-or-less standalone block of video that can be accessed independently. Scenes with a great deal of motion, or many cuts may require more "I" frames, and/or more bits per pixel (Jack, 1996, pp. 459-461).

SO WHAT'S THE POINT?

We often must significantly reduce the quantity of digital information in order to store the intellectual creation it represents. Frequently, we can only attain the required compression level by using mathematical transforms to remove data. Without an exact knowledge of the transforms and how they are applied, the data cannot be retrieved. The issue for society to consider is whether any of these techniques will be available, or even remembered, in the distant future.

One may argue that, as new formats are developed, they incorporate backwards compatibility and conversion. For instance, machines are available that play both digital video formats such as DVD's, as well as older analog Laserdisc formats. It is certainly possible to translate a laserdisc, or a VHS video cassette into a DVD format. Compact Discs can be converted to MP3 files, and these, in turn, can be converted into any one of a dozen other digital audio formats. So in the short term, there is no problem.

But, backward compatibility has a limited time horizon: Eventually the overhead needed to retain compatibility hampers the effectiveness of a system. In light of falling demand, the resources used to support an obsolete format become better utilized for other purposes. The technology-based recording landscape is littered with abandoned formats from Edison cylinders through monaural reel-to-reel tape recorders to Betamax videocassettes.

The digital revolution has further compressed the time scale. Tremendous gains in hardware and software capability have come at the expense of unprecedented rates of obsolescence. Our conversion to digital, software-driven data storage does not free us from the cost of backward compatibility. In fact, the rapid pace of innovation will cause abandonment to happen more quickly. For example, in both popular personal computing formats the operating systems have migrated to 32-bit code. Eventually, backward compatibility with older 16-bit code had to be abandoned, and this transition has occurred in a mere 20 years. If these 16-bit programs were used to process or encode data according to a unique format, the ability to retrieve this data may well be lost once the last 16-bit-compatible system is "upgraded."

New generations of artists and creative personalities use technology-based formats the way their ancestors used quill-and-ink, or paint and canvas. While most intellectual creations of the popular culture offer little of lasting value, a few will be judged significant enough to be studied and preserved far into the future. The difficulty arises from the fact that human society does not always recognize immediately the importance or significance of an intellectual work. The creator may, indeed, be ridiculed during his or her productive period, and fall into obscurity for decades or even centuries. A cursory search through an encyclopedia (Good, 1994) reveals the following examples from many fields of human endeavor. In the sciences, although Gregor Mendel's discoveries are fundamental to the field of genetics and, despite the fact that his papers reached major libraries, Mendel's discoveries remained virtually unknown for almost 30 years. In literature, Herman Melville's last short novel, *Billy Budd*, was not published until more than 30 years after his death. Indeed most of Melville's works fell into obscurity for several decades until American Literature students rediscovered them after World War I. In the arts, painter Sandro Botticelli's works remained little-known from the late 1400s until the 19th century. In religion, the Dead Sea Scrolls, which included books of the Jewish Torah and Christian Old Testament 1,000 years older than the previously known oldest translations, remained unknown for over 1,900 years. Although the scrolls are badly deteriorated and fragmented, scholars have been able to devise ways to reconstruct and read much of the text.

Additionally, much can be observed about a given societal period by observing its popular culture creations. However this cannot be done objectively until, at least, several decades have passed. Even then, critiques and judgments may go through generations of modification and revision before any consensus is reached.

MINDSETS: CREATORS OF TECHNOLOGY VERSUS CREATORS OF IDEAS

As we discussed previously, technology creators operate in a human activity where value is obtained from innovation. Corporate profits, and professional employment, cannot be maintained once a technology "matures," and a "shakeout" era ensues in which profit margins collapse. With physical goods, some continued profitability is possible because things wear out and must be replaced. With software, however, especially in digital form, infinite replication is possible. Thus, barring legal impediments, there is virtually no value to creating additional copies of the same product. Even where legal instruments, such as copyrights, provide some protection, others are free to change details, and create software that operates differently but accomplishes the same goal. It should come as no surprise, then, that the mindset of technology creators could be viewed as a "cult of the new." Obsolescence is the fuel for continued employment and profitability.

There is some similarity in the realm of intellectual creations. One would not expect artists, writers, actors, and musicians to rest on past achievements; they are driven by a "vision" which they share with others through their creations. However, since their creative expressions embody a combination of knowledge, ideas and interpretation, they continue to have value after they are produced: most have some lasting value to their creators. More importantly, a few will have lasting value to society. Remember, however, there is no necessary correlation between time and perceived value. Intellectual works must prove their lasting value repeatedly through decades and centuries of cultural change.

The problem is that, increasingly, these works are created through a technological process that need only prove itself until the next "better" innovation comes along. If an intellectual work has the potential for tremendous value in the distant future, that value may never be realized if the creation is embodied in a technical process that has zero value five years on.

Economists would view this dilemma in terms of *externalities*. The rediscovery of an author's body of work in the distant future has little supportive value to the author in the present, but the future value to society may be quite high. The author has derived some economic and moral satisfaction from production of material within their lifetime, and their estate may continue to profit in the near future, but these time scales may be quite short compared to the point where the works' ultimate value to society is realized. In the previous section, we presented several examples of the potentially long time periods between the "loss" and subsequent "rediscovery" of intellectual works.

If the creator derives no present value from future societal worth, then the "encoder"—the producer of the technology in which artists embodied their work, derives even less. The encoding technology was sold, at one point in time, as both a medium and a creative tool. There is no value derived from the tool/medium once it is sold. In the past, the medium survived regardless of the intentions of its original manufacturer. The medium was directly observable; deterioration could often be detected in a timely fashion, sometimes providing the opportunity to preserve the intellectual creation before it could be substantially lost. For reasons we have outlined above, however, when intellectual works are created through modern technology, the "medium" is both the physical storage object, and the software/hardware systems used to encode the idea onto the object. Even if the storage object can last centuries, the ability to retrieve it is governed by individual and corporate entities that have, if anything, a *dis*-incentive to ensure continued accessibility in the very long term. This leaves society with no way to ensure that the positive externalities of intellectual creations can be realized in the distant future.

RESPONSIBILITY FOR THE FUTURE

While it is unfair to lay all responsibility for long-term accessibility at the feet of technology creators, it is clear that the nature of innovation in the digital fields fosters the problem. Among engineering ethicists, there is general agreement that those who create technology have a unique insight into potential side-effects. This implies a responsibility for technology creators to envision possible consequences and, at the very least, take steps to inform others of their existence and nature. This is especially true where the complexity of the technology is transparent to the end-user.

Thus, while it may not be the sole responsibility of digital technology creators to ensure future accessibility of works expressed through their technology, we would argue that they do have a responsibility to enter into dialogues as how best to preserve accessibility, and to design their encoding technology with an eye to preservation.

We may be able to preserve some parts of the machines of creation for centuries: A microprocessor chip, after all, is a monolithic piece of silicon. Conversely, other pieces of machinery clearly have a limited shelf life: Mechanical systems are subject to physical deterioration, and wear effects from continued use.

The following list is an example of steps that technology creators could take to ensure society continued access to intellectual works: This list is by no means exhaustive or even optimal. It is meant to stimulate thought about the critical importance technology has assumed in the embodiment and storage of society's intellectual creations.

1. Help create the means to archive critical hardware components to minimize deterioration over time.
2. Document technical details of deterioration-prone hardware so they can be restored or newly manufactured for future information retrieval.
3. Document encoding/decoding software in a format that facilitates translation and implementation in the distant future.
4. Be explicit about the implementation of algorithms and models embodied in software and, in some cases, hardware. Provide this information in a format that will engender its future use.

5.   Use technology leadership status to influence societal decision makers, since they must ultimately provide the support for future retrieval of technologically-encoded information.
6.   Think beyond generational time frames. Become aware of the importance of the intellectual historical record across time and cultures.
7.   Think outside the technology. Envision technology as a "means" rather than an "end."

ANOTHER IMPORTANT PROBLEM: ENVIRONMENTAL EFFECTS

In this chapter, we have concentrated primarily on the effects of rapid technical innovation on the ability of future generations to retrieve intellectual works encoded in rapidly obsolete formats. We wish to point out, however, that there are other undesirable externalities to rapid technological obsolescence. For instance, the growing quantities of obsolete information technology (IT) equipment result in staggering amounts of waste, including toxic materials. Matthews and Matthews estimate the amount of obsolete personal computing equipment in the U.S. alone would occupy a volume equivalent to a football field stacked 1.5 km high (Matthews & Matthews, 2001). The toxic materials in this mass of obsolete equipment include heavy metals, such as the cadmium in nickel-cadmium batteries, and the lead used in cathode ray tubes (CRTs.) Much of the material is difficult or, at least, not cost-effective to recycle. Worse, the obsolete equipment is frequently sent to poorer nations where economic recovery of some materials is possible due to low labor rates. However, the remaining uneconomically recoverable materials, especially lead in CRT's and circuit board solder connections, are frequently dumped in uncontrolled landfills. This action would be illegal in the U.S. Over time, the toxic materials can leach into the groundwater supply and be consumed by humans. Beyond waste, the accelerated manufacturing of replacement equipment uses energy and natural resources, and creates pollution. Distribution of products to retailers and consumers also uses energy and creates pollution, and additionally generates product packaging waste.

Once again, the people who create new technologies are in a unique situation to address the problem. Careful analysis of the product lifecycle should be performed at the start of product development. This results in material and design choices that minimize environmental impacts through reduced energy usage, more efficient packaging and transportation of the finished product, and greater ease of recycling at end of life.

CONCLUSION

We hope that this chapter will stimulate some thought and discussion, especially among technology creators, about the broader implications of rapid technological obsolescence in digital formats and systems. If the present culture does not solve the problem of obsolescence, future societies will be forced to bear the cultural effects of lost intellectual creations. Technologists cannot ignore their responsibility in this regard because they are the ones who create the technology and, usually, the only ones capable of fully understanding it. If they are not clear and explicit about documenting this knowledge for future generations, then much of our present culture may be irretrievable in as little as a century. It is ironic that, at a time when recording media may have the greatest long-term survival potential in human history, the information recorded on them may become impossible to retrieve due to the perishable nature of the methods used to encode and store it.

REFERENCES

Abbott, P. (1994, November/December). Video formats and resolution. *Nuclear Plant Journal,* 39-46.

Carasso, M., Peek, J., & Sinjou, J. (1982). The Compact Disc digital audio system. *Philips Technical Review, 40*(6), 151-156.

Chinn, H. (1957, August). Splicing video tape. *Industries & Tele-Tech,* 79.

Freed, L. (1995). *The History of Computers.* Emeryville, CA: Ziff-Davis Press.

Goedhart, D., van de Plassche, R., & Stikvoort, E. (1982). Digital to analog conversion in playing a Compact Disc. *Philips Technical Review, 40*(6), 174-179.

Good, D. (ed.) (1994). *Compton's Interactive Encyclopedia 1995.* Cambridge, MA: SoftKey International, Inc. (CD ROM).

Harris Jr., C. Pritchard, M., & Rabins, M. (2000). *Engineering Ethics: Concepts and Cases* (2nd ed.) Belmont, CA: Wadsworth.

Heemskerk, J. & Schouhamer Immink, K. (1982). Compact Disc: System aspects and modulation. *Philips Technical Review, 40*(6), 157-164.

Hochheiser, S. (1992). What makes the picture talk: AT&T and the development of sound motion picture technology. *IEEE Transactions on Education, 35*(4), 278-285.

Hoeve, H., Timmermans, J., & Vries, L. (1982). Error correction and concealment in the Compact Disc system. *Philips Technical Review, 40*(6), 166-172.

Jack, K. (1996). *Video Demystified: A Handbook for the Digital Engineer* (2nd ed.). San Diego, CA: HighText Publications.

Lenk, J. (1991). *Lenk's Video Handbook: Operation and Troubleshooting.* New York: McGraw-Hill.

Malone, M. (1995). *The Microprocessor: A Biography.* Santa Clara, CA: TELOS.

Matthews, H. & Matthews, D. (2001, September 1). IT, PC's and the environment. In *The Green PC* (Publication pending.)

Moore, G. (1991, 1999) *Crossing the Chasm: Marketing and Selling High-Tech Products to Mainstream Customers.* New York: HarperBusiness.

Reitan, Jr., E. (May, 1984). Preserving the history of television at UCLA: The collection of television technology and design. *IEEE Transactions on Consumer Electronics, CE-30* (2), 46-61.

Saussure, F. (1974). *Course in general linguistics.* In C. Bally & A. Sechehaye (Eds.) and W. Baskin (Trans). London: Fontana.

Schinzinger, R. & Martin, M. (2000). *Introduction to Engineering Ethics.* New York: McGraw-Hill.

Shima, S. (1984, May). The evolution of consumer vtr's – technological milestones. *IEEE Transactions on Consumer Electronics, CE-30*(2), 66-69.

Wayner, P. (1997). *Digital Copyright Protection.* Chestnut Hill, MA: Academic Press.

White, R. (2002). *How Computers Work* (6th ed.). Indianapolis, IN: Que.

Chapter XV

Compliance with Data Management Laws

Jack S. Cook
Rochester Institute of Technology (RIT), USA

Laura L. Cook
State University of New York at Geneseo, USA

ABSTRACT

This chapter exposes professionals to laws dealing with data management. Both positive and negative aspects of legislation are highlighted. The purpose of this chapter is to expose the reader to some of the more interesting legal issues and provide insight into how information systems professionals and businesses may protect themselves from the negative ramifications of not complying with current legislation and the related negative publicity from such non-compliance. The increased ubiquitous nature of computing, coupled with the vast quantities of data gathered, increases the need for legislation to force companies and governmental agencies to take privacy seriously.

INTRODUCTION

Companies regularly manage and mine their data to explore the contents of data warehouses. These companies look for trends, relationships and outcomes to enhance their overall operations and discover new patterns that theoretically allow them to better serve their customers. However, with this great ability, concerns exist regarding social, ethical and legal issues associated with data management and data mining. For example, a recent article started out by asking the question "What if your refrigerator knew too much? More specifically, what if the company that made your refrigerator knew too much, automatically sucking in data about food purchases you make?" (Carr, 2002). Does this sound farfetched? It is not. Whirlpool, along with IBM, is pilot testing to resolve security and privacy concerns with such a system (Carr, 2002). Otherwise, what if the data gathered from the refrigerator is passed along to a business partner such as an online grocery supplier, which, based on alcohol consumption, concludes someone in the house has a drinking problem and then sells that information to insurance companies.

The increased ubiquitous nature of computing, coupled with the vast quantities of data gathered, increases the need for legislation to force companies and governmental agencies to take privacy seriously. Rapid advances in information technology have made the capturing of almost any desired information not only possible, but much easier, faster and cheaper than before. Privacy has become increasingly difficult to enforce since data transfers across jurisdictions are so simple. Vast amounts of personal information are being sold and exchanged at an alarming rate.

What is legal and what is ethical are often not the same. Laws protecting privacy and preventing data management abuses are unlikely to keep up with rapid advances in technology. However, laws do exist that apply to specific situations, particularly in healthcare and the financial industry, as well as concerning how governmental agencies manage data. Information systems (IS) professionals must be aware of what is required to comply with these laws. Ignorance of the law does not constitute a defense in a court of law. Sadly, formal IS education and training rarely addresses ethical and legal concerns in any systematic manner. Therefore, IS professionals must educate themselves concerning existing laws, and be aware of potential future regulation so that they design flexible systems that can adapt to regulations. Furthermore, by being informed of the legal environment in which they must operate, situations can be prevented that contribute to the social pressure for further government-imposed restrictions.

The objective of this chapter is to expose professionals to how laws typically limit data management. This chapter highlights both positive and negative aspects of legislation. This topic is broad and warrants an entire book on the subject itself. Therefore, the purpose of this chapter is to expose the reader to some of the more interesting legal issues and provide insight into how IS professionals and businesses may protect themselves from the negative ramifications of not complying with current legislation and the related negative publicity from such non-compliance. The more experience with, and exposure to, legal concerns with respect to data management, the better prepared one will be to prevent future legal troubles. Before examining these issues, it is helpful to understand more about data management and privacy concerns.

DATA MANAGEMENT

Many definitions of data management exist. Some IS professionals define data management in terms of its objective. It is the process of making the *right* data available, to the *right* person, at the *right* time, in the *right* place, in the *right* format. The most important as well as most difficult word to define in this definition is *"right."* How does one define *"right?"* It is, of course, application specific. One important aspect of applications is the source of data. Data management can also be defined in terms of activities that must be accomplished, such as the acquisition, analysis, storage, retrieval and distribution of data.

Whichever perspective is preferred, it is important to keep in mind that data has no ethics (Berinato, 2002a). A data set does not care how it is used. "It will not stop itself from spamming customers or sharing personal, identifying details with third parties. It cannot decide to delete or preserve itself" (Berinato, 2002a). Therefore, chief information officers (CIOs) must develop guidelines on how to manage data. Company policies should clearly state what type of data can be collected, why it is collected, what are appropriate uses of that data, who can view and receive it, and how long data is retained.

Businesses must make much of their data publicly available. For example, online catalogs contain product description, price, weight, taxes, and shipping costs. However, individuals typically prefer to keep their personal affairs private. Some examples of personal data include health history, marital status, education history, employment history, telephone record history, cash withdrawal information, purchases by credit card or check, e-mail messages, and World Wide Web browsing behavior (Cate, 1997). The line is blurring between personal and non-personal data. Where does it end? How can we protect individual rights and what laws currently exist?

Ethics and Data Management

Ethics deals with more than just stealing or lying. Good intentions are not enough. Ethics are standards of conduct that are agreed upon by cultures and organizations. Supreme Court Justice Potter Stewart defined ethics as knowing the difference between what you have a right to do and what is right to do. It is important that IS professionals act according to the highest ethical standards. With the increasing prevalence and reliance on data, one cannot separate technology and its uses and still be ethically and socially responsible. As a professional, one must explore how the data you create will be used.

CIOs and IS professionals encounter ethical dilemmas regularly. Of course, they must adhere to the law. But ethics are often more restrictive than what is called for by the law. Sadly, there are a number of IS professionals who either lack an awareness of what their company actually does with data, or purposely come to the conclusion that it is not their business. They are enablers in the sense that they solve management's problems. What management does with that data is not their concern. Some of the difficulties with that attitude are illustrated in Table 1.

Approaches for dealing with such dilemmas vary. Creating a position titled "corporate ombudsman," someone with direct access to the board of directors, and whom employees can contact anonymously concerning ethical dilemmas, is a step in the right direction (Ewalt, 2002). This approach is much less expensive than a catastrophic ethical failure. Other companies are appointing chief privacy officers (CPOs) to deal specifically with privacy concerns.

Laws provide guidelines. How a company decides to comply with the law always has social, legal and ethical consequences. Any action or set of actions can be either potentially harmful or helpful. However, unexamined actions and their corresponding assumptions are more likely to be problematic. Ethics is de facto based on group norms. Increasing complexity and diversity in society decreases the cohesiveness of social norms and ethical decisions are increasingly negotiated within and between groups. CIOs, responsible for the technology that collects, maintains and destroys corporate data, must responsibly traverse this ethical quagmire (Heller, 2002).

Table 1. Ethical Dilemmas

- A manager believes a key employee is hunting for another job, and she wants you to examine his email for verification (Holtzman, 2002).
- A junior marketing manager has made a deal to provide customer information to a strategic partner and he wants you to collect and send the information within a week (Holtzman, 2002).
- After years of hard work, you are finally promoted to CIO. The job is great, the pay fantastic, and the opportunities for professional development are numerous. One day, the CFO asks you into his office. Handing over a long list of financial data and details--all sales over the past 18 months, dealing with a particular company--he asks you to search out all the related records and purge them from the company's systems (Ewalt, 2002).
- A video surveillance system is installed outside your building and upon reviewing the digital video security files, you realize that employees are fooling around in the parking lot after hours (Holtzman, 2002).

Table 2. Six Commandments of Ethical Data Management (Heller, 2002)

Principle	Support
Data is a valuable corporate asset and should be managed as such, like cash, facilities or any other corporate asset.	100%
The CIO should partner with executive peers to develop and execute the organization's data management policies.	100%
The CIO is responsible for bringing technological knowledge to the development of data management practices and policies.	99%
The CIO is responsible for controlling access to and use of data, as determined by governmental regulation and corporate policy.	73%
The CIO is steward of corporate data and is responsible for managing it over its life cycle--from its generation to its appropriate destruction.	72%
The CIO is responsible for preventing the inappropriate destruction of data.	69%

With the help of more than 100 CIOs, members of the CIO Best Practice Exchange, CIO Magazine generated and then debated a set of ethical principles for ethical data management (Heller, 2002). As a result of online discussions and follow-up telephone interviews, six principles ultimately received the support of more than 50% of the CIOs involved. See Table 2 for a description of each of these six principles, ordered by the support they received from CIOs.

All the CIOs agreed that data is a valuable corporate asset. However, only 72% thought they should be responsible for the health of that asset (Heller, 2002). Interestingly, if the CIO is not responsible, then who should be?

The retention and destruction of data also raises ethical concerns. Clear-cut corporate policies are needed, as evidenced by recent events at Enron, WorldCom and Arthur Andersen. Most companies, on the advice of corporate counsel, destroy data on a regular basis (Heller, 2002). The CIO should be responsible from ensuring that data are not destroyed in order to eliminate incriminating evidence. It is the CIO's responsibility to raise objections if someone requests data to be destroyed in a manner inconsistent with corporate policy and particularly, if it violates the law (Berinato, 2002b).

A principle that CIOs did not agree upon is that "The CIO is responsible for maintaining the accuracy and integrity of data" (Heller, 2002). Fifty-two percent of the CIOs did not agree with this principle. It was noted that CIOs can build systems that force users to conform to format but that does not ensure they will enter accurate data, only properly formatted data.

Businesses often encounter ethical dilemmas while trying to balance privacy concerns with demands from marketing and other functional areas within the business that would like to gain access to the vast quantities of transaction data that reside within a corporation. According to a KPMG survey, the number one risk associated with privacy issues is risk to reputation (64%), followed by loss of customers (44%), and litigation (34%) (Zolkos, 2001).

It could be said that these risks are interdependent. A company could experience a loss to reputation following a privacy blunder. Due to the loss of reputation, the company could lose customers. Some customers could be deeply affected by the blunder and seek damages. The ensuing legal battle would involve litigation. Consequently, by identifying those risks as their top three items, companies are really saying that they fear any major privacy blunder.

PRIVACY

According to a Forrester Research survey of more than 10,000 North American Internet-savvy youths, 40% between the ages of 16 to 22 do not shop online because of privacy concerns (George, 2002). This study found 73% of adults do not buy online out of concern for privacy. However, adults fret over credit card fraud whereas teens worry their privacy will be invaded by unsolicited marketing (George, 2002). Whatever the concern, privacy is important to individuals of all ages.

Spending on privacy is hard to gauge, since it is intermixed among IT, training and customer-support budgets, rather than as a line item of its own, even for internal budgeting (Whiting, 2002). Much of privacy spending has focused on regulation compliance (Whiting, 2002). Although security and privacy are not the same, secure systems are needed in order to ensure privacy. Due to the importance of security for ensuring privacy, CPOs work closely with chief security officers (CSOs) (Carr, 2002).

Security started out as a low-level technology driven issue that eventually rose to such importance that CEOs became concerned with the topic. Privacy, on the other hand, began as a non-technical issue that primarily dealt with setting policies and complying with regulations, often in response to legislation and high-profile scandals (Whiting, 2002). Businesses are still grappling with the meaning of privacy at the IT level. Few software tools exist to help businesses manage privacy issues. IBM and Zero-Knowledge Systems are two of the few companies selling privacy management tools (Carr, 2002).

Privacy policies must be developed that define the organization's guidelines for dealing with privacy matters. Privacy statements, often found on corporate web sites, must be made more readable, primarily by stripping away the legalese. The purpose should be both to inform those affected by data collection and protect the organization from liability. Statements must explain in plain, not necessarily simple, language the scope and purpose of data collection practices. However, well-constructed privacy statements are not valuable if the business has not instituted procedures to protect privacy.

Some companies permanently damage their reputation by failing to carry privacy policies. Such was the case with Eli Lilly & Co. The company began a customer relationship management (CRM) effort in which they "started an e-mail campaign reminding more than 600 users of its depression, bulimia and obsessive-compulsive disorder medications to take their dosages" (Dobrow, 2001). When the company decided to shut down the list, they sent a final e-mail to their list members. Unfortunately, in sending the e-mail, all 600 e-mail addresses of the members were revealed to every recipient (Dobrow, 2001). While releasing the e-mail addresses themselves would have been a serious privacy violation, the fact that all of the address owners were known to have a very private medical condition compounded the seriousness of the violation. This incident resulted in an investigation and subsequent settlement with the Federal Trade Commission (Carr, 2002). As a result of similar situations, state, federal and international laws have been enacted to address data management and privacy issues.

DOMESTIC LEGISLATION PERTAINING TO DATA MANAGEMENT

Many laws exist that restrict data management practices. Laws designed to ensure that data management practices safeguard records and data have been enacted at the county, state, federal and international level. These laws are designed to protect consumers and citizens from improper use, abuse or loss of data. Some of the states that have passed laws to protect an individual's right to privacy are Virginia, Utah, New York, and Oklahoma. The Virginia Right to Privacy Act, passed in 1974, protects an Individual's personal information such as name, picture or other information. This law prevents any firm, corporation or government from using this information for advertising purposes. A corporation cannot use someone's picture to advertise a product without that person's permission. Is a web site a form of advertising? How does content management differ from data management? How many web sites in Virginia are probably in violation of this Act?

Some counties within states have even gone as far as to enact ordinances designed to protect privacy. For example, "California's San Mateo County adopted an 'opt-in' data privacy ordinance requiring banks and other financial institutions to get the consent of customers before sharing personal information with third parties. The measure, approved by the county's board of supervisors, is based on legislation in California's State Assembly that would impose a similar requirement statewide" (Computerworld, 2002, p. 12).

Privacy officers say a sizable part of their job is keeping up with the dozens of proposed and approved state and federal privacy-related laws (Whiting, 2002, p. 36). Kirk Herath, CPO for Nationwide Mutual Insurance Co. tracks about 150 state and federal privacy related laws (Whiting, 2002). To comply with a new

California law designed to combat identity theft, Nationwide spent about $130,000 reprogramming its IT system so that no mail from the company contains a customer's social security number (Whiting, 2002, p. 36). A good example of a federal law for which states have passed tighter restrictions is the Gramm-Leach-Bliley Act.

Gramm-Leach-Bliley Act (GLBA)

The Gramm-Leach-Bliley Act (GLBA) was adopted by Congress in November 1999. The GLBA states that financial institutions can only share information with affiliate and nonaffiliated companies after giving customers the option to "opt-out" of certain disclosures. Therefore, organizations must notify individuals when they are planning on sharing private information outside the scope of typical financial transactions. That would include selling it to others who plan on using it for data mining purposes. Enforcement began July 1, 2001. When financial institutions sent out federally mandated privacy notices in the summer of 2001, only 2% to 3% of all consumers opted out (Thibodeau, 2002).

The privacy provisions of Title V of the Act apply only to non-public personal information about individuals who obtain financial products or services for personal, family or household purposes. They do not apply to companies or individuals obtaining products or services for business purposes (Hirsch, 2000). In addition, the law requires that both stored and transmitted information be encrypted if security cannot be guaranteed. The following federal agencies have responsibility for enforcing the Act: the Federal Trade Commission, the Department of the Treasury, the Comptroller of the Currency, the Federal Reserve System, the Federal Deposit Insurance Corporation, the National Credit Union Administration and the Securities and Exchange Commission.

Privacy policies, although complicated, are just words. The GLBA has produced a mountain of mail for consumers and a great deal of expense for financial institutions. That is because companies are focused on the agenda of regulators (Whiting, 2002). Companies must examine the issue of privacy from a consumer's perspective in order to benefit from compliance with the GLBA. This might require them to re-examine their position on opt-out versus opt-in. If they do not, states are going to force the issue anyway. States were ordered to comply with GLBA, although the law did not preempt states from adopting more strict privacy standards. Several states have enacted legislation that provides greater privacy protection than the GLBA. For example, North Dakota passed the Disclosure of Consumer Information Law. "The North Dakota statute imposes a duty of confidentiality upon its financial institutions to ensure the protection of customer information" (Clark, 2001, p. 2). Under this statute, a financial institution cannot disclose information unless the customer has consented or "opted in" (Clark, 2001, p. 2). The North Dakota law provides greater protection to customer information than the GLBA, which acts as a floor or minimum protection for consumers' privacy (Clark, 2001, p. 2).

Other states, such as Vermont, have enacted similar laws that require financial services companies to obtain opt-in permission before they share consumer data among business units (Whiting, 2002). Complying with such state laws will require institutions to have flexible data management systems. Vermont has taken a much stronger position than the federal statute by requiring, as of February 15, 2002, financial institutions to acquire affirmative customer consent (opt-in) of its citizens before personal data can be shared with others.

Insurance trade groups retaliated against Vermont by filing suit on January 30, 2002, and threatening price increases (Thibodeau, 2002). In response to industry complaints, Elizabeth Costle, Commissioner of the State Department of Banking, Insurance, Securities, and Health Care Administration stated, "The industry can just assume that everyone with a Vermont ZIP code has opted out. That's the easy way to fix your computers" (Thibodeau, 2002, p. 16). Vermont's rules are a broader application of the State's existing banking privacy laws and not a result of legislative action (Thibodeau, 2002, p. 16). The insurance industry argues in its suit that the banking commission usurped legislative authority. Opt-in requires companies to convince consumers of the benefits of sharing their personal information with others.

Vermont and North Dakota are not alone concerning "opt-in." According to the Internet Alliance, 13 other states have pending opt-in privacy bills—Arkansas, California, Florida, Hawaii, Illinois, Iowa, Massachusetts, Minnesota, Missouri, North Dakota, New Hampshire, New Jersey, and New York (Thibodeau, 2002). New Mexico is considering regulatory action similar to Vermont's. When acquiring data, differences in state laws and regulations like Vermont's opt-in policy will play a role in acquiring data that can be legally used. Another law with broad reaching implications is the Health Insurance Portability and Accountability Act (HIPAA).

Health Insurance Portability and Accountability Act (HIPAA)

HIV and mental health information is extremely private. Even common medical problems are sensitive to some individuals. The Health Insurance Portability and Accountability Act (HIPAA), enacted in 1996, is a set of federal transaction and data protection regulations for healthcare providers, plans and clearinghouses (Bednarz, 2002, p. 9) designed to ensure data remains private but accessible. This regulation has three major purposes: (1) To protect and enhance the rights of consumers by providing them access to their health information and controlling the inappropriate use of that information; (2) to improve the quality of health care in the U.S. by restoring trust in the health care system among consumers, health care professionals and the multitude of organizations and individuals committed to the delivery of care; and (3) to improve the efficiency and effectiveness of health care delivery by creating a national framework for health privacy protection that builds on efforts by states, health systems, organizations and individuals (HHS, 2002, p. 82464). Penalties for privacy violations start at $100 per violation (Zipperer, 2002). Certain violations, such as knowingly disclosing protected health data, can result in a $50,000 fine and a year in prison (Zipperer, 2002).

The deadline for HIPAA compliance for privacy regulations is April 2003 (Zipperer, 2002). Compliance with HIPAA is challenging but possible. The Military Health System (MHS), the U.S. Department of Defense's healthcare organization, provides medical services to the Army, Navy, Air Force and related services such as the Coast Guard. It has almost 9 million beneficiaries worldwide (Zipperer, 2002). MHS "managed more than 35 million appointments last year, as well as millions of claims and referrals" (Zipperer, 2002, p. 40). Another large health industry organization is the National Account Service Company (NASCO), based in Atlanta. It handles health-benefits processing for 27 Blue Cross Blue Shield-affiliated plans, processing 75.7 million claims for more than 6 million members last year (Bednarz, 2002). Both of these organizations are HIPAA compliant. As a result, these and other healthcare organizations will experience cost savings over the long run. Other examples of Federal regulations are provided in Table 3.

Electronic Communications Privacy Act

For those interested in locating a truly private means of communicating information, e-mail should not be one of the alternatives considered. Although e-mail offers some interesting and indisputable benefits, the law provides little protection for e-mail privacy. With respect to e-mail, the Electronic Communications Privacy Act (ECPA), a federal law passed in 1986, is most relevant. The purpose of the ECPA was to expand the federal eavesdropping law that was passed in 1968 to cover e-mail and other emerging media. The ECPA classifies protected communications into three categories: oral, wire and electronic. The Act defines wire communications as any wire-borne communication involving voice.

The distinction between wire and electronic is critical since the ECPA affords far greater protection to wire-borne voice communication. A federal prosecutor who wishes to wiretap a suspect's phone must first seek the approval of the U.S. attorney general before the request can even be submitted to a federal judge. Phone-taps are only granted in connection with the investigation of certain ECPA-designated federal crimes. On the other hand, a prosecutor who desires a warrant to eavesdrop on electronic communications does not need

Table 3. U.S. Federal Regulations that Protect Privacy (Adapted from Caudill & Murphy, 2000)

Act	Year	Description
Fair Credit Reporting Act	1970	Consumers may correct errors in their credit reports.
The Privacy Act of 1974	1974	Government officials may not maintain secret files or gather information about people irrelevant to a lawful purpose.
Right to Financial Privacy Act	1978	Government officials need a warrant to obtain a bank's copies of checks.
Electronic Transfer Funds Act	1978	Banks must notify customers when disclosing records to third parties.
Privacy Protection Act	1980	Government officials are restricted in their ability to seize records of the print media.
Cable Communications Act	1984	Cable companies may not disclose choices consumers make or other personal information without consent.
Family Education and Privacy Right Act	1984	Government officials are restricted in their ability to reveal to third parties information gathered by agencies or educational institutions.
Electronic Communications Privacy Act	1986	Telephone, telegraph, and other communications services are prohibited from releasing the contents of messages they transmit (only the recipient of the message can be identified).
Computer Security Act	1987	All government agencies should develop safeguards for protecting sensitive data stored in their computers.
Video Privacy Protection Act	1988	Video rental companies may not disclose choices customers make or other personal information without consent.
Computer Matching and Privacy Protection Act	1988	Governmental officials are allowed to increase the amount of information they gather if the safeguards against information disclosure also increases.
Telephone Consumer Protection Act	1991	Telemarketers are prohibited from using automatically dialing telephone calls or facsimile machines to sell a product without obtaining consent first.
Drivers' Privacy Protection Act	1993	Places restrictions on state government agencies and their ability to sell driver's license records.
Health Insurance Portability and Accountability Act (HIPPA)	1996	Inefficiencies are reduced in the healthcare industry by reducing paperwork, controlling abuse in the system, providing privacy protection for individuals, and ensuring health care coverage for even those with pre-existing conditions.
The Gramm-Leach-Bliley Act	1999	Information can be shared by financial institutions with affiliate companies, and with nonaffiliated companies after giving customers the option to "opt-out" of certain disclosures.
Children's Online Privacy Protection Act (COPPA)	2000	Rules are set for online collection of information from children.

the approval of the Department of Justice. In fact, suspicion of any federal felony is all that is needed to seek such a warrant.

The ECPA also makes a distinction between seizure of "stored" communications and "live" eavesdropping, and affords more severe penalties to the latter. Realistically, it is much easier to gain access to email once stored than it is to intercept a message during transmission. Hence, email will almost always be classified as a stored communication, except in those very rare occasions where a message is intercepted during transmission.

Steve Jackson Games vs. U.S. Secret Service

The most cited ECPA case involving stored communications is *Steve Jackson Games vs. U.S. Secret Service* (No. 93-8661, United States Court of Appeals). In this case, the Secret Service executed a search warrant at the offices of a game publisher. Pursuant to its investigation, the Secret Service seized a computer that served both as a development platform and a server for a public bulletin board system (BBS). Contained within the memory of this computer was the email of some 300 BBS customers, none of whom were the targets of the probe. The ECPA sets standards for government seizures and makes it a crime to obtain, alter or prevent access to stored communications without authorization. Furthermore, it creates a private right of action that lets victims of unauthorized invasions bring civil suits for money damages. As stated earlier, the ECPA makes a distinction between stored communications and communications in the process of transmission. The statutory minimum for invasions of stored communications is $1,000, whereas it is $10,000 for victims of illegal "interceptions." In this case, the distinction made a substantial difference monetarily to the 300 BBS plaintiffs.

Steve Jackson Games and its customers filed a civil suit claiming that the government's action violated the ECPA because the Secret Service took none of the preliminary steps required by the ECPA. The court agreed but declined to rule the email had been intercepted. Rather, the court concluded the email had reached its destination and hence it was stored communication. As a result, each plaintiff received only $1,000—the statutory minimum for invasion of stored communication.

Not all laws are designed to protect privacy. Recent events have produced laws that actually allow government agencies to invade privacy (see Table 4). The USA Patriot Act is an example of the broadening of powers to investigate and observe individuals.

USA Patriot Act of 2001

The Uniting and Strengthening America by Providing Appropriate Tools Required to Intercept and Obstruct Terrorism (USA Patriot) Act of 2001 is not

Table 4.   U.S. Federal Regulations that Invade Privacy

Act	Year	Description
Foreign Intelligence Surveillance Act (FISA)	1978	Law enforcement is provided special authority when investigating state-sponsored terrorism or espionage.
Communications Assistance for Law Enforcement Act (CALEA) of 1994	1994	Law enforcement agencies are guaranteed access to telecommunications carriers' networks.
USA Patriot Act of 2001	2001	Law enforcement agencies granted the right to use Carnivore. This law was enacted as a result of the September 11 attack on the World Trade Center and signed by President Bush on October 26, 2001.

a single new law but rather an omnibus piece of legislation that amends dozens of existing laws (B. Fausett, 2001, p. 10). It "greatly expands the right of law enforcement officials to wiretap the web, including information transmitted over the Internet, corporate in-house networks and voice mail systems. It also lets them search stored e-mails and voice mails to collect evidence that may be useful in prosecuting criminals, including terrorists" (M. Scott, 2001, p. 82). Unlike the Electronic Communications Privacy Act which requires a subpoena or search warrant, Section 212 of the Patriot Act "lets a system operator voluntarily disclose customer information along with the content of stored e-mail messages to a governmental entity if the provider reasonably believes that an emergency involving immediate danger of death, or serious physical injury to any person justifies disclosure" (M. Scott, 2001, p. 82). Section 210 of the Act requires an email system operator to disclose the means or source of payment for the provider's services, records of session times and durations, and any temporarily assigned network addresses—quite a data management task. The hope is that such information may help locate terrorists and those who fund them. The Act can produce a wealth of information on suspected criminals and terrorists that law enforcement agencies can merge with other data overlays in order to data mine candidates for intense scrutiny.

LEGISLATION IN OTHER COUNTRIES PERTAINING TO DATA MANAGEMENT

Data protection is very important worldwide. One of the major goals of data protection is to guarantee an individual's privacy rights while removing obstacles to data movement. Many countries have laws dealing with data protection. Some of the more well-known data protection laws are discussed below. These laws and acts embrace similar data protection principles governing the collection, retention and use of personal data. Table 5 summarizes a representative sample of other country's laws designed to regulate data management practices and enhance privacy. The discussion begins by examining a country not typically noted for its protection of individuals' right to privacy, Russia, and its data management law—The Russian Federation Law on Information, Informatization, and Information Protection Act.

The Russian Federation Law on Information, Informatization, and Information Protection

The Russian Federation Law on Information, Informatization, and Information Protection of 1995 sets requirements dealing with personal data and draws guidelines for future development of e-commerce in Russia (Kim, 2000). This law sets forth that personal data should be: (1) obtained and processed fairly and lawfully; (2) stored for specific and legitimate purposes; (3) be adequate, relevant and not excessive in relation to such purposes; (4) be accurate and up-to-date; and (5) permit identification of the data subjects for no longer than is required by the purpose of storing (Kim, 2000).

The UK Data Protection Act of 1998

The UK Data Protection Act contains many regulations that must be adhered to with regard to the collection and distribution of personal information. This act supercedes the Data Protection Act of 1984 and addresses many of the inadequacies of that Act. According to the 1998 Act, any company using equipment or property within the UK to collect or process data must adhere to these new regulations.

Companies storing or processing information must register with the Data Protection Commissioner. Failure to do so is a prosecutable offense unless the company qualifies under an exemption (Dyer Partnership, 2000). This act gives individuals more power to discover what information is being collected and held about them. A person has the right to request information being held by any source for which they are the subject. However, current enforcement of this Act

Table 5.   Selected Non-U.S. Laws that Protect Privacy

Year	Act
1995	The Russian Federation Law on Information, Informatization, and Info. Protection
1998	The UK Data Protection Act
1993	The New Zealand Privacy Act
1995	EU Data Protection Directive
1996	The Hong Kong Personal Data Ordinance

rests mainly on people who believe their information is being used improperly contacting the Data Protection Commissioner. A recent article states that the UK's Data Protection Commission plans on increasing enforcement of this law, which has been "spotty" thus far (ComputerWorld, 2002, p. 54). U.S. companies operating in Europe should understand that they will be forced to comply with this law limiting data sharing. The penalties for non-compliance can be large fines, with no monetary limit (Dyer Partnership, 2000). In addition, businesses that transmit data to a country outside of the European Union cannot do so unless that country guarantees a level of protection for the personal data.

Closed circuit television recordings are also regulated by the 1998 Act (Dodd, 2002). Previously, no permission was required from individuals pictured in closed circuit television (CCTV) before being sold. In one such case, a man's attempted suicide was captured on CCTV. The footage was later sold to BBC's Crime Beat program and aired on national television (Dodd, 2002). There was nothing he could do to prevent this from happening. Tougher regulations were needed to prevent such violations from happening, and this new Act ensured this right of privacy would not be infringed upon (Dodd, 2002).

The New Zealand Privacy Act of 1993

The New Zealand Privacy Act of 1993 "regulates the dissemination of personal information in both the public and private sectors. It also grants to individuals the right to have access to personal information held about them by any agency" (Electronic Privacy Information Center, 2002, p. 277). Personal information with respect to this Act is "any information about an identifiable individual, whether automatically or manually processed" (Electronic Privacy Information Center, 2002, p. 277). This Act has been amended several times since it was enacted in 1993. The legislation is based on the following 12 Information Privacy Principles (Caslon Analytics, 2002) that cover the:
1. Purpose of collection of personal information;
2. Source of personal information;
3. Collection of information from subject;
4. Manner of collection of personal information;
5. Storage and security of personal information;
6. Access to personal information;
7. Correction of personal information;
8. Accuracy of personal information to be checked before use;
9. Agency not to keep personal information for longer than necessary;
10. Limits on use of personal information;
11. Limits on disclosure of personal information;
12. Unique identifiers.

The 1995 European Union Data Protection Directive

The 1995 European Union (EU) Data Protection Directive was agreed upon on October 24, 1995, by the member states of the EU. There are currently fifteen member states: Austria, Belgium, Denmark, Finland, France, Germany, Greece, Ireland, Italy, Luxembourg, The Netherlands, Portugal, Spain, Sweden, and the UK (http://www.eurunion.org/states/home.htm). The main objective of the EU Data Protection Directive was to allow for the free flow of information and data among the member states while protecting an individual's privacy (Cate, 1997). With an open market and a single currency, European businesses now have clients all across Europe. But non-European businesses operating in these regions, such as the U.S., must also adhere to this directive. In addition, national laws "enacted in compliance with the directive must guarantee that 'processing of personal data' is accurate, up-to-date, relevant, and not excessive. Personal data may be used only for the legitimate purposes for which they were collected and kept in a form that does not permit identification of individuals longer than is necessary for that purpose" (Cate, 1997, p. 37).

The Hong Kong Personal Data (Privacy) Ordinance of 1996

The Hong Kong Personal Data Ordinance came into effect on December 20, 1996. "It aims to protect the individual's right to privacy with respect to personal data. It also safeguards the flow of personal data to Hong Kong from restrictions by countries that already have such laws" (The Government of Hong Kong, 2002). This Ordinance also established an office of the Privacy Commissioner for Personal Data. This Privacy Commissioner receives any complaints about misuse or disclosure of personal data and seeks possible prosecution. From 1996 to 2001, the Privacy Commissioner received 2,655 complaints from individuals. Of those complaints, the Commissioner found violations of the Hong Kong Personal Data Ordinance in 143 cases, and referred 18 of them for possible prosecution (http://www.freeconomy.org/freeconomy/eng/text/page_b45.html).

BENEFITS OF DATA MANAGEMENT AND DATA MINING

Although consumers need legal protection concerning how their data is used, not all uses of data and exchanges among trading partners of data result in negative consequences. Table 6 details but a few of the benefits consumers realize when companies, as well as government agencies, are able to properly manage data and mine it for "nuggets" that help better serve individuals. These

Table 6. Benefits to Consumers

Category	Benefits
Presale	Increased understanding of customer needs
	Faster reaction to changes in consumer demand
Sale	Personalization of products and services
	Different treatment of more valuable customers
	Enhanced customer satisfaction with goods and services
Post-Sale	Rapid access to integrated systems and information concerning consumer transaction purchase history
	Acceleration of the process of re-purchasing products and services
General Benefits	Decreased cost of products and services
	Better customer relationships

benefits have been placed into four general categories: presale, sale, post-sale, and general benefits.

Data management and data mining help those who provide products and services better understand what potential customers need. For the selling process, proper data management allows companies and government agencies to personalize their products and services and in the process, they are economically able to provide customers what they need in the most cost efficient manner.

After a sale is made, consumers may benefit from data management if the process of re-purchasing products and services is simpler and more time efficient. For example, many retail catalog companies have a customer number that is printed on each flyer sent to consumers in the mail. When the consumer calls, the company has already captured the consumer's address, billing information and shipping information from previous purchases. Hence, this makes subsequent purchases easier. In addition, these systems allow rapid access to integrated systems and information concerning consumer transaction purchase history. The overall general benefits to consumers include decreased cost of products and services through efficiency and better customer relationships.

Over-regulating the environment in which companies operate can increase costs, decrease costs or ultimately not impact costs at all. An example where proposed legislation is expected to ultimately decrease cost is in the banking industry. "After bundles of paper checks were stuck in grounded airplanes for days after September 11, 2001, Congress took up a bill to require that all banks transfer and clear checks electronically. The bill is expected to pass when the new Congress takes office next year. In addition, banks are dealing with laws that require them to keep records of the identity of customers who open accounts, as well as archive transactions, to make it more difficult for terrorists to launder money" (Garvey, 2002, p. 24).

As a result of this proposed legislation, Sterling Savings Banks has begun a pilot project for handling all check processing electronically. This project will cost $5,000 for new hardware and $600 per month for increased bandwidth. It will cost between two to four cents per check for processing (based on volume). Currently, Sterling Savings pays three to seven cents to process checks using its current system. In addition, it takes four days to clear checks (Garvey, 2002, p. 24). With the new system, check processing will shrink to four hours, ultimately allowing the bank to respond more quickly to bad check writers.

Even though regulations exist that govern data management, ample opportunities still exist for businesses to profit from data management and data mining. For a relatively extensive list of benefits to companies, see Table 7. Practically all functional areas within a company can benefit from data mining and definitely from data management. Marketing and product development are two areas that have much to benefit from data mining. However, particularly for marketing, privacy concerns must be constantly at the forefront of any decisions made relating to how data is managed and mined. Since the focus of this chapter is not on data management and mining per se, but rather on the legal environment in which firms operate, each one of these benefits will not be discussed in detail.

Table 7.   Potential Benefits to Companies

Tailor offerings to specific customer needs
Determine product and service features that are important to customers
Engage in customer prospecting and market segmentation
Develop better customer relationship management
Increase money and time savings
Find, attract, and retain the best customers
Distinguish preferred from marginal customers
Customize marketing plans to specific markets
Identify new market opportunities
Enhance productivity
Improve and enhance product and service offerings
Make intelligent, accurate decisions in a timely manner
Maintain a competitive edge in a volatile marketplace
Understand current customer buying patterns
Develop insight into changing customer requirements
Reduce risk
Identify customers interested in new products or services
Analyze delivery channels
Enhance target pricing
Manage portfolios
Identify customers who repeatedly purchase particular products or services

Rather, they have been provided in the previous table to illustrate that even within the growing complexities and restrictions of the legal environment, numerous benefits to companies exist.

As seen in previous sections, most laws concerning data govern the healthcare and financial industries as well as governmental agencies. Ultimately, such laws as the Health Insurance Portability and Accountability Act that govern the healthcare industry and the Gramm-Leach-Bliley Act that, among other laws, govern the financial industry, should eventually improve the competitiveness of companies in both industries. As Table 8 shows, better data management and data mining can result in better healthcare for all. Particularly in today's security conscious environment, using data to identify criminals and terrorists provides for a safer and more secure society. Table 8 provides a number of very specific examples of how government agencies from the Department of Justice to the Center for Disease Control and Prevention can use data mining to benefit society.

FUTURE TRENDS

As the world becomes more interconnected, it is probable that detailed electronic profiles on practically anyone will exist. Because of emerging technologies and recent terrorists' threats, authorities now have more power to inspect Internet files and other media, which is possibly an invasion of privacy. In recent years, the amount of personal data that can be monitored and recorded has vastly expanded. "As a result, there is increased danger that personal

Table 8. Benefits to Society

Improved Healthcare
• Improved patient treatment
• Improved patient satisfaction
• Decreased healthcare fraud
• More accurate budgets
• More efficient deployment of medication

Improved Governmental Services
• Increased law enforcement identification of criminals and terrorist
• Improved ability to find patterns and trends in crime enabling the Department of Justice to reallocate resources
• Enhanced prediction of patient demographic changes allowing Veterans Affairs to create more accurate budgets
• Improved identification of customer needs by the Internal Revenue Service
• Enhanced identification of plane crash patterns by the Federal Aviation Administration to prevent future problems
• Improved tracking of reactions to vaccines by the Center for Disease Control and Prevention
• Improved prediction of service retention by the Marine Corps

information originally disclosed to friends and colleagues may be exposed to, and misinterpreted by, a less-understanding audience" (Rosen, 2001, p. 19). However, due to changing global conditions, future legislation may in fact invade privacy rather than protect it.

CONCLUSION

As technology is changing rapidly, so are the laws governing it. Responsible professionals should keep informed about evolving laws. Protecting privacy can be strategically advantageous, but it requires IT to be flexible in order to adapt to changing consumer attitudes and legislation. Data management and the privacy that results from regulatory compliance is not enough. The focus must be on building closer ties with customers without being unethical and breaking laws. "Creating a privacy-conscious culture that encourages ethical considerations and discourages dubious database dealings is not only an excellent precaution, it helps prevent customer problems from escalating into front-page news stories" (Holtzman, 2002, p. 28).

The more experience with, and exposure to, legal concerns with respect to data management, the better prepared one will be to prevent future legal troubles.

REFERENCES

Bednarz, A. (2002, November 4). IBM tailors wares for HIPAA readiness. *Network World*, 9.

Berinato, S. (2002a, July 1). Take the pledge: The CIO's code of ethical data management. *CIO, 15*(18). Retrieved November 5, 2002 from the World Wide Web: <http://www.cio.com/archive/070102/pledge.html>.

Berinato, S. (2002b, July 1). To preserve or not to preserve, that is the question. *CIO, 15*(18). Retrieved November 5, 2002 from the World Wide Web: http://www.cio.com/archive/070102/pledge_sidebar_2.html.

Carr, D. (2002, November). Closing a door on data. *Baseline*, 13 and 16.

Caslon Analytics. (March 2002). Caslon Analytics Privacy Guide. Retrieved October 25, 2002 from the World Wide Web: http://www.caslon.com.au/privacyguide5.htm.

Cate, F. (1997). *Privacy in the Information Age*. Washington, DC: Brookings Institution Press..

Caudill, E. & Murphy, P. (2000, Spring). Consumer online privacy: Legal and ethical issues. *Journal of Public Policy & Marketing*, 7-19.

Clark, D. (2001, June 28). Letter to the Honorable Gray D. Preszler. *Federal Trade Commission Online*. Retrieved October 28, 2002 from the World Wide Web: <http://www.ftc.gov/os/2001/06/northdakotaletter.htm>.

Department of Health and Human Services (HHS). Retrieved November 9, 2002 from the World Wide Web: <http://www.hhs.gov/ocr/part1.txt>.

Dobrow, L. (2001). Tread carefully on privacy. *Advertising Age, 72*, 6.

Dodd, V. (2002, September 14). Still life: For your eyes only. *The Guardian*. Retrieved October 25, 2002 from the World Wide Web: <http://www.guardian.co.uk/Print/0,3858,4498823,00.html>.

Dyer Partnership. (2000). *The UK Data Protection Act 1998*. Retrieved November 9, 2002 from the World Wide Web: <http://www.netaccountants.com/dataprotection/>.

Electronic Privacy Information Center. (2002). *Privacy and human rights 2002: An international survey of privacy laws and developments*. Retrieved October 30, 2002 from the World Wide Web: <http://www.privacyinternational.org/survey/phr2002/phr2002-part3.pdf>.

Ewalt, D. (2002, September 24). Fall conference: Ethical dilemmas: Panelists discuss CIO's role in the financial-reporting process. *InformationWeek*. Retrieved November 13, 2002 from the World Wide Web: <http://www.informationweek.com/story/IWK20020924S0001>.

Fausett, B. (2002, February). Becoming a Patriot. *Web Techniques*, 10-12.

Garvey, M. (2002, November 11). Rules to buy by. *InformationWeek*, 22-24.

George, T. (2002, July 8). Privacy matters: Teens and technology. *InformationWeek*, 53-56.

Government of Hong Kong, The. (2002, June). *Privacy protection for personal data*. Retrieved October 30, 2002 from the World Wide Web: <http://www.info.gov.hk/info/perdata.htm>.

Heller, M. (2002, July 1). The six commandments of ethical data management. *CIO, 15*(18). Retrieved November 5, 2002 from the World Wide Web: <http://www.cio.com/archive/070102/pledge_sidebar_1.html>.

Hirsch, R. (2000). The other privacy law: Preparing for the Gramm-Leach-Bliley Act. Davis Wright Tremain LLP. Retrieved August 1, 2001 from the World Wide Web: <http://www.dwt.com/related_links/adv_bulletins/HLABMarch2001.htm>.

Holtzman, D. (2002, November). Charting ethical waters. *CSO Magazine*, 28.

Hong Kong and the pursuit of economic freedom website. Personal Data Privacy. Retrieved October 30, 2002 from the World Wide Web: <http://www.freeconomy.org/freeconomy/eng/text/page_b45.html>.

Johnson, D. (n.d.). Electronic communications privacy: Good sysops should build good fences. Electronic Frontier Foundation, Wilmer, Cutler & Pickering, Washington, D.C. Retrieved November 10, 2002 from the World Wide Web: <http://www.eff.org/Publications/David_Johnson/good_fences_johnson.article>.

Kim, A. (2000, May). *The legal environment for e-commerce in Russia*. BISNIS Bulletin. Retrieved October 10, 2002 from the World Wide Web: <http://www.bisnis.doc.gov/bisnis/bulletin/0005bull2.htm>.

Rosen, J. (2001, December 1). Privacy, reconsidered: An interview with Jeffrey Rosen. *CIO Insight*, 18-24.

Scott, M. (2001, December). War's new front. *CIO Insight*, 82-83.

Thibodeau, P. (2001, March 26). FTC examines privacy issues raised by data collectors. *ComputerWorld*, 36.

Thibodeau, P. (2002, February 11). Vermont opt-in rules spur suit. *Computer World, 36*(7), 1 and 16.

Thibodeau, P. (2002, August 16). California County 'Opts in' On Data Privacy. *ComputerWorld*, 12.

U.K. to Toughen Privacy Laws. (2002, November 4). *ComputerWorld*, 54.

Whiting, R. (2002, August 19). Making privacy work: Developing a policy to protect customers is only the beginning. *InformationWeek*, 30-36.

Zipperer, J. (2002, October). Military fights to protect data. *Internet World*, 38-40.

Zolkos, R. (2001, July). Privacy-related risks reviewed. *Business Insurance, 35*, 3-4.

Section IV

Further Implications

Chapter XVI

The Central Problem in Cyber Ethics and How Stories Can Be Used to Address It

John M. Artz
George Washington University, USA

ABSTRACT

The central problem in Cyber Ethics is: how do you establish ethical standards in a professional field that is defined by a rapidly evolving technology where the consequences of the technology and the impact of any ethical standards cannot be known in the time frame in which the standards must be established? Stories play a very important role in addressing this issue. This chapter explores the role of stories in Cyber Ethics.

INTRODUCTION

Several years ago, I was teaching an undergraduate computer literacy class and decided to liven things up a bit with a heated discussion on some current and relevant topic from the field of computer ethics. I thought I would start by asking if any of the students had "borrowed" software to do the homework assignments, rather than go to the lab, and, if so, did that make them thieves? Or, I would ask if privacy on the Internet was really all that important. After all, doesn't privacy restrict the free flow of information and hence represent a benign form of censorship? When I offered these ideas to the class I was confronted with the same intellectual lethargy that you get when presenting a topic which the students have already decided is irrelevant to their goals in life. I looked across the faces in the class with a combination of confusion and amazement. Personally, I think that discussions of this type can be intellectually stimulating and challenging. They involve complex issues, competing values, competing interests and often times important but razor thin distinctions. So, I asked the class why I had received such a lukewarm response to my suggestions. After the customary shuffling in their seats, avoidance of eye contact, and stalls that may allow somebody else to speak, a student offered the following insight—"Ethics are just a bunch of rules that tell you what not to do." And therein lies a serious problem.

Shortly after that, I was attending a conference at the *Computer Ethics Institute* in Washington, D.C. and had an opportunity to see the "Ten Commandments of Computer Ethics." All 10 statements were stated in the negative. Don't do this. Don't do that. Don't do the next thing. The student was right. Computer ethics really was just a bunch of rules that tell you what not to do. In fact, after reading over the "Ten Commandments," I concluded that the most ethical thing I could do would be to get out of the computer field lest I transgress one of these daunting rules. How did computer ethics ever get into this dismal state?

Certainly one of the reasons is that computer ethics (now Cyber Ethics) has been dominated by a collection of unchallenged claims prescribing ethical behavior, or at least behavior that is considered to be ethical by prominent voices in the field. We have all heard most of these claims: you must not copy software, you must not violate the privacy of individuals, you must not use computer technology to exploit workers, you must not allow society to evolve into technological haves and have-nots, etc., etc. And these values are often reinforced by empirical studies that show repeatedly that undergraduates, men and women and even professionals often come up short on ethical behavior (Kreie & Cronan, 1998, 2000; Prior, M. et al., 2002). The problem arises when you challenge one of these claims and ask—why is copying software unethical? Or why is it so important to protect privacy? The problem is that there seems to be little critical thought behind these positions.

While these and many other similar issues are clearly important to both computing professionals and computer users, and are being discussed at length (usually from one side), I would argue that they are merely examples of a much larger issue that is not being discussed at all. I see the central problem in Cyber Ethics to be the means of determining ethical standards. Stated more clearly, the central problem in Cyber Ethics is: how do you establish ethical standards in a professional field that is defined by a rapidly evolving technology where the consequences of the technology and the impact of any ethical standards cannot be known in the time frame in which the standards must be established? Stories play a very important role in addressing this issue. Specifically, stories provide a means of exploring ethical issues for which the full range of consequences is not currently known. But, in order to justify this claim, quite a bit of explanation is in order.

BACKGROUND

The word "story" evokes a wide variety of different meanings. For example, if a student claims that he cannot turn in his homework because his dog ate it, you might question the veracity of this claim by asking, "Is that true, or is that just a story?" The implication is that there is truth and there are stories and never the twain shall meet. But true versus fictitious is not the same as true versus false; and a story can contain important truths, as we shall see, while still being wholly fictitious. Yet, there is a strong, and very unfortunate, bias in the modern world against the use of stories in the pursuit of truth. To some extent we can trace the blame for this bias to Plato, who replaced stories (Greek myths) with reasoned discourse and went on to claim that storytellers should be expelled from the ideal society. We now view the modern age as a testament to the value of rationality and reasoned discourse and any argument that promotes the use of stories sounds like an undesirable throwback to irrational, mythic pre-Socratic times. While Plato was certainly correct in his view that stories are imprecise representations of objective reality, he frequently used stories in conveying his own philosophical beliefs, showing both some ambiguity in his position and a realization that stories are an important tool for exploring philosophical ideas.

If we are looking for precise intellectual truths, then perhaps stories are not the best medium for exploration. However, in areas where our understanding is unclear, either because we do not fully understand a phenomenon, or the phenomenon is not available for study because it exists in a possible world, stories play a very important role in advancing our understanding. To put a finer point on this argument, science and logic fail miserably at telling us what could be or more importantly what should be. In these two areas stories are powerful vehicles for intellectual explorations.

A story, for the purposes of the current discussion, is a rendition or a telling of a series of true or fictitious events, connected by a narrative, in which a set of characters experience and react to a set of actions or events and in doing so reveal something about the human character or condition. In order to see the value of stories for the exploration of issues in Cyber Ethics, three prior arguments must be made. First, one must first recognize the fact that there are two distinct modes of thinking which humans use to organize and make sense out of their experiences. These two modes of thinking are logical thinking and narrative thinking. Both modes provide meaningful structures for organizing experiences with the goal of making sense out of them. Both are legitimate and both are productive. Today we tend to favor logical thinking as a more legitimate mode of sense making, while ignoring the vast abundance of instances where logic fails us miserably and we have to resort to narratives of some kind. This argument is important because it allows us to see how stories provide a legitimate alternative to rational discourse for situations in which rational discourse fails to deliver satisfying results. Second, we need to understand the role of emotion in reasoning. We often believe that emotion has no role in reasoning. In fact, we believe that emotions cloud our reasoning. Yet reasoning without emotions is seriously flawed, and one could go as far as to say that reasoning effectively and productively without emotions is simply not possible. This argument is important because stories tend to connect with the reader emotionally, whereas reasoned arguments do not. If emotion is necessary for valid reasoning, then stories provide us with a means of exploring the emotional aspects of an issue as well as the rational aspects, thus providing a richer and fuller exploration. Third, stories allow us to experience possible worlds. We do not know the full set of consequences that may result from various positions on issues in Cyber Ethics and stories provide us with a means of exploring those issues. Each of these arguments will be addressed in turn.

NARRATIVE VS. LOGICAL THINKING

Rational utilitarianism, which is the dominant mode of ethical reasoning in Cyber Ethics today, was coming into vogue in the mid 19th century (Mill, 1861). Charles Dickens, who was alive and writing at the time, was appalled by this kind of reasoning and frequently made fun of it in his novels (Abbott& Bell, 2001). One of the most dramatic examples can be found in *Hard Times* in the character of Thomas Gradgrind, the schoolmaster. The book opens with Gradgrind proclaiming:

"Now, what I want is, Facts. Teach these boys and girls nothing but Facts. Facts alone are wanted in life. Plant nothing else, and root out everything else. You can only form the minds of reasoning animals upon Facts: nothing else will ever be of service to them. This is the principle on which I bring up my own children, and this is the principle on which I bring up these children. Stick to the Facts, Sir!"

The stark, sterile, monotonous and one-dimensional character of Thomas Gradgrind appalls us. He is colorless, without feelings, empathy, warmth or compassion. He is without doubts in his extreme intellectual myopia. Even his name suggests that the graduates of his school are "ground" out like so much social sausage from the social sausage factory rather than enlightened and enlivened with a love of learning. They are as consistent in their thinking as sausage is in its texture. But more importantly, Dickens counters the logical reasoning of rational utilitarianism with a narrative argument. Nobody in their right mind would aspire to be like Thomas Gradgrind, and hence, the narrative argument leads us to the inescapable conclusion that nobody in their right mind would aspire to rational utilitarianism.

Granted there is nothing like a clear, tight, well-developed logical argument—context independent and objectively verifiable to the extent that anyone with some basic instruction in logical reasoning can verify the conclusions. And once we have an argument reduced to a formal logical structure (the extreme, of course, being a mathematical representation), we feel as though the issue is well understood. Logical reasoning provides us with an intellectually economical means of making sense out of the world around us in a manner that can be shared with other people and verified individually. It would be great if all of our vexing problems could be reduced to logical arguments. We could simply articulate the assumptions, follow the rules of logical reasoning, and adopt the conclusions. Unfortunately, life is not that simple.

Narrative and logical reasoning represent two distinct methods of making sense out of the world around us. They are both legitimate and rigorous. Sometimes they provide alternative paths to truth and understanding. Sometimes one or the other provides the only path. This dichotomy is described by Bruner (1986), who offers, "There are two modes of cognitive functioning, two modes of thought, each providing distinct ways of ordering experience, of constructing reality. ...A good story and a well-formed argument are different natural kinds. Both can be used as a means for convincing another" (p. 11). Robinson and Hawpe (1986) also describe this dichotomy between logical or propositional thinking and narrative thinking:

"In both, the goal is the establishment of cause and effect relations between factors. Both are attempts to organize and give meaning to human experience, to explain and guide problem solving. But the products of these two modes of thought, story and principle respectively, are quite distinct. The product of scientific theorizing is a principle, or law. These principles are general, context-free, usually abstract, and testable only by further formal scientific activity. The product of narrative thought, story, is context-bound, concrete, and testable though ordinary interpersonal checking." (p. 114)

They go on to say:

"Perhaps the most radical difference between scientific and narrative thinking is in cast of mind: the scientist strives to eliminate ambiguity and uncertainty and is uncomfortable when there are two equally credible theoretical accounts of some phenomenon. In contrast, in our everyday reasoning about social reality we live comfortably with apparent contradictions. We want explanations which are convincing enough to be accepted as true, but recognize that there could be alternative accounts which tell a different but equally persuasive story." (p. 115)

Logical reasoning is general, context independent, objective and leads to a single conclusion. Narrative reasoning is specific, context dependent, open to subjective interpretation, and potentially leads to multiple conclusions. The characteristics of narrative reasoning are considered flaws when applied to logical reasoning. But the reverse applies also. A story that has only one interpretation and means the same to everyone is not much of a story. The point of generality, however, is a little confusing. Great literature is great because of its timelessness. But timelessness and generality are not the same. The situation described in a good story tends to resonate with a ring of truth with readers perhaps centuries later. Yet, while the sequence of events may be very common to many people, the situation itself is usually very specific.

While narrative and logical reasoning are different kinds of reasoning, different ways to organize our experiences and make sense out of the world, they are not mutually exclusive. A good narrative is also often quite logical in structure, and a good logical argument can often be better understood with a good narrative example. Narrative reasoning can also be inductive or deductive. It is inductive when it provides us with experiences that we use to formulate our opinions about life. It is deductive when it establishes a model of behavior that we wish to follow. Thus, logical and narrative reasoning are not either/or approaches to reasoning. They are complimentary alternative modes of thinking that provide different paths to truth and understanding.

A concern, some may have, about narrative reasoning is that it may not be as rigorous as logical reasoning. After all, syllogisms are syllogisms, and stories are stories. However, much of this concern results not from a lack of rigor in narrative reasoning, but from the lack of documentation and refinement of the rules of narrative reasoning. Logical reasoning was not rigorous until Aristotle began codifying it. George Boole took it further in his classic book on logic, *Investigation of the Laws of Thought*. Each of these efforts were attempts to make logical reasoning more rigorous, which is to say that logical reasoning is not inherently any more rigorous than narrative reasoning. Today, we refine our reasoning abilities by studying logical fallacies and logical reasoning under the popular heading of critical thinking. It is interesting to note that Boole believed that he was actually codifying the "laws of thought." Subsequent research in the psychology of deductive reasoning shows that people are not inherently logical: logical rigor is learned. Similarly, narrative rigor can also be refined and learned.

Narrative reasoning has similar rules, which are being articulated today under the name of narratology (Bal, 1997). Narratives must follow specific structural rules. They must have a plot, believable characters and a meaningful setting. There must be a coherent temporal sequence told from a consistent point of view. And the temporal sequence must embody some sort of causality. The often-quoted E.M. Forster (1927) offers the following observation:

"A plot is a also a narrative of events, the emphasis falling on causality. 'The king died and then the queen died' is a story. 'The king died, and then the queen died of grief' is a plot. The time-sequence is preserved, but the sense of causality overshadows it." (p. 86)

In fact, if someone were to tell the story—"Bill won the lottery and Bob filled his car up with gas"—the listener would automatically wonder what the connection was between Bill and Bob. If the storyteller were to say that there is no connection, the listener would dismiss the story instantly as being silly. Thus, stories, if they are to be believable, if they are to convince us of their "lifelikeness," must follow the rules of narrative.

Certainly stories can be used to mislead, but so can logical arguments. The many books published on critical thinking and logical fallacies are a testament to vagaries of logical reasoning. There are fallacies in narrative reasoning as well, only they have not been identified and named with the same diligence as logical reasoning fallacies have been. Yet, at bottom a logical argument must "make sense" and so must a narrative argument. If a story is not believable, then the characters are not acting in a way that we believe people would behave, based on our own experiences.

To some extent, logical and narrative reasoning address different domains. Logic is well suited to mechanistic processes that can be reduced to logical description. Logic is good for articulating general principles and deductive reasons. Logic is useful for describing and explaining. While logic is good for describing "what is," narrative is good for exploring "what could be" and figuring out "what should be." Narratives are a useful means for understanding the complex and ambiguous issues in human affairs. They allow us to explore possibilities and experience situations vicariously. Narrative reasoning is particularly well suited to Cyber Ethics because many issues are not well understood and the goal of Cyber Ethics is not to discover truth about the physical world, but truth about human nature. Narrative fiction gives us a means to explore and discover truths about what could be and what should be. Through narratives we can explore possible consequences of technology, construct alternative worlds and select the one in which we would like to live.

Critics of the use of narrative in ethics point out that after exploring narratives you always have to come back to principles. Ethics, they argue, is too messy without principles and discussion of narratives does not lead to consistent conclusions. This view misses the point of narratives. First, principles are developed by extracting the principles from experience. Narratives provide some of these experiences vicariously. Hence, narratives can be used in the development of principles. Second, it is often unclear which principles apply in given situations. Narrative explorations provide insight into situations allowing us to determine the governing principles. And narratives can be used to explore the consequences of principled decisions to determine if the outcomes are indeed what are intended. Finally, narrative reasoning does lead to conclusions—very specific conclusions about very specific situations. Narrative reasoning is lacking in generality, as was mentioned before, not lacking in conclusions.

The relationship between principled and narrative ethics is similar to the relationship between theoretical and empirical science. Theories need data for validation. In turn, theories are needed to make sense out of data. It does not make sense to ask whether theory construction or data collection is more important. It only makes sense to ask which is appropriate at a given point in an investigation. Similarly, it does not make sense to ask whether principled logical reasoning or narrative reasoning is more appropriate for understanding ethical situations. It only makes sense to ask which is appropriate at the current point in the investigation. Since principled reasoning breaks down in situations where outcomes cannot be known and values have not been determined, now is a good time to look to narrative reasoning to advance the state of Cyber Ethics.

THE ROLE OF EMOTION IN REASON

It is a widely held belief that once you become emotional in an argument you have lost the argument. After all, reasoning should be dispassionate and free from emotional influences that may cloud our reasoning. We try to reason in an objective and dispassionate manner so that we are not influenced by our feelings, which will only lead us astray in our thinking. However, reasoning without emotional influence is often seriously flawed, and we need to understand the role of emotions in reasoning if we are going to make legitimate and appropriate moral decisions.

There is a well-known argument against utilitarianism in which there are several patients in a hospital in need of organ transplants. One needs a heart, one a liver, one a kidney and so forth. A healthy person comes to the hospital to visit an ailing friend and the hospital staff decides to sacrifice the healthy person to save the lives of the patients who need transplants. After all, this meets the fundamental tenant of utilitarianism—the greatest good for the greatest number of people—five or six people get to live and only one has to die. Logically it works, but its visceral repugnance forces us to go back and reexamine our reasoning.

Emotions are our connection with the real world. Logical reasoning uses abstract principles that must ultimately be grounded in how we feel about the world. Thus, reasoning free of emotion is often incomplete. Thomas Gradgrind, the Dickens character who was mentioned earlier, is a caricature of this flawed approach. Stories connect with us emotionally and allow us to include emotion as an important component in our moral reasoning. If you were the patient in the scenario above, would you rather have your fate decided by rational utilitarians or by people that had to square their decision with their gut feeling?

Although it is difficult to find it written anywhere, there is a prevailing belief that decisions should be made based on reason, rather than emotion. The unfortunate and unwarranted implication is that emotions have no place in reasoning. While there is some basis for this widely held belief, it completely misses the subtle and important relationship between reasoning and emotions. This becomes particularly troublesome when one observes that stories are more likely to invoke an emotional response than an intellectual one. After sorting out their emotional reactions, readers may refine an intellectual response, but their emotional reaction is primary. Hence, if emotion has no place in reasoning, then stories have no place in Cyber Ethics, but that, of course, is not the case.

There is some basis for the belief that emotions get in the way of reasoning. For example, if you lose your temper in the middle of an argument and start flinging ad hominem remarks at your opponent, most rational people would not consider you as having advanced your position. Most would say that you lost the argument when you lost your temper.

Another obvious example, in which emotions can interfere with reasoning, can be found in advertising where emotional appeals are often used to cloud the reasoning of consumers. We purchase status, social acceptance, quality of life and the possibility of meaningful relationships in the form of automobiles, deodorant, toothpaste, beer and jewelry. A dispassionate observer would easily see that when you buy deodorant, all you are getting is deodorant. If you want social acceptance, you would have to do other things. However, this perspective is often lost on a viewer who is caught up in the emotional appeal of the advertisement.

This can easily be turned around to show how reasoning clouds emotions. Perhaps a gifted piano player was brought up with the belief that music is a frivolous, unproductive activity. This person may secretly enjoy producing beautiful music while feeling guilty about being frivolous and unproductive. Again, a dispassionate observer may claim that this person should not feel guilty and perhaps should feel great joy and satisfaction. However, this reaction is lost upon the poor piano player who only feels guilt over wasting time. In this case, reasoning has interfered with an appropriate emotional response. Yet, few people would make the claim that reasoning has no place in emotions.

At the extreme, reasoning can interfere with appropriate emotional responses and emotions can interfere with clearheaded reasoning. However, in the middle where most of life occurs, reasoning and emotions inform each other. Reasoning helps us to refine our emotions and emotions help us to evaluate and validate our reasoning. In order to see this more clearly we need to see how both our reasoning and our emotions are means to understanding the world around us, but either one by itself is incomplete.

There is considerable debate about the exact nature of emotions. The philosopher Robert Solomon (1994) offers one very useful observation that "emotions are judgments about the world." If you are walking down a path in the woods and it is getting dark, you might start to get a little nervous and walk a little faster. If you hear an unfamiliar noise or a rustling in the leaves your heart may begin to beat a little faster as you experience the emotional reaction of fear. This fear is a judgment about the world in which you have judged your current situation as unsafe. You did not arrive at this judgment through a rational process. Specifically, you did not think: "It is dark and hungry animals or possibly monsters come out when it is dark. I just heard a noise that I cannot identify and therefore there could be a hungry animal near me. If I walk a little faster, I might get away before the animal gets me. If I am wrong then all I have done is walked a little faster. If I am right, I might avoid being eaten. Hence, it is logical and reasonable for me to walk faster." In fact, you probably didn't think at all. You just felt scared and increased your pace. If asked later why you were walking so quickly you might come up with a reasonable explanation. But that reasonable explanation is certainly constructed after the fact.

Lazarus and Lazarus (1994) add the additional insight that "one general principle operating in any emotion is that there must be a goal at stake for an emotion to be aroused." In the preceding example, the goal, of course, is to stay alive or at least to stay out of harm's way. Suppose that in the previous example you were in the woods looking for a lost child. The rustling sound may have resulted in excitement, relief or happiness instead of fear, as the possibility of a hungry animal is replaced by the possibility of a found child. So, emotions are not only judgments, they are goal oriented judgments. Simply because neither the goals nor the linkages between the current situation and the goal have been articulated does not diminish the fact that our emotions present us with a nonverbal, preconscious assessment of our current situation.

We know that seemingly rational judgments are not always reliable. By employing logical fallacies we can lead an unwitting person to an erroneous conclusion that appears to be rationally sound. Even in scientific research we employ heuristics that, hopefully, prevent us from making erroneous conclusions about the implications of our data. For example, if I take a large sample of people and weigh them once a week for ten years, I might conclude two things: that the pull of gravity is stronger in the winter and that the pull of gravity is increasing over time.

There is nothing in the formal process of deduction that will prevent me from drawing those conclusions. It is, instead, the refinement process that prevents me from making this error. In a research methods class, I may have studied shadow variables or confounding influences. In presenting my paper to peers, I may have been challenged on these conclusions. In trying to apply this conjecture to other objects such as rocks, I may have found that it did not hold up. We know that rational reasoning alone is not reliable, so we build a process of refinement around it that will, hopefully, catch the most egregious errors.

We also know that emotional judgments are not reliable, yet we make little effort to refine the process of making emotional judgments. I attended a stress management class several years ago where the instructor claimed that one of the main causes of unnecessary stress in the office is the misinterpretation of the thoughts and motives of others. Let's say that you are sitting at your desk during lunch reading the paper. Your boss walks by and makes a face of some kind. You interpret the facial expression as disapproval. Either he doesn't like you to eat at your desk, or he does not like you reading the newspaper. Maybe he just doesn't like you and is planning to get rid of you as soon as possible. It may turn out that he had burritos for lunch and the grimace had everything to do with the burrito and nothing to do with you. The stress management experts tell us not draw erroneous judgments like these because they increase our levels of stress unnecessarily.

Unfortunately, there are few examples beyond stress management where we attempt to refine our emotional judgments about the world. When we are happy, we rarely analyze the circumstances to determine whether or not we should be happy. In our many relationships with other people we rarely evaluate our feeling through independent corroborative data. When a relationship fails we are much more likely to just try and forget the #!@* rather than evaluate our emotions and determine whether or not we made good judgments. However, emotions are judgments about the world, and as such can be refined. And the refinement, as with rational judgments, is simply in the process. We need to identify the sources of erroneous emotional judgments and we need to continually evaluate our judgment to improve them.

Perhaps we have conceded at this point that emotions are judgments about the world and that they can be refined. The obvious question is "So What?" Why do we care and why should we bother to make an effort refining our emotional judgments? From a strictly personal level, making better judgments about the world improves our ability to survive and succeed in the world. However, from a philosophical standpoint, emotional judgments are important because purely rational judgments are incomplete.

Damsio (1994) describes the case of a young man who, after suffering damage to part of his brain, was no longer able to feel emotions. The unexpected side effect of this malady was that he was also unable to make good decisions or assign importance to competing tasks. He seemed normal in every other way and seemed to have his intellectual facilities fully intact. Yet he seemed no longer able to feel emotions and, as a result, he was unable to function as a normal person. When we make a decision we evaluate alternatives. If we are unable to feel emotions, we are unable to place values on the different alternatives. If we cannot place values on the different alternatives then there is no difference between the alternatives and decision-making becomes seriously flawed. Hence, without emotions rational decision-making may not be possible.

Meaning in life is derived emotionally, not rationally. When we attach significance to something we attach feelings, not conclusions. Even the most ardent rationalist pursues knowledge because it is satisfying or because it feels good to discover things. Emotions drive us in our quest for knowledge and without the feelings that we derive from pursuing knowledge we would not pursue it. Emotions make our lives meaningful and the constant pursuit of meaning is the driving force behind our pursuit of knowledge. Hence, without our emotional responses, there would not be any reason to do anything.

So, if emotions are the driving force behind our pursuit of knowledge, then emotions should play a role in the decisions that we make regarding what knowledge to pursue and what to do with the knowledge once we have obtained it. Rationalism, with its carefully developed processes, can only tell us what is. Emotion is required in the reasoning process to tell us what should be.

A good story about an ethical issue is much more likely to draw an emotional response that an intellectual one, whereas an abstract analysis is more likely to yield an intellectual response. Ultimately, ethical decisions are emotional decisions because they embody human values. For this reason, examining ethics from a purely rational perspective completely misses the point.

IMAGINATION AND POSSIBLE CONSEQUENTIALISM

One of the problems in establishing standards of ethical behavior in a field driven by technology is that the consequences of the technology and reactions to the technology often cannot be known. Looking to the past to provide guidance is ineffective because the past provides few clues. Marshall McLuhan is often attributed with the famous observation that looking to the past to provide guidance for the future is like driving by looking in the rear view mirror. Although it is disputed as to whether he ever said that or not, it is a rich metaphor for understanding how we should think about the future in times of rapid technological change.

Imagine you are driving down a highway in the desert. The road is as straight as an arrow for as far as you can see. You are driving along at a modest speed and if you happen to veer slightly off onto the shoulder, no harm is done. With a minor correction, you can be back on the road again. Now imagine that you try looking in your rear view mirror and use the information about where you have been to direct your steering. It probably isn't so bad. As long as the road is straight and you don't drive too fast you can learn to steer the car based upon where you have been. The road behind you is the past and as long as the road in front of you is just like the road behind you, steering by looking in the rear view mirror might be okay.

Now imagine that you have reached the edge of the desert and are entering a passage through the mountains. The highway becomes curvy with steep drop-offs so that steering becomes more difficult and the penalty for a mistake is much greater. Further imagine that the car begins to accelerate forcing you making steering corrections more and more frequently. Most people, at this point, would have given up the silly idea of using the rear view mirror and would have concentrated on the task of steering by looking ahead.

The insight that can be taken from this example is that as long as the road is straight and our progress is slow, we can look to the past to understand the future. However, when the world is changing and those changes are coming at us with increasing rapidity, we have to look ahead to prepare for the future. There are minor examples, such as the Internet Worm and the Y2K bug, and major examples, such as the Cold War and nuclear brinkmanship, that suggest we have come closer than we would like to swerving off the road. Yet in this age of rapid technological change, we still look to the past to understand where we are going.

Imagination is the key to understanding the future. The problem though, in using imagination to understand the future, is that we have a cognitive bias against understanding the future. We feel quite comfortable that we understand the past, but the future is the domain of prophesies. Yet assertions about the past are never testable because the past is gone, never to return, while assertions about the future are testable. So one could argue, on the basis of the testability criterion, that the future is more knowable than the past. However, that discussion is for another time.

Consider imagination as the creative capacity to think of possibilities. Imagination lets us see the world not as it is, but as it could be. Seeing the world as it could be allows us to make choices about how it should be. It is this ability to see possibilities that drives us to build technologies to bring about or implement our preferences about possible worlds. Stories are both a product and a tool of our imaginations. Using stories in moral reasoning provides a means for a slightly different view of ethics that could be called "possible consequentialism." Whereas the consequentialist evaluates actions based upon their consequences, the possible consequentialist evaluates actions based upon their possible outcomes. The possible outcomes are described in stories and the likelihood of the outcome is determined by the believability of the story given our understanding of current conditions and human nature. As the literary critic Northrop Frye (1964) points out, "The fundamental job of the imagination in ordinary life, then, is to produce, out of the society we have to live in, a vision of the society we want to live in" (p. 140).

We often think of imagination as the source of our internal worlds of make believe; the factory of fabula from which we construct our daydreams and fantasies. Yet imagination is an important cognitive function. Specifically, "Imagination is generally held to be the power of forming mental images or other concepts not directly derived from sensation" (Manser, 1967, p 136). Think of the last time you drove to work. Most likely you see yourself in your car driving down the road. When you actually drove to work, you saw the road in front of you, and maybe the dashboard of the car. But you certainly did not see your car or yourself. It is your imagination that has presented this picture to you even though you never really saw it.

Imagine yourself in your car again, the last time you drove to work. Hopefully, this time you don't actually see yourself, unless, of course, you were floating along outside of the car in a disembodied form at the time. Look down and see what kind of shirt you are wearing. Chances are there is no shirt in your imagined view. You probably were wearing a shirt of some kind but it was not significant so it isn't included in this imagined scene. The point is that we routinely interact with our imagination in scenes that have been constructed based on something other than perceptions and are quite incomplete from the perspective of sensory perceptions. Yet we think of these scenes as reality.

The capacity to see possible worlds and then select between them is a uniquely human feature. It is also an awesome responsibility that weighs heavily on the minds of the human race. In the myth of Prometheus we see the titan punished for bringing fire to mankind. The name Prometheus means foresight, or the ability to see possibilities—or imagination. The fire he brings represents technology. For his trouble he is sentenced by Zeus to be chained to a rock and have an eagle peck out his liver every night for the rest of eternity. This is his punishment for being able to see into the future.

There are many instances in literature that explore our fear of the products of our imagination. For example, in *Forbidden Planet*, a science fiction take off on Shakespeare's *Tempest*, an ancient civilization discovered a way to convert imagined objects into real objects. Monsters are created from the dark corners of their imaginations (monsters of the id) who in turn destroy them. The message is clear. We fear the power of the imagination and like to keep it contained, lest it destroy us. One of the ways we keep it contained is to deny its value. Truth is truth and imagination is imagination and never the twain shall meet. In the next few paragraphs I would like to define a concept that I call "Imaginary Truth," which may give us a way to harness the power of the imagination while still containing its destructive power.

Our modern notion of truth is dominated by scientific truth. A fact is true (in the scientific sense) if it can be observed repeatedly by any number of different unbiased observers. We like this view of truth because if a person does not believe that a fact is true they could always (theoretically) check it out for themselves. However, a fact such as Columbus discovered America in 1492 cannot be repeatedly observed by any number of different unbiased observers. So does this mean that this fact cannot be true? Not at all! Instead we have another kind of truth (which I will call historical truth) that says that a fact is true if some number of reviewers looking over the historical evidence are likely to come to the same conclusion. Historical truth and scientific truth different in validation approaches, but agree that rigor lies in method and agreement.

Now consider the following: A friend of yours is reading a copy of *Huckleberry Finn*. Halfway through the book, she throws it down in disgust and says, "I don't think that is a true story. I don't think that really happened at all!" You would look at her in amazement thinking that she had completely missed the point. A novel does not need to adhere to the criteria of scientific or historical truth. It must adhere to the criteria of literary truth. A novel contains literary truth if the characters, in a believable situation, act in a way that is consistent with our understanding of human nature. Whether or not the events really occurred is of little importance. In fact, many true stories that we hear may be historically true because they actually occurred, but false in a literary sense because they are not consistent with our understanding of human nature and they give us no insight into our own lives.

When we imagine, we are constructing possible worlds in order to choose between them. I will define imaginary truth as the likelihood that a given scenario could occur given a believable set of assumptions and our understanding of human nature. Truth, in order to have value, needs some element of rigor. In order to bring rigor to imaginary truth, we need to understand how rigor is brought to other kinds of truth. Instead of the usual true/false dichotomy, consider truth as being on a scale from soft truth to hard truth. As truth becomes harder, it moves toward the unattainable limit of absolute truth. As truth becomes softer it moves toward the unattainable limit of absolute uncertainty.

Further, let's say that a statement is a soft truth if it is plausibly or possibly true. Similarly a statement is a hard truth if it is very likely that it is true. Now, let's apply this to the kinds of truth above. A fact is a soft scientific truth if it is possibly true. It is a hard scientific truth if it is very likely to be true. A fact moves from a soft scientific truth to a hard scientific truth by having someone gather data that either supports or refutes the fact. Thus, when we say truth, we are really asserting the likelihood that the fact will not be overturned for some time into the future.

A fact is a soft historical truth if it is possible that things happened that way. It moves to hard historical truth as more historians comb over the facts and come to the same conclusion. As with scientific truth, there is always the possibility that a piece of evidence will come along at any point that does not fit the current view and the current view may be overturned. Historical truth is less stable than scientific truth. For example, Richard III was considered a villain by Shakespeare and represented as such in the play named after him. Recent interpretations suggest that this portrayal was simply a result of Shakespeare's allegiance to the Tudors. So the truth-value of a fact is measured on the soft to hard scale by numbers of unbiased observers over time.

A story is a soft literary truth if it is plausible that characters in that situation may have behaved that way. It is a hard literary truth if it is likely that any ordinary person in those circumstances would have behaved that way. Here we see the metrics of truth even more clearly. A cyberpunk science fiction novel, when read by a cyberpunk person may have a high degree of believability. However, if I read the same story I might feel that the characters made no sense at all. Thus, such a story would have only soft literary truth. Many of the classics of literature are such because they have a message of enduring value. Different people over many different generations and times see meaningful truths in these stories, giving them a high degree of hard literary truth.

Using this dimension of soft and hard truth, I would define an imaginative scenario as a soft imaginary truth if it could possibly happen. A scenario would be a hard imaginary truth if it is likely to occur given the setting and assumptions in the scenario. A scenario would move from soft to hard imaginary truth by being examined rigorously over time by unbiased evaluators to determine if they also believed that it is likely to occur given the assumptions. For example, the books *1984* by George Orwell and *Brave New World* by Aldous Huxley are soft imaginary truths if readers believe that the worlds presented in these stories could possibly happen. They become hard imaginary truths if critical readers examine the assumptions and agree that these outcomes are quite likely to happen given our understanding of human nature.

When we examine issues in Cyber Ethics, we cannot examine them in terms of consequentialist ethics because the consequences are not known. However, through the use of stories we can construct imaginative scenarios and examine possible consequences. Possible consequentialism may be a preferable approach to computer ethics because we can look at possible outcomes, assess the likelihood of each, and select the outcome we prefer. Imagination provides us with a means of fully examining possible outcomes and stories provide us with the means of sharing our imaginings. By writing stories and sharing them we can explore possible consequences and, through social debate, derive imaginary truths. These imaginary truths allow us to choose the kind of world that we would like to live in.

WHY NOT CASE STUDIES?

A reasonable question to ask at this point is, "If stories are the way to explore Cyber Ethics, then what is wrong with the case studies that we have been using all along?" This is a reasonable reaction and needs to be addressed before closing.

A case study is an economical abstraction of an ethical situation that focuses on the elements of the dilemma so that the reader or discussant can explore and weigh the competing factors. The competing factors can result from conflicting roles, values or responsibilities. But case studies focus almost exclusively on the elements of an ethical dilemma. They are abstracted and lacking in context. Yet the ethical dilemmas that we face are never abstracted or lacking context. And the decisions we make often result from the context in which the dilemma is embedded. Further, the characters in a case study are usually two-dimensional without being archetypical. This means that they are not fully developed people, nor do they represent essential types of people. A typical case study character is Bob Smith who is a manager for Acme Corporation. But what did Bob have for breakfast that morning. How does he treat his kids? What experiences in his formative years had the greatest impact on his worldview? We don't know. Yet if Bob were really in a situation in which an ethical dilemma must be resolved these issues as well as a host of others would come into play.

Ethical problems exist in a temporal, cultural and personal web. Characters have families and friends and conflicting obligations. They have character traits and values that affect their ethical reasoning. Yet the elements that are most likely to affect an ethical decision are usually missing from a case study. A good case study discussion leader will often toss in more details as the discussion progresses, providing more context for the case and making the characters more real. In fact, the good case study discussion leader moves the case study toward being a story.

In the introduction to *Jurassic Park*, Michael Crichton states, "The commercialization of molecular technology is the most stunning ethical event in the history of science." And, despite the fact that most people see *Jurassic Park* as a high tech thriller, it is really an exploration of the ethical implications of biotechnology. It was not the first story to explore the ethical implications of technology. Other notables include Mary Shelly's *Frankenstein*, Kurt Vonnegut's *Player Piano*, and, of course, Charles Dickens' *Hard Times*, to name a few. To really see the difference between case studies and stories, imagine presenting the elements of any of these stories in a one to two thousand word case study and see what is lost.

So does this mean that case studies have no value for exploring ethical issues? Not at all. In situations where we are clear on the appropriate ethical behavior, case studies allow us to present the elements of the dilemma and work towards an (usually predetermined) acceptable outcome. However, when facing ethical issues, such as many of the issues in Cyber Ethics, where we do not know the appropriate ethical stance, case studies are simply not rich enough to allow us to explore the issues. In these cases we need stories.

CONCLUSIONS AND FUTURE DIRECTIONS

The central problem in Cyber Ethics is not, as many may suppose, how to prevent software piracy or how to protect privacy on the Internet. It is instead: how do you establish ethical standards in a professional field that is defined by a rapidly evolving technology where the consequences of the technology and the impact of any ethical standards cannot be know in the time frame in which the standards must be established? Stories play an important role in addressing this problem by providing a means of exploring ethical issues for which the full range of consequences are not known. Stories allow us to construct narrative arguments to explore issues that we do not fully understand. They allow us to explore the emotional as well as rational aspects of a situation. Stories allow us to explore worlds that do not currently exist which, in turn, allows us to examine possible consequences and make choices about the world in which we would like to live.

But the role of stories does not stop here. Stories play an important role in moral development. They can confront the reader with moral dilemmas which require the reader to reexamine his or her beliefs, especially when those beliefs do not square with a given situation. The Platonic dialogues are certainly one of the best-known examples of using stories to promote moral development. But the exact role of stories in moral development is not well understood and future research is needed in this area so that we can understand it better.

Sadly, there are few good examples of great stories that can be used in moral development, especially in the area of Cyber Ethics. This then leads to another direction for future research. Do we have to rely on the whims of short stories writers who may, at some point, decide to write a story to examine an issue in Cyber Ethics? Or can we construct stories to examine ethical dilemmas? The answer to these questions still lies in the future.

REFERENCES

Abbott, R. & Bell, C. (2001). *Charles Dickens: A Beginner's Guide*. Hodder & Stoughton.

Artz, J. (1998). Narrative vs. logical reasoning in computer ethics. *Computers & Society, 28*(4).

Artz, J. (1998). The role of stories in computer ethics. *Computers and Society, 28*(1).

Artz, J. (1998). Using the Socratic Method to teach computer ethics. *Journal of Information Systems Education, 9*(1).

Artz, J. (2000a). Narrative versus logical reasoning in computer ethics. Reprinted in R. Baird, R. Ramsover, & S. Rosenbaum (Eds.), *Cyberethics: Social & Moral Issues in the Computer Age*. Prometheus Books.

Artz, J. (2000b). The role of emotion in reason and its implications for computer ethics. *Computers & Society, 30*(1).

Artz, J. (2001). Imagination, truth and possible consequentialism. *Computers & Society, 31*(3).

Bal, M. (1997). *Narratology: Introduction to the Theory of Narrative*. Toronto, Canada: University of Toronto Press.

Bruner, J. (1986). *Actual minds, possible worlds*. MA: Harvard University Press.

Damsio, A. (1994). *Descartes' Error: Emotion, Reason, and the Human Brain*. Avon Books.

Dickens, C. (1854). *Hard Times*. London: Bradbury & Evans.

Egan, K. (1992). *Imagination in Teaching and Learning*. Chicago, IL: The University of Chicago Press.

Forester, E.M. (1927). *Aspects of the Novel*. New York: Harcourt Brace & Company.

Frye, N. (1964). *The Educated Imagination*. Bloomington, IN: Indiana University Press.

Gardner, J. (1991). *The Art of Fiction*. New York: Vintage Books.

Goleman, D. (1995). *Emotional Intelligence*. Bantam Books.

Hill, R. (1987). *Writing in General and the Short Story in Particular*. Houghton Mifflin Company.

Kreie, J. & Cronan, T. (1998). How men and women view ethics. *CACM, 41*(9), 70-76.

Kreie, J. & Cronan, T. (2000). Making ethical decisions. *CACM, 43*(12), 66-71.

Lazarus, R. & Lazarus, B. (1994). *Passion & Reason*. New York & London: Oxford University Press.

Manser, A. R. (1967). Imagination. *The Encyclopedia of Philosophy*, 136-139.

Mill, J. S. (1957). *Utilitarianism*. New York: The Library of Liberal Arts, Macmillan Publishing Company. (Original work published 1861).

Prior, M., Rogerson, S., & Fairweather B. (2002). The ethical attitudes of information systems professionals: Outcomes of an initial survey. *Telematics and Informatics, 19*(1), 21-36.

Robinson, J.A. & Hawpe, L. (1986). Narrative thinking as a heuristic process. In T.R. Sarbin (Ed.), *Narrative Psychology: The Storied Nature of Human Conduct* (pp. 111-125). New York: Praeger.

Solomon, R. (1994). Love and vengeance: A course on human emotion (Superstar Teachers Series). Chantilly, VA: The Teaching Company.

About the Authors

Linda L. Brennan is a member of the faculty of Mercer University in Macon, USA. She received her PhD from Northwestern University, her MBA from the University of Chicago, and her BIE from the Georgia Institute of Technology. Building on her extensive experience in the Management of Knowledge Work and Information Technologies, she conducts research and consults in the areas of Project Management and Control, Process Assessment and Design, and Technology Impact Assessment and Implementation. Her focus is on achieving organizational performance through individual effectiveness. Dr. Brennan's prior work experience includes management positions at The Quaker Oats Company and marketing and systems engineering experience with the IBM Corporation.

Victoria E. Johnson is Professor of Management in the School of Business at Mercer University in Atlanta, Georgia, USA, where she previously held the position of Associate Dean. She received her DPA from the University of Georgia, and her MPA and AB from Georgia State University. In addition to her extensive administrative experience, Dr. Johnson has also published numerous articles in the areas of Organizational Design and Development; Ethics and Social Responsibility; Human Resource Development, and International Management. She currently continues to consult and to conduct research in these areas.

*   *   *

John M. Artz, PhD, is an Associate Professor of Management Science at The George Washington University in Washington, D.C., and the Director of the Master of Science in Information Systems Technology degree program. He teaches classes in Systems Development, Database, Data Warehousing, Programming, and Social and Ethical Impacts of Information Systems. His research interests include Philosophical Foundations of Information Systems and the Role of Stories in Computer Ethics.

Jordan "Jody" M. Blanke is a Professor of Computer Information Systems and Law at the Stetson School of Business and Economics at Mercer University in Atlanta, Georgia, USA. He has taught a wide variety of courses in Computer Science, Computer Information Systems and Law during his 20 years of college teaching. His areas of interests include Privacy, Copyright and Trademark Law, and Human Factors in design. He lives in Roswell, Georgia, with his wife, Charlene, their three children, Ilani, Zack, and Melanie, and their two dogs, Ralph (part kangaroo) and Richie (part termite). He describes himself as "an aging softball pitcher."

Jack S. Cook is an Associate Professor of Information Systems at the Rochester Institute of Technology (RIT), USA. His specialties are Electronic Commerce, Information Systems and Production/Operations Management. Jack's extensive experience teaching and training over the last two decades includes more than 50 conference presentations and numerous journal articles. Jack has an entertaining approach and is known for bringing theories to life. Dr. Cook is a Certified Fellow in Production and Inventory Management (CFPIM). His education includes a PhD in Business Administration, an MS in Computer Science, an MBA, an MA in Mathematics, and a BS in Computer Science.

Laura L. Cook works for the Computing & Information Technology Department at the State University of New York at Geneseo, USA. She is currently a graduate student in Information Technology at the Rochester Institute of Technology. Laura has four journal publications and has given numerous presentations. She also volunteers as the Webmaster for the Rochester, NY chapter of APICS. Laura has taught Electronic Commerce for the Jones School of Business and Computers in Education for the School of Education at SUNY-Geneseo. She has also taught many technology workshops on various topics.

J. Carl Ficarrotta is an Assistant Professor of Philosophy at the United States Air Force Academy. He has published a number of articles on problems in theoretical and applied ethics in such diverse venues as *Public Affairs Quarterly*, *Armed Forces and Society*, the *Encyclopedia of Applied Ethics*, and with the NDU Press (*Ethics and National Defense: The Timeless Issues,*

Gaston & Hietala Eds., 1993). He edited *The Leader's Imperative* (Purdue University Press, 2001) and is currently writing a book on Ethics and International Relations.

John Gallaugher is an Associate Professor of Information Systems at the Wallace E. Carroll School of Management at Boston College, USA. His research interests include Strategic Information Systems, Electronic Commerce, Network Effects, and Global Information Systems. Prof. Gallaugher's research has appeared in leading publications including *CACM*, *IJEC*, and *MIS Quarterly* and he serves on the editorial board of the *Journal of Electronic Commerce in Organizations*. He has been an invited speaker at several organizations including Accenture, Staples, State Street, and the U.S. Information Agency. He can be reached online at http://www.gallaugher.com, where he publishes a regular digest of technology-related business news.

Gerald M. Hoffman is a consultant, author and educator. He is an Adjunct Professor of Industrial Engineering and Management Sciences at Northwestern University and President of The Gerald Hoffman Company LLC. His recent book, *The Technology Payoff*, is about things that executives can do to help their organizations realize the benefits of their investments in information technology. He has been President of both The Society for Information Management and The Institute of Management Science, and has served on advisory boards at Columbia University, Illinois Institute of Technology, and the American Management Association. He holds BS and MS degrees in physics from Purdue University, and a PhD in Industrial Engineering and Management Sciences from Northwestern University.

Chuck Huff is Professor of Psychology at St. Olaf College, USA. He has published research in the areas of Moral Reasoning, Computing and Education, Gender and Computing, Social Aspects of Electronic Interaction, and Ethics in Computing. He is Associate Editor of the journals *Computers and Society* and *Social Science Computer Review*. He is currently doing empirical research on the moral development of computer professionals in collaboration with the Centre for Computing and Social Responsibility at Demontfort University in Leicester, UK.

Marianne M. Jennings is a Professor of Legal and Ethical Studies in the WP Carey School of Business at Arizona State University, USA. She has taught there since 1977. She has served as a consultant to companies, government agencies and educational institutions. She writes a weekly column that is syndicated around the country. She is the author of *Business Ethics: Case*

Studies and Readings (4ᵗʰ edition), as well as the forthcoming *A Business Tale: A Story of Choices, Success, Ethics and A Very Large Rabbit.*

Deborah G. Johnson is the Olsson Professor of Applied Ethics in the Department of Technology, Culture, and Communication at the University of Virginia, USA. She is the Author/Editor of four books including *Computer Ethics*, now in its third edition, and *Computers, Ethics, and Social Values* (co-edited with Helen Nissenbaum). Johnson co-edits the journal *Ethics and Information Technology* as well as a new book series on Women, Gender, and Technology. She is past President of the Society for Philosophy and Technology and current President of a new professional association, the International Society for Ethics and Information Technology (INSEIT).

Mark Kieler, MS PE, graduated with a BS double major in Electrical Engineering and Engineering and Public Policy from Carnegie Mellon University in 1982. He received his MS in Engineering and Public Policy from Carnegie Mellon in 1992. He has worked as an Electrical Engineer in the civilian and naval nuclear power industries. Additionally, he has operated a one-person instrumentation laboratory where he designed custom equipment to support neurobiology and ophthalmology researchers. Currently he is Assistant Department Head for Undergraduate Affairs and Lecturer in the Department of Engineering and Public Policy at Carnegie Mellon University, USA.

William J. McIver, Jr. is Assistant Professor in the School of Information Science and Policy at the University at Albany, State University of New York (SUNY), USA. He has done research in the areas of Digital Government, Database Integration, Telecommunications Applications, Agent-Based Systems and Software Reusability. William is co-holder of a U.S. patent for his work in telecommunications. He is Co-Editor with Ahmed K. Elmagarmid of the book: *Advances in Digital Government: Technology, Human Factors, and Policy* (Kluwer, 2002). William has held research positions at US WEST Advanced Technologies (now Qwest Communications), the University of Colorado at Boulder, Purdue University and Brown University. He has a BA degree from Morehouse College and a PhD from the University of Colorado at Boulder, both in Computer Science.

Keith W. Miller is a Professor of Computer Science at the University of Illinois–Springfield, USA. Dr. Miller's research interests include Software Engineering, especially testing; and Computer Ethics, especially Professional Ethics. Dr. Miller was part of the team that developed a code of ethics for software engineers, a code approved by both the IEEE Computer Society and the ACM, and adopted by companies and organizations internationally. This chapter grew from discussions Drs. Huff, Johnson, and Miller had while all three were working on the DOLCE project, work supported by an NSF grant, DUE 9952841.

Emma Rooksby is Research Fellow at the ARC Special Research Centre for Applied Philosophy and Public Ethics (CAPPE), Australia. She has published in the areas of Computer Ethics, Political Philosophy and Urban Planning Theory. Her primary research focus is Computer Ethics, including Internet Democracy, the Ethics of Text-Based Communication, and the Digital Divide. Her most recent publication is *E-mail and Ethics* (Routledge, 2002). Forthcoming publications include "How to be a responsible slave: Managing the use of expert systems" (*Ethics and Information Technology* 5(2)) and "Election as a mandate" in D. Cryle and J. Hillier (Eds.), *Consent and Consensus* (Queensland University Press, 2003).

Richard A. Spinello is an Associate Research Professor in the Carroll School of Management at Boston College, USA. Prior to joining the faculty of Boston College he worked as a Programmer and Marketing Manager in the software industry. He has written and edited five books on Information Technology Ethics, including his most recent work, *Regulating Cyberspace: The Policies and Technologies of Control.* He has also written numerous articles and scholarly papers on Ethics and Management.

Robert D. Sprague, BSBA (Economics), MBA, JD, teaches Business Law and law-related classes in Eastern New Mexico University's College of Business, USA. Professor Sprague's current research includes Liability for Defective Software, Online Defamation, Workplace Privacy, and the Evolution of State Statutes regarding strategic lawsuits against public participation. Professor Sprague has more than two dozen papers and publications covering topics including Software Copyrights, Privacy and the use of Advanced Technology in the delivery of legal services. Prior to joining academia on a full-time basis, Professor Sprague held senior management positions with Internet-related companies in Silicon Valley. Professor Sprague has several years of experience consulting in the area of Legal Automation, as well as practicing law, primarily representing clients in the computer industry.

Sandra Waddock is Professor of Management at Boston College's Carroll School of Management, USA, and Senior Research Fellow at Boston College's Center for Corporate Citizenship. She has published extensively on Corporate Responsibility, Corporate Citizenship, and Multi-Sector Collaboration in journals such as *The Academy of Management Journal, Academy of Management Executive, Strategic Management Journal, The Journal of Corporate Citizenship, Human Relations,* and *Business & Society*. Her latest book is

Leading Corporate Citizens: Vision, Values, Value Added (McGraw-Hill, 2002). She a founding faculty member of the Leadership for Change Program at Boston College.

John Weckert is Associate Professor of Information Technology in the School of Information Studies, a Principal Research Fellow at the Centre for Applied Philosophy and Public Ethics (CAPPE), at Charles Sturt University, and a Visiting Fellow at the Australian National University. At CAPPE he is Manager of the research programme "Emerging technologies: IT and nanotechnology." His main research interests currently are in Computer Ethics and in the emerging field of the Ethics of Nanotechnology. He has published widely in Computer and Internet Ethics, has recently been involved in consultancies with government departments on electronic corruption in the public sector and on the digital divide.

Michael J. West is Principal Lecturer in the Modern Languages Department at Carnegie Mellon University, USA. After receiving his doctorate in French from the University of California, Santa Barbara, in 1989, he joined Carnegie Mellon. He has taught and published in areas including Cultural Criticism, particularly the cultural construction of national identity. He has also worked in the private sector in technology training. Current research interests include Language Pedagogy and the Ethical Dimensions of Technology.

David Wiencek is a graduate of the University of Illinois at Chicago Circle and the University of Virginia. He has been a practicing IT professional for 30 years in the educational, consulting and commercial sectors. In addition, he has taught MIS and Technology Management at the graduate and undergraduate levels. His research interests include Ethical Decision-Making, IT Risk Management and Asset Life-Cycle Analysis.

Marsha Woodbury, PhD, is a Lecturer in the Department of Computer Science at the University of Illinois at Urbana-Champaign, USA, and the former National Chair of Computer Professionals for Social Responsibility. She wrote *Computer and Information Ethics* (Stipes Publishers, 2002) and was a curriculum developer and faculty member of the Information Group at International Women's University in Germany in 2000. She teaches Computer Ethics and Professional Responsibility as well as Intellectual Property along with her large lecture course. Her involvements and interests are available on her home page, http://www.cpsr.org/~marsha-w/. She received her undergraduate education at Stanford and her master's and doctorate at Illinois. As an active computer professional, she is involved in teaching, writing and working to encourage more women to study computing. A member of the ACM and IEEE, she lectures on how the September 11 disaster has influenced the field of computer ethics.

Index

G

G8 nations 11
gambling 60
gaming 60
geo-politics 155
glass ceilings 131
glass walls 131
global environment 131
global interdependencies 2
global presence 51
globalization 145
Gramm-Leach-Bliley Act (GLBA) 258
group communication 60
guilty mind 105

H

hactivism 135
harm 103
Health Insurance Portability and
    Accountability Act 259
hidden surveillance devices 77
Hippocrates 122
Hong Kong Personal Data (Privacy)
    Ordinance 266
human expression 237
human needs 12
human rights 6
human-centered information society 9

I

IM traffic 62
imagination 285
immediacy of information 52
implied warranty of fitness 187
implied warranty of merchantability 187
individual corporation 150
individual development opportunities
    151
information and communication tech-
    nologies (ICTs) 2, 30
information systems (IS) 252
information systems professionals 118
information technology applications 49
insider crime 67

instant messaging (IM) 62, 75
Institute of Electrical and Electronics
    Engineers 205
integrity 124
intellectual capital 143
intellectual capital creation 157
intellectual creations 234
intellectual property 14
interactive relationships 132
international communication 66
International Radio-Telegraph Union 6
International Telecommunication Union
    6
International Telegraph Union (ITU) 6
Internet 60, 223
Internet Corporation for Assigned
    Names and Number 10
Internet governance 10
Internet-enhanced social activism 137
interpersonal communication 60
IT manager 146
IT professionals 126

J

Japan 66
Judeo/Christian cultures 121

K

keystroke monitoring 70
knowledge sharing 13

L

LambdaMOO 99
language 235
least developed countries (LDCs) 14
legal protection 187
license agreement 186
licensure 204
licensure resistance 213
linguistic diversity 14
linguistic preservation 7
logical thinking 277
lossy encoding 241

NEW Titles
from Information Science Publishing

- **Instructional Design in the Real World: A View from the Trenches**
  Anne-Marie Armstrong
  ISBN: 1-59140-150-X: eISBN 1-59140-151-8, © 2004
- **Personal Web Usage in the Workplace: A Guide to Effective Human Resources Management**
  Murugan Anandarajan & Claire Simmers
  ISBN: 1-59140-148-8; eISBN 1-59140-149-6, © 2004
- **Social, Ethical and Policy Implications of Information Technology**
  Linda L. Brennan & Victoria Johnson
  ISBN: 1-59140-168-2; eISBN 1-59140-169-0, © 2004
- **Readings in Virtual Research Ethics: Issues and Controversies**
  Elizabeth A. Buchanan
  ISBN: 1-59140-152-6; eISBN 1-59140-153-4, © 2004
- **E-ffective Writing for e-Learning Environments**
  Katy Campbell
  ISBN: 1-59140-124-0; eISBN 1-59140-125-9, © 2004
- **Development and Management of Virtual Schools: Issues and Trends**
  Catherine Cavanaugh
  ISBN: 1-59140-154-2; eISBN 1-59140-155-0, © 2004
- **The Distance Education Evolution: Issues and Case Studies**
  Dominique Monolescu, Catherine Schifter & Linda Greenwood
  ISBN: 1-59140-120-8; eISBN 1-59140-121-6, © 2004
- **Distance Learning and University Effectiveness: Changing Educational Paradigms for Online Learning**
  Caroline Howard, Karen Schenk & Richard Discenza
  ISBN: 1-59140-178-X; eISBN 1-59140-179-8, © 2004
- **Managing Psychological Factors in Information Systems Work: An Orientation to Emotional Intelligence**
  Eugene Kaluzniacky
  ISBN: 1-59140-198-4; eISBN 1-59140-199-2, © 2004
- **Developing an Online Curriculum: Technologies and Techniques**
  Lynnette R. Porter
  ISBN: 1-59140-136-4; eISBN 1-59140-137-2, © 2004
- **Online Collaborative Learning: Theory and Practice**
  Tim S. Roberts
  ISBN: 1-59140-174-7; eISBN 1-59140-175-5, © 2004

Excellent additions to your institution's library! Recommend these titles to your librarian!

To receive a copy of the Idea Group Inc. catalog, please contact 1/717-533-8845, fax 1/717-533-8661,or visit the IGI Online Bookstore at: http://www.idea-group.com!

Note: All IGI books are also available as ebooks on netlibrary.com as well as other ebook sources. Contact Ms. Carrie Skovrinskie at <cskovrinskie@idea-group.com> to receive a complete list of sources where you can obtain ebook information or IGP titles.

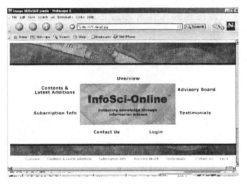